Romans Through History and Cultures
Receptions and Critical Interpretations

CRISTINA GRENHOLM AND DANIEL PATTE, SERIES EDITORS

›mans Through History and Cultures includes a wealth of information regarding the :ceptions of Romans throughout the history of the church and today, in the "first" and e "two-thirds" world. It explores the past and present impact of Romans upon ›eology, and upon cultural, political, social, and ecclesial life, and gender relations.

In each volume, the authors contribute to an integrated practice, "Scriptural riticism," which takes into account, with contemporary biblical scholars, that different :adings can be grounded in the same text by different critical methods; with church storians and practical theologians, that the believers' readings inter-relate biblical text ıd concrete life; and with theologians, that believers read Romans as Scripture.

The cover art skillfully represents that any interpretation of a scriptural text is framed three ways: a) by an *analytical frame* that reflects each reader's autonomous choice of textual dimension as most significant—see the individual studying the text; b) by a *ntextual/pragmatic frame* shaped by a certain relational network of life in society and ›mmunity—see the people joining hands; and, c) by a *hermeneutical frame* inspired by a :rtain religious perception of life—see the bread and chalice and the face-to-face ıcounter.

By elucidating the threefold choices reflected in various interpretations of Romans rough the centuries and present-day cultures, the volumes in the series—which nerge from a three-year Society of Biblical Literature Consultation and an on-going ЗL Seminar—raise a fundamental critical question: Why did I/we choose this terpretation rather than another one?

s in previous volumes the markings of **C** (contextual/pragmatic frame), **A** (analytical ame), **H** (hermeneutical frame), and **I** (interplay between frames), are selectively added footnotes as a guide to readers concerning the heuristic tool of scriptural criticism.

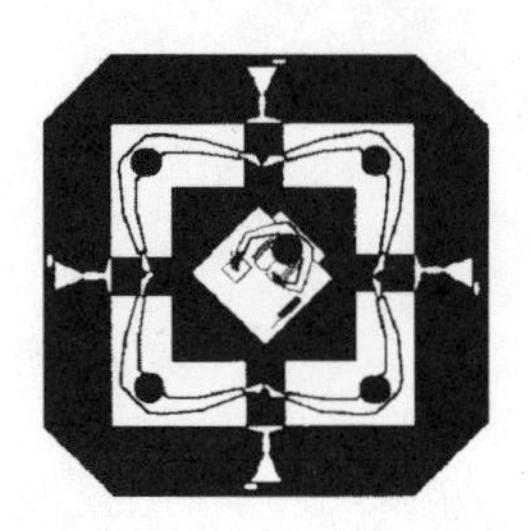

Romans Through History and Cultures Series

Reformation Readings of Romans

Edited by

Kathy Ehrensperger and R. Ward Holder

t&t clark

T & T Clark International
80 Maiden Lane, New York, NY 10038

T & T Clark International
The Tower Building, 11 York Road, London SE1 7NX

www.continuumbooks.com
www.tandtclarkblog.com

T & T Clark International is a Continuum imprint.

Cover art by Elizabeth McNaron Patte

Library of Congress Cataloging-in-Publication Data

Reformation Readings of Romans / edited by Kathy Ehrensperger and R. Ward Holder
p. cm. -- (Romans through history & culture ; 8)
Includes bibliographical references and index.
ISBN-13: 978-0-567-02714-6 (pbk. : alk. paper)
ISBN-10: 0-567-02714-7 (pbk. : alk. paper) 1. Bible. N.T. Romans--Criticism, interpretation, etc. I. Ehrensperger, Kathy II. Holder, R. Ward III. Title. IV. Series.

BS2665.52.M43 2007
227'.1060902--dc22

2007034748

Printed in the United States of America

Table of Contents

— INTRODUCTION —

Romans in the Light of Reformation Receptions

R. Ward Holder

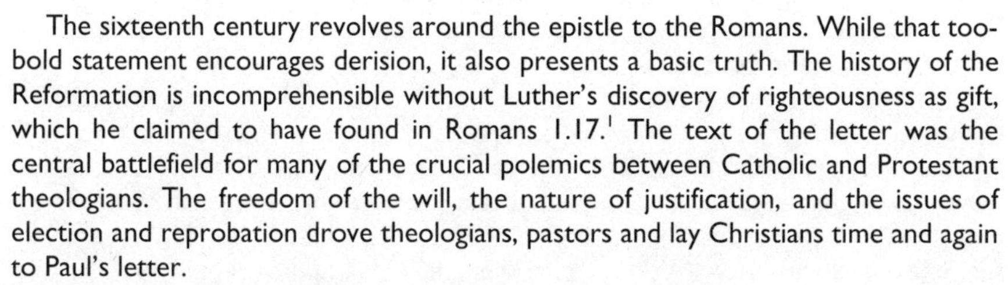

The sixteenth century revolves around the epistle to the Romans. While that too-bold statement encourages derision, it also presents a basic truth. The history of the Reformation is incomprehensible without Luther's discovery of righteousness as gift, which he claimed to have found in Romans 1.17.[1] The text of the letter was the central battlefield for many of the crucial polemics between Catholic and Protestant theologians. The freedom of the will, the nature of justification, and the issues of election and reprobation drove theologians, pastors and lay Christians time and again to Paul's letter.

Further, many of the most widely-regarded theologians of that time clearly saw that Romans was the key text in their own seeking out of Christian truth. Philip Melanchthon (1497–1560) commented upon Romans more than any other book of the Bible. John Calvin (1509–1564) saw it as the most necessary book for understanding the message of scripture. Wolfgang Musculus (1497–1563), Martin Bucer (1491–1551), Heinrich Bullinger (1504–1575), and Georg Major (1502–1574) are just a few of the company of exegetes who took up the task of commenting on it.[2] This commenting upon the book was not confined to Protestant exegetes, as significant Roman Catholic figures essayed it as well. Cardinal Jacopo Sadoleto (1477–1547) wrote a commentary on Romans that so emphasized human freedom that he was censured. John Colet (1466?–1519), Erasmus (1466?–1536) and Cardinal Thomas de Vio Cajetan (1469–1534) took up this epistle as well. They were hardly the only Roman Catholics to come to the text. Counting both Protestants and adherents of Rome, over seventy commentaries on Romans were published in the sixteenth century.[3]

Thus, the editors need make no argument for including a volume on the Reformation in the Romans through History and Cultures series. On quantity of output alone, the Reformation would merit inclusion. But the Reformation period saw far more significance for the understanding of the letter to the Romans than simple numbers. Though books could be (and have been) written on the topic, this essay will concentrate upon three facets that make our consideration of the epistle to the Romans in the Reformation worthwhile. First, many theologians of the Reformation period used Romans, either consciously and explicitly or unconsciously, as the entrance to the scriptures. Second, it is in the Reformation period that we see the foundational moves that allowed New Testament scholarship to take on its modern form. Dependence on original language manuscripts and editions,[4] examination of historical context,[5] and a variety of types of rhetorical analysis all proceed from the Reformation era, in its debt to Renaissance humanism. Finally, when we look at the impact of the Reformation upon our own day, we see that the Reformation period's engagement with Romans crystallized certain understandings of this epistle, and of Paul, that New Testament scholars and theologians still examine today. The Reformation period proposes a set of thinkers and ideas about Romans that make the conversation between historians of the exegesis of the period and modern Paul scholars especially fruitful.

In the Reformation, Romans served as the door to the scripture and the correct understanding of the Christian religion. To many thinkers in the Reformation, the epistle to the church at Rome went far beyond a helpful collection of doctrine and prooftexts that addressed some of the most pressing issues of the first century, and by happenstance illumined some of the issues of their own day. For thinkers such as Luther, Bullinger, Calvin and Melanchthon, Romans presented the most efficient and truest way to enter the scriptures. This ideal presents our first issue – Romans as a key or door to the scriptures. We shall concentrate upon Luther and Calvin, but other reformers took this same tack.

Martin Luther never wrote a 'Protestant' commentary on Romans. His lectures on Romans that were published as his commentary were written in 1515 and 1516. If we cannot state with the bullet-proof confidence that this occurred before his conversion,[6] we can state unequivocally that it predates the indulgence controversy that proved to be the spark of so large a conflagration.[7] Late in his life, however, in the preface to his Latin Writings published in 1545, Luther would look to his understanding of Romans 1.17 as the key to his evangelical breakthrough. He wrote,

> ...but a single word in Chapter 1 [:17], 'In it the righteousness of God is revealed', that had stood in my way. For I hated that word 'righteousness of God', which, according to the use and custom of all the teachers, I had been taught to understand philosophically regarding the formal or active righteousness, as they called it, with which God is righteous and punishes the unrighteous sinner.... Thus I raged with a fierce and troubled conscience. Nevertheless, I beat importunately upon Paul at that place, most ardently desiring to know what St. Paul wanted.
>
> At last, by the mercy of God, meditating day and night, I gave heed to the context of the words, namely, 'In it the righteousness of God is revealed, as it is written, 'He who through faith is righteous shall live." Then I began to understand that the righteousness of God is that by which the righteous lives by a gift of God, namely by faith. And this is the meaning: the righteousness of God is revealed by the gospel, namely, the passive righteousness with which merciful God justifies us by faith, as it is written, 'He who through faith is righteous shall live'. Here I felt that I was altogether born again and had entered paradise itself through open gates. There a totally other face of the entire Scripture showed itself to me.[8]

Luther called this revolution a hermeneutic event – immediately the whole of the scriptures seemed new and different. Contemplating upon Romans 1.17, motivated by existential urgency, Luther found the key to the whole of the gospel within the first chapter of Romans. He noted that this was a contextual and theological discovery, and he invited his readers to share it.

However, the early commentary and Luther's evangelical breakthrough were not the only times Luther considered Romans. Luther wrote prefaces to the books of the Bible for his German translation of the scriptures.[9] They were first published in

1522. In the Romans preface, Luther wrote, 'This epistle is really the chief part of the New Testament, and is truly the purest Gospel'.[10] In Romans, Luther found the heart of the gospel, the part that any reconciling effort would have to place in theological priority. Luther established a biblical hermeneutic for his German readers of the scripture: 'Interpret what you read according to Romans'. The brevity and clarity of this preface, and the intended broad audience, increased its impact far beyond that of a possible lengthier treatise written in traditional Latin for university trained scholars. Luther provided the tools for reading the gospel. Chief among them was Romans, as Luther understood it.

Luther had company in seeing Romans as central to scripture. The younger French reformer, John Calvin, would make the same move. Calvin displayed an early concern for the reader who attempted to navigate through scripture without a guide.[11] He proposed his *Institutes of the Christian Religion* as a particularly helpful guide to reading scripture. However, Calvin did not make this argument based on his own abilities, or his rhetorical brilliance, or even his alignment with the most sober fathers. Instead, he encouraged his readers to test him according to scripture.

For Calvin, one of the most basic *loci* in the scripture for establishing religious orthodoxy and grasping the meaning of God's revelation was Romans.[12] He contended that in his *argumentum* to the commentary. He wrote: 'Therefore, it will be better for me to come now to the argument itself. This will establish beyond any controversy that among other exceptional endowments the Epistle has one in particular which is never estimated highly enough. It is this – that if the true understanding of it is followed, we will have an open door to all the most concealed treasures of Scripture'.[13] Calvin was certain that this particularly Pauline lens presented in Romans offered the best way into scripture, the clearest road that would keep the reader from stumbling or wandering to and fro.[14] As numerous authors have pointed out, Calvin saw the scriptures themselves as "spectacles" which allowed believers to understand God's revelation in the world around them better.[15] But, to extend the metaphor, Romans acted as the cleanser for those spectacles.

The Reformation period also bequeathed significant gifts to the scholarly engagement with the scriptures. In 1516, Erasmus published his *Novum Instrumentum*. The theological world would never be the same. Erasmus was not actually lionized for his accomplishment – he would spend the rest of his life defending himself against the attacks that his revelation of the actual text behind the Vulgate harmed doctrine and the faith. Further, Erasmus was not the only scholar to present the Greek original to the scholars of the sixteenth century. The Complutensian Polyglot actually beat Erasmus's edition into print, though it would not be published until 1520.[16] But through doctrinal and academic battles, through argumentation and the countering decrees of the Council of Trent, the die was cast. Biblical scholarship had to rest on engagement with Greek and Hebrew. The return to the sources, the battle cry of *ad fontes*, demanded the engagement of serious biblical scholarship with the original languages.

The modern or postmodern world takes far too much for granted in presuming the superiority of this approach, and thus the ease of the transfer.[17] The inertia of a millennium dragged against the reform of biblical study; the carefully managed sense or senses of the text were clearly based on the Vulgate. Sixteenth century exegetes frequently were faced with a bewildering array of textual options, a set of options made more difficult because of the lack of standardized linguistic and historical tools.

But beyond the difficulties with establishing the most correct texts, the antecedent interpretive tradition was based upon the glossed Vulgate. The Vulgate did not immediately lose its authority, and even Protestant interpreters would call it the 'old interpreter'. The battles of the Reformation era set biblical scholarship on a path that led more clearly to the present, one that established a level of differentiation between biblical-textual work and theological-doctrinal work that was hitherto unknown.

Finally, the Reformation readings of Romans created a set of interpretive solutions that still resonate today. If Barth's commentary on Romans was a bomb set off in the playground of the theologians, Luther's discovery of righteousness as gift in Romans was a supernova in the midst of the Church – a cosmic event whose rays are still only arriving before our eyes. Some of the articles in this collection will continue the effort to come to grips with what Luther or Calvin meant, and why their solutions still seize our imaginations. While we may argue that as postmodern thinkers the Reformation is not our own time, we may never escape its impact.

Since the middle of the last century, biblical scholars and historians of Christianity have been painfully aware of the manner in which certain 'orthodox' understandings and interpretations of Romans have channeled the modern interpretation. Krister Stendahl's 'The Apostle Paul and the Introspective Conscience of the West' set out this pattern, noting that a particular (and incorrect!) reading of Paul had cemented ways of reading Romans in Western culture. This way of appropriating Paul had become normative in the theological stream of the West, buttressed by the centrality of Augustine and Luther to the theology of that culture.[18] Since Stendahl's article, many others have traced such 'mis-readings'.

Later scholars have continued the effort to uncover Paul from the theological frameworks that have kept the 'real Paul' away from view. To give just a single well-known example, E. P. Sanders has noted that Paul was not working out the theologies of individual salvation that became cherished in medieval and early modern theological interpretations, but rather was working in a framework of 'covenantal nomism' taken from the context of traditional Judaism.[19] These efforts of New Testament scholars worked to replace the worldviews of later readers with the most likely senses that Paul and his first century readers would have shared.

These discoveries within modern New Testament scholarship correspond to the breakthroughs of the history of exegesis school in examining pre-modern interpretation. The history of exegesis school has been able to demonstrate that the questions various interpreters asked of a pericope, or the theological loci which they believed corresponded to a pericope, had been established by the prior exegetical tradition.[20] Thus, the history of exegesis school frequently demonstrates that there is far greater continuity between the early modern and medieval traditions than modern historians, especially those under the sway of confessional considerations, had previously noted.

While the insights generated by careful textual and historical work on the real Paul of the first century world offer valuable correctives against reading too confidently in our modern efforts at both understanding and the task of Pauline theology, these insights also offer up a question. Given that we now know many things that the early modern exegetes did not, should our research into Paul and Romans simply work at setting aside the distortions of Paul and especially Romans which their work introduced or strengthened in our tradition?

Though that may sound like a tempting option, its promises are more chimerical than actual. First, scholars of hermeneutics have suggested that the effort at attaining a presuppositionless stance of reading is impossible. It is only the presuppositions which we bring to any text that allow understanding to be created.[21] Second, while our own understanding of Paul in his own time definitely outstrips that of the sixteenth century, we should not be unwilling to have our own presuppositions about the meaning of Romans challenged. By entering into a conversation with a set of texts from a world that is not our own, we are challenged to consider why our own scholarship makes the choices it does. We live in a world where biblical scholarship and systematic theology are separate disciplines – a division that would have been impossible to contemplate for the Reformation era thinkers. Finally, in examining the interpretations of the Reformation, and the theological statements they drew from those interpretations, we can begin to come to a better understanding of our own tradition, for we have ourselves been formed by the imprint of those thinkers.

With these thoughts in mind, we turn to the essays. Laurel Carrington opens the collection of essays with her treatment of Erasmus's interpretation of Paul, in her 'Erasmus's Readings of Romans 3, 4, and 5 as Rhetoric and Theology'. Frequently scholars rightly include Erasmus in the history of biblical interpretation, because of the incalculable significance of his textual work, especially his *Novum Instrumentum*, first published in 1516. Carrington moves beyond that stance to see Erasmus working not only as a text critic, but also as a biblical interpreter and theologian. She notes the careful tasks which Erasmus set for himself, first among which is that of taking Paul out of his context in the first century so that he could be met and grasped by men and women of the sixteenth century. Paul's message would be met in the simple faith that rejected the philosophy of the schoolmen, but paradoxically that message was wrapped in the manifold senses of scripture, inviting the learned reader to continual engagement. Secondly, Carrington considers the very different ways that Erasmus and Luther were reading the third chapter of Romans. Finally, in his struggles against his Catholic critics over the nature of original sin, Erasmus demonstrated a sensitivity to the nuance of the Pauline text that took priority over the traditional Augustinian rendering of the doctrine.

Two considerations of Martin Luther's interpretation of Paul follow. Deanna Thompson offers 'Letting the Word Run Free: Luther, Romans, and the Call to Reform', while Ekkehard Stegemann presents 'The Alienation of Humankind: Rereading Luther as Interpreter of Paul'. Thompson considers Luther's own sense of how Romans 1.17 transformed his entire theology. She finds that the background to this Copernican theological revolution is evident even in Luther's pre-1517 biblical work. However, it is with the commentary on Romans that Luther's freeing of God's word springs fully into view. Ironically, this same freeing of the word so that the spiritual realm would more closely resemble God's desires in the world resulted in a freeing of the word that impacted the temporal realm, causing even Luther himself to recoil against those who would destroy the traditional patterns of lord and servant. This led Luther to resist some of the fuller implications of his own theological breakthroughs, and invites further engagement even today.

Stegemann's article takes up our first two figures, Erasmus and Luther, and uses their debate to frame the ways that Luther was reading Paul in the sixteenth century. With an eye to Krister Stendahl's critique, Stegemann asks a different question. How was it that Luther made Paul so Lutheran? He sees the debate between the two as a clash of civilizations, as two world-views that each demand something of the Pauline text which denies the possibility of the other. Stegemann finds in Luther's *simul* an echo of a very different simultaneity in Paul's own thought. For Paul, the simultaneous issue was the existence of two worlds, or two ages. Paul believed that this situation must end soon. Luther, adopting the stance of the sixteenth century, redrew that time-frame to include his own life.

Edwin Woodruff Tait takes us away from Luther with a consideration of Martin Bucer's interpretation of the law in Romans. His 'The Law and its Works in Martin Bucer's 1536 Romans Commentary' takes up the issue of the law in Martin Bucer's mature theology. Tait situates this work between Wittenberg and Geneva. Differently from the Wittenberg theology, Bucer finds a unity in justification's effect, the making of the sinner righteous, which includes both the legal declaration of righteousness, and the actual making the person righteous. On the other hand, Bucer adopts a position on the law which sees the entire scripture as law, a position that differentiates him from both Luther and Calvin. His emphasis on identity, Tait argues, makes him a more congenial conversation partner for the 'new perspectives on Paul' movement than his contemporaries Martin Luther and John Calvin, who have received more attention by the present generation. Tait offers the chance that perhaps this character to his biblical interpretation will open a new chapter in Bucer studies and appropriation.

Two articles specifically dealing with John Calvin's interpretation of Romans follow. Both the articles consider the issue of hermeneutics in Calvin's thought. First, Gary Neal Hansen contributes 'Door and Passageway: Calvin's Use of Romans as Hermeneutical and Theological Guide'. Hansen makes the bold claim that the book of Romans functioned for Calvin as a guide to his theology and his hermeneutics. To demonstrate this, Hansen meticulously sets out the instances of Calvin's citation of Romans in the *Institutes*, and in the Genesis commentary. He demonstrates the preponderance of Romans citations over almost all other books of scripture, and suggests that the underlying structure of Calvin's doctrine is the structure of Romans.

R. Ward Holder's 'Calvin's Hermeneutic and Tradition: An Augustinian Reception of Romans 7', offers a different avenue into the issue of Calvin's hermeneutic and the book of Romans. Holder examines Calvin's interpretation of Romans 7, and his choice of the reading of the later Augustine as the correct reading. Calvin chose the later Augustine as correct, believing that Paul's cry represented the believer *coram Deo*, rather than a representation of a man before the law, prior to grace. Holder carefully traces the 'untold story', demonstrating that the choice of the later Augustine was also the rejection of the interpretation of Chrysostom. This rejection of Chrysostom becomes more significant when the reader sees that Calvin himself praised Chrysostom as the better exegete, better than Augustine. Holder finds the answer to this interpretive choice in Calvin's hermeneutical stance that rather uncritically accepts Augustine as truly orthodox. Thus, in Romans 7, Calvin abandons his own exegetical stance and the interpretation of his favorite exegete, so as to maintain orthodox doctrine – presenting a case where hermeneutics overwhelmed exegesis.

G. Sujin Pak furthers the book by adding an article which takes three of the giants of the Reformation and compares their interpretation of Romans. Her 'Luther, Melanchthon, and Calvin on Romans 5 and 13: Three Reformation Approaches to Reading Romans', examines the two Wittenberg theologians and the reformer of

Geneva in their approach to the fifth and thirteenth chapters. Pak sees the value of the comparative task as having to do with determining different approaches to the same material. She discerns a variety of readings, labeling Luther's approach contextual, Melanchthon's theological and Calvin's analytical. Carefully pointing out the historical contexts which informed the different commentaries, Pak notes several substantive differences between the authors. She finds that Luther has not moved beyond the medieval stance of the form of the commentary, nor has he left the thought-world of late Augustinianism. Implicitly, she argues that the Reformation breakthrough Luther scholars so assiduously search for cannot yet be seen in the Romans commentary. Melanchthon, however, writing in 1540, informs his exegesis with the dynamic of Law and Gospel; while Calvin, writing in the same year, demonstrates a concern for providence and election. Pak finds that the distinctive theological emphases that correlate to their confessional identities also exercise an influence upon the interpretive choices that each theologian makes.

Peter Opitz takes us into another Reformed figure, the Zürich theologian Heinrich Bullinger. Here we see the Reformed stream that precedes Calvin. Opitz carefully demonstrates those interpretive influences that others, including Calvin, might have taken from Bullinger. Further, Opitz establishes Bullinger's approach to Romans as occasional, rather than the more frequent approach to the epistle as a theological treatise. For Bullinger, Romans was most truly a proclamation of '*solus Christus*' and '*sola fide*', understood against the horizon of the Hebrew tradition of promise. This would always serve the homiletical needs of the present – to make Paul's message timeless.

The final contribution to the volume is Mark Elliott's 'Romans 7 in the Reformation Century'. Elliott essays a survey approach, examining the treatments of the seventh chapter in twenty different commentaries from the era. Beginning with John Colet's exposition from 1497, Elliott traces the wideness of the interpretive streams in the Reformation. Time and again, we see in his work that the modern analyst cannot predict the interpretive stances and decisions that a particular exegete would make simply by knowing his confessional stance or his educational pedigree. Elliott finds anticipations of some of the 'new perspectives' on Paul especially in their denial of the individualism that is so frequently attributed to the Protestant Reformation. The article demonstrates the promise inherent in comparative work that takes into account a wider field of study than that of one or two or even three interpreters. In comparisons of this scope, conversely, the analyst can begin to see the issues which are constant, and those which are ephemeral, in the Reformation century.

The Editors of this volume have chosen to include brief response articles as companion pieces to the essays noted. We do this because this was the style of the seminar sessions, but also because it brings greater coherence to the volume. Frequently a historian was answered by a New Testament specialist, or the Pauline scholar was responded to by a historical theologian. The different perspectives of our own research and thought added to the richness of the dialogue, and to the consideration of the hermeneutical and exegetical issues of addressing Romans in the sixteenth century, and in our own day's acceptance, rejection and transformation of those theological and exegetical complexes. Because these critiques are included, the Editors have been able to avoid our own critical evaluations and engagements with the essays.

The essays in this volume all originated as peer-reviewed Seminar papers that were prepared for, presented, and discussed at the Society of Biblical Literature 'Romans through History and Culture' panel sessions, presented in 2005 and 2006. We present them in the hope of furthering both modern biblical exegesis, and the study of historical exegesis.

Notes

[1]True, Luther wrote that long after his insight. But he believed that this was the locus of the central insight that turned him from hatred of God to grateful acceptance of God's mercy. See his Preface to the Latin Writings, LW vol. 34, WA 54.

[2]See the article by Mark Elliott within this volume.

[3]Timothy George notes this in his 'Modernizing Luther, Domesticating Paul: Another Perspective', in D. A. Carson, Peter T. O'Brien and Mark A. Seifrid, eds., *Justification and Variegated Nomism,* Wissenschaftliche Untersuchungen zum Neuen Testament, 181 (Tübingen, Mohr Siebeck, 2004), p. 440.

[4]Jerry Bentley, *Humanists and Holy Writ: New Testament Scholarship in the Renaissance* (Princeton: Princeton University Press, 1983).

[5]See especially Irena Backus, *Historical Method and Confessional Identity in the Era of the Reformation (1378–1615)* (Leiden: Brill, 2003).

[6]The date of Luther's conversion is a matter of on-going interest to Luther scholars. Dates as early as 1514 and as late as 1520 are proposed.

[7]See the article by Sujin Pak, 'Luther, Melanchthon, and Calvin on Romans 5 and 13:Three Reformation Approaches to Reading Romans', in this volume.

[8]Martin Luther, Preface to his Latin Writings. LW 34.336ff, WA 54.185f.

[9]I am indebted to Dr. Mickey Mattox for pointing out the significance of the biblical prefaces to me. See his article on Luther and Paul in *The Reception of Paul in the Reformation,* forthcoming from Brill Academic Publishers.

[10] WADB 7.2: ‚Dise Epistel ist das rechte hewbtstuckt des newen testaments, und das aller lauterst Euangelion'. The sentence is retained, with minor changes, in the edition of 1546.

[11]See my *John Calvin and the Grounding of Biblical Interpretation: Calvin's First Commentaries* (Leiden: Brill Academic Publishers, 2006).

[12]On this point, see especially Gary Neal Hansen's 'Door and Passageway: Calvin's Use of Romans as Hermeneutical and Theological Guide', contained in this volume.

[13]John Calvin, Commentary on the Epistle to the Romans, argument. T. H. L. Parker, ed., *Iohannis Calvini Commentarius in Epistolam Pauli ad Romanos* (Leiden: E. J. Brill, 1981), 5.6–11. 'Ergo iam ad argumentum ipsum transire satius fuerit: unde citra controversiam protinus constabit, praeter plurimas alias, et eas eximias dotes, hanc ei proprie competere, quae nunquam pro dignitate satis aestimetur: quod siquis veram eius intelligentiam sit assequutus, ad reconditissimos quosque Scripturae thesauros adeundos habeat apertas fores'. Parker has argued that this sense of Romans as the key, and by extension, the rest of Paul, explains why Calvin did not follow the canonical order in his commenting.

[14]T. H. L. Parker saw this as Calvin's reason for commenting upon the Pauline epistles first, rather than working through the New Testament in canonical order. See his *Calvin's New Testament Commentaries.* 2nd ed. (Louisville: Westminster/John Knox Press, 1993), pp. 31–35. Barbara Pitkin has noted Calvin's tendency to interpret texts according to Paul in her

What Pure Eyes Could See: Calvin's Doctrine of Faith in Its Exegetical Context (Oxford: Oxford University Press, 1999), pp. 82–83.

[15]See David Steinmetz, *Calvin in Context* (Oxford: Oxford University Press, 1995), and most recently, Randall Zachman, *Image and Word in the Theology of John Calvin* (Notre Dame University Press, 2007).

[16]Jerry Bentley, p. 71.

[17]See David Steinmetz, 'The Superiority of Pre-critical Exegesis', *Ex Auditu* 1 (1985) 74–82.

[18]Krister Stendahl, 'The Apostle Paul and the Introspective Conscience of the West', *Harvard Theological Review*, 56 (1963) 199–215.

[19]E. P. Sanders, *Paul and Palestinian Judaism* (Philadelphia: Fortress Press), 1977.

[20]See the work of especially David C. Steinmetz, Timothy Wengert, John Thompson, Craig Farmer, and Barbara Pitkin.

[21]See especially Hans-Georg Gadamer, *Truth and Method*, 2nd rev. ed., translated and revised by Joel Weinsheimer and Donald G. Marshall (New York: Crossroad Publishing, 1989).

— ONE —

Erasmus's Readings of Romans 3, 4, and 5 as Rhetoric and Theology

Laurel Carrington

◆

C In late 1517, at the point when Luther first voiced publicly his critique of the Roman church, his elder Erasmus was at the height of his fame as a humanist and advocate of reform. In 1516 he had published his first edition of his New Testament, the *Novum Instrumentum*, and was at work on a second edition, to appear in 1518.[1] He also had completed and published a paraphrase on Paul's letter to the Romans, the first in what would be a series of paraphrases on the whole New Testament. He had won great praise for these works, but he also had become the target of harsh criticisms. The list of his detractors is substantial: the young English biblical scholar Edward Lee, Chancellor Nöel Béda of the University of Paris, and bodies of Franciscan, Dominican, and Carmelite critics, to name but a few.[2]

Erasmus thus felt that he was under siege even before the onset of the evangelical reform polarized Europe beyond anything he could have imagined. As Luther's criticisms of the ecclesiology and theology of the Roman church gained support, Erasmus's work became the center of yet more controversy, partly because many of the people who went over to the reform had been his admirers and even collaborators in his New Testament scholarship. He was unwillingly drawn into debates with Martin Luther, Martin Bucer, and, indirectly, with Melanchthon, Oecolampadius, Pellican, and Leo Jud. The best known of these is the debate with Luther over the freedom of the will, which Erasmus launched with the publication in 1524 of his *Diatribe on the Freedom of the Will*, a direct refutation of the doctrine that was central to Luther's position. Luther would rely extensively upon his own interpretation of Paul's letter to the Romans in refuting Erasmus's arguments. We find that on examining Erasmus's comments on significant passages of that epistle, we can achieve further insight into the basis for Erasmus's quarrel with Luther.

It is not surprising that Luther and his party would accuse Erasmus of Pelagianism. What is less well known is that Erasmus's Catholic critics made the same accusation, based not on his *Diatribe* but on his translation and annotation of Romans 5:12 in his New Testament. Erasmus defended himself vigorously against all such accusations, in lengthy *Apologia* and in each new edition of the New Testament as well. This paper will examine Erasmus's readings of significant passages from Romans 3, 4 and 5, with a view to clarifying his true position not only in the eyes of his critics, but in the context of his own principles of interpretation. We turn first to the two works that are the foundations of Erasmus's New Testament scholarship.

C Erasmus's work and fame in the context of European theologians.

Erasmus's New Testament Scholarship: the *Novum Instrumentum* and the Paraphrases

AC Erasmus was originally inspired to turn his attention to a philological study of the New Testament by a 1499 trip to England, where he became acquainted with Thomas More and John Colet. At that time, Colet was presenting a series of lectures at Oxford on Paul, including the Romans epistle. Erasmus was impressed with Colet's humanist learning and with his opposition to the approach of the Scholastics, but he also felt keenly the need to know Paul's letters in their original language, Greek. Erasmus thus determined to master that language himself. A further source of inspiration for his work came from his discovery in 1504 of a copy of the *Adnotationes in Novi Testamenti* of Lorenzo Valla, a set of notes on scripture based on a linguistic and historical analysis of the Greek original.[3] This piece became a model for Erasmus's philological method, as well as a resource for his editorial decisions.

Erasmus's first task was to use his expertise in Greek to assemble as complete a collection of Greek manuscripts as possible, and try to produce through careful comparative analysis an authoritative edition of the Greek New Testament.[4] He had arrived at the conviction that it was impossible to understand Scripture without a clean and authoritative rendering of the text, which over the centuries had suffered from scribal errors and from near universal ignorance of the original language. Next, he decided to offer a Latin translation that was intended as both an alternative and an improvement on the Vulgate. Finally, there were extensive annotations, explaining decisions he had made in favor of one reading over another. The first edition appeared in 1516, and the criticisms quickly followed.[5]

His Paraphrases followed a different trajectory. Erasmus had begun work on a commentary on Romans in 1501. He labored on it off and on over the course of two decades, and yet never completed it. In 1514 he turned his attention instead to paraphrase.[6] Paraphrase, the act of recasting the language of a text while retaining its meaning, is a technique that teachers of rhetoric from antiquity had utilized in helping their students become proficient in verbal *copia*, abundance and variety of expression. In the dedicatory letter to his Paraphrase of Paul's letter to the Romans, Erasmus wrote: 'I thought I should be doing something worth while if I could make Paul speak to men who are now pure Romans and adult Christians, not only in the Roman tongue but more intelligibly; if, in fact, he could talk Latin in such a way that one would not recognize the Hebrew speaking but would recognize the Apostle'.[7] As a rhetorical exercise, Erasmus's paraphrase of Romans provides a special service in allowing the apostle to shift out of the limits of his historical context to speak to modern audiences, 'pure Romans and adult Christians', leaving behind the Jew whose law has been eclipsed by the Gospel.[8]

Erasmus's letter is dated November 13, 1517, at exactly the same time that Luther's 95 Theses were beginning to circulate. Thus the evolution of his New Testament work took place alongside of the beginnings of the Protestant reform. We should look next at the principles underlying Erasmus's interpretations.

A Analysis of the origin of Erasmus's philological interest.

C In a particular context, under specific circumstances.

Erasmus's Hermeneutical Principles

Manfred Hoffmann in his groundbreaking study, *Rhetoric and Theology: The Hermeneutic of Erasmus,*[9] defines Erasmus as a rhetorical theologian. As a humanist, Erasmus believed in the crucial importance of rhetoric as a foundation both for knowing the truth and doing what is right. In contrast to sterile arguments expressed in technical language, he stressed the transformative power of language, which can act upon the soul to turn a person's life towards God and away from things of the flesh. Erasmus was particularly caustic in his characterization of the scholastic philosophers and theologians, who were among his most obstreperous critics. These were the people who were so wrapped up in their technical definitions and wrong-headed literal interpretations of a flawed Vulgate that they had lost sight of Jesus himself, the goal (*scopus*)[10] of all our faith. Erasmus's *philosophia Christi* was his answer to the philosophers of the schools: a philosophy consisting of a simple faith in Christ, and a willingness to follow His teachings.[11] Erasmus wanted the mediation of Christ to replace Aristotle's metaphysics and syllogistic logic as a means for gaining insight into scripture.

A Of course, not even the most sublime language could accomplish this if human beings were unable to respond to it. Erasmus adopts from Origen, one of his favorite theologians, the division of the human being into three components: flesh, soul, and spirit.[12] It is the middle part, the soul, that is open to persuasion through language that is rightly used.[13] For Erasmus, the soul is the mediator between the body and the spirit, just as Jesus Christ mediates between human and God. Language in particular is a mediator, between speakers and hearers as well as writers and readers. In the case of scripture, divine language communicates divine meaning to humans who cannot understand it directly. Thus Erasmus views God as the heavenly rhetorician, capable of accommodating His language to the limited ability of humans to hear and understand. The four levels of meaning in scripture, historical or literal, allegorical, tropological, and anagogical, are necessary because no human being can leap directly from his or her limited earthly vision straight to the ultimate sense of scripture. The two middle levels are thus of particular importance as the mediators between heaven and earth. They are able to fulfill this function through scripture's extensive use of metaphors.

Metaphor is a term or trope that mediates between two unlike things by drawing a parallel, thus rendering them like each other. Metaphor is the model for the mediating activity of scripture, which brings together those who are unlike, God and humans. According to Erasmus, the language of scripture is not simply a technical correspondence between word and thing, which the interpreter needs only to read to know immediately what it means. It is a bridge between disparate entities, which takes into account their distinct positions in history, in society, and in the cosmos. Thus, Erasmus's introduction to the Romans paraphrase, 'I thought I should be doing something worthwhile if I could make Paul speak to men who are now pure Romans and adult Christians', acknowledges that the original context for Paul's letter is different from that of Erasmus and his contemporaries. The Paul of history spoke to people who were recently converted to Christianity, not the 'adult Christians' of almost 1500 years later; he likewise used Greek in a manner that bore 'the admixture everywhere of Hebrew idiom'.[14] Erasmus wanted his own contem-

---

A Analysis of Erasmus's perception of rhetoric.

poraries to be able to hear Paul the apostle, not Paul the Jew. Erasmus acknowledges that there will be those who object, conceding that 'he who rejects any change in the letter of Holy Writ may use it as a commentary, while he who is free from such superstition may hear the voice of Paul himself'.[15]

Thus Erasmus's paraphrase, as it replicates Paul by transforming his language, mediates between Paul in his earthly, historical identity as a Jew and his spiritual, eternal identity as an apostle. **A** The term 'Jew' in Erasmus's vocabulary has a specialized meaning: the Jew is the one who is bound to the letter of the law, which in Erasmus's terms equates with superstition and a failure to allow the language its mediating function.[16] **C** Those who rejected any change in the letter of Holy Writ in Erasmus's day were the Paris theologians and the monastic orders who tormented him with criticisms; in his eyes they are parallel to the Jews who rejected the saving grace of Christ in the newborn church.

Erasmus's paraphrase does indeed alter the language of Paul the Jew in ways designed to separate him from his origins, as for example at the end of his paraphrase of Romans 3:26 and beginning of the paraphrase of 3:27. The biblical verses are:[26] 'it [Christ's sacrifice] was to prove at the present time that he himself is righteous and that he justifies him who has faith in Jesus.[27] Then what becomes of our boasting? It is excluded. On what principle? On the principle of works? No, but on the principle of faith'.[17] Erasmus's paraphrase begins: 'Tell me, therefore, *you Jew*, where is your boasting? Of course this boasting was taken away from *you* after the divine will made all the races of the world equal with respect to the gospel' (emphasis added).[18] Another example is the paraphrase of Romans 3:31: 'Do we then overthrow the law by this faith?' which begins, 'But here *some Jew* will say: How can this be, Paul?'[19]

To summarize, Erasmus in his hermeneutic moves in two opposing and yet complementary directions: towards simplicity in his rejection of the theology of the schools, and towards complexity in his recognition of the layers of meaning that unfold for the experienced reader. The principle of accommodation, which Paul himself embodies in his missions to all kinds of people, allows for both movements to occur together. Scripture accommodates itself to readers at all levels, drawing those who have innocent minds into the mysteries a little at a time, as they are prepared to understand them.

Erasmus's Debate with Luther

Erasmus illustrates these hermeneutical principles in his famous debate with Luther, as the combatants clash in their respective understanding of faith and works, freedom of the will, and original sin. Luther for his part will explicitly reject Erasmus's hermeneutic, laying out not only a different set of beliefs or interpretations, but an opposing approach to the discernment of theological truth. For example, at the beginning of *De libero arbitrio*, Erasmus remarks: 'For in Holy Scripture there are some secret places into which God did not intend us to penetrate very far, and if we attempt to do so, the farther in we go the less and less clearly we see',[20] indicating that even experienced readers who are mature in faith

---

A Analysis of the term 'Jew' in Erasmus's understanding.

C Contextual dimension of the above analysis

are limited in what they can know. For Luther, however, scripture is almost transparent, even to the beginner:

> But that in Scripture there are some things abstruse, and everything is not plain – this is an idea put about by the ungodly Sophists,[21] with those lips you also speak here, Erasmus; . . . I admit that many passages in Scriptures are obscure and abstruse. But that is due to our ignorance of certain terms and grammatical particulars, and not to the majesty of the subject. This ignorance does not in any way prevent our knowing all the contents of Scriptures.[22]

AH Luther is bluntly dismissive of Erasmus's understanding of human beings as trichotomous: 'I, too, am familiar with Origen's fable about the threefold disposition of flesh, soul, and spirit, with soul standing in the middle and being capable of turning either way, toward the flesh or toward the spirit'.[23] He asserts in its place a stark dualism, based largely on his readings of Paul: 'What else is the meaning of 'You are not in the flesh if the Spirit of God is in you' (Rom. 8:9) but that those who do not have the Spirit are necessarily in the flesh? And if anyone does not belong to Christ, to whom else does he belong but Satan? Clearly, then, those who lack the Spirit are in the flesh and subject to Satan'.[24] In contrast, Erasmus in his paraphrase of this same passage writes,

> One who is void of the Spirit is alien to Christ. But if Christ is in you, since he is nothing other than purity, truth, temperance, and other virtues, what place is there for vices in you? *One who has Christ must express him* ... We express Christ if the body, that is, that baser part of ourselves which tempts us to deadly things by the attractions of desire, is dead and free from all passion for sinning; and if the spirit lives, that is, the better part of ourselves, enticing us to the good, carrying us off by its own force to those things that belong to righteousness (emphasis added).[25]

It is clear that for Erasmus, the individual is not simply one or the other, 'of Christ' or 'of Satan', but rather is capable of expressing Christ's virtues through imitation when Christ dwells within. We are 'enticed' to the good, 'carried off by its own force'. Such terminology speaks of persuasion, attraction, and response, language that belongs to the art of rhetoric.[26] Indeed, Erasmus in his examination of the scriptural evidence for free will in his *Diatribe* points to one passage after another in which believers are exhorted to turn away from evil and toward righteousness: 'Nearly the whole of Scripture speaks of nothing but conversion, endeavor, and striving to improve. All this would become meaningless once it was accepted that doing good or evil was a matter of necessity'.[27]

Luther rejects Erasmus's understanding of such exhortations as instances of persuasion, understanding them rather as statements of fact that the just will recognize and the unjust ignore. He turns to Paul for confirmation of his view, as for example in Romans 3:21–25:

> But now the righteousness of God has been manifested apart from law, although the law and the prophets bear witness to it,[22] the righteousness of God through faith in Jesus Christ for all who believe. For there is no distinction, [23] since all have sinned and fall short of the glory of God,[24] they are justified by his grace as a gift, through the redemption which is in Christ

---

AH Analysis of divergent hermeneutical presuppositions of Luther and Erasmus.

Jesus,[25] whom God put forward as an expiation by his blood, to be received by faith. This was to show God's righteousness, because in his divine forbearance he had passed over former sins.

Luther's comment on this passage is that 'Paul's words here are absolute thunderbolts against free choice',[28] directly interpreting Paul's opposition between faith and law as a repudiation of free will. For Erasmus, however, there is no such necessary connection between God's free gift of faith and humans having an unfree will, because humans can be led to abandon their reliance on the law through the mediating power of the language of the gospel. Erasmus's paraphrase of 3:27 describes the dichotomy between faith and works: 'Salvation and righteousness are conferred also on the gentiles. Through what law then? Through that old Mosaic law which prescribes *ceremonies*? Not at all, but *through a new law which demands nothing except faith in the Son of God*' (emphasis added).[29] Erasmus explicitly upholds the teaching of justification by faith, but expresses the contrast between faith and law as being between *faith* and *ceremonies*, a distinction that he understands in his own context as that between the *philosophia Christi* and the kind of superstition that is manifested in pilgrimages, worship of relics, masses for the dead, and many practices typical of the religious orders.

We can see another example of the same interpretation in his paraphrase of the beginning of Romans 3:1, 'Then what is the advantage of the Jew?' 'But here someone will say to me: *If the whole matter depends on a pious life and innocent character and on faith in Christ*, what then is left to the Jew by which he excels the heathen?' (emphasis added).[30] This is the essence of the *philosophia Christi*: a pious life, innocent character, and faith in Christ. We are brought to all of these things by the mediation of scripture. For Luther, however, we are brought out of sin into righteousness only through the intervention of Christ in an act of redemption that we are powerless even to accept or reject. Luther's concept of sin is all-encompassing, completely destroying in man any possibility of goodness without Christ's redemption. As we look to Erasmus's reading of Romans 5:12, we will see that his concept of sin is substantially different not only from Luther's, but from that of many in his own church as well.

Controversies over Erasmus's Rendering of Romans 5:12

Erasmus's paraphrase of Romans 5:12: '[t]herefore as sin came into the world through one man and death through sin, and so death spread to all men because all men sinned …' is as follows:

> And it was provided by the wonderful and secret plan of God that the way by which our well-being was restored would correspond to the way in which we had suffered ruin. Accordingly, through Adam alone, who first transgressed the law of God, sin crept into the world, and sin dragged along death as its companion inasmuch as sin is the poison of the soul. And so it happened that the evil originated by the first of the race spread through all posterity, *since no one fails to imitate the example of the first parent* (emphasis added).[31]

To describe sin as the poison of the soul suggests that the soul has been adversely affected by sin, especially insofar as sin leads to death. But Erasmus describes the effects of Adam's sin in its spreading to all his descendants as being manifested in their *imitation* of Adam's example. We have encountered another term for imitation, *exprimere*, in Erasmus's paraphrase of Romans 8:9: 'one who has Christ must express him'.[32] The concept of *imitatio Christi*, which is the title of Thomas à Kempis's famous handbook, was well known among Erasmus's contemporaries; however, for Erasmus to speak of sin being transmitted by imitation of Adam was another matter, for it raised the possibility of Pelagianism in the minds of theologians.

C For Erasmus, however, there is an additional layer of significance to the notion of imitation: imitation of models was an essential component of rhetorical training during the Renaissance, something Erasmus not only understood but also was moved years later, in 1527, to feature in a work entitled *Ciceronianus*, a repudiation of a theory of imitation then in vogue among Roman intellectuals. What these individuals had done was adopt the prose style of Cicero as a model that they imitated slavishly. In the *Ciceronianus* Erasmus pokes fun at these fanatics for clinging to the outer details of Ciceronian rhetoric, failing to incorporate into themselves the principles that were the source of Cicero's excellence. **A** Erasmus's preferred approach to imitation was assimilation, which allowed the individual to be himself and yet at the same time express what was worthy in the model. In the case of imitating Christ also, Erasmus wished his readers not to focus on the outer appearance of piety through adherence to ceremonies, but rather to assimilate Christ so that they could express Him in their very being.[33] Conversely, as descendants of Adam, humans have assimilated Adam's sin as it has spread to his posterity, and as a consequence, express this sin through imitation.

The means by which rhetoricians assimilate Cicero is through extensive reading of his works; likewise, Christians assimilate Christ through reading scripture. But how might people learn to imitate Adam's sin? We can find an answer in Erasmus's annotation to his translation of Romans 5:12: Translating the Greek ἐφ’ ῷ πάντες ἥμαπρτον, Erasmus chooses *quatenus omnes peccaverunt* ('inasmuch as all have sinned'), over the Vulgate version, *in quo omnes peccaverunt* ('in whom all have sinned'). Erasmus's translation suggests that all people have sinned without specifying that sin lies at the very basis of postlapsarian human nature, whereas the Vulgate shows the sin of Adam as automatically transferring itself to all of his descendants. In his note to this verse, Erasmus writes: 'But if sin here is understood as the withdrawal of the divine grace that was in Adam before he sinned, or a certain natural propensity to commit sin, which seems ingrown in all (*although I think [this propensity] proceeds from example rather than from nature*) – these are the punishments for sin more truly than they are sin [itself]'[34] (emphasis added). We imitate Adam's example through our assimilation of the sin that we learn from observing others.

Unfortunately for Erasmus, this approach to original sin was at odds with the accepted teaching of the church. He was immediately taken to task following the publication of the 1516 edition by Edward Lee, an Englishman who had taken a post in the theological school at Louvain.[35] Lee's criticism led to a protracted battle, as Erasmus tried to justify his interpretations through a series of *Apologiae* and through expanded annotations on that verse in subsequent editions of the New Testament. Erasmus claims the support of Origen – '[Origen demonstrates] with proofs that individuals have sinned by their own sins', with the exception of Christ, who alone

---

C Significance of contextual factor for understanding Erasmus's emphasis on *imitatio*.
A Analysis of Erasmus's perception of imitation.

repulsed sin; concluding, 'I think it is clear enough from these words that Origen interpreted this passage in terms of the sin of imitation, as did the scholiast'.[36] However, Erasmus immediately qualifies these remarks by pointing out that he does not question the existence of 'some original sin',[37] and adds that he does in fact condemn Pelagius's view, but that 'the dispute is concerned only with the sense of this passage, whether properly it refers to original sin'.[38] While it may seem that he is dodging the issue, his comment in fact reflects his belief that interpreting any passage from Scripture should reflect the context of the passage in relation to the chapter and book in which it appears, and ultimately all of Scripture; **H** interpretation should not be a mining of individual passages for doctrine.

Erasmus's annotation cites examples from the Fathers – Ambrose, Theophylact, Chrysostom – in support of his contention that Rom. 5:12 does not necessarily lead to any conclusions about either the nature of sins (whether they be freely committed by individuals in imitation of examples) or the sin of infants. His argument is that the passage supports more than one interpretation, and that for him to suggest an alternative does not threaten or injure church teaching in any way.[39] This being said, however, it is clear that Erasmus did not uphold a fully Augustinian doctrine of original sin, which claims that sin is not just a propensity, but rather an the elemental corruption of the very nature of all human beings, including infants.

Conclusions

Erasmus's interpretation of Paul's Letter to the Romans, based on what we have observed here, is an illustration of his most deeply-held convictions. First, we clearly see reflections of Erasmus's belief that language has the power to bring harmony out of disorder, including out of the disordered relationship between humans and God. Second, he believes that humans, even in all our weakness, are able to participate in the discourse that brings us closer to God. In our capacity for sin we are strongly inclined to learn how to imitate the examples of those around us, who in turn imitate their predecessors, all the way back to Adam. As a remedy for sin, Erasmus focuses on Christ's mediation between heaven and earth and the reconciliation He has effected, so that our souls may be brought to turn away from the flesh and toward the things of the spirit. Erasmus's respect for the teachings of the church does not preclude his openness to more than one interpretation of any given passage of Scripture; indeed, his very belief in the freedom of grace enables us to explore the multiple dimensions of scriptural language without fear of violating strict rules. Because we are justified by our faith, we can live with the knowledge that God's love is steadfast, and that our slavery to ceremonies has been superceded by the free gift of the Gospel.

Abbreviations

CWE: *The Collected Works of Erasmus* (Toronto: University of Toronto Press, 1974)

LB: Jean Leclerc, ed., *Desiderii Erasmi Roterodami Opera Omnia* (Leiden, 1703; repr. Hildesheim: Georg Olms Verlagsbuchhandlung, 1962)

H Hermeneutical presupposition of Erasmus's reading of scripture.

LW: *Luther's Works* (Philadelphia: Fortress Press, 1955–1975)

WA: *Martin Luthers Werke, Kritische Gesamtausgabe* (Weimar, 1883–1966)

Notes

[1] The title of the 1518 and subsequent editions was changed to *Novum Testamentum*.

[2] See Erika Rummel, *Erasmus and his Catholic Critics* (Nieuwkoop: De Graaf Publishers, 1989), 2 vols.

[3] Erasmus found the manuscript at the Premonstratensian Abbey du Parc, near Louvain, and published an edition of the work in the following year.

[4] See Jerry Bentley, *Humanists and Holy Writ: New Testament Scholarship in the Renaissance* (Princeton, N.J.: Princeton University Press, 1983) and Albert Rabil, Jr., *Erasmus and the New Testament: The Mind of a Christian Humanist* (San Antonio: Trinity University Press, 1972).

[5] For a discussion of Erasmus's annotations as they evolved through the five editions published in his lifetime, see Erika Rummel, *Erasmus' Annotations on the New Testament: From Philologist to Theologian* (Toronto: University of Toronto Press, 1986).

[6] See the introduction to CWE 42 by John B. Payne and Albert Rabil, Jr. Erasmus's paraphrases did not meet with the same resistance as his New Testament.

[7] CWE 42, p. 2: 'videbar mihi facturus operae pretium, si effecissem ut Paulus jam mere Romanis, ac plene Christianis, non solum Romane, verum etiam explanatius loqueretur: atque ita loqueretur Romane, ut Hebraeum quidem non agnoscas, agnoscas tamen Apostolum loqui' (LB VII 771).

[8] For a discussion of Erasmus's use of the Jew as a symbol of bondage to rules as opposed to the freedom under grace of Christ, see Shimon Markish, *Erasmus and the Jews* (Chicago: University of Chicago Press, 1986).

[9] Toronto: University of Toronto Press, 1994.

[10] See Marjorie O'Rourke Boyle, *Erasmus on Language and Method in Theology* (Toronto: University of Toronto Press, 1977), pp. 72–81 for an analysis of Erasmus's use of this term.

[11] Erasmus developed this concept in several of his most significant works, including the *Enchiridion militis Christi*, a handbook for a pious life that he first published in 1503 and later in 1518, and the *Paraclesis*, his introduction to the first edition of his New Testament.

[12] Origen *Commentarius in Epistolam ad Romanos* 1.5 and *De Principiis* 3:4.

[13] As we shall see, the fact that the soul is capable of responding to teaching is the basis for Erasmus's belief in free will.

[14] CWE 42, p. 2: 'admixtam Hebraei semonis proprietatem' (LB VII 771).

[15] CWE 42, p. 3: 'ut ei, qui nolit quicquam in sacris Litteris immutari, commentarii vice sit futurum; rursus ei, qui vacet hujusmodi superstitione, Paulus ipse loqui videatur' (LB VII 771).

[16] See n. 8, above.

[17] All biblical citations are from *The New Oxford Annotated Bible, Revised Standard Version* (New York: Oxford University Press, 1977.

[18] CWE 42, p. 25: 'Dic igitur Judae, ubi gloriatio tua? Nimirum ademta est tibi, posteaquam divini voluntas omnes orbis nationes aequat in negotio Evangelii' (LB VII 787B).

[19] CWE 42, p. 26: 'Verum, hic dixerit Judaeus quispiam: Quid ais Paule?' (LB VII 787D). It should be pointed out that there are some passages where Erasmus's Paul does refer to himself and the Jews in the first person; e.g. Romans 3:9: 'Sed ut ad rem redeam: quid dicemus? Num Judaei potiores sumus Ethnicis?' (LB VII 786B).

[20] CWE 76, p. 8.

[21] Luther is referring to the scholastic theologians.

[22] LW 33, p. 25: 'Sed esse in scriptura quaedam abstrusa et non omnia exposita, invulgatum est quidem per impios Sophistas, quorum ore et tu loqueris hic Erasme ... Hoc sane fateor, esse multa loca in scripturis obscura et abstrusa, non ob maiestatem rerum, sed ob ignorantiam vocabulorum et grammaticae, sed quae nihil impediant scientiam omnium rerum in scripturis' (WA 18 606).

[23] LW 33, p. 275: 'Nota est ad mihi fabula Origenis de triplici affectu, quorum unus caro, alius anima, alius spiritus illi dicitur. Anima vero medius ille, in utram partem vel carnis vel spiritus vertibilis' (WA 18 774).

[24] LW 33, p. 274: 'Quid enim aliud hic vult: Vos non estis in carne, si spiritus Dei in vobis est, quam necessario in carne eos esse, qui spiritum non habent? Et qui Christi non est, cuius alius quam Satanae est? Stat igitur, qui spiritu carent, hos in carne et sub Satana esse' (WA 18 774).

[25] CWE 42, p. 46, amended: 'quo qui vacat, is a Christo est alienus. Quod si Christus in vobis est, cum is nihil aliud sit, quam castitas, quam veritas, quam temperantia caeteraeque virtutes, quis est vitiis locus? Christum exprimat oportet, qui Christum habet. ... Hunc sic exprimimus, si corpus, hoc est, crassior illa pars nostri, quae cupiditatum lenociniis ad mortifera sollicitat, sortua sit, et omni peccandi libidine careat, vivat autem spiritus, hoc est, melior pars nostri, ad honesta sollicitans, et ad ea, quae sunt justitiae, impetu suo rapiens' (LB VII 801F–802A).

[26] Cf. Quint. *Inst. Or.* XII.x.61, in reference to the abundant style: 'Sat ille, qui saxa devolvat et ponem indignetur et ripas sibi faciat, multus et torrens iudicem vel nitentem contra feret cogetque ire, qua rapiet'.

[27] CWE 76, p. 36.

[28] LW 33, p. 263: 'Hic Paulus mere fulmina loquitur adversus liberum arbitrium' (WA 18 757).

[29] CWE 42, p. 25 (italicized portion added in 1532): 'Defertur et Gentibus salus ac justitia. At per quam tandem legem? Num veterem illam Mosaicam, quae ceremonias praescribit? Nequaquam, imo per novam legem, quae nihil exigit nisi fidem erga Filium Dei' (LB VII 787C).

[30] CWE 42, p. 22 (italicized portion added in 1532): 'Sed dixerti hic quispiam, si summa rei pendet a pietate vitae et innocentia morum, ac fide in Christum, quid igitur reliquum fit Judaeo, quo praecellat Ethnicum?' (LB VII 785B).

[31] CWE 42, p. 34: 'Itaque miro et arcano Dei consilio curatum est, ut restitutae salutis ratio, cum accepti exitii ratione congrueret. Proinde quemadmodum per unum Adam, qui primus praetergressus est Dei praecesciptum, peccatum irrepsit in mundum, peccatum autem mortem comitem secum traxit, quandoquidem peccatum animae venenum est, atque ita factum est, ut malum a principe generis ortum, in universam posteritatem dimanaret, dum nemo non imitatur primi parentis exemplum' (LB VII 793A-B).

[32] See p. 8 above. CWE 42 translates this term as 'imitate'.

[33] It is important to note that the meaning of 'to imitate' is not exactly the same as the meaning of 'to express'. To express Christ suggests a stronger sense of identification with the example than the imitation of the sin of Adam.

[34] CWE 56, p. 140: 'Quod si peccatum accipitur pro subtractione gratiae divinae, quae fuit in Adam antequam peccaret, aut pro naturali quadam pronitate ad peccandum, quae videtur omnibus insita, quanquam arbitror hanc magis ab exemplis proficisci, quam a natura, haec sunt poena peccati verius quam peccatum' (LB VI 585C–D).

[35] For a thorough discussion of this controversy, see Robert Coogan, 'The Pharisee against the Hellenist: Edward Lee Versus Erasmus', in *Renaissance Quarterly*, 39.3, (Autumn, 1986), 476–506. See also John B. Payne, 'Erasmus: Interpreter of Romans', in *Sixteenth Century Essays and Studies*, 2 (Jan., 1971), 1–35.

[36] CWE 56, p. 144: 'declarans argumentis singulos pecasse suis peccatis ... Ex his arbitror satis liquere, quod Origines hunc locum interpretatus est de peccato imitationis, quemadmodum ille Scholiastes' (LB VI 587A). The 'scholiast' is a commentator on Paul's letters bearing Jerome's name, but although Erasmus included the commentary in his Froben edition of Jerome, he knew that it was pseudonymous. The author has been shown to be Pelagius, although Erasmus did not realize this.

[37] CWE 56, p. 144: 'aliquod peccatum originis' (LB VI 587B).

[38] CWE 56, p. 144: 'tantum de huius loci sensu disputatio est, an proprie pertineat ad peccatum originale' (LB VI 587B).

[39] CWE 56, p. 148, 150; LB VI 588E.

Response to Laurel Carrington

Cynthia Briggs Kittredge

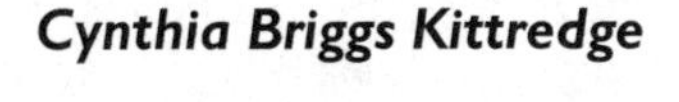

Laurel Carrington reviews Erasmus's contribution to New Testament scholarship with his publication of his edition of the New Testament, the *Novum Instrumentum* and his paraphrase of Paul's letter to the Romans. She presents Erasmus's hermeneutical principles: his understanding of the multiple levels of scriptural meaning, the role of the soul in mediating between spirit and body, and the contrast he makes between Christ as the goal of the faith and the use of metaphysics and scholastic logic. Her explication of the paraphrases of Romans 3:26–31 and 5:12 illustrates Erasmus's principles of scriptural interpretation and illuminates his dispute with Luther about reading scripture and about free will. Dr. Carrington's lucid paper describes the texture of theological and exegetical debate in this period. In the biblical scholarship of Erasmus and his contemporaries textual criticism, translation, commentary, polemics, social criticism, and satire were all mixed up together and they defy the careful distinctions that we in modern historical biblical studies attempt to keep today. This sequence of studies of Reformation readings makes vivid the way that readings of Romans are in explicit connection with the urgent disputes in theological and political context of their time. When we study those at an historical distance, the operation of the hermeneutical circle is more clearly visible than it is in our own. This study raises four questions for contemporary understanding of the relationship between biblical scholarship and readings of Romans.

The first is Erasmus's understanding of the role of the biblical scholar. Through translation of the texts in their original languages Erasmus and other Renaissance humanists attempted to get closer to the origins of Christian faith. With many early historical critics, they shared the impulse to circumvent accumulated traditions and readings and gain less mediated access to origins of faith. Erasmus's ambitions were not confined to illumination of the past, but included the retrieval of meaning into the present. Paraphrase allowed Erasmus to bridge the gap between the past and the present. His description of the goal of his paraphrases of Romans expresses the aspirations:

> I thought I should be doing something worthwhile if I could make Paul speak to men who are now pure Romans and adult Christians, not only in the Roman tongue but more intelligibly; if, in fact, he could talk Latin in such a way that one would not recognize the Hebrew speaking but would recognize the Apostle.

At the same time understated and extraordinarily ambitious, Erasmus's words convey recognition of the changed context and identity of his contemporary readers.

But unlike modern scholarship on Paul where the weight is placed on reading Paul in his Jewish context, for Erasmus, in order for Paul to speak to the present, he must be detached from his identity as a Hebrew. While for some modern critics who situate Paul firmly in the first century, it is not necessary for Paul to 'speak' in the present, for others the challenge is to bring Paul's voice into the present yet in a way that does not disregard his own context. While not many modern scholars would claim to be a channel for the voice of Paul as boldly as Erasmus does, many take on the task of "translating" Paul into the present and inviting him to weigh in on contested issues of the modern world.

Erasmus envisioned his project in the *Paraphases* to be a rhetorical exercise in which he as translator and commentator brought Paul's meaning into the present. Erasmus became a channel for the voice of the apostle, but Erasmus acknowledged the way that translation must necessarily transform Paul's own text. Furthermore, the ultimate aim of Erasmus's paraphrase, was like Scripture itself, to act on the soul and turn a person's life toward God. The view that the soul is open to persuasion through language and that the biblical scholar might persuade through her commentary is not common among biblical scholars but is the foundational confidence of most biblical preaching.

Next, Carrington's analysis of Erasmus's principles of interpretation shows how they depend on his understanding of language and of anthropology. His belief in multiple levels of scriptural language, adapted from Origen, Augustine, and others, allowed him to conceptualize how the language of scripture could function as God's mediation between heavenly and earthly realities. Erasmus's stress on the mystery of scripture and its multivalence is in distinct contrast to Luther's confidence in scripture's transparency and clarity. While Luther is very optimistic about the efficacy of scripture and of Christ, Erasmus is more hopeful about human effort and ability to progress. Modern views of language range from one-to-one correspondence models to language as infinite play of meanings, but not all biblical interpreters reflect on the view of language which underlines their interpretations. Those biblical interpreters today who conceive of biblical studies as a rhetorical enterprise acknowledge its exhortatory character and its explicit ethical aims.[1]

Likewise, beliefs about anthropology, derived not from the text but from the world view of the culture or theological convictions of the interpreter, significantly shape the reading of Romans. The role played by cultural categories in interpretation is exemplified by the discussion of Luther and Erasmus about the freedom of the will based on Romans 5:12. It seems clear to me, and to Erasmus, that whether the human will in absolutely bound or free cannot be determined by appeal to Romans 5:12 alone. Rather, readings of Augustine, disputes with Pelagius, and constraints of the theological debates of the time shape the reading of the text of Romans itself. In our interpretive context contemporary ideas of the human self, as free or bound, individual or corporate, autonomous or not, heterosexual, homosexual, transgendered, male, female, slave, or free influence readings of ancient texts. How these ideas obscure, reinforce, or contradict the anthropology expressed in the text is a complex problem to untangle. Even if they can be sorted out, the problem of translation remains a significant challenge for theologians and critics who take on that task.

Laurel Carrington's analysis raises the third question of how to read Paul's dualism. She presents the contrast between Erasmus's tripartite anthropology and Luther's dualistic one. Corresponding to the three-part picture of human being is

Erasmus's view of the robust and active role of language as a mediator between human and God. In contrast, Luther's literalism and resistance to the idea of mediation correspond to his view that the human is made up of flesh and spirit. Here Luther finds an ally in Paul, who provides plenty of evidence to support Luther's view. Although my own working anthropology is closer to that of Erasmus, I acknowledge that Luther's more closely resembles Paul's.

Related to the general question of reading Paul's dualism is the perpetuation of rhetorical forms and their interpretation through history. Erasmus's paraphrases of Romans 3:27, 31 presents a clear instance of the problem of reading Paul's dualistic rhetoric. The powerful rhetorical device of the diatribe's rhetorical questions and the stark opposition Paul makes between flesh and spirit are strengthened and made more tenacious through centuries of commentary. The oppositional dynamic is reinforced and historical people are supplied as representatives of that dualism. Carrington shows how Erasmus supplies the addressee 'you Jew' in his paraphrase of Romans 3:27, 31. Stanley Stowers has traced how the history of this view of the audience of Romans as including Jews has skewed the reading of the letter. Such an anti-Jewish reading would not have made sense in its original context to Paul's first century audience.[2] The interpreter's contemporary foes take their place in the oppositional dynamic. Erasmus's substitution of the word 'ceremonies' for 'works' reads the anti-Catholic polemic of Erasmus's time back into Paul's text. This rhetorical technique, of supplying a real contemporary opponent who is analogous to Paul's historical rhetorical opponent, survives to this day in Christian preaching and biblical argument. Inscribed patterns of rhetoric against Jews as 'other' standing for the particular, the ethnic, the exclusive, the carnal were repeated with deadly effect in the anti-Semitic writings in twentieth century Europe. Feminist critics of Romans have drawn attention to the position of woman/wife/female/*hypandros* in the symbolic universe of Romans and to the effects of this rhetoric in reinforcing a kyriarchal social structure.[3] In the afterword to *Erasmus and the Jews*, Arthur Cohen argues that the anti-Judaism in Erasmus's writing was part of the unquestioned fabric of thought in European intellectual circles. Since the work of Krister Stendahl and others, many of us contemporary scholars of Paul have worked to dismantle the simplistic translation of the rhetoric of flesh and spirit to that of Jew and Christian or for Erasmus, Paul as Hebrew and Paul as Apostle.[4] But arguments about the ahistorical character of such readings, no matter how convincing intellectually, do not remove their power. Even if it were possible to make an argument that Paul's view of female/male subordination embedded in Romans is not historical, its power would not be diminished.

Finally, Carrington's depiction of Erasmus's rhetorical conception of the task of the biblical scholar suggests to me that Erasmus's model is in some respects a distant kin to the model of rhetorical biblical studies, articulated by Schüssler Fiorenza and developed in my own work. Rather than promising to deliver the true, real, or original meaning of the text or accurate historical situation, this model seeks to articulate the visions within the text which are in competition with one another and with other compelling visions of humanity and ultimate value. This model stresses the responsibility and accountability of the interpreter for her readings. It highlights the role of language in moving hearts and wills, and it understands those who hear and receive the arguments of biblical scholars as active judging agents who are capable of offering counterarguments, of modifying, challenging, and improving the inter-pretations of scholarship. I am grateful for Carrington's sensitive and articulate description and analysis of Erasmus's interpretation of Romans which so suggestively illuminates the modern landscape of reading this letter.

Notes

[1] See the work of Elisabeth Schüssler Fiorenza, particularly *Rhetoric and Ethic: The Politics of Biblical* Studies (Minneapolis: Fortress 1999).

[2] Stanley K. Stowers, *A Rereading of Romans: Justice, Jews, and Gentiles* (New Haven, CT: Yale, 1994).

[3] See the essays assembled in Cristina Grenholm and Daniel Patte, eds., *Gender, Tradition and Romans: Shared Ground, Uncertain Borders,* Romans through History and Cultures (T. & T. Clark, 2005).

[4] Krister Stendahl, *Paul Among Jews and Gentiles* (Philadelphia: Fortress, 1976).

— TWO —

Letting the Word Run Free: Luther, Romans, and the Call to Reform

Deanna A. Thompson

'Here the door is thrown open wide for the understanding of Holy Scriptures, that is, that everything must be understood in relation to Christ ...'.[1] Martin Luther spoke these words to his students in Wittenberg when lecturing on the opening verses of Paul's epistle to the Romans in 1515. Within a few years, this devout, secluded monk came to ignite a reformation that swept through Europe and radically altered religious thought and practice. **H** Luther's reforming instinct has to do, in part, with the way in which he re-imagined Christian existence. Luther came to reject much of the worldview of late-medieval Christianity, pursuing instead an intensely personal understanding of religion. Toward the end of his life, Luther explained it this way: 'Not reading and speculation, but living, dying, and being condemned make a real theologian'.[2] One of the key influences for Luther on becoming a 'real theologian' lay in his fascination with the one he considered the first real theologian, the apostle Paul, most particularly in the words he wrote to the church in Rome.

In fact, Luther himself attributes his breakthrough to a new way of seeing Paul's words in Romans 1:17, 'The righteous shall live by faith'.[3] This paper will trace Luther's training, immersion in the biblical text, and new approach to understanding scripture. Then we will examine how Luther uses Paul's letter to the Romans as one of the essential underpinnings of his new theological vision. Finally, we will investigate how this approach was received by those around him.

The Stirring of Luther's Theological Imagination

C At twenty-one years old, Luther entered the order of Augustinian monks. Luther devoted himself whole heartedly to both serious academic study and the severe ascetic practices for which the Augustinians were known. While scholastic texts were required reading, Luther was drawn to the biblical text. While inside the text, he wrestled with images of an angry God and a judgmental Christ. As a monk he tried desperately to live a godly life, but his conscience refused to let him believe that placating this God was actually possible. It also troubled him that the adherents

---

H Hermeneutical presuppostition of author reading in Luther.

C Contextual factor in Luther's life.

to scholasticism seemed unaware of the terror he called *Anfechtung* that pervaded his own encounters with God.

While he failed to find comfort in the scholastic texts, Luther did embrace other aspects of late medieval thought. For instance, Luther followed humanists in their insistence upon returning to scripture itself – in its original languages – rather than relying solely on the *scholia* (commentaries written by medieval theologians). **A** While Luther could not have become the biblical scholar he did without building on the scholastic tradition, he also followed humanism as he grew to rely more on personal impressions and their intersections with the biblical text rather than on the *scholia* as his primary source for reflection.[4]

Luther also shared with humanists a wariness of the scholastic appetite for Aristotle and what he came to regard as an overly formulaic approach to theology. While many humanists preferred Cicero and other Latin writers to Aristotle, Luther favored the Bible above all other sources. In his inaugural lectures on the Psalms (1513–1515), Luther relied predominantly on the *quadriga*, the accepted fourfold scholastic method of interpretation. In his lectures on Romans, the reliance is less apparent. And by the time he entered the national stage with his public protests of the Church, Luther had abandoned the *quadriga* and many of scholasticism's fundamental assumptions.

Finally, one can argue that the humanist fascination with rhetorical eloquence influenced Luther's own exegetical and theological expression. While at times humanists regarded eloquence as an end in itself, Luther always intended his rhetorical creativity to serve the preaching and proclaiming of God's Word.[5] Moreover, Luther captured the imagination not only of his students but of average folk throughout Germany by speaking with an eloquence accessible to any and all Christians. 'You must ask the mother at home, the children in the street, and the common man in the marketplaces, and see on their own lips how they speak, and translate [the biblical text] accordingly, so that they understand it and realize that you are speaking German to them'.[6] For Luther, writes Peter Matheson, 'human speech itself was a sacrament'.[7]

C In his earliest days of writing and lecturing, Luther's exegesis and theology was both grounded in the tradition he inherited as well as reflective of movements such as humanism, which did not go unnoticed by humanists themselves. Prominent scholars like Erasmus provided Luther critical support for his vision, thus bolstering his influence both within and outside the church.

The Totally Other Face

Luther received his doctorate in theology and joined the faculty at the university in Wittenberg. It was there, in his post as professor of biblical theology, that Luther would begin to envision a theological universe quite different from the one in which he had been raised. His early lectures on Psalms, Romans, Galatians, and Hebrews propelled him more deeply into Scripture, where he began to glimpse something other than the God of the medieval portraits surrounding him. While steeped in the lament and praise of the Psalms, Luther encountered a poet whose writings bespoke

---

A Analysis of the development of Luther's theological thinking.

C Context of Luther's reading of scripture.

the *Anfechtung* he knew so well. The Psalmist's words not only spoke to his besieged conscience; Luther also heard them bear witness to the *Anfechtung* of Christ. Luther's own terrified conscience inspired him to embrace a new theological vision, one that originated at the foot of the cross.

In his early interpretations of Psalms, Luther employed the fourfold meaning of scripture, but he altered the scholastic conventions. Infusing the process with his existential emphasis, Luther instead revived the Pauline distinction of the letter versus the spirit of the text, which, as Gerhard Ebeling suggests, had come to be used very differently within medieval biblical interpretation. Luther, writes Ebeling,

> did not regard the literal meaning as such as the 'letter that kills', and the allegorical, tropological, and anagogical interpretations [elements of the fourfold method of interpretation] imposed upon it as the 'life-giving Spirit'. Instead, he based the fundamental distinction between the letter that kills and the life-giving Spirit on the substance of what was expressed in the whole fourfold meaning of scripture. The whole can be the letter that kills, or the whole can be the life-giving Spirit, depending upon whether the understanding is oriented toward Moses or towards Christ.[8]

Luther's insistence that an entire Psalm can preach letter or spirit signaled his first significant break with medieval biblical interpretation. This letter/spirit distinction later gives way in Luther to the law/gospel dialectic, and it is here that Luther begins to grasp at a new imaginative universe. In his lectures on the Psalms, we see a Luther striving to understand the Psalms as communicating more than mere letter. Immersed in the Psalter's laments, Luther discovers a text concerned with 'Christ himself', finding in the Psalms details of Christ's suffering, all the way to his experience of abandonment by God. It is through this immersion, writes Ebeling, that Luther prepares the way for his new theological vision.

Lecturing on Romans, Luther worked to inculcate in his students this process of becoming immersed in the biblical text itself. Twice weekly for two years Luther moved through this epistle. For his lectures, he required his students to have their own copies of the Bible in class, so that 'the experience of the Word could be lived and felt'.[9] Even though Luther began with the glosses and moved on to the *scholia*, Luther continued to push up against the boundaries of the traditional fourfold method. As Walther von Löwenich asserts, Luther's theology was 'more than academic, it was a confession of faith'.[10]

In these early lectures, we see Luther repeatedly grappling with an understanding of God's righteousness that seemed to counter prevailing views of the role of righteousness in one's relationship with God. **A** For Luther, a crucial error for scholastic theologians was their appropriation of Aristotelian categories within the realm of grace. The problem was not that scholastics claimed that persons could become righteous before God *without* grace; for Luther the error involved the use of Aristotle's concept of *habitus*, or formation of an inner disposition, to claim that grace was imparted as an *inner quality*[11] which then was made manifest by the believer *externally*. Why exactly did Luther believe it necessary to reject such an approach? Luther's own struggles with his conscience convinced him that a focus on human cooperation with God's righteousness only left one in a state of fear. 'Have I done enough?' Luther would ask, petrified that he had not satisfied God's daunting

---

A Analysis of Luther's rejection of Aristotelian categories.

expectations. Toward the end of his life, Luther recalled these early days as a time not of loving God but of despising the one who would demand the impossible of sinners:

> [U]ntil [his lectures on Romans] it was not the cold blood about the heart, but a single word in chapter 1 [:17], 'In it the righteousness of God is revealed', that had stood in my way.... As if, indeed, it is not enough that miserable sinners, eternally lost through original sin, are crushed by every kind of calamity by the law of the Decalogue, without having God add pain to pain by the gospel and also by the gospel threatening us with his righteousness and wrath.[12]

In Luther's mind, to speak of grace as something within is to assert that a person is justified only to the extent to which that grace is realized *externally*, within works.[13] To direct our gaze inward, toward the quality of the believer's inner life, left Luther with a God of whom he was terrified; he could do nothing other than hate the God he longed to love and serve.

The saving vision that struck Luther came through the very same verse in Romans that had initially caused him terror: 'The righteous will live by faith' (1:17). **C** Luther's mentor Johann von Staupitz, then dean of the faculty at Wittenberg, encouraged him to see that scripture ultimately testified to a more encompassing view of righteousness than he encountered in scholasticism.[14] Thus Luther came to hear anew these words in Romans – words that carved a path for him through God's terrifying wrath. It is from this word of grace that Luther re-envisioned the church's doctrine of justification. No longer would he embrace the scholastic approach: that humans must 'do what is in them' (*quod in se est*) to achieve a state of worthiness before God. **A** Instead Luther discovers through Paul a God whose righteousness comes to humanity not in humanly expected form of punishment or reward, but as an undeserved gift given to sinners by grace. Luther writes, in response to Paul's self-reference as a 'servant of Jesus Christ' in Romans 1:1: 'God does not want to redeem us through our own, but through external righteousness and wisdom, not through one that comes from us and grows in us, but through the one that comes to us from the outside'.[15] God justifies humanity not as a reward for humble living, as Luther initially feared, but rather through grace alone.

But to really realize that we cannot achieve a state acceptable to God does entail suffering. In his commentary on Romans 5, where Paul insists that Christians 'rejoice in their sufferings ...'. Luther notes that the cross of Christ 'puts to death everything we have'. To really accept this claim entails a kind of suffering, for our 'iniquity tries to keep itself and its possessions alive'.[16] Once we are brought low by the cross, Luther comes to see, we learn 'that of ourselves and our own powers it is impossible, but that it is a gift of love which is given by the Holy Spirit'.[17] Here Luther lingers over Paul's image in Romans 5:5: 'God's love has been poured into our hearts through the Holy Spirit'. Luther continues: '*Into our hearts*, that is, into the depths and the midst and center of our hearts, not on the surface of the heart, as foam lies on water'.[18] Luther basks in this claim that God gifts sinful humanity with grace, righteousness, and love, setting us free from the power of sin to define our lives.

This gift of God's righteousness places the sinner as one who stands before God clothed in divine righteousness. The magnitude of this realization for Luther cannot

---

C Contextual dimension in Luther's theological development.
A Analysis of Paul's role for Luther.

be underestimated: 'I felt that I was altogether born again and had entered paradise itself through open gates. There a totally other face of the entire scripture showed itself to me'.[19] This totally other face is neither remote nor even external; this face of scripture dynamically engages the hearer, placing the believer *coram Deo*. Set free by this new insight, Luther is liberated from the problem of human attempts at justification before God. **AH** He embraces the vision he finds in Paul: that the gospel reveals God's righteousness as rendering sinners righteous through the death and resurrection of Christ.

Transformed by this new vision, Luther's views emerge as pointedly in opposition to both his predecessors and his contemporaries. Late-medieval scholastic theologians interpreted the righteousness of Christ as ushering in a new law for Christians. For them, Christ replaced Moses as lawgiver, and although Christ initiates the process of justification in the believer, the law still needs to be fulfilled. In this vision, God's righteousness remains distant, conferred upon sinners only after fulfillment of the new law. Luther's new vision of justification, however, offered a radical alternative. As Luther says when commenting on Romans 1:17, 'For the righteousness of God is the cause of salvation.... [This is] the righteousness by which we are made righteous by God'.[20] Grace does not equip human beings to become righteous; rather, the gift of grace fundamentally alters the situation for humanity *coram Deo*. Luther reasserts Christ's redemptive role, for *Christ himself* is the righteousness of God. Christ's life, death, and resurrection, Luther writes, guarantees 'our own spiritual resurrection and life'.[21] **H** Here he uses the term 'spiritual' to indicate 'the category of true understanding', wherein living in the Spirit means to live in faith.[22] Consequently, our spiritual relationship to God's work in Christ is one of radical receptivity, where righteousness is received by us through the gift of grace. Luther states: 'The righteousness of God is completely from faith, but in such a way that through its development it does not make its appearance but becomes a clearer faith according to that expression in 2 Cor. 3:18: 'We are being changed ... from one degree of glory to another. ...'.[23] Therefore Luther counsels sinners to 'believe at least your own experience', for by the law you deserve God's wrath, but by grace you have been saved through faith.[24] This 'totally other face of scripture' seen first in Romans caught Luther in its gaze and never let him go.

Letting the Word Run Free

It was only a matter of time before Luther's new vision pushed him to publicly oppose the prevailing views of his day. Luther declares, 'I have learned nothing [from the scholastics] but the ignorance of sin, righteousness, baptism, and the whole of Christian life. I certainly didn't learn there what the power of God is ... Indeed, I lost Christ there, but I have found him again in Paul'.[25] **H** Equipped with this new understanding of God's Word, Luther spoke out, calling the church and the academy away from Aristotle and back to the encounter with God through the Word. Therefore, Luther repeatedly claims he is 'duty bound' to speak out publicly against the church hierarchy. Early on he contradicts the claim, voiced repeatedly by his opponents, that only the pope can interpret scripture. Luther intentionally subverts

---

AH Analysis of Paul's role in Luther's perception.
H Reference to Luther's hermeneutical clarification.
H New understanding of God's word as hermeneutical presupposition of Luther's activity.

that mandate throughout his treatises, claiming himself a fool on the order of Paul's playing the fool, and insists that the Word cannot be held captive by the papacy, but rather must be allowed to run free.

In his 1518 Heidelberg Disputation, with help from Paul's words in Romans, Luther develops further the link between righteousness and the freedom it affords all who receive it. In thesis 25, Luther refers again to Romans 1:17, using it to explain that the righteous person understands that 'works do not make him [sic] righteous, rather his righteousness creates works'.[26] Luther reinforces the point that our righteousness is God-given when he states in thesis 26 that 'through faith Christ is in us, indeed, one with us'.[27] This portrait of what a justified life looks like leads Luther to quote Paul in Romans 13:8: 'Owe no one anything, except to love one another'. In his Romans lectures, Luther says of this verse: 'It is truly the best freedom and one which is the peculiar property of Christians'.[28] This conviction – that righteousness leads to freedom from rules and regulations – leads Luther to yet another conviction: that Rome has no real jurisdiction over him. **HC** Thus the church could discipline him, but they could not rob him of his freedom to preach Christ.

It is also important to stress, however, that for all Luther's talk of Christian freedom, he repeatedly invokes Romans 13.1–7 and Paul's discussion of obedience to earthly rulers, claiming that Christian freedom *coram Deo* does nothing to alter one's necessary obedience to temporal authorities. Going even further, Luther insists that Christians are to be subject not just to rulers, but to *all* others. To experience the death of our outer, sinful self with Christ is to experience a shattering of all pretense. Living *coram hominibus*, where self-absorption has been broken, gives Christians what Otto Pesch calls 'freedom of conscience': Christians are freed to serve others without being forced to trust in the works themselves.[29] Being subject to all, then, offers its own version of freedom – the freedom of keeping track of one's deeds toward others. Any scorekeeping ultimately coaxes one back to a preoccupation with self over others. It is important to acknowledge, however, that 'we only begin to make some progress in that which shall be perfect in the future life'.[30]

C In the face of ecclesial opposition, Luther repeatedly refused to recant. In 1521 he was summoned to the Diet of Worms, where he was given one last chance to change his position. He declared, 'I am bound by the scriptures I have quoted and my conscience is captive to the Word of God. I cannot and will not retract anything, since it is neither safe nor right to go against conscience'. Then he added, 'Here I stand. I can do no other. God help me! Amen'.[31] Here Luther makes it clear that he stands accountable, not first to spiritual authorities, but ultimately to the Word of God.

Luther's understanding of faith given by God freed him to follow his conscience rather than the external commands he believed contradicted God's Word. Walther von Löwenich frames the significance of these words for Christian history: 'For the first time, the principle of freedom of conscience was exposed publicly before the highest ranking representative of the church and the world. One could make demands of everything else, but not of faith, for faith was a matter of conscience, [and conscience was] bound to God's Word'.[32] For Luther, the transforming claim of the gospel – that we are saved by faith – becomes so deeply engraved in one's being

---

HC Hermeneutical presuppositions have contextual effects.

C Implications of theological insights upon Luther's life and the lives of his contemporaries.

that conscience can and must go against any authority who threatens the gospel's proclamation. It is difficult to overestimate the force with which these visions of freedom permeated the imagination of the German people, from the monasteries to the farmlands.[33] Thousands were captured by the image of freedom, understanding its relevance to their lives in ways that would shock even the reformer himself.

As quickly became clear, not everyone embraced the sharp distinction Luther did between the spiritual and temporal realms. Authorities rightly feared that Luther's ecclesiastical disobedience could spawn civil disobedience, unrest, and even outright rebellion throughout society. **C** While Luther was forced into seclusion after the Diet of Worms, it was not long before his vitriolic calls for ecclesiastical reform fanned flames of unrest among Wittenberg students, professors, and parishioners.[34] Protestors destroyed icons, altars, and relics in area churches, prompting authorities to close city schools for fear the violence would spread. When Luther heard of the rioting and upheaval, he quickly returned to Wittenberg. While he likely prevented the Reformation from becoming an insurrection in Wittenberg, the reverberations of unrest extended far beyond his city. Heiko Oberman places the situation in context, noting that 'the roots of unrest had long been present in European history as a non-violent impulse for reform ... The new foment of the reformation proved to imply political radicalization by a biblical-spiritual opposition to the secular power of the church'.[35] **H** Using his interpretation of Paul as a guide, Luther declares that the Word is set free, and counsels bold action in the spiritual realm. It is clear Luther was single-mindedly focused on exposing and changing abuses in the ecclesial realm. Meanwhile, setting the Word free also was interpreted by many who heard or read his words as heralding a civic or temporal freedom as well.

It is clear that in Luther's early career, his concerns over abuse of authority and the limitations on freedom are focused on the *spiritual* rather than the *earthly* rulers. From his invectives against the Roman hierarchy in his Lectures on Romans forward, Luther sees church authorities as the real danger for Germans. **C** Nevertheless, as the unrest in the countryside grew, Luther knew he needed to clarify his own position on the relationship between reform of the church and reform of the state.

While Luther remains a steadfast supporter of Paul's words in Romans 12–13 regarding Christian obedience to earthly rulers, he also articulates what he sees as the limits of temporal authority. He begins his treatise on Temporal Authority with the words, 'we must provide a sound basis for the civil law and sword so no one will doubt that it is in the world by God's will and ordinance'. The passages which do this are the following: Romans 12 ...'.[36] He acknowledges that rulers possess authority to legislate behavior and action, but it is beyond their authority to legislate beliefs. Matters of faith belong to the spiritual kingdom; 'thoughts are free', Luther insisted.[37] In addition to overstepping their authority on matters of faith, Luther also admonishes the princes for over-taxation and harsh treatment of the peasants under their rule. Here he sounds a prophetic note about the bloody Peasant Uprising looming on the horizon:

> The common man is learning to think, and the scourge of princes ... is gathering force among the mob and with the common man. I fear there will be no way to avert it, unless the princes conduct themselves in a princely manner

---

C Implications of theological insights upon Luther's life and the lives of his contemporaries.
H Luther's interpretation of Paul as hermeneutical guide.
C Context of social unrest led to Luther's writings about the role of earthly rulers.

> and begin again to rule decently and reasonably. Men will not, men cannot, men refuse to endure your tyranny and wantonness much longer.[38]

Princely rule, Luther made clear, stood in need of serious reform. But before the peasants could use his words as a rallying cry for social change, Luther quickly invoked the biblical imperative of 'turning the other cheek' when encountering abuse. Likely Luther called for such restraint in order to '[strengthen] the state, the instrument he relied on for reform of the church, against the secular powers of the papacy'.[39] This point is crucial to understanding Luther's relationship to the rulers. Without temporal power on his side, his words might have incited uprisings, but dramatic reform would have come much more slowly. But Luther repeatedly cautioned princes against their abuse of power, imploring them to 'mete out punishment [of evil doers] without injuring others'.[40]

Despite Luther's efforts to preach reform and passive resistance around Germany, his consistent attempts to let the Word run free significantly impacted many who caught wind of this call to freedom and reform. **A** While Luther's defiant words and actions alone did not stir German peasants to action, it can be argued that Luther functioned as 'a symbol, a beacon, a sign of the times' for the peasants,[41] and that his theological vision equipped them with a lens through which they could interpret and protest their experience of oppression. Although Luther repeatedly invoked Paul's words in Romans 12–13, preaching patience and endurance of trials inflicted by unjust rulers, his noisy disobedience in response to papal injustices fueled the imaginations and religious zeal of the peasants set on ushering in the reign of God on earth. Buoyed by Luther, the peasants demanded better treatment by the rulers. As priests and lords of all, they argued, should they not have the right to control their economic and social affairs as well? Luther responded quickly, admonishing both peasants and princes to practice restraint. He tells the peasants: 'The word of Paul in Romans 3 [:8] applies, "Why not do evil that good may come? Their condemnation is just". It is true that rulers do wrong when they suppress the gospel and oppress you in temporal matters. But you do far greater wrong when you not only suppress God's word, but tread it underfoot, invade his authority and law, and put yourselves above God'.[42] But his admonition did not have the calming effect that he had hoped, and peasants became more violent. Many followed the rallying cry of radical reformer (and former student of Luther) Thomas Müntzer, who proclaimed, 'Kill a prince for Christ!' Müntzer and others were fighting for a revolution and calling for the gospel to be wedded tightly to the sword. Such a vision not only thoroughly confused the two realms, Luther believed, but it – not unlike the medieval Church – held the gospel captive to a dangerous theology of glory that emphasizes freedom without any thought of sin and the necessity of external restraint.

CH These developments pushed Luther over the edge. He positions himself squarely behind the princes, berating the peasants for stopping 'at nothing short of revolution and overthrow of the existing social order'.[43] Because the peasants resort to violence in the name of Christ, Luther accuses them of 'blaspheming God'. While such a response is consistent with his understanding of the proper separation of

---

A Analysis of the implications and role of Luther's notion on 'freedom' in relation to concrete social and political events.

CH Political and social events provoke Luther to clarify his theological position in relation to political authorities.

earthly and spiritual powers, Luther needlessly rants against the peasants, repeatedly invoking Paul's words in Romans:

> And Romans 13 [:1] says, 'Let every person be subject to the governing authorities'. Since [the peasants] are now deliberately and violently breaking this oath of obedience and setting themselves in opposition to their masters, they have forfeited body and soul, as faithless, perjured, lying, disobedient rascals and scoundrels usually do. St Paul passed this judgment on them in Romans 13 [2:] when he said that those who resist authorities will bring a judgment upon themselves. This saying will smite the peasants sooner or later, for God wants people to be loyal and do their duty.[44]

Luther emboldens the princes by recommending that they punish the peasants without a trial, in order to hasten the end of the ordeal. Most unfortunately, this pamphlet was not published until after the Uprising had been quelled. Nevertheless, the rulers invoked Luther's words and plundered the peasants brutally.

As many as one hundred thousand peasants lost their lives in the uprising.[45] Amidst the bloodshed Luther intoned that 'God would save the truly innocent'. In the wake of continued atrocities committed by the rulers in the revolt's aftermath, Luther's position came under attack by friends and foes alike. He finally published what was supposed to be a retraction of his position. But Luther stood firm in his unrepentance, refusing to accept any responsibility for the behavior of the rulers, depicting their actions merely as proof of the reality of God's wrath. Again he relies on Paul: 'And in Romans 12 [13:2], 'Whoever resists God's authority will incur judgment'. Why is not St Paul merciful? If we are to preach God's word, we must preach the word that declares his wrath, as well as that which declares mercy'.[46] To the peasants he explains, 'You must take your turn, and die without mercy'. This, many argue, was Luther at his worst.

A What are we to make of this transformation of Luther the proclaimer of freedom to Luther 'the hammer of the poor'?[47] Peter Matheson helps set the stage for a response, suggesting that 'when a great shattering takes place and an enchanted world is lost, it can free us up to step out in new directions but can also toss us into the abyss. Dreams and nightmares frequently interweave. There is a nightmarish dimension to the Reformation, too'.[48] **H** Indeed, Luther's stance against the peasants qualifies as one of the nightmarish aspects of his life. He refused to rein in his rhetoric and disregarded his own admonition to the rulers that they must 'deal justly with evildoers'. Why couldn't the Reformer see what seems so clear to us? Jürgen Moltmann faults Luther for his inability to see that 'church and society were too closely bound for the church to be reformed without consequences for society as well'.[49] A key insight of the Reformation, Moltmann continues, is Luther's vision that the reformation of life necessarily follows from the reformation of faith. Indeed, we hearken back to Luther's delight in Paul's claim in Romans 5.5, that our hearts will be filled with love poured in by the Spirit, which, Luther insisted, 'makes us free, joyful, almighty workers and conquerors over all tribulations, servants of our neighbors, yet lords of all'.[50] It is clear that the peasants overstepped their bounds in the violent uprising, but it remains deeply troubling that Luther could not still see them – especially after the princes had regained control – as neighbors to be loved in Christ.

A Analysis of the development of Luther's theologizing concerning the role of political authorities.

H Hermeneutical presupposition of author qualifies Luther's stance.

Despite his continued insistence that faith transforms the sinful self, altering the way the believer acts in the world, in the context of the Peasant Uprising this sheltered monk could not yet envision a more nuanced relationship between the limits of temporal rulers and the limits of Christian freedom in matters of life in the world.

It is true that Luther 'opened wide the door' to understanding a new way of interpreting the biblical text – indeed, a new way of being in the world – but in letting the Word run free it quickly ran away from his control. One of Luther's most enduring contributions to the history of Christian thought is his telling, again and again, the story that he found in Paul: that the gospel message gives us "grace and mercy" and the gospel, as Luther discovered through Romans, is full of claims about 'how great this is for us'.[51] While Luther himself resisted the full implications of his understanding of Christian freedom, his breakthrough with Paul's letter to the Romans and his subsequent rethinking of how the righteousness of God sets humanity free leads to a powerful theology of reformation whose potential has yet to be fully realized even today.

Notes

[1] *LW* 24:4, footnote 4.

[2] *LW* 34:388.

[3] According to contemporary scholarship, Paul utilized the genre of Greek scholastic diatribe when writing Romans. In that light, it is interesting to note that in stressing Paul's words in 1.16–17, Luther is actually identifying the basic thesis of the letter as a whole. See Stanley Stowers, *The Diatribe and Paul's Letter to the Romans* (Atlanta: Scholars Press Dissertation Series, 1981). I am indebted to my Hamline colleague Timothy Polk for this insight.

[4] Martin Brecht, *Martin Luther: His Road to Reformation*, 1483–1521, trans. by James L. Schaaf (Philadelphia: Fortress Press, 1985), p. 82.

[5] Alister McGrath makes this point in *Luther's Theology of the Cross: Martin Luther's Theological Breakthrough* (Oxford: Basil Blackwell, 1985), p. 51.

[6] As quoted in Gerhard Ebeling, *Luther: An Introduction to His Thought*, trans. by R. A. Wilson (Philadelphia: Fortress Press, 1970), p. 58.

[7] Peter Matheson, *The Imaginative World of the Reformation* (Minneapolis: Fortress Press, 2001), p. 28.

[8] Ebeling, p. 104.

[9] David Jasper, *A Short Introduction to Hermeneutics* (Louisville: Westminster/John Knox, 1989), p. 58.

[10] Walther von Löwenich, *Martin Luther: The Man and His Work*, trans. by Lawrence W Denef (Minneapolis: Augsburg Publishing, 1982), p. 86.

[11] Ebeling, p. 156.

[12] *LW* 34:37.

[13] Ebeling, p. 156.

[14] Rowan Williams, *Christian Spirituality: A Theological History from the New Testament to Luther and St. John of the Cross* (Atlantic: John Knox, 1980), p. 143.

[15] *LW* 25:136.

[16] *LW* 25:292.

[17] *LW* 25:293.

[18] *LW* 25:294.

[19] *LW* 34:337.

[20] *LW* 25:151.

[21] *LW* 25:45.

[22] Ebeling, p. 106. Here we see Luther's strong emphasis on the subjective genitive, that is, on our dependence on the righteousness of *God* rather than on our own ability to be righteous. But as Arland Hultgren insists and as we shall see later on in this essay, 'Luther himself didn't carry out the implications of his insight consistently'. See Hultgren's *Paul's Gospel and Mission* (Philadelphia: Fortress Press, 1980), p. 17.

[23] *LW* 25:153.

[24] *LW* 25:145.

[25] *WA* 12:414, as cited in Wilhelm Pauck, 'General Introduction', in Martin Luther, *Lectures on Romans,* Library of Christian Classics 15 (Philadelphia: Westminster Press, 1961), p. xxxix.

[26] *LW* 31:55.

[27] *LW* 31:56.

[28] *LW* 25:474.

[29] Otto Pesch, 'Free by Faith: Luther's Contributions to Theological Anthropology', in *Martin Luther and the Modern Mind: Freedom, Conscience, Toleration, Rights,* vol. 22, Toronto Studies in Theology, ed. by Manfred Hoffman (Lewiston, N.Y.: Mellen, 1985), p. 45.

[30] *LW* 31:370. Of course here is where we see the objective genitive interpretation at work, which is definitely a minority position represented by Luther, but it harkens us back to Hultgren's point that Luther did not work out this distinction in a fully consistent way.

[31] *LW* 32:123.

[32] Von Lowenich, p. 195.

[33] Matheson, p. 38.

[34] Martin Brecht, *Martin Luther: Shaping and Defining the Reformation: 1521–1532,* trans. by James Schaaf (Minneapolis: Fortress Press, 1990), pp. 30-39.

[35] Heiko Oberman, 'The Gospel of Social Unrest: 450 Years after the So-Called 'German Peasants' War' of 1525', in *The Dawn of the Reformation: Essays in Late Medieval and Early Reformation Thought,* ed. by Heiko Oberman (Grand Rapids: Eerdmans, 1992), pp. 155–178.

[36] *LW* 45:85.

[37] 'Secular Authority: To What Extent It Should be Obeyed', in *Martin Luther: Selections from his Writings,* ed. by John Dillenberger (Garden City, N.Y.: Anchor Books, 1961), p. 385.

[38] *LW* 45:106.

[39] *LW* 45:106.

[40] Luther, *Selections from his Writings*, p. 397.

[41] Oberman, p. 161.

[42] *LW* 46:26.

[43] *LW* 46:48.

[44] *LW* 46:50.

[45] Robert Schultz, Introduction to 'On the Robbing and Murdering Hordes of Peasants', *LW* 46: p. 59.

[46] *LW* 46:66.

[47] Matheson, p. 97.

[48] Matheson, p. 77.

[49] Jürgen Moltmann, 'Reformation and Revolution', in Manfred Hoffman, ed, *Martin Luther and the Modern Mind: Freedom, Conscience, Toleration, Rights,* Toronto Studies in Theology, v.22 (New York: Edwin Mellon Press, 1985), p. 186.

[50] *LW* 31:367.

[51] *LW* 25:43.

Luther's Reimagining of Christian Existence Through a Romans - Shaped Hermeneutic

Response to Deanna A. Thompson

Kurt Anders Richardson

Theological exegesis of scripture, shaped by doctrinal, moral, apologetical, political, and mystical interests dominated Christian commentary for over a millennium by the time Martin Luther was installed to teach Bible and theology at Wittenberg. These interests persisted during and after his lifetime, but became more consciously utilized as they were engendered by the critical engagements of intra-Christian conflict in Germany. With Luther, much of this conflict would be centered on the interpretation of Romans and its doctrine of justification. Indeed, to the extent that Luther's interpretation of this doctrine – 'by which the church stands or falls' – became the central doctrine of Protestantism, a kind of Romans-shaped hermeneutic emerged as well. Slowly and begrudgingly, modern Christianity adopted varieties of historical critical method with echoes of this hermeneutic in order to rescue the ancient religious documents from a despised 'timeless' theological reading and from the apologetics of 'supernaturalism' so characteristic of scholastic defensiveness. In recent years however, without sacrificing the critical outlook, exegetes seek to recover a theological step that had been missing for so long.

When returning to the historic exemplars of theological exegesis, Luther looms large. One discovers, of course, that there are no neat divisions between 'pre-modern', 'modern' and 'post-modern' exegesis, and the interest to investigate the legacy of Luther's believing intellect suggests not merely a node in the history of interpretation but an event of the text finding a willing exponent. The provocative definition of church history by Gerhard Ebeling as the history of the interpretation of scripture only begins to hint at this. Luther became an expert reader of Romans and, while not exactly pioneering the doctrine of *sola fide* in justification, one is struck by the larger biography as someone who was as much 'read by' the great epistle as one who 'read out' a great number of meanings, assembling them into religiously and politically revolutionary doctrines and movements.

Deanna A. Thompson's 'Letting the Word Run Free: Luther, Romans, and the Call to Reform' is an historical theological introduction to Luther's reception of the great Pauline letter. Her sense of method in Luther's Christological exegesis opens the set of reflections on Luther sources such as the *Lectures on Romans* (1515), along with various autobiographical statements. The paper orients itself to the Reformer's beloved *locus classicus*, Romans 1:17, and highlights the intensity of personal appropriation by which he would 'reimagine Christian existence'.

Thompson makes reference to Luther's narratival signifiers such as *Anfechtung* and the intensely personal way in which exegesis and the encounter with God were combined in his writings. Luther eschewed medieval *scholia* in favor of first-hand exegesis of the biblical text, dispensing with its particular four-fold exegetical method (*quadrigia*). Some caution is required here, however, since Luther would not dispense with typological, allegorical method but actually fashioned one that suited his own reforming agenda – a fourfold Christological hermeneutic. *Sensus literalis* – a 'literal' approach to scripture did not militate against fourfold exegesis if shaped by a Romans-hermeneutic as he understood it. Thompson sees a kind of humanist exegetical method in Luther that advanced 'rhetorical eloquence'. By 'rhetorical' she means something which is oriented to proclamation of the Gospel. Thompson highlights this by providing a sense of the common touch in Luther that went beyond theological polemics and was directed to the entire lay audience of the churches. Luther's approach on this point could be seen as extending even beyond literacy to an orality of his work of reimagining.

Thompson acknowledges, with the aid of Ebeling, Luther's use of four-fold exegesis, but sees practicing it as a function of 'his existential emphasis' – the life-giving Spirit in and through the text throughout this exegetical approach. As important as this beginning 'break' with the medieval tradition was, Thompson lays greatest stress upon the Law/Gospel distinction as the guiding framework for the task of reimagining. The existential, according to Thompson, is the source of Luther's 'life-giving' reading of the Psalms, displaying a kind of 'immersion' in the text. This is the source of his Christological reading of scripture establishing a new confessional theological vision. Said to reject the Aristotelian notion of habitual righteousness as 'external' and gradually internalized through ecclesially prescribed acts of habituation, Luther would come to emphasize a righteousness that only the gospel of Christ could engender. This comes as the unmerited gift of grace. One might add that the forensic character of Luther's interpretation of Paul's doctrine of justification becomes prominent at this point. Rather than ritual prescriptions bridging the gap between the external and the internal in religious experience, it is trust in the irrevocably promissory Word of the almighty God that creates a cognitive, affective experience of confidence in God. This experience of confidence or certainty in God who is *extra nos* ('outside us'), according to Luther, is acquired through exposure to scripture's message, particularly that of Paul through Romans. Hearing this gospel and internalizing it through trust is precisely the existential moment Thompson perceived in Luther's expositions.

Much of what Thompson presents is rather straightforward narration of Luther's theological development. With a contrasting focus upon Romans 5:5 and the outpouring of love by the Spirit, Luther's reading is a 'transformational' one acquired through knowledge of the death and resurrection of Christ. Thompson's interest is in retelling the autobiographical and biographical narrative of Luther shaped by his reading of Romans (again, esp., 1:17) and the rest of the Pauline corpus. Thompson writes from a deeply sympathetic view of Luther – with the advantages and disadvantages of such an approach. On might wish for more elaboration on such terms as *coram deo*, 'the two realms', theology of glory', but the paper seeks to cover many fronts. There is some discussion of the problem of Luther's political views related to Romans 13 and the disastrous Peasant's Revolt. The theme of 'letting the Word run free' persists throughout Thompson's confident notes on Luther. Acknowledging Luther's lack of mercy during the Revolt, Thompson can also state, 'It is clear that the peasants overstepped their bounds in the violent uprising…' – does that mean Luther's opposition to rebellion in principle is to be adopted as scriptural? Thompson seems to suggest that this would fall under her concluding statement that Luther actually resisted the full implications of freedom in Christ as he understood it.

Luther's remarkable career as exegete of Romans is notable, not merely for raising the justification doctrine to ultimate status, but also for re-centering theology itself, sometimes seen as its 'concentration' in the soteriological dimension of scripture. Rather than the ratiocinated hierarchical, cosmological systems of being of much medieval theology, Luther, rewrote much of theological tradition according to the history of salvation. But as above, Luther with a unique set of interpretive advantages, not least the powerful political patronage of Philip of Hesse, his promulgation of justification by faith was an elevation of exegetically derived notions among a few voices in late-medieval theology. Actually, as Heiko Oberman has pointed out, the great contribution of Luther is the *simul iustus et peccator* doctrine, based upon interpretation of texts like Romans 7.

Essential to Luther's arguments with his papal interlocutors as they utilized the 'faith and works' passage of James 2, his dictum 'simultaneously righteous and sinful' had immense consequences both for theological anthropology and for understanding the nature of the church. Although founded by Christ and his apostles, Luther presupposed its fallibility as an institution. Anthropologically, Luther's contribution at this point called into question all Christian claims of perfectionism, past and future. His extensive polemics against monasticism, as well as the relativization of tradition as never more than ancillary, all stem from this fundamental dictum. Finally, the office of pope became Luther's target as he had been targeted, whereby the very insistence upon infallibility claims was itself evidence of fallibility before God.

Luther also raised to a new level, quite consistent with the forensic tendency of his theology, the Pauline doctrine of *metanoia*, repentance, to an epistemological one. Repentance became, in Luther's soteriology, the greatest act of human worship. In repentance the human being does something that truly corresponds to the Word of God by agreeing with it that God is 'right' and the human being, as sinner, is 'wrong'. The self-critical principle that becomes operative here was to be directed against every human knowledge and moral claim, thereby gaining epistemological status in the course of time. It is precisely this realization that grounded the already rampant late-medieval epistemology of nominalism which Luther is so suspected of unleashing upon Western culture. Here also is an aspect of Luther's rejection of mystical theology, or as he called it, *theologia gloriae*, in that the human being is simply not capable of mentally or spiritually transcending body and sense to a perfect vision of the deity. At this point, one could say that Luther is quite anti-Augustinian, in favor of Pauline fallibilism. All human knowledge was for him a function of its own embodiment and requires an understanding of revelation so appropriately conveyed through Jesus, the embodiment of God, in this conveyance and in no other. Repentance, guided by a *theologiae crucis* of the gospel, made the knowledge of God always a humble claim of the conscience, on account of the humiliation of God for human salvation.

Perhaps Luther's greatest, most abiding contribution from his Romans hermeneutic is his *Freiheit eines Christenmeschen* – 'Freedom of the Christian'. In this short tract, profoundly indebted to the Pauline ethical arguments of Romans 12–15 (as well as Gal. 5), Luther argues for a simultaneous embrace of freedom and enslavement in the bonds of the love of Christ. There appears yet another aspect of the divide with classic medieval soteriology at the point of ethics: moral behavior motivated not by the threat of demerit, but by the promise of divine favor toward the believer. Indeed, the human agent herself embraces the esteemed promise through the work of the Holy Spirit so that acts of love are the result not of obedience as much as of voluntary submission for the sake of the greater good and imitation of Christ. In this essay, he effectively removes necessity from the soteriological logic of sanctification as obedience. Sanctification is necessary, but it is caused by God or not at all and certainly comes about ultimately through resurrection. Again, this is all partly about motivation, but it is also essential to understanding the very human life of faith. That which is necessary belongs entirely to the divine side of the exchange that is at the heart of salvation.

Luther's hermeneutic was inseparably linked to a model of divine and human relations whereby nothing which the human can do includes the condition of necessity. Creaturely finitude precludes the necessary, just as it precludes perfection. But based upon the divine determination of self-disclosure through the creaturely, there is also, until the new creation, a non-necessity, or contingency, about revelation. Luther's sense of Paul in Romans elicits for him a perception of gracious divine will that reveals and therefore creates whatever it wills, not bound by any higher principle or value. This was so much at the heart of his rethinking of 'righteousness' as he understood Romans 1:16–17 which he saw as the thematic text of the entire epistle. When he had thought of the divine attribute of 'righteousness', he wrote that he had regarded it according to metaphysical 'perfections' inherited from classical metaphysics and also mystical theological traditions. The order of salvation seemed to require human perfection in faith and action. This occasioned, according to Luther, his most severe awareness of *Anfechtung*. His 'reimagining' of Romans, however, reoriented him to a twin focus upon divine speech and action. At the heart of the Romans hermeneutic, Luther's soteriological concentration of theology is God's freedom and power in his word to call the sinful human being that which it was not, i.e., righteous. Just as in the doctrine of *creatio ex nihilo*, God's almighty Word called into being that which did not exist. This perhaps was the reimagining that for Luther spelled the proper Pauline understanding of divine righteousness in salvation.

— THREE —

The Alienation of Humankind: Rereading Luther as Interpreter of Paul

Ekkehard W. Stegemann

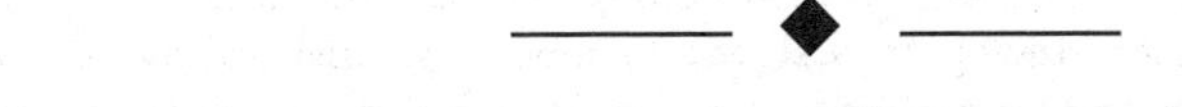

A new Perspective on Luther after a New Perspective on Paul

H Since Krister Stendahl's famous essay on 'The Apostle Paul and the Introspective Conscience of the West' (*HThR* 56, (1963), 199–215), it has become a truism that our image of Paul has to undergo a kind of de-Lutherization. If we try to read him in the context of his own culture we have even to be cautious about following Luther's main teacher among the fathers, Augustine, too, although he was far more part of the culture of Paul's antiquity than Luther. But he 'stands at the threshold between the ancient and the medieval worlds',[1] and he is also suspected to have contributed to the shaping of the introspective conscience and individualism so typical of the modern Western mind. I do not doubt that these constraints have given birth to the formation of a New Perspective on Paul with a lot of pretty new children of research. But what about turning the tables? **H** What about rereading Luther as interpreter of Paul in his times, asking perhaps not so much how Pauline he was but what he made of Paul and how he could make him so Lutheran. For after all, Luther's key has opened the lock to Paul's letters and especially to the letter to the Romans for centuries and for millions of Protestant readers at least.

To sharpen our eye on Luther will compare him to Erasmus and look at their dispute on free or captive will, on the *liberum* or *servum arbitrium*.[2] **A** Taken at face value, this was more a discourse about an already well established Christian doctrine of the will and its biblical proofs than especially on Paul or in fact on Romans 7. Erasmus's polemical *diatribe* used Paul as one authority among many other scriptures to prove his thesis on the freedom of will. And Luther's response in *De servo arbitrio* is rather restrained on Paul, although he was the 'Achilles' of his case, as he put it (WA 18,783). But since the discourse on the doctrine of free or captive will was traditionally and mainly shaped by Augustine it is originally a matter of interpretation of Paul and not at least of Romans 7. And Augustine is known to have changed his mind on it himself. His first interpretation of Romans 7 has been more in the path of Erasmus, but his later reinterpretation was the basis of Luther's lecture on Romans 7. So the *Wirkungsgeschichte* of Paul and especially of Romans 7 is part and parcel of the concept of free or captive will anyway. To read Paul as a witness of free will or captive will has depended since Augustine, exegetically on the decision whether to read Romans 7 as spoken by the *homo sub lege* or by the *homo sub gratia*, man under

---

H Hermeneutical presupposition of reading Luther's reading of Paul.

H Stegemann's presupposition of reading Luther.

A Analysis of Erasmus's and Luther's debate on free and captive will.

law or under grace.[3] But this was not Erasmus's point against Luther and vice versa. Their readings of Paul were more than exegetical worlds apart. And if all the signs are believed, Erasmus was not quite wrong to claim Paul for his case and Luther was right to do so, too. But before you remind me of the joke about the rabbi who listens to the complaints of two feuding parties and said to each of them 'you are right' and gave to the answer a third one who was listening and asking, 'Rabbi, they are at odds, how can they both be right?', 'You are right, too', I will admit: **H** One of the feuding parties with which we will deal now was more Pauline than the other.

Erasmus's Christian Philosophy as a Reshaping of Practical Philosophy in the Footsteps of Plato and Epictetus

As movements of scholars and erudition the European Humanism and Reformation had elective affinities. This is especially true for those of the Humanists like Erasmus who were named by Cornelius Augustijn 'Bible Humanists' (*Bibelhumanisten*). And the reforming movement in Switzerland came almost totally from Humanists of these kinds.[4] But there was nonetheless a decisive difference between Erasmus and the reforming Humanists like Zwingli or Melanchthon, his former disciples. For it was the firm negation of a free will that made the difference. Zwingli even responded to Erasmus's *diatribe* earlier than Luther himself. It was of course also a matter of different readings of scripture. But at the centre of the dispute stood the conflict about human nature and the different concepts of the effect of education and erudition. **H** The centerpiece of the anthropology of Humanism is erudition in its original Latin meaning of e-*ruditio*, which means de-brutalization or deprivation of roughness by education and the studies of ancient wisdom (*paideia* or *humanitas*). A human being is educable and has to be educated, morally and intellectually. His educability corresponds to his responsibility. And that's why humankind has to have a free will. For a human being without a free will could not be held responsible for his actions. Of course, Erasmus is a *Christian* Humanist. He was not unaware of the concept of grace and the doctrine of sin and the inheritance of a certain weakness because of the primordial sin of Adam and Eve. Therefore Erasmus admits that nothing good could be perfected without God's support, without the *auxilium divinum* (III c.12). And he adds as a proof for it Romans 8:26: 'In the same way the Spirit helps us in our weakness'. So without the assistance of God, of the Spirit, of God's grace, a free will is without effect. But the consequence of this is not *igitur nulla sunt hominis opera bona* ('therefore there are no good actions/works/deeds of a human being'), but *igitur omnia opera hominis possunt esse bona* ('therefore all actions/works/deeds of a human being *could* be good'). The Christian is able to lead his life according to the well-known demands of a good life (*bene vivendi praecepta*: Ia9 14/15) with the assistance of the sacramental tools of the church, the *remedium paenitaentiae*, confession and absolution, and God's merciful help, *ac domini misericordia* (Ia8). Of course he admits that the faculty of judgment is darkened by sin. That is why compared to the mainstream of Greek and Roman philosophers of antiquity it is not the *logos* or the *nous* or the faculty of reasonable judgement alone that is able to choose the path to the good life. Reason needs God's

H Author's evaluation.

H Hermeneutical presupposition decisively shapes perception of free and captive will along pro- and contra- Reformation lines.

grace or spirit as a permanent assistance in the Christian's struggle for righteousness (IIa3). And indeed the struggle is in itself a good action. For when Paul says in Romans 7:18, 'To will is available for me but the *perfection* of the good I do not find' (note the translation is from the Vulgata 'nam velle adjacet mihi, *perficere* autem bonum non invenio'), Erasmus reads it as expression of the faculty of free will, for if Paul wrote 'the will to do good is adjacent to me' he is already doing a good work, since the opposite, the will to do evil is already a bad work, as the example (which Erasmus took of the Sermon on the Mount) shows that the will to kill is already an evil deed, *opus malum* (IIb5). **A** Once again: for Erasmus free will needs support at least sometimes by the Spirit or the grace of God. But although there is flesh and its desires there is reason and its capability to command them, too. In one passage Erasmus directly hints at Plato and Epictetus and their concept of self-mastery and self-control through those parts of the soul which is called *ratio* or *hegemonikon* (IIIb4)[5]. Paul, the father of a Christian philosophy, as Erasmus said in his *Enchiridion militis Christiani* – 'Handbook of a Christian Soldier (or Fighter)' – speaks about the weakness of the human being, but he shows 'the most excellent way' (1 Cor. 12:31b). The philosophy of Christ is the 'restoration of human nature, which is actually good in itself', a 'rebirth' or *renaissance*, as Christ said (John 3), or a 'new creation' as Paul put it (2 Cor 5:17). So for Erasmus the art of living, which Christian philosophy is teaching, is a better way of self-mastery than the one of Epictetus, but it is a way of self-mastery with a possible successful outcome. Progress is possible – not only for the individual Christian but for Christian Europe under guidance of its elites. And reforms are necessary. But unfortunately there is this Augustinian barefoot monk.

Luther's Apocalyptic Radicalisation of Paul

For Erasmus a free will is a self-evident and basic principle of human nature or of being a human being. And because of the certain weakness and roughness of its nature a human being needs erudition and of course divine assistance.[6] These are basic and self-evident principles as well for him. **A** For Luther, that is all ridiculous (WA 18,679.718). There is not such a thing as Erasmus's human being. And there is not such a thing as Erasmus's God. For God's almightiness and providence do away with the doctrine of free will totally (718). Of course there is such a thing as moral or civil righteousness, a righteousness of works or by deeds as a reason of human honour. Paul himself admits it, as Luther says, in his remarks on Abraham in Romans 4:1ff. But Paul, Luther stresses, adds: *not before God*. God rejects all these works, even the good ones as evil before him (771s). Erasmus therefore underestimates the misery of mankind and its recognition. By persisting in the illusion of free will he bars the only possible way out of it: to recognize the misery and to call for salvation. 'The misery which is acknowledged, the crying misery', as Luther says alluding to Romans 7:24 ('Wretch that I am, who will rescue me from this body of death?') will find God's mercy (679). And recognition of humankind's misery is at same time recognition of God's majesty and submission to it and to God's grace. For Erasmus, Luther paints a cruel picture of God and a barbaric image of humankind. For Luther,

---

A Analysis of aspects of Erasmus's perception of human nature and free will.

A Luther's perception of human nature.

Erasmus has a distorted image of God and is playing down his terrifying power as judge and his pitiful and merciful power as savior as well. Erasmus paints for Luther at the same time a harmless picture of human nature. Humankind is not more or less capable of being moral and rational and God is not more or less its helper. For Luther a human being, and corrupted by the history of the *peccatum radicale*, the radical sin, is rather the battlefield of temptations and dangers, is in distress and despair, beset by the devil and an army of 'evil spirits of whom each individual is stronger than all human beings together, so that nobody could be saved' (783). But since God has taken from humankind the burden for its *eternal* salvation, the agonizing uncertainties and doubts and gloomy introspective conscience have come to an end. There is only one certainty, namely that without God's grace and mercy a human being, miserable, ill, mortal and sinful as it is, is doomed to eternal decline.

Luther criticizes Erasmus for leaving out of his *diatribe* a discussion of Romans 7:14ff. But he himself only mentions Paul as a teacher who has explained 'that even those who belong to God and are pious are not able to do what they want to do', since human nature is 'so evil, that it is hostile to the good even in those who are new born by the spirit' (WA 18, 783). Here we get an impression of the consequences of which Luther's exegetical decision. But it is not the reading of Romans 7 as a witness of the *Ego* of Paul and as a paradigm of a Christian's life even under grace, *sub gratia*, that makes as such the difference from Erasmus, since Erasmus is not at odds with Luther on this issue. **H** The area of dispute is rather that Luther followed in the later Augustine's footsteps. Therefore it is not by chance that Luther took Romans 7:25b in his lectures on Romans as the most adequate expression of the description of a Christian's life: 'See, that one and the same human being serves both the law of God and the law of sin, he is a righteous one and he sins at the same time'.[7] The *simul iustus est et peccat* marks the decisive point, since 'it is one and the same human being, Paul, who declares both for himself, each time concerned with different relations: under grace he is spiritual, but under law he is carnal, and yet he is each time one and the same Paul' (*Against Latomus*: WA 8,119)[8]. To sharpen the argument: For Luther Paul has to speak in Romans 7 as the paradigmatic human being under grace since as a carnal human being *sub lege*, under the law, he would not be able to recognize that he does not do what he wants to and does do what he detests (Romans 7:15). Only the spiritual human being under grace could 'agree that the law is good' and could 'delight in God's law', since he knows of his misery and believes in God's rescuing him from his doomed body.

The Divided Paul

C It is of course Luther's own life-story 'between God and the devil' (H. A. Oberman) which he transformed to the story of 'Man between God and the devil' (Oberman 1990). But it is really about the devil and it is really about God and his majesty and it is really about the human being as the *mount* ('*Reittier*'), as the animal used for riding either by the devil or by God. Each individual human being is a battlefield of God and Satan, without free will, without the capability to choose, without autonomy and self-determination. If we compare this figure to Plato's simile

H Luther's hermeneutical choice to interpret Romans 7 following the later Augustine.
C Context as shaping/influencing Luther's interpretive choice.

in his dialogue *Phaedrus* of the tripartite soul and the *nous* as the charioteer of the obedient and the unruly horse we get an idea of the difference between Luther and Erasmus's humanism. From the perspective of Luther, Erasmus has deprived God of his power, but he himself deliberately deprived man of power, totally, and that on the eve of the greatest scientific discoveries and technical inventions in European history.

The late Heiko A. Oberman has always challenged an image of Luther which for him was a Protestant myth or even an idol of German nationalism and ideology. Oberman has drawn a picture of Luther as a prophet of the end, the end of the world and the end of the time, as a prophet of a chaotic apocalyptic drama between God and the devil, between true Christians and the Antichrist. And he has not left out the delusions of Luther and especially his idiosyncratic anti-Jewish mania (no less disgusting in this respect was Erasmus).[9] Maybe Oberman has made his case a little bit too strong. But what concerns the interpretation of Paul is that Luther indeed took up an apocalyptic perspective, which Paul outlines first and foremost in Romans. But Luther changed Paul at the same time radically.

AH The drama of humankind as Paul has seen it is not the drama which Luther has seen. And what separates them is precisely the Lutheran motto: *simul iustus est et peccat.* This is absolutely not the password to enter Paul's world. Indeed, for him it would have been an abomination to claim both at the same time for one person. For Paul you are either a righteous one or a sinner but not both at the same time. Of course, Luther's *iustus* is a righteous one *in spe*, not *in re*. But that is just the result of the inversion of Paul´s concept. In his terms, stamped by his apocalyptic-encoded hellenistic-Jewish culture, Christ is the turning point in history, who changed the destiny of all humankind. Threatened already by the wrath of God as a last and devastating judgement coming soon from heaven to earth, the Gospel as God's saving power is already at work on earth, namely by creating faith and by faithfulness righteousness and participation in salvation. It is not only a promise of future saving from the devastating last judgement to come, it is not an accounting as righteous in the eyes of God, but a making righteous and so a being righteous. And as manifestation of God's own righteousness working on earth through revelation in the Gospel, it is the righteous made faithful 'who lives on the basis of Jesus's faithfulness' (Romans 3:26 according for example to Stowers (1994, p. 223[10]) and has achieved reconciliation with God (Romans 5:1–11), which means: Since he is no longer a sinner, God is no longer his enemy (5:10).

A So what Luther could not see was, that the transition of humankind from the outrage under the power of sin and flesh to liberation from 'enslavement to passions and desires' and by this to 'fulfilment of the demands of the law', has already taken place for those in Christ. If one fails to understand Paul's anthropology in its setting, in its dramatization of his present day as the end of the time, that means as a time of co-existence of the 'new creation' (represented by believers) and the old humankind, you will either dissolve the dramatic situation like Erasmus or shift it to a drama of the individual Christian split into the co-existent *simul iustus et peccator,* like Luther. There is a dramatic difference in all humankind's situation before and without the gospel. But although the revelation of salvation by faith has brought a change only to a part of humankind, the believers, who are already affected by the gospel and its

---

AH Analysis of the similarity and difference between Luther and Paul guided by the author's presupposition of reading Paul as an apocalyptic theologian.

A Analysis of Luther's reading Paul in relation to the author's perception of Paul.

saving power, participate in it. In other words: for Paul the encounter of the 'ends (or turning points) of the ages' (1 Cor. 10:11) divided humankind into two parts, namely the ones still enslaved to passions and desires of the flesh and the other ones already liberated from it. And this division in humankind is at the same time a division in their own life-story. Erasmus has lost Paul's dramatization of the situation of (divided) humankind by taking a simple post-eschatological position of Christian normalcy. But Luther's re-apocalyptization of Paul has renewed the drama of humankind even for and in fact especially for the believers.

The Alienation of Humankind

One can take the conflict between Luther and Erasmus not only as a theological disputation on the concept of free or captive will but as an expression of a 'clash of civilizations' embedded in the cultural and historical settings of the Occident with its roots in Jerusalem *and* in Athens or Rome and revived by the hero of the Protestants from Wittenberg and the prince of the Humanists from Rotterdam. One can perhaps call it a conflict between those whose experiences lead them to describe humankind and human being as a strange, frightening, eerie and unpredictable entity, and who have, to quote Freud, a feeling of uneasiness in culture ('Civilization and its Discontents'). That is what I mean by 'the alienation of Humankind', in German: *Das Befremdliche am Menschlichen*.

C But there are at the same time those traditions in occidental culture that have confidence in the capability of man to do good which is mostly linked to reason and its power of self- and world-mastery. In Athens and Rome you will find both traditions and in Jerusalem, too. And you can find it in Paul, too. The irony is that Paul describes in Romans the alienation of humankind in a biblical and Jewish perspective and language (of course already mediated with Hellenistic culture and rhetoric) and in the language and perspective of the Greek tragedy, too. The last one is to be found mainly in Romans chapter 7. The first one is dominates chapters 1:19–3:20, the last or 'final account' (as Krister Stendahl called his last fine book on Romans) on humankind, Jews and Gentiles alike. Judged according to the cardinal commandments of God's law (εὐσέβεια and δικαιοσύνη), both of them are an outrage: 'The whole world may become accountable to God' (3:19). This law is actually discernible for Gentiles by their mind or reason or by their hearts as the *Sitz im Leben* of the reasonable potential (!) of human nature now darkened and made futile. And the Jews even are in the possession of the written incorporation of the knowledge and the truth of God in the Torah given to them through Moses by God. But they failed also, especially in their mission to the Gentiles as teachers of God's truth and will.

So the judgment is framed by the cardinal commandments with respect to trespassing: 'There is no one righteous, not even one' (3:10 taking up the opposite of δικαιοσύνη mentioned in 1:18: ἀδικία) and 'There is no fear of God before their eyes' (3:18 taking up the opposite of εὐσέβεια mentioned in 1:18: ἀσέβεια). Therefore on balance the conclusion Paul is drawing is: No one, not even one, could expect to be proved to be righteous in God's Last Judgment. And this last judgment is already written in the Torah. But Paul coined this result not as the New English

---

C Contexts of tradition which are seen as present in Paul as well as Western culture.

Translation has it: 'For *no one* is declared righteous before him by the works of Law', or as the RSV translates: 'For no *human being*[11] will be justified in his sight by works of the law' (saving by the way the unrevised Standard Lutheran Version on Paul). But: 'Therefore *no flesh* is proved righteous before God'. The point is that Paul does use πάσα σάρξ and not the neutral expression πάσα ψυχή, *every (single) person* or *everybody* (as in Romans 13:1) or πᾶς ἄνθρωπος for *every (single) human being* (as in Romans 3:4) or something else. And that is on the one hand readable in connection with the divine judgment before the Flood (there are some allusions to it in Romans 3:9ff.): 'And God said to Noah: "I have determined to make an end of *all flesh*"' (πάσα σάρξ in the Septuagint; I cannot go here into details of Paul's alluding here to the first decline of humankind and its meaning for the last and definite one, how interesting it would be to do). **A** And on the other hand the term *flesh* (σάρξ) as metonymy for a human being or humankind in the first place is remarkable, since it hints at the anthropological side of the coin. The divine verdict in the Torah names it as that which is responsible in a human being or in mankind for the enslavement to sin or the dependency on or subordination to sin (3:9: ὑφ' ἁμαρτίαν εἶναι).

And on the anthropological explanation of this dependency one has to switch to chapter 7 and especially to verses 14 to 25. For here Paul takes up the discourse on self-mastery in Greco-Roman rhetoric, the speech-in-character so often recognized in research and brilliantly set out last by Stanley K. Stowers (1994, 260ff.[12]). And it is not the optimistic concept of self-mastery of Plato or Epictetus and the mainstream, but its tragic version starting with Euripides's *Medea*, to which Paul is alluding. This Medea-discourse (a kind of a discourse on free or captive will in antiquity) in its tragic version, in its negation of the possibility of self-control or self-mastery, makes it possible for Paul to illustrate the desperate situation of humankind under the constraints of flesh and desire. But unlike Medea, who killed her children while overwhelmed by the storm of emotions or passions and despite her capacity for clear and reasonable recognition of the evil she was doing, the ἐγὼ δέ σαρκινός εἰμι, the 'I, which is out of flesh', 'sold in bondage to sin' like a slave of Romans 7:14f., cannot 'accept' or 'approve' (perhaps better for γινώσκω here than 'understand': already Augustine, and among the modern interpreters for example Barrett, Cranfield[13]) that, what the 'I' actually does. That means: Medea, overwhelmed by her desire to take revenge on Jason, really wanted to kill her children, although she was able to see the evil she was about to do. The Ego of flesh, however, really wants to do the good, but instead does the non-desired, detested evil (7:19). This shifting of the discourse is due to the reaction to the Medea-discourse in the Stoa of the early Roman Principate. For it is Epictetus, who argues: 'Every ἁμαρτήμα transgression (or: error?) involves a contradiction. For since he who transgresses does not wish to transgress (οὐ θέλει ἁμαρτάνειν), but to be right, obviously he is not doing what he wishes (δηλὸν ὅτι ὁ μεν θέλει ποιεῖν οὐ ποιεί)' (Diss. II, 26,1). The context of this is the conviction that a human being is able to lead his life according to the divine laws and his mind (cf. Bendenmann p. 55).

A Quite comparably we find in Romans 7:22 the delight in 'God's law' which the 'inner human being' is concerned with[14] and in 7:23 the 'law of my *mind*'. But nevertheless neither God's holy law nor the νοῦς, the human mind in consent with

---

A 'Flesh' is reference to anthropological aspect.

A Analysis of Pauline discoursein the light of Euripides's tragedy.

God's law, is able to realize the Good and to let the good order of God to become a reality in humankind. That is the tragic reality, the alienation of humankind. And that is the reason why 'the wrath of God is being revealed from heaven against every kind of ungodliness and unrighteousness of human beings' (1:18) and why mankind is doomed to decline except those who are made faithful and righteous by God's power of salvation (1:16f.). It is *flesh* that is responsible for the enslavement to sin and humankind's being doomed to failure. It is really the 'stuff' out of which humankind was made whose power made him weak. But at the same time it is the weakness of God's holy law, its powerlessness (8:3). And therefore there is for Paul no other way out than a 'new creation', starting on earth with a transformation from living according to the flesh to living according to the spirit and assisted by its power and ending in heaven with a new body not of flesh and blood. But since Paul is in fact thinking of the 'new life' (6:4) as a 'serving' of God's law in 'the newness of the spirit' (7:6) and of believers as being enabled to fulfil the requirement of righteousness of the law (8:4) he actually declares self-mastery to be possible. That is the *particula veri* of Erasmus. But more important for the reading of Romans, I believe, was Luther's *simul*. Paul's *simul*, however, is a *simul* of co-existing worlds or humankinds. Of, for Paul, course this encounter of two aeon-ages will soon cease. **H** But there is in this mythical apocalyptic concept something which tends to dissolve the tendency of mythical concepts, namely that human nature is eternal and unchangeable. That is not untypical for hybrid cultures.[15] It has obviously always been a discourse of different concepts and it will presumably always remain such a pluralistic discourse. Perhaps not?

Notes

1 Stanley K. Stowers, *A Rereading of Romans. Justice, Jews and Gentiles* (Yale University, 1994), 1.

2 We cite Luther's *De Servo Arbitrio* according to the Weimarer Ausgabe (WA 18) and Erasmus's *De Libero Arbitrio diatribe, sive collatio* (1524) according to: Erasmus von Rotterdam. Ausgewählte Schriften. Vierter Band, ed. Winfried Lesowsky, Darmstadt 1969, and the usual division in chapters and subparts. The translations are mine.

3 Cf. Hermann Lichtenberger, *Das Ich Adams und das Ich der Menschheit: Studien zum Menschenbild in Römer 7* (Tübingen, 2004).

4 Cf. Gottfried W. Locher, *Die Zwinglische Reformation im Rahmen der europäischen Kirchengeschichte* (Göttingen and Zürich,1979).

5 Nec tamen omnis affectus hominis est caro, sed est, qui dicitur anima, est, qui dicitur spiritus, quo nitimur ad honesta, quam partem animi rationem vocant aut hegemonikon, id est principalem, nisi forte in philosophis nullus fuit ad honesta nixus…

6 Cf. for the following Heinrich Bornkamm, *Das Jahrhundert der Reformation. Gestalten und Kräfte,* (Göttingen 2. Auflage 1961), pp. 36–54; Gerhard Ebeling, 'Luthers Kampf gegen die Moralisierung des Christlichen', in: G. Ebeling, *Lutherstudien* III, (Tübingen 1985), pp. 44–73.

7 Hoc omnium expressissimum est. Vide, ut unus et idem homo simul servit legi Dei et legi peccati, simul iustus est et peccat (WA 56,47).

H Author's presupposition of reading 'flesh' from the perspective of discourse of self-mastery in the Greco-Roman tradition.

H Author's evaluation of comparative analysis of Luther's and Paul's discourse.

[8] Unus est homo Paulus, qui utrunque de se confitetur, alio et alio respectu, sub gratia est spiritualis, sed sub lege carnalis, idem idem Paulus utrobique (WA 8,119).

[9] Heiko A. Oberman, *Luthe:. Man between God and the Devil*, (New Haven: Yale University Press 1990); David Daniell, ed., *The Two Reformations: The Journey from the Last Days to the New*, (New Haven: Yale University Press, 2003).

[10] Cf. path-breaking for this interpretation Morna D. Hooker, ΠΙΣΤΙΣ ΧΡΙΣΤΟΥ *NTS* 35,1989,321-342.

[11] Even Joseph A. Fitzmyer in his commentary (p. 333); correct translation, as nearly always, C.E.B. Cranfield (p. 137); laudable also is J. Dunn (p. 145).

[12] Cf. also Reinhard von Bendemann, *Die kritische Distanz von Wissen, Wollen und Handeln. Traditionsgeschichtliche Spurensuche eines hellenistischen Topos in Römer 7, ZNW* 95, 2004, 35-63.

[13] Cf. Ovid, Metam. 7,17ff.: video meliora *proboque* deteriora sequor.

[14] Cf. Hans Dieter Betz, The concept of the "Inner Human Being" (ὁ ἔσω ἄνθρωπος) in the Anthropology of Paul, *NTS* 46, 2000, 315-341.

[15] Cf. Homi K. Bhabba, *The Location of Culture*, (London 1994).

Two Kinds of Self

A Response to Ekkehard W. Stegemann

Stanley K. Stowers

Ekkehard Stegemann's balanced and insightful article asks not so much how Pauline was Luther, but how Luther read Paul in his own context and what about his appropriation of Paul marked it as distinctively Lutheran. Of course, posing the question this way requires having and using an understanding of Paul's thought in his own time apart from Luther. Professor Stegemann succeeds in this balancing act so as to illuminate both Luther's appropriation of Romans and aspects of Paul's thought and context that were foreign to Luther.

The article proceeds by comparing Luther and Erasmus. In this analysis, both Luther and Erasmus got some important things right about Paul and both also made some interpretations that added distinctive moves away from Paul's thought. Stegemann strategically focuses on their differences about freedom of the will, a debate for which the interpretation of Romans 7 had been central in Western Christianity since Augustine. The ancient church had been virtually unanimous in supporting free will, and this included Augustine in his earlier writings. The later Augustine's denial of free will, his doctrines of original sin and radical grace raise Krister Stendahl's famous and brilliant question: Did the genius of Augustine finally uncover the real Paul that had been misunderstood by the whole ancient church or did Augustine radically adapt Paul's message to a different time?[1] Luther, Calvin and other reformers had John Chrysostom's writings and the free will tradition of ancient Christianity available to them, but chose Augustine's Paul for the centerpiece of reformed exegesis and theology. Salvation came entirely from God without the mediation of the church or any connection with human piety or morality.

As Stegemann stresses, both Luther and Erasmus took the voice in Romans 7 to belong to Paul – another departure from the ancient church that generally took the voice as *prosopopoiia*. The latter is imitative speech that ancient commentators understood to be a person who was not yet in Christ.[2] Stegemann says that Erasmus saw that self-mastery was possible for the person who was in Christ and who had been changed by the *pneuma* – in my view poorly translated as spirit or ghost – of God. But as Stegemann argues persuasively, Erasmus's humanistic educational model lacked Paul's and Luther's apocalyptic context in which humans were deeply gripped by evil, in Luther's case so deeply that they are unable to do good or to cooperate with God. Luther, however, did not understand Paul's two ages in which believers had been brought from the old evil age to the new and liberated from sin. Thus Luther made the Christian individual a battleground between God and Satan, simultaneously a sinner and justified.

Our attempts to understand Luther's exegesis of Paul's letters necessarily requires that we tell various stories about what we think Paul meant in Romans 7, what Augustine and other commentators such as Chrysostom made of Paul and how the Reformers related to these predecessors in their interpretations. I will therefore comment on Stegemann's very helpful account by suggesting some modifications to traditional stories of interpretive relations between this cast of characters. My argument will be that the stories make better sense if we place Paul in the company of philosophers and moralists, if we note Augustine's revolutionary innovations on their common moral psychology, and if we conclude that Luther's apocalyptic thought was wedded to a revolutionary kind of subjective interiority. This story is a kind of genealogy in which each protagonist turns out to be a creature of his own time.

Romans 7 displays the central features of the moral psychology that was common to thinkers in Paul's age, Greek, Roman and Jewish. I want to join a growing chorus of scholars who deny that the picture of the person in Romans 7 is fundamentally unique and *sui generis*, without significant analogy in its ancient context.[3] In spite of what Romans 7 is likely to seem to us with our modern subjectivism, the self here is reason, the ability to have reflective desire and volition regarding God's law. This person is not a subject in the modern sense.[4] There is no value given to inwardness or the first person point-of-view. Paul's self is not a Cartesian mental subject epistemologically and ontologically cut off from a wholly other external world of objectivity. Plato, Stoics, Philo, and no writer before Augustine, except perhaps Plotinus, have this privileged inner space because the object of reason or the mind is something external, and certainly not the post-Cartesian mental objects that subjectively represent the world.[5] Nor is there some neo-Platonically inspired predecessor of these mental objects. Rather, the mind's object is the higher immaterial order in Plato, the providential order and the normative propositions of practical reason for Stoics, and God's law in Romans 7. Here Paul refers to reason as the *nous* (mind), the 'I', and the inner person. The latter is a metaphor for reason that comes from book 9 of Plato's *Republic*.[6] The 'I' in chapter 7 speaks, reflects on its situation, understands the good and God's law, and has volition. All of the operations of the 'I' are attributes commonly given to reason in ancient moral psychology.

Recent persuasive and important scholarship by Emma Wasserman makes great advances in more precisely understanding this moral psychology and its significance for interpreting Paul's letters.[7] It is easy to take the divided person in Romans 7 as a simple depiction of *akrasia*, weakness of will, as I have done in the past.[8] This is the problem usually attributed to Medea. The chapter indeed depicts psychological division that may be seen as the extreme form of *akrasia* and properly illustrated by Medea, but there is also more to the picture. Wasserman shows that the person depicted is the case of extreme moral failure (sometimes called the *akolastes*). Hellenistic ethical thinking worked within the bounds of two limiting cases, the sage and the sage's opposite, the case of complete moral failure. The *akrasia* here is more than weak volition, as Stegemann astutely points out in noting Medea's tragic character. It is not that the person here often fails to do what reason, the inner person, knows to be good, but that the person is unable to do the good at all. Erasmus, I think, took the situation of chapter 7 as one of normal *akrasia*. But the *akolastes* cannot do the law because by definition he can do no good at all. His reason is totally enslaved by passion and desire.

Wassermann shows that the Platonic tradition of moral psychology in such cases spoke of the passions and desires as conquering, imprisoning, enslaving, deceiving and confusing reason. Some texts also speak of this situation as one in which the good only incites the passions and desires that have conquered reason. Wasserman also argues convincingly that Paul uses a related tradition seen especially in Philo about the death of the soul, a metaphor for reason that is totally dominated by passion and desire. So Paul speaks of sin first being dead then coming to life, killing the 'I' and working death. In this tradition the passions and desire are associated with the body or the flesh. Reason, the 'I,' can speak of its own flesh to which it is captive. In other words Romans 6–8 exhibits the essential elements of a version of Hellenistic moral psychology, in this case depicting the *akolastes* totally dominated by sin. Paul here defines sin as passion and desire allied with the flesh or as manifestations of the flesh, the weak stuff of the body inherited from Adam (1 Cor. 15:45–47). I do not believe, however, that Paul thought all humans to be in a state of complete moral failure. I have argued that the person in Romans 7 is not every human being without Christ, but the idolatrous and morally degenerate Gentile of 1.18–32.[9] The Western Christian tradition made Paul's claims concerning the idolatrous rejection of God causing the degenerate moral constitution of the non-Jewish peoples into a doctrine of universal human nature.

I have been convinced by scholars, including Charles Taylor and Phillip Carey in his recent book, *Augustine's Invention of the Inner Self*, that the great theologian created a new kind of self focused on an inner space.[10] Here the first, person point of view replaces reason's focus on the order of the cosmos, God's law or God's economy of salvation. What is most important in this new kind of self is awareness of one's awareness of God. One's own experience becomes the inward road toward God. I would argue that it is Augustine's neo-Platonic ontology that predisposed him to read Paul's letters as being about radical sin and grace. The entire creation including humans has its being by participation in the Ideas of God. But in the fallen condition of creation, human memory of God is at best completely clouded. Only a self-knowledge that one's entire being is sustained by God's power and grace can turn one's awareness toward God. Such a being who is an emanation of God's being, but who lives as if self-sufficient, is deeply riven in will and desire. Self-knowledge that is knowledge of God can only be the result of strenuous inner struggle granted by God's grace.

Calvin and Luther were not neo-Platonists and were in many ways far removed from Augustine's intellectual milieu, but they inherited his inner space as the site of Christian selfhood. John Chrysostom, by way of contrast, operated with and saw in Paul's letters the same basic moral psychology that I have attributed to Paul and Hellenistic thought. For Luther to have followed Chrysostom and the ancient church against Augustine, seeing Romans 7 as about degenerate pre-Christian experience, would have meant losing this powerful new Christian self that would become the basis for modern subjectivity and subjectivism. Luther skillfully used the new inward self against Erasmus who was in some ways closer to Chrysostom. Stegemann is right to insist that Luther's and Paul's apocalyptic frameworks distanced their thinking from Erasmus's, but Luther's kind of inwardness also distanced him from Paul.

Stegemann persuasively speaks of Luther's 'apocalyptic radicalization of Paul'. The latter's reading of Romans 7 as the Christian struggle should be set in this apocalyptic context that was very personal for him. The human being is dominated, even controlled, by the Devil and hosts of evil spirits. In Stegemann's reading, Paul and Luther agreed on the radical enslavement of humanity to sin, but whereas Paul had Christians receiving the *pneuma* of God and thus moving to the new age from the old, Luther made the apocalyptic struggle go on even for the one who was in Christ.

I want to make some qualifications of this helpful formulation, by way of addition. There are some important differences that distinguish Paul's and ancient Jewish apocalyptic thinking from late medieval and early modern apocalyptic thought. While Paul and Jewish apocalyptic writings have sinful and sin-provoking beings, they do not thereby take away 'free will'.[11] Satan tempts but cannot normally take away one's ability to choose for God and do the good. There is nothing in Jewish apocalyptic writings like the 'powers' sometimes – in my view falsely – attributed to Paul. The crucial difference here is that for Jewish writers, for Paul and for ancient Christian thinkers such as Chrysostom, the evil beings are external to one's true self or reason and normally cannot forcibly corrupt it. Even for the degenerate Gentiles of Rom. 1:18–32, it is not Satan who has corrupted their moral rationality, but God as a punishment for idolatry (i.e., vv. 24, 26, 28). Unlike in later Western thought, reason and the will are not inherently prone to sinful motives and evil allegiances. The evil beings are not normally part of the self, just as the good, the law and God are outside the self. Struggle with the Devil was absolutely central to much of fourth and fifth century Christian thought and piety, but the powers were external and Christians could exercise their God-oriented reason to reject their temptations and deceit.

For Luther, however, the site of the apocalyptic struggle has been transferred to the inner space created or at least decisively developed by Augustine. Now reason, unlike in Romans 7, does not intrinsically delight in the good and want to do God's law. The self is a dark and obscure battleground and all of its parts are up for grabs. Now the most important function of the law is not to communicate God's will to humans, but to show humans how evil and helpless they are. It is difficult to imagine more radical opposites than Paul's and Luther's conceptions of reason, appetite and emotion. Luther writes, 'And doubtless that ignorance and contempt [of God] are not seated in the flesh, in the sense of the lower and grosser affections, but in the highest and most excellent powers of man, in which righteousness, godliness and knowledge and reverence of God should reign – that is, in reason and will, and so in the very power of "freewill," is the very seed of uprightness, the most excellent thing in man'.[12]

Paul by contrast has the person speaking in Romans 7 say in conclusion (v. 25), 'Therefore then, I serve the law of God with my mind, but I serve the law of sin with my flesh'. Though helpless because of its conquest by the flesh, 'the bodily parts' that are the seat of passion and appetite, the 'inner person' delights in God's law (7:22). The Medean verses about willing and doing emphasize that reason wills the good. This 'I' should own and control its own flesh, but does not, so that it cannot bring about what it wills. There is nothing wrong with reason's willing! Paul locates contempt of God's law in the flesh. The 'you shall not desire' of the law only challenges the emboldened ruling appetites of the Gentile *akolastes* to greater evil desire. Luther and Calvin only read Romans 7 with any plausibility at all by making the speaking person a Christian who by grace has been made able to recognize his sinful nature.

Luther accomplishes this transfer of the sinful nature to the inner man partly by distinguishing the sinful act – 'the work' – from the will and the motivation, and by making these two the source of sin. In Paul's and Hellenistic psychology there is no faculty of the will. Stoics, Epicureans and others thought that reasoning and desiring were holistically integrated in morally healthy people, and for Platonists, each part - the reason, the emotional part and the appetites - had its own desires.[13] Following the lead of Augustine, later western medieval thinkers after Aquinas more and more treated the will as a distinct faculty.[14] Luther writes that what God wants are not works as such, but 'he wants them to be performed gladly and willingly. And when there is no joy in doing them and the right will and motive are absent, then they are dead in God's eyes'.[15] Again following Augustine, who probably got the notion from Plotinus's account of the turning from the One and fall because of a certain pride, Luther strongly emphasized that the essence of sin is pride characterized by total self-centeredness and self-reliance.[16] One function of the law might be the control of bodily lusts, but its true purpose is to reveal the fallen human essence of self-reliant pride that characterizes the intellect and its will. The Jews, for example, could keep the law to all external appearances and seem to be good and godly people, but their motivation was an evil pride.

Luther's radical apocalyptic cosmos with humans in bondage to demonic beings must be brought together with a psychology that locates human evil in subjectivity, in the mind, and not in the passions and appetites that belong to the external physical world of the body. Paul, later Platonists and Christian thinkers all depart from the ancient philosophies and move toward Descartes and Kant in alienating desire from the true self, but Paul does not make that self evil.

It seems to me that Stegemann's apt appeal to Luther's apocalyptic thinking ought to be considered together with the Reformer's concept of the two kingdoms that builds on Augustine's two cities. I am certainly not knowledgeable enough about Luther's complex use of these ideas to outline any firm conclusions, but some differences from Paul's apocalyptic thinking seem clear. The kingdoms reflect the social-political-religious order that the West had developed. On one side there is the secular order with the realm of the social, political, the legitimate realm of reason, morality and the law in its several Lutheran forms. On the other side is the spiritual that is the realm of the individual, the gospel and grace, and activity motivated by love and not reason. Luther places the two in sharp contrast. God is the legitimate governor of both, but due to the fall, the Devil in this age strongly contests God's rule in both domains. I believe that this order reflecting a Christian empire, a church that had negotiated a division of labor with a social political realm descending from the Roman empire and so on is utterly foreign to Paul's world and his thinking. So yes, Paul and Luther do stand together over against Erasmus in their apocalyptic thinking, but it is also important to stress the ways that the apocalyptic visions differ.

Finally, I heartily agree with Ekkehard Stegemann that the most basic problem for Paul is that humans are made of flesh, a weak material concocted from earth (1 Cor. 15:45–49). This is why Paul locates sin in passion and desire that he and Platonists associated with the body, emotion and desire. The solution will come when God replaces flesh with *pneuma*, a stuff of a vastly superior quality that God has granted humans by means of participation in Christ's post-resurrection *pneuma*.[17] This connection of physics and ethics fits perfectly with Hellenistic thought. Luther and Calvin's inner space, lacking Augustine's Platonic ontology, breaks the ancient hierarchical continuity of the physical and the mental, and looks forward to the absolute divide and subjective autonomy of the spiritual from the physical of René Descartes and modernity. But the development of the self from ancient moral psychology to Augustine and then Luther and Calvin could not have occurred in the way that it did without the rich interpretive opportunities of Romans 7.

Notes

1 'The Apostle Paul and the Introspective Conscience of the West', *HTR*, 56 (1963), 199–215.

2 See my *A Rereading of Romans: Justice, Jews and Gentiles* (New Haven: Yale University Press, 1994), pp. 264–69, and 'Apostrophe, *Prosopopoiia* and Paul's Rhetorical Education', in John T. Fitzgerald, Thomas Olbricht and L. Michael White (eds.), *Early Christianity and Classical Culture: Comparative Studies in Honor of Abraham J. Malherbe* (Leiden: Brill, 2003), pp. 351–69.

3 One prominent example is Troels Engberg-Pedersen, *Paul and the Stoics* (Louisville, Kentucky: Westminster John Knox, 2000).

4 Stanley Stowers, 'Paul as Hero of Subjectivity', in Hent De Vries and Ward Blanton (eds.), *Paul and the Philosophers* (Durham: Duke University Press, forthcoming).

5 The point about the external focus has been developed by Charles Taylor, *Sources of the Self: The Making of the Modern Identity* (Cambridge, Massachusetts: Harvard University Press, 1989), pp. 124–145. On Plotinus as the creator of this interiority, see Richard Sorabji, *Self: Ancient and Modern Insights about Individuality, Life, and Death* (Chicago: University of Chicago Press, 2006), especially pp. 51–53.

6 Theo Heckel, *Der Innere Mensch: Der paulinische Verarbeitung eines platonischen Motivs* (WUNT 2.53; Tübingen: Mohr Siebeck, 1993); Christoph Markschies, 'Innerer Mensch', *RAC*, 18 (1997), 266–312.

7 *The Death of the Soul in Romans 7: Sin, Death, and the Law in Light of Hellenistic Moral Psychology*, (Wissenschaftliche Untersuchungen zum Neuen Testament; Tübingen: Mohr Siebeck, forthcoming); 'The Death of the Soul in Romans 7: Revisiting Paul's Anthropology in Light of Hellenistic Moral Psychology', *Journal of Biblical Literature*, forthcoming; 'Paul Among the Philosophers: The Case of Sin in Romans 6–8', *Journal for the Study of the New Testament*, forthcoming.

8 *Rereading of Romans*, pp. 261–80.

9 *Rereading of Romans*, pp. 273–84. I have been followed by a number of scholars in identifying the person as a Gentile, including Wasserman and most recently Andrew Das, *Solving the Romans Debate* (Minneapolis: Fortress, 2007), pp. 203–35.

10 Carey (New York: Oxford University Press, 2000); Taylor, *Sources of the Self*, pp. 127–42.

11 This is argued by Wassermann, who reviews all of the evidence in apocalyptic writings in her forthcoming book.

12 *The Bondage of the Will* (trans. J. I. Packer and O. R. Johnston; Old Tappan, New Jersey: Revell, 1957), pp. 280–81.

13 For an excellent comparative account of these psychologies, see Christopher Gill, *The Structured Self in Hellenistic and Roman Thought* (Oxford: Oxford University Press, 2006).

14 Perhaps most relevant for Luther in this regard are Duns Scotus and Ockham. Treating will as a distinct faculty was important both for their conceptions of morality and their radically voluntaristic teachings about God that were crucial for Luther and his obsession with God's omnipotence.

[15] 'Sermon on the Three Kinds of Good Life', in Jaroslav Pelikan and Helmut T. Lehman (eds.), *Luther's Works*, (Philadelphia: Fortress, 1955), vol. 44, p. 240.

[16] On Augustine's use of the fall from Plotinus, see Robert J. O'Connell, *St. Augustine's 'Confessions': The Odyssey of the Soul* (Cambridge, Massachusetts: Harvard University Press, 1969).

[17] Stanley Stowers, 'What is Pauline Participation in Christ', in Susannah Heschel and Fabian Udoh (eds.), *New Views of Jewish and Christian Self-Definition: Essays in Honor of E. P. Sanders* (Notre Dame University Press, forthcoming).

— FOUR —

The Law and Its Works in Martin Bucer's 1536 Romans Commentary

Edwin W. Tait

Introduction: Context and Structure of the Commentary

Martin Bucer's 1536 commentary on Romans, published the same year as the first edition of John Calvin's *Institutes,* is the Strasbourg Reformer's most extended and systematic theological work.[1] It marks the end of a decade of exegetical productivity, including commentaries on the Gospels, the Psalms, and Romans. These massive works go beyond exegesis of the text to provide detailed theological discussion of a host of important 'loci'. The Romans commentary is the most thorough and mature example of this method, prompting Calvin's criticism that it was far too long and difficult for the average pastor.[2] Calvin himself chose to separate the discussion of theological loci from the continuous exposition of Scripture, engaging in the latter in his commentaries and the former in his *Institutes.* Calvin's criticism is perhaps justified by the fact that he is widely read and translated today, while Bucer is not. Clearly the combination of systematic theological reflection with Biblical exposition proved indeed to be too confusing for most people.

There are other reasons for the relative neglect of Bucer for most of the past five hundred years. Not only are his commentaries chaotic in structure, but his style is difficult, sometimes impenetrable. **C** Furthermore, his career was spent in the service of a cause that ultimately proved elusive – the construction of a common front of reformist Christians, including Lutherans, Reformed, and even Catholics (detached from their allegiance to the papacy), to promote the reign of Christ on earth. The future lay with those, like Calvin, who were willing to construct a sharply defined identity against other Christians rather than attempting to pitch as broad a tent as possible.

In the past twenty years, there has been a resurgence of interest in Bucer, and while his fame is a long way from overtaking Calvin's, his work is no longer regarded as a mere rung on the evolutionary ladder leading to the 1559 *Institutes*. Some of the qualities that contributed to his neglect now look like virtues. His persistent search for consensus commands the admiration of an ecumenical age. His attempt to reduce doctrinal disagreements to matters of semantic definition, once regarded as contemptible verbal juggling, now evinces a sophisticated awareness of the complexity of theological 'language games'.

C Aspects of Bucer's ecclesio-political activities and aims as contextual factors for relative neglect of Bucer's commentary.

The Romans commentary was published in the year of Bucer's greatest success in the field of religious diplomacy – the signing of the Wittenberg Concord, which marked Bucer's reconciliation with the Lutherans and his acceptance of a somewhat vaguely worded doctrine of the real presence of Christ in the Lord's Supper. At the time, the Concord appeared to be merely a step to greater things – the inclusion of the Swiss in the pan-Protestant front, for one thing, and the formation of reformist national churches in Germany and France, for another. Neither of these prospects ever materialized. In the long run, all Bucer had done was move Strasbourg into the Lutheran camp and thus ensure that eventually his own legacy would be rejected in the confessionalized atmosphere of the late sixteenth century.[3]

C Bucer's other major New Testament commentary, on the Gospels, was first published in 1527–28 and revised in 1530 and 1536. These revisions reflect Bucer's theological development during nine crucial years, but even the final edition remains a work of 'early' Bucer with significant later patches.[4] The Romans commentary, on the other hand, was written from scratch in 1536 and reflects Bucer's mature thought. Most students of Bucer's theology have concluded that his thought did not develop significantly after 1536.[5] It can certainly be said that Bucer's work between 1536 and his exile from Strasbourg in 1549 was primarily of an occasional and pragmatic nature – the scale and pace of his increasingly futile efforts to reform European Christianity left him little time for theological reflection. His closing years in England produced lectures on Ephesians and his most famous work, *De Regno Christi,* but they form a coda to his career. Thus, the Romans commentary represents the pinnacle not only of Bucer's influence and diplomatic activity but arguably of his thought as well.

The structure of the commentary reflects Bucer's systematizing and harmonizing agenda. Bucer treats the text on several levels. Each section receives an *exposition* – a summary of what Bucer thinks Paul is trying to say in this particular passage – and a more detailed *interpretatio,* which follows Paul's argument verse by verse. The *interpretatio* is usually followed by a discussion of patristic interpretations of the passage, though this may occur elsewhere. Next, if Bucer thinks that this particular passage provides the best opportunity to discuss some major doctrinal issue, he will insert a detailed discussion of that issue here (and refer to it at other points in the text where the same issue arises). These more detailed discussions are called *quaestiones* or, if they deal with an apparent conflict between the passage under discussion and some other part of Scripture, *conciliations.* Finally, Bucer goes back over the text and offers further observations on specific verses (these observations typically deal with edification rather than with scholarly exegesis, though the distinction between them and the *interpretatio* is not always clear).

The commentary as a whole is divided into three books. The first book, comprising 220 out of a total of 595 pages in the first edition, deals with the first three chapters of Romans. The second book covers chapters 4–11, and comprises a further 308 pages. The last five chapters of Romans receive a much more cursory treatment, comprising a mere 67 pages. This 'front-loading' of the commentary is typical of Bucer (his 1527 commentary on Matthew was printed in two volumes, with the first volume running only through chapter 7). In part, it was the result of the great haste in which he wrote his commentaries – he generally began to deal with the text in great detail and had to become more concise as time grew short.

C Contextual location of Bucer's Romans commentary within his career and other major writings.

However, this structure also results from Bucer's exegetical method. Because he usually dealt with theological issues the first time they arose in the text, the earlier portions of his commentaries contained far more detailed discussion of these issues. Later on, he was content to refer the reader with increasing frequency to his earlier discussion of theological points in the text.

In this essay, I will focus on the first book of the commentary, and on a single interpretive question which dominates the book: what are the 'works of the law' which Paul declares cannot save? This question was of central importance in the sixteenth century and continues to loom large in modern interpretations of Romans. Bucer's approach to this issue offers a bridge between the standard Protestant interpretation of Romans as a polemic against human self-righteousness and the contemporary 'new perspective' that identifies ethnic particularism as Paul's primary target.

The Law in Bucer's Theology: An Overview

After his first enthusiastic encounter with Luther at the Heidelberg Disputation in 1518, the young Martin Bucer wrote an account of Luther's theses to his friend Beatus Rhenanus. According to Bucer, one of the central principles maintained by Luther in the disputation was the inability of the law to justify, because the law was a merely external force and could not bestow the motivation to keep the precepts it proclaimed. **H** The Spirit, according to Bucer, could also be called 'law', and this internal law of the Spirit conferred grace.[6] The 'law of the Spirit' remained at the heart of Bucer's theology for the rest of his career. In his 1527 Gospel commentary, he insisted that the word 'Torah' meant primarily 'teaching' (*doctrina*), and hence in its fullest sense embodied both command and promise – what Lutherans referred to as 'Law' and 'Gospel'.[7] **A** Bucer did not reject the theological point the Lutherans were making about the relationship between command and promise, but as a matter of philological accuracy he did not think that 'law' should be used primarily to refer to the exclusively condemnatory aspects of divine *doctrina*.[8] The old and new covenants, Bucer argued, are in fact one and the same, except that the new covenant no longer needs the outward regulations that were added to the essential teachings of the old covenant.[9] Bucer interpreted the distinction drawn between Old and New Covenants in Hebrews as applying not properly speaking to the two covenants themselves, but to the external trappings of the Old Covenant on the one hand and the inner, eternal teaching common to both covenants on the other.[10]

In the Romans commentary and the 1536 version of the Gospel commentary, Bucer moves toward a more traditional understanding of the relationship between Old and New Covenants in which the Old Covenant has a more external quality owing to the 'uncultivated' nature of the people with whom it was dealing.[11] Whereas in 1527 he had argued that the New Covenant *lacks* external regulations and ceremonies (except for those explicitly instituted by Christ as 'free' signs of the inner disposition of the worshippers), he now cites Augustine's view that the New Covenant is characterized by fewer, simpler, and clearer ceremonies.[12] Furthermore, in the light of the Wittenberg Concord, Bucer attempted to clarify his understanding

---

H Spirit as Bucer's hermeneutical guide.

A Bucer differentiates 'Lutheran' perception of 'law' as referring primarily to Torah as doctrine.

of law and Gospel and harmonize Lutheran theology (particularly as represented by Melanchthon) with his own position and that of the Fathers. This latter development did not represent any significant change in Bucer's theology, but merely a more careful use of language.

In the preface to the Romans commentary, Bucer distinguishes several senses in which Paul uses the term 'law'. Most broadly, he sometimes uses it to refer to Scripture as a whole.[13] On the other hand, when Paul speaks disparagingly of the 'works of the law' as a basis for salvation, he is referring specifically to the ceremonial regulations of the law. Most prominently, the 'law' denotes the Torah, the 'doctrine of God' revealed to Moses and delivered by him to the ancient Hebrews.[14] The Torah, Bucer argues, is the centerpiece of the entire Old Testament, to which the former and latter prophets and the Psalms alike refer. The Torah deserves all the accolades it receives in the Old Testament, but it cannot justify in and of itself, since it has no power to create the internal dispositions of faith and love in which alone true righteousness consists.[15]

At the same time, Bucer takes into account Paul's affirmation in Romans 2:13 that those who 'do the law' will be justified. He defines doing the law as a zealous attention (*studium*) to its teachings,[16] shifting the weight from the actual performance of every law to the law-doer's attitude toward the teachings of the law. **A** This forms a sharp contrast with the standard Lutheran interpretation, in which the law's commands cannot possibly be obeyed in anything remotely approaching an adequate fashion. It furthermore raises the question of just who can do the law, and how this 'doing the law' is related to the doctrine of justification by faith, which Bucer affirms to be the central theme of Romans.

The Law Written on the Heart

According to Bucer, the primary theme of Romans 1–3 is that no one can possibly be saved apart from Christ.[17] Paul constructs the argument so as to make it clear that he is not singling out his own people, while at the same time demolishing the Jews' false belief that simply possessing the Law gave them superior access to the means of salvation.[18] On the other hand, Paul's discussion of Gentile knowledge of God in chapter 1 demonstrates that the Gentiles too have a kind of law.[19] For the Greeks, and for other cultured Gentiles (*cultiores*; Bucer explicitly mentions the 'Asiani' as honorary 'Greeks'), this law consisted of philosophy. For the barbarians (i.e. all human beings who were not Jews or Greeks), it consisted solely of the law written on the heart.[20] Bucer thus (with patristic support) transforms Paul's Jew/Greek dichotomy into a Jew/Greek/barbarian trichotomy, which reflects the high value Bucer placed on classical culture.[21]

This knowledge of God, of course, serves primarily to condemn those who do not act on it. Bucer argues, like Calvin after him, that a purely natural knowledge of God (without the special revelation that comes only from the Spirit) gives just enough light to condemn but not enough to save.[22] Bucer is working with an essentially intellectualist psychology – he believes that if human beings see the truth clearly enough, they will inevitably love it.[23] As in Thomist philosophy (which Bucer had studied as a Dominican friar), the intellect and feelings (*affectus*) influence each other, but the intellect has the last word. The *affectus* can sway the intellect and

A Analysis of contrast to Lutheran interpretation of 'doing the law'.

keep it from reaching a firm conclusion, but once it does so the *affectus* (and corresponding actions) must follow in their turn. Sinful humans have a weak 'judgment' and depraved *affectus*, and as a result they distort the truth and fail to act on it.[24] At the same time, because they are not completely ignorant, they remain culpable.[25] Their problem is not that they lack information about who God is, but that they have been handed over to a reprobate mind so that they judge as good what is in fact evil.[26] As a result, they fail to acknowledge God as the source of all good and to worship him as he deserves.[27] This resistance to the truth, however, can never give peace or certainty – the wicked remain continually tormented by doubt, because they have based their lives around the rejection of a truth that they cannot wholly suppress.[28]

H Some human beings, however, have received the gift of the Spirit, leading them to recognize God as the source of all goodness and to manifest a *studium* for his law as it has been revealed to them – whether in the fuller form of the Torah, or in the various less perfect forms received by the Gentiles.[29] This is how Bucer interprets the law/Gospel distinction so central to Lutheranism. The Spirit is tied to the proclamation of the Gospel and not to the teaching of the law – hence, Bucer claims, a person can be justified by faith without ever having heard of the law.[30] Thus, paradoxically he gives less place to the law in this instance than do the Wittenberg theologians, for whom the law was the necessary precursor to the Gospel.

Bucer understands the 'Gentiles who do the law by nature' (Rom. 2:14) to be not Christians (as Ambrose and Augustine argued, though Bucer tries to play down this disagreement) but pre-Christian Gentiles to whom God revealed himself and gave the gift of the Spirit.[31] The fact that some Gentiles could be saved through the knowledge of God revealed to them apart from the Law (and before the coming of Christ) demonstrates, in Bucer's view, that the Gentiles were not compelled to sin and that those who persisted in sin did so because of their own 'wicked will' (*prava voluntas*).[32] While the Law (whether Torah or the more imperfect 'law' known to the Gentiles) cannot itself save, the *studium* for its precepts which is implanted in the elect by the Holy Spirit does lead to salvation.

Justification by faith in the Romans commentary

But if this is so, what becomes of the cardinal doctrine of justification by grace alone, which Bucer believes to be the central theme of Romans?[33] Bucer addresses this problem in a seven-page *conciliatio* inserted into his discussion of Romans 2:6, 'he will repay according to each one's deeds'. **A** He argues that while salvation does depend solely on God's gratuitous mercy as its ultimate cause, God has chosen to use our good works as cooperative and partial causes in the process of salvation.[34] Indeed, it must be said – since Scripture affirms it in many places – that good works are rewarded by God and evil works are punished, and that these rewards and punishments include eternal salvation and damnation.[35] Scripture affirms this not because our works are the decisive factor – they are not – but because God accommodates revelation to our understanding, and is seeking to lead us to love God and regard him as the source of all good things. The purpose of the Scriptural

---

H The spirit is Bucer's guiding hermeneutical principle to interpret law/gospel distinction.
A Analysis of Bucer's interpretation of the process of salvation.

threats and promises, then, is to inculcate dependence on God rather than primarily to elicit specific actions.

Bucer can affirm emphatically that we are not saved by good works – in the first place because even our good works depend ultimately on God's grace and are valuable only insofar as God is working them in us, and in the second place because our works always remain imperfect and never provide a solid basis for confidence in our relationship with God. This issue of confidence is key to Bucer's understanding of justification by faith. In Bucer's theology, faith is a firm 'persuasion' (*persuasio* – it could also be translated 'conviction') that God is gracious to us. Without this persuasion, our consciences cannot find peace and we cannot truly begin to love God and do good works. Justification by faith, then, lays the necessary basis for the work of sanctification, rather than (as in Luther's theology) itself uniting us to God.

Bucer addresses the topic of justification at some length in the preface to the commentary, with the primary purpose of showing the essential agreement between himself, the Fathers, and evangelical contemporaries (principally Melanchthon). The Fathers (including Augustine and Chrysostom but not Ambrose) generally understood 'to be justified' as 'to be made [intrinsically] righteous'.[36] This, Bucer suggests, is based on the actual usage of Paul in passages such as Romans 3:26, which says that God's righteousness is demonstrated by his ability to justify those who believe. Paul's reference to the 'demonstration' of God's righteousness shows that he must be thinking of the actual behavior of believers. **H** Therefore, Bucer argues, in this context 'justify' means to make (rather than simply declare) righteous.[37]

At the same time, Bucer agrees wholeheartedly with Melanchthon's rejection of the (Catholic) idea that faith is simply the 'beginning' or basic principle of righteousness, with the transformed life of the Christian as the actual basis for her standing before God.[38] No fruit of the Spirit in the Christian's life can be the basis for justification in any sense, precisely because all the Christian's good works are free gifts from God. They follow rather than preceding divine acceptance of the believer. For Bucer, this acceptance guarantees final justification, because he does not believe that anyone except the elect ever has true faith or receives the gift of the Spirit.

In his comments on the 'righteousness of faith' in chapter 3, Bucer defines justification as remission of sins and eternal life.[39] He does not deny imputation, but he does not heavily stress it.[40] The 'first effect' of justification is the 'communication of righteousness' (by which Bucer appears to mean actual, inherent righteousness) and all the *rationes* of justification are contained in this effect.[41] Therefore, he does not see any necessary conflict between the view that 'justify' means to declare righteous legally and the view that it means to 'make righteous'. Each is an appropriate formula in different circumstances.

Works of the Law and the role of ceremonies

Bucer interprets the 'works of the law' mentioned in Romans 3:20 as the ceremonies of the OT law.[42] In this he takes his stand with the bulk of the patristic tradition and with contemporary Catholics over against Augustine in the early Church and contemporary evangelicals such as Melanchthon.[43] But he does not interpret this as a restriction of Paul's critique of the law – rather, Bucer argues that

---

H Bucer with some Fathers and Protestant contemporaries on understanding of 'to be justified'.

Paul is focusing on the ceremonial law because this was the part of the law in which his opponents were trusting.[44] Paul's claims that the law cannot justify, that it brings death, that indeed it is the cause of condemnation, are deliberate paradoxes that appear to contradict the praise of the Law found throughout Scripture. Paul is stating things this way in order to refute those who were trying to make Gentiles observe the law for salvation.[45] The 'works of the law' in question (the ceremonial *mitzvoth*) cannot justify *because* the whole law cannot justify.[46] Bucer's explanation for why the law as a whole cannot justify is more or less the standard Protestant view, with the strong pneumatological twist characteristic of his own theology. No one can follow the commands of the law without the Spirit. Therefore, on its own the law simply convicts its hearers of their sinfulness and inability. This is true not only of those parts of the law which condemn sin directly, but even for the proclamation that God is 'your savior and your highest good'. This promise comes together with the threat of damnation if you fail to love and obey him with all your heart. The 'ceremonies' of the law, in which first-century Jews trusted, also fall under this category, because they are signs of the covenant promising God's favor to those who keep the *entire* law.[47]

A Bucer's emphasis on the unity of the law, often seen as a point of distinction between himself and the Wittenberg theologians, thus serves to harmonize these two rival interpretations of the 'works of the law'. The Lutherans are right in saying that the whole law condemns precisely because *all* Scripture is 'law' in the sense of *doctrina*.[48] Interpreting 'works of the law' as ceremonies does not weaken this teaching, because ceremonies are effectual signs of the entire covenant.

Thus, Bucer's interpretation of 'works of the law' as 'ceremonies' does not indicate a purely hostile attitude to ceremonies in the Christian life.[49] Rather, Bucer draws on Augustine's theory of signs in *De Doctrina Christiana* to explain the role of ceremonies in the Christian life. The signs of both Old and New Covenants, according to Bucer, are signs of a present rather than an absent reality. The reality signified by both is the covenantal relationship in which God promises to be the God of those who put their trust in him. Speaking of circumcision in particular, Bucer says, 'For he calls it not only a sign, but the covenant itself. For the covenant of the Lord, as was said earlier, is in it – the covenant by which he presents himself to us as God, and we are his people. Therefore God offered by this sign the thing that he was promising, namely that he would be God to those who were circumcised, and then accepted them among his own, using for this, as he was accustomed, the ministry of his Church'.[50]

For Bucer, there is no meaningful distinction between the signs of the Old Covenant and those of the New, except that the latter are clearer, and of course that they look back whereas OT signs look forward. Standard medieval theology had held that the sacraments of the Old Law and the sacramentals of the New conferred grace based on the disposition of the one receiving grace, while NT sacraments conferred grace *ex opere operato*. For Bucer, on the other hand, all covenantal signs operate at essentially the same level, transmitting to believers the heavenly realities they signify.

Bucer manages to conscript Augustine for this position over against the medieval theologians, although at least some of the medievals (Thomas Aquinas and Nicholas of Lyra, for instance) actually have a more positive evaluation of the Old Law than

---

A Author's analysis of Bucer's perception of the law compared with the Wittenberg theologians.

Augustine does. Bucer relies heavily on Augustine's debate with Faustus the Manichee (which primarily concerned the value of the Old Testament, totally denied by Faustus), to portray Augustine as a champion of the essential unity between the Testaments.[51] Bucer also cites Augustine's argument in *De Doctrina Christiana* that only some people in the Old Testament (patriarchs, prophets, etc.) perceived the spiritual meaning of the Law. The others (the *vulgus*) were held in 'servitude' to the outward commands, so that they would at least worship the one God and would (as a people) be prepared for clearer revelation later.[52] After quoting this passage, Bucer immediately adds: 'Blessed Augustine therefore judges that so much was revealed to the people in the sacred ceremonies, that they served their God by observing them – the God who had promised those who lived for him in these observances that he would be their God and would give them eternal life, and in this way they received this usefulness from those ceremonies, that those signs which were imposed for a time to servants, kept in this way as under a pedagogue, would bind them over to the worship of the one God who made heaven and earth'.[53]

Bucer's skill as a harmonist is evident here. By focusing on Augustine's point that the believers of the Old Testament at least recognized the one God, he slurs over the questions whether they perceived the spiritual meaning behind the outward observances, and whether such observances have any value in the absence of an understanding of their meaning.[54] On the other hand, Bucer follows his citation of Augustine with the claim that 'even the multitude' possessed a knowledge of Christ that was 'not obscure', and suggests that this Christocentric (i.e. Messianocentric) teaching was orally passed down through the Sabbath instruction of the scribes (*periti legis*).[55] Only such a tradition, Bucer argues, can account for the confidence with which early Christians in the New Testament affirm that Moses and the prophets taught of Christ.[56] This directly contradicts Augustine's position that only a few spiritual people understood the meaning of the signs and symbols of the Old Testament. Bucer is willing to use the language of 'bondage' to describe the Old Testament, but the bondage he describes is far less severe and less universal than that portrayed by Augustine. For Bucer, it was not the Torah that was temporary but the benign servitude of outward signs not yet fully understood.

Conclusion

H Bucer's understanding of the entire Scripture as law arguably provides a resolution to the ambiguity pervading many other Reformers' treatment of the relationship between law and Gospel. Luther, Melanchthon, and Calvin all vacillate to some degree between the traditional identification of the law with the Old Testament (and hence the Gospel with the New) and the insistence that both law and Gospel are found in both Testaments. In the light of modern Pauline scholarship, I suggest that Bucer's understanding has many merits when compared with that of his more influential contemporaries. **H** Bucer's interpretation of the 'works of the law' anticipates some of the themes of the contemporary 'new perspective'. **C** In

---

H Bucer's presupposition of entire scripture as law renders law/Gospel dichotomy less ambiguous in author's view.

H Author draws conclusion from his analysis in relation to contemporary understanding /discourse.

C Contemporary issues may be illuminated by Bucer's reading.

particular, Bucer identifies the issue between Paul and his opponents as one of *identity*. Who are in fact God's people? Those who practice the ceremonial laws and thus partake in God's promises, or those who perceive the spiritual meaning behind the signs of the covenant, receiving in faith the saving reality that those signs represent? At the same time, Bucer agrees with his fellow Reformers that Paul's overarching purpose is to describe how human beings are saved, rather than simply to address questions of ethnic particularism and the boundaries of the chosen people. In this, Bucer has much in common with Stephen Westerholm.[57] Perhaps, as Bucer's variant of Reformation theology becomes better known, he may continue to promote his harmonizing agenda five hundred years after his death.

In spite of the significant differences between the Romans commentary and Bucer's earlier work, the theme of restoration and transformation through the pedagogy of divine *doctrina* remains central. For all his concern to harmonize, for all his willingness to modify and moderate his formulations, Bucer remains remarkably faithful to the fundamental vision he had expressed in his earliest German works and in the 1527 Gospel commentary. Indeed, he can compromise on matters that might seem essential to some precisely because the truth he is concerned to preserve lies elsewhere. Whether the 'works of the law' are ceremonies or moral precepts is not of ultimate importance, because both are impotent without the life-giving power of the Spirit. The Old Testament Law can be spoken of as 'shadow' and 'servitude' because it points toward a clearer and fuller revelation, but this revelation is identical with the substance of the Old Law itself. The only thing that matters, in the end, is to listen to the teaching of the Spirit and reject the smug self-righteousness propounded by the 'false prophets' of every age.

Notes

[1] *Metaphrasis et Enarratio in Epist. D. Pauli ad Romanos* (Basel, 1562). For a thorough examination of Bucer's Romans commentary as a work of exegesis, see Bernard Roussel, *Martin Bucer, Lecteur de l'épitre aux Romains* (unpublished doctoral dissertation, Strasbourg, 1970).

[2] Calvin, Epistle to Simon Grynaeus, preface to *Commentary on Romans*, in *Romans and Thessalonians* (David and Thomas Torrance (eds.), Ross Mackensie (trans.); *Calvin's Commentaries*, 8; Oliver and Boyd Ltd., 1960; reprinted Grand Rapids: Eerdmans, 1995), 2. For a detailed comparison of Bucer's and Calvin's interpretations of Romans, see Joel Kok, *The Influence of Martin Bucer on John Calvin's Interpretation of Romans: A Comparative Case Study* (unpublished doctoral dissertation, Duke University, 1993).

[3] See James Kittelson, *Toward an Established Church: Strasbourg from 1500 to the Dawn of the Seventeenth Century*, Veröffentlichungen des Instituts für Europäische Geschichte Mainz, Abteilung abendländische Religionsgeschichte 182 (Mainz: Von Zabern, 2000); and Lorna Jane Abray, *The People's Reformation: Magistrates, Clergy, and Commons in Strasbourg, 1500–1599* (New Haven, Conn.: Yale University Press, 1985). The most authoritative general biography on Bucer is Martin Greschat, *Martin Bucer: A Reformer and His Times* (Munich: Beck, 1990; Stephen Buckwalter (trans.); Louisville: Westminster John Knox, 2004).

[4] *In Sacra Quatuor Evangelia Enarationes Perpetuae* (Strasbourg, 1527, 1530, 1536). The most thorough and comprehensive study of the Gospel commentary remains August Lang, *Der Evangelienkommentar Martin Butzers und die Grundzüge seiner Theologie* (1900; reprinted Aalen: Scientia, 1972). See also Edwin Tait, *A Method for the Christian Life: Martin Bucer and the Sermon on the Mount* (unpublished dissertation, Duke University, 2005).

[5] See Lang, *Evangelienkommentar*, pp. 299–374, esp. pp. 371–72; and W. P. Stephens, *The Holy Spirit in the Thought of Martin Bucer* (Cambridge: Cambridge University Press, 1970), p. 162. Stephens furthermore notes that the mid-1530s marked both the maturing of 'Bucer's theology of the Spirit and the Church' and (no doubt as part of that maturity) a greater appreciation for the role of the Church, and particularly of the Fathers, in interpreting Scripture (p. 137). This claim is supported by Irena Backus; see 'Ulrich Zwingli, Martin Bucer and the Church Fathers', in *The Reception of the Church Fathers in the West*, vol. 2, *From the Carolingians to the Maurists* (Leiden: Brill, 1997), pp. 627–660.

[6] Bucer, ep. 3, in *Correspondance, jusqu'en 1524* (Jean Rott (ed.); *Martini Buceri opera omnia*, series 3: *Correspondance*, vol. 1; Leiden: Brill, 1979), p. 62: 'huiusmodi sententiam ad quamcunque legem deducit, quae modo foris manens quicquam faciendum praescribat, de nulla non lege, sive data esset auctore Deo sive homine, scripta aut tantum animo complexa, se loqui testabatur. Nam mentem lex huiusmodi, quaecunque illa sit, erudit quidem, at affectui nullam praebet efficaciam implendi eius quod praecipit in gloriam Dei, eoque manet foris nec in cor ipsum instar ignis penetrat perinde ac lex Spiritus; enimvero est quoque lex Spiritus, quae eadem lex gratiae dicitur et digito Dei, divino nimirum Spiritu, cordibus hominum non membranis aut codicillis insculpitur . . . sed spirituali afflatu illustrans, purificans pariter et ad bonum peficiendum impellens et perficiens legemque adimplens'. Bucer does not mention the theology of the Cross, which looms so largely in the printed version of Luther's theses. This has led Karl Koch to argue that Bucer selected only those theses that fit his own agenda (largely influenced by Thomistic rationalism and Erasmian humanism), fundamentally distorting Luther's theology. See Koch, *Studium Pietatis: Martin Bucer als Ethiker* (Neukirchen-Vluyn: Neukirchener Verlag, 1962), pp. 12–15. Thomas Kaufmann persuasively defends the essential accuracy of Bucer's account: 'Bucers Bericht von der Heidelberger Disputation', *Archiv für Reformationsgeschichte*, 82 (1991): pp. 147–70.

[7] Bucer, 1527 Gospels, 1:148–9.

[8] Bucer, 1527 Gospels, 1:1–2. Koch argues that this is more than a matter of philology – Bucer sees all of Scripture as law and thus fundamentally rejects the Lutheran distinction (*Studium Pietatis*, p. 66).

[9] Bucer, 1527 Gospels, 1:177.

[10] Bucer, 1527 Gospels, 1:149–51.

[11] See for instance *Enarratio in Romanos*, p. 65 (discussing Rom. 1:21: 'they did not glorify him as God'), where Bucer argues that God's people in the Old Testament was 'rudior' (less cultivated, presumably by comparison with Christians, or perhaps simply in comparison with unspecified more cultivated people!), so that the Israelites needed the outward display of gold, gems, etc., in worship in order to draw them to God.

[12] Bucer, *Enarratio in Romanos*, p. 156.

[13] See for instance *Enarratio in Romanos*, p. 180: 'ex ipsa lege, hoc est, Scriptura'.

[14] Bucer, preface to *Enarratio in Romanos*, cap. 10, p. 23: 'Lex enim Dei tradita per Mosen, de qua agit, dum contendit fide nos, non lege iustificari (nam legis nomine alicubi etiam totam Scripturam divinam intelligit) ea lex est, quae simplex & absoluta est, & animam sibi studentium restituit, testimonium de Deo certum, quo sapientiam confert rudioribus, edicta recta, quae exhilarent cor, praecepta pura, quae illuminant oculos, doctrina religionis casta, quae aeternum perstat, decreta vera, in quibus nihil est iniquitatis, expetibilia prae auro & gemmis preciosissimis, dulciora melle, & distillante favo, quibus solis servus Dei ritè instituitur, cumque illis studet, mercedem accipit infinitam'. See also p. 109. For Bucer's understanding of the term 'Torah' see 1527 Gospels, 1:148–49.

[15] Bucer, preface to *Enarratio in Romanos*, cap. 10, p. 23: 'Lex per se interna, fidem & dilectionem, quibus vera iustitia constat, conferre nequit'.

[16] Bucer, *Enarratio in Romanos,* p. 118: 'qui legem fecerint, hoc est, legis praeceptis seriò studuerint'. See also preface, cap. 10, p. 23, which defines 'facere legem' as 'primis legis praeceptis, quibus fides docetur & charitas, studere'; and p. 131, which defines keeping and breaking the law as the presence or absence of *studium* respectively. *Studeo* and its related noun *studium* have a wide range of meanings, from intellectual study (as in the English cognate) to zeal or enthusiasm.

[17] Cf. Bucer, *Enarratio in Romanos*, p. 122.

[18] Bucer, *Enarratio in Romanos*, pp. 122–24; see also preface, cap. 7, pp. 8–10.

[19] Bucer interprets Paul's statement (Rom. 2:12) that the Gentiles did not possess the Law as meaning simply that they lacked the perfection of the Mosaic Torah – it did not mean that they were entirely without Law: *Enarratio in Romanos*, p. 109.

[20] Bucer, *Enarratio in Romanos*, pp. 107–8.

[21] Bucer, *Enarratio in Romanos*, pp. 45–46.

[22] Bucer, *Enarratio in Romanos*, pp. 59–61, 111–12. For a comparison of Bucer's interpretation of the knowledge of God in Romans 1 with Calvin's, see David Steinmetz, 'Calvin and the Natural Knowledge of God', in *Calvin in Context* (Oxford: Oxford University Press, 1995), pp. 23–39.

[23] See Bucer, *Enarratio in Romanos*, p. 59; Bucer argues that sinful human beings (without the gracious illumination of the Spirit) can 'recognize' (*agnoscere*) that there is nothing better than to worship God, but cannot 'see it clearly' (*pervidere*). Bucer explains his intellectualist psychology and its soteriological consequences more fully in the Gospel commentary, 2:18, 21–22; see also the preface to the 1530 edition of the Gospel commentary (p. 3), which claims that all sin arises from mistaken ideas.

[24] Bucer, *Enarratio in Romanos*, p. 61.

[25] Bucer, *Enarratio in Romanos*, pp. 59, 63.

[26] Bucer, *Enarratio in Romanos*, p. 96.

[27] Bucer, *Enarratio in Romanos*, pp. 64–65.

[28] Bucer, *Enarratio in Romanos*, p. 96, commenting on Rom. 2:8: 'those who are self-seeking' (NRSV). Bucer's 'Metaphrasis' of the text renders this 'Hos vero, quos agit contentio' (those whom contention leads, p. 2), and in the commentary he uses the phrase 'ex contentione' (from contention), which he explains as meaning 'based on contention' (p. 96). This 'contention' is both the struggle against the witness of divine truth and the inner uncertainty caused by this struggle.

[29] Bucer, *Enarratio in Romanos*, pp. 111–12, 132.

[30] Bucer, *Enarratio in Romanos,* 185: 'Ad praedicationem siquidem Euangelij, etiam vbi nihil de lege auditum erat, cum ea fide recipiebatur, aderat spiritus domini, diuini fauoris arrhabo'. Bucer's identification of the 'works of the law' primarily with the ceremonial *mitzvoth* supports this view, since, as he points out, 'Gentes ceremonias Mose ignorant … Igitur fide sine operibus legis contingit hominibus iustificatio' (212).

[31] Bucer, *Enarratio in Romanos*, pp. 111–13.

[32] Bucer, *Enarratio in Romanos*, pp. 111–12. This is the most obvious difference between Bucer's view of the knowledge of God and Calvin's.

[33] See Bucer, *Enarratio in Romanos*, p. 99: 'Iam D. Paulus totis viribus hoc ubique defendit, & docet, neminem iustificari apud deum, id est, in iudicio dei absolvi, interque beandos numerari, factis suis, sed omnes sola clementia dei, peccata propter se ipsum remittentis, & gratia Christi apud deum, propter quem scilicet deus peccata remittit'.

[34] Bucer, *Enarratio in Romanos*, pp. 100, 103–4.

[35] Bucer, *Enarratio in Romanos*, pp. 99–103.

[36] Bucer, preface to *Enarratio in Romanos*, cap. 10, pp. 12–13.

[37] Bucer, *Enarratio in Romanos*, p. 12.

[38] Bucer, *Enarratio in Romanos*, p. 13.

[39] Bucer, *Enarratio in Romanos*, p. 182.

[40] Bucer does speak of believers being 'accepted as righteous' ('& pro iustis acceptat', p. 185). He notes that Melanchthon defines God's righteousness (described in Rom. 3:21) as his acceptance of human beings (*pro acceptatione accipit*) and grants that this interpretation is valid inasmuch as it identified God's righteousness with 'incomparabilem illam Dei bonitatem in Christo exhibitam, qua & peccata condonat, & iustitiam imputat, & vitam aeternam largitur, eamque hic adspirando mentem nouam, ac pietatis stadium, auspicatur' (p. 186).

[41] Bucer, *Enarratio in Romanos*, p. 183: 'In sequentibus adfert quidem aliquot rationes huius, Iustificari electos dei per solam fidem in Christum. . . verum omnes eae rationes in iustificationis primo effectu, qui est communicatio iustitiae, hoc est, sortis diuinae, continentur'.

[42] Bucer, *Enarratio in Romanos*, pp. 179, 183.

[43] Bucer, *Enarratio in Romanos*, *p*. 184.

[44] Bucer, *Enarratio in Romanos*, p. 184. Bucer interprets Romans through the lens of Galatians (which he regarded as written after Romans – see p. 2), arguing that the latter epistle shows that Paul's opponents were specifically relying on the ceremonies of the Torah, not 'works of the law' in a more general sense.

[45] Bucer, *Enarratio in Romanos*, p. 180.

[46] Bucer, *Enarratio in Romanos*, p. 185.

[47] Bucer, *Enarratio in Romanos*, p. 181: 'Sicut vbique enim Deum tibi praedicat vnum seruatorem tuum & summum bonum: ita requirit sub aeternae damnationis comminatione, vt illum tanquam Deum tuum ex toto corde, tota anima, totis viribus colas: hoc quoque sacris ceremonijs nominatim profiteris'.

[48] Bucer, *Enarratio in Romanos*, p. 210: 'Omnis doctrina Dei lex est: vocat enim ad recta, & reuocat a prauis: vbique ergo peccatum ostendit'.

[49] The 1527 Gospel commentary had come much closer to expressing such a view (arguing that the New Covenant was essentially the Old without its outward ceremonies), but Bucer backed away from this radical position in later editions of the commentary. See Bucer, 1527 Gospels, 1:150–52; 1530 Gospels, p. 49; 1536 Gospels, p. 122; Tait, 'Method', pp. 74–76, 206–9.

[50] Bucer, *Enarratio in Romanos*, p. 150F: 'Nam vocat eum non solum signum, sed ipsum quoque foedus. Iam foedus Domini, vt dictum, in eo est, quod praestat se nobis Deum, nos sumus illi populus. Ergo exhibuit hoc signo Deus id quod pollicebatur, se nimirum circuncisis fore Deum, iamque eos inter suos accepit, vsus ad id, vt solet ministerio Ecclesiae suae'.

[51] It is certainly true that Augustine regards the substance of the two Testaments as the same. But Augustine identified the Old Testament with the 'lesser righteousness' of external commands (Cf. *De Sermone Domini* 1.1.2, CCL 35:2.32–34, 38–39), whereas Bucer considered the internal righteousness of the New Covenant to be present also (though less clearly) in the Old.

[52] Augustine, *De Doctrina Christiana* 3.6.10.

[53] Bucer, *Enarratio in Romanos,* p. 157: 'Tantum ergo in sacris ceremonijs vulgo reuelatum fuisse D. Augustin. arbitratur, quod illarum obseruatione Deo suo seruirent, qui promiserat se ipsis in hisce obseruationibus sibi viuentibus, futurum Deum, & aeternam vitam largiturum, & hoc pacto eam ex illis ceremonijs vtilitatem percepisse, quod eos illa signa, quae temporaliter imposita errant seruientibus, hoc pacto quasi sub paedagogo custoditos, ad vnius Dei cultum, qui fecit coelum & terram, religarent'.

[54] And Bucer's discussion of infant baptism a few pages later admits the value of sacramental participation even for those (elect infants in this case) who have no understanding of the meaning of the action (a view that would have been anathema to the Bucer of 1527). Bucer, *Enarratio in Romanos,* p. 161.

[55] Bucer, *Enarratio in Romanos,* pp. 157–58: 'Atqui dum considero quid Prophetae de significatione ceremoniarum populo obiecerunt, & perpendo quam non fuerit obscura Christi future cognition, etiam vulgo, cuius profecto permulta sunt in Euangelicis historijs indicia, omnino existimo per sabbata a peritis legis populum, quid singulae etiam ceremoniae sibi vellent, saltem in genere, diligenter fuisse institutum. De eo quod ad Christum omnia relata sunt, perparum quidem expressum est in literis prophetarum, at non permulta huius rei tradita fuisse per manus, & in hoc gente, ceu primum mysterium, religiose fuisse abscondita: id vero neminem dicturum arbitror, qui obseruarit quantam Christi cognitionem fuisse in populo veteri, Euangelicae & Apostolicae literae clare admodum indicant'. Bucer makes a similar argument for a Messianic oral tradition in his discussion of Rom. 1:5 (on the name of Jesus), pp. 22–23.

[56] Bucer, *Enarratio in Romanos,* p. 158.

[57] See for instance Westerholm's essay 'Bucer and the Law in Romans 9–11', in James D. G. Dunn (ed.), *Paul and the Mosaic Law* (Tübingen: J. C. B. Mohr, 1996; Eng. Trans. Grand Rapids: Eerdmans, 2001), pp. 215–37 (236): 'Jewish convictions about God's goodness and sovereignty over the affairs of humankind found expression long before Paul in the notions that God accomplishes his (ultimately benevolent) purposes independently of human designs or activity and that, given the recalcitrance of the human heart, divine deliverance must be rooted in divine goodness and faithfulness, not in the merits of the delivered. Such notions are the very pith of the Pauline gospel and, at the same time, a crucial element in his argument in Romans that "flesh" cannot be "justified" by human observance of the law'.

Questions of Reception

Response to Edwin W. Tait

Troy W. Martin

Introduction

Questions arise from traditions. Both the logic and the relevance of questions are supplied by the tradition that poses and shapes them. Traditions even play a role in the answers to questions not only by raising and formulating the questions in certain ways but also by providing a sociology of knowledge that informs the answers. Put the other way around, traditions are characterized by the questions they ask and the answers they provide. Our own Society of Biblical Literature is a good example. Formed to create a forum in which certain questions could be raised about the biblical text, the earliest sections, groups, and seminars put questions of a literary and historical nature to the Bible. The Historical Critical Method characterized the early SBL, and questions outside the purview of this method were considered inappropriate for the Society. Many of us have witnessed the expansion of our Society in the past three decades to include new groups asking different questions related to gender and the Bible, the Bible and modern media, and the Bible in non-Western contexts. Even our own group, 'Romans through History and Cultures', was formed to pose questions not raised elsewhere in our Society. Certain questions, therefore, characterize not only our Society as a whole but also our group as well.

In responding to Tait's competent paper, I shall focus on the questions he asks and the answers he gives as a Reformation scholar and compare and contrast these questions and answers with those of interest to someone in Pauline studies. Indeed, Tait's essay (pp. 59, 64) suggests such a comparison by briefly considering Bucer's understanding of Romans 'in the light of modern Pauline scholarship' and in particular the 'new perspective' on Paul. The questions Tait raises in his essay are questions appropriately raised by a Reformation scholar, and the answers he provides contribute greatly to an understanding of the Reformer Martin Bucer. These questions, however, do not address many issues of interest to Pauline Studies. Examining these questions reveals at least three different levels of reception. There is Bucer's reception of Paul's Letter to Rome in his Romans commentary. There is Tait's reception of Bucer's commentary in his paper. There is my reception of Tait's essay in my response. At each level of reception, the questions asked and the answers given may reveal more about the receiver than the received.

Reformation Questions

The first question Tait addresses in his essay is why Bucer's commentaries and especially his commentary on Romans are not 'widely read and translated today' (pp. 57-8). Tait answers this question by writing that they are 'too confusing' and 'chaotic in structure' because they combine exegesis with theological discussion (pp. 57-8). The preferred method was to separate 'the continuous exposition of scripture' in a commentary from 'the discussion of theological loci' in theological works (p. 57). Tait contrasts Bucer with John Calvin, who clearly differentiated between his commentaries and his *Institutes* and assessed Bucer's Romans commentary to be 'far too long and difficult for the average pastor' (p. 57). This critique is somewhat amusing, for many modern Pauline commentaries, if not confusing and chaotic, are often 'far too long and difficult'.

Two further answers Tait gives to the question of the neglect of Bucer's Romans commentary are its 'difficult', 'impenetrable' style and its participation in a lost cause. Tait explains that Bucer published his Romans commentary in 1536, 'the year of Bucer's greatest success' in his attempts to create a pan-Protestant front that included 'Lutherans, Reformed, and even Catholics' (pp. 57-8). The Romans commentary 'was written from scratch' in that year and 'reflects Bucer's mature thought' and his 'systematizing and harmonizing agenda' to create this ecumenical front (pp. 58-9). Bucer's efforts enjoyed their greatest success in 'the signing of the Wittenberg Concord' in 1536 but were ultimately 'rejected in the confessionalized atmosphere of the late sixteenth century' (p. 58). Because of its chaotic structure, impenetrable style, and participation in a lost cause, therefore, Bucer's Romans commentary has been neglected 'for most of the past five hundred years' (p. 57).

Having answered this first question about the neglect of Bucer's Romans commentary, Tait explains, 'In this essay, I will focus ... on a single interpretive question ... what are the "works of the law" which Paul declares cannot save' (p. 59). As Tait responds to this 'single interpretive question', he clearly is more interested in how Bucer understands works of the law than in what Paul may have meant in Romans. The headings in Tait's paper are instructive. After posing this 'single interpretive question', Tait immediately describes 'The Law in Bucer's Theology: An Overview' (p. 59). Tait then turns to a discussion of Bucer's understanding of 'The Law Written on the Heart' (p. 60) and of Bucer's conception of 'Justification by Faith in the Romans Commentary' (p. 61). Finally, Tait addresses 'Works of the Law and the Role of Ceremonies' (p. 62) and concludes, 'Bucer interprets the "works of the law" mentioned in Romans 3:20 as the ceremonies of the OT law'. Tait's answer to this 'single interpretive question' clearly demonstrates that Bucer, not Paul, is the real subject of the question about the works of the law.

As Tait answers this 'single interpretive question', we learn much more about Bucer than Paul. We learn about the 'law of the Spirit' as the heart of Bucer's theology (p. 59). We learn about Bucer's theology in dialogue with and in contrast to other reformers (pp. 59-60). We learn of Bucer's 'intellectualist psychology' (p. 60) and his Thomistic affinities (p. 60). We learn of Bucer's 'law/Gospel' distinction and how it differs from the Wittenberg theologians' (p. 61) as well as his position on justification by faith as inclusively accepting both imparted and imputed righteousness (pp. 61-62). Finally, we learn how Bucer's understanding of 'works of the law' is situated in the Reformation debate. In the end, we learn much more about Bucer and his interpretive context than we do about Paul. We may appropriately wonder whether Bucer transforms not only 'Paul's Jew/Greek dichotomy into a Jew/Greek/barbarian trichotomy' but other aspects of Paul's thought as well (p. 60).

A final question Tait raises in the conclusion of his paper is what significance Bucer's thought has among the Reformers and for contemporary scholars (pp. 59, 64-5). In answering this question, Tait now shifts from a descriptive mode to an apologetic mode and argues that 'Bucer's understanding of the entire Scripture as law' allows Bucer to avoid the vacillation of 'other Reformers' treatment of the relationship between law and Gospel' (p. 64). Whereas they refer to the Old and New Testaments as Law and Gospel respectively, they admit that both Testaments contain sections of both Law and Gospel. In contrast, Bucer understands 'the entire Scripture as law', the 'divine *doctrina*' or teaching that embodies 'both command and promise' and is revealed in both Testaments (pp. 59-60). According to Tait, Bucer's view is both more consistent and preferable to the positions of the other Reformers.

Regarding contemporary scholars, Tait suggests that Bucer's understanding has 'many merits' and 'anticipates some of the themes of the contemporary "new perspective"' (p. 64). Tait states that similarly to some advocates of the 'new perspective', 'Bucer identifies the issue between Paul and his opponents as one of *identity*' (p. 64). Unlike these advocates, however, Bucer refuses to limit the issue to identity but 'agrees with his fellow Reformers that Paul's overarching purpose is to describe how human beings are saved, rather than simply to address questions of ethnic particularism and the boundaries of the chosen people' (p. 65). Tait thus presents Bucer as 'a bridge between the standard Protestant interpretation of Romans as a polemic against human self-righteousness and the contemporary "new perspective" that identifies ethnic particularism as Paul's primary target' (p. 59). Tait proposes that Bucer's 'harmonizing agenda' may indeed continue 'five hundred years after his death' (p.65)

Considering the questions Tait raises, I would say that these are questions appropriately raised by a Reformation scholar working in the tradition of Reformation studies. As a result of Tait's questioning, we know much more about Bucer and his thought than about Romans and what Paul may have thought. Tait's paper thus demonstrates the general observation that an investigation of reception reveals much more about the receiver than the received. In the end, Tait's investigation of Bucer's reception of Romans reveals much more about Bucer than about Romans. I would also say that my investigation of Tait's reception of Bucer reveals quite a lot about Tait's interests as a Reformation scholar, and my response cannot help but reflect my interests in Pauline studies.

Pauline Studies Questions

In response to Tait's question of why Bucer's Romans commentary is neglected, I cannot disagree with the reasons he gives but would emphasize as a determining factor Bucer's identification of 'works of the law' in Rom 3:20 with the ceremonial law rather than law as a whole. Indeed, a large portion of Tait's paper recognizes the importance of this identification in answering the other questions Tait raises but not as a reason for Bucer's neglect. From the standpoint of Pauline Studies, however, Bucer's identification of 'works of the law' with ceremonies locates Bucer on the minority side of the ensuing debate dominated by those who understand this phrase as referring to the whole law. The stakes in this debate are high, for at issue is not only the proper understanding of Paul and the law but also the universal relevance and truth of Paul's gospel.

For Luther and the dominant Lutheran interpretation of Paul, understanding 'works of the law' as the whole law rather than only the ceremonial Jewish law is crucial. Luther describes the understanding of this phrase as ceremonial law to be a fundamental error, for this understanding cannot explain how all are unrighteous from works of the law.[1] Only by interpreting 'works of the law' as the whole law can this phrase describe the plight of all humanity in attempting to assert their own righteousness in place of the righteousness God provides. For the Lutheran position in the debate, limiting 'works of the law' to Jewish ceremonies restricts Paul's critique of the law to a specific historical situation that renders his gospel irrelevant for the rest of humanity. The strength of the Lutheran position is its ability to describe the universal human problem of attempting to earn salvation by quantitatively or qualitatively fulfilling the law. The weakness is its preference for theological over historical concerns for interpreting this phrase.

Recent attempts to 'delutheranize' Paul represent the other side of this debate and focus precisely on the phrase 'works of the law' as understood in its historical rather than Reformation context. Whether 'works of the law' are seen as stipulations for 'staying in' the covenant (Sanders) or as boundary markers (Dunn), the important issue in interpreting this phrase is its historical context in first century Judaism. This historical emphasis leads precisely to the fundamental error feared by Luther, and those on this side of the debate face the serious problem of the relevance of Paul as a universal guide to faith and conduct. Francis Watson, a participant on this side of the debate, clearly articulates the implication by asking, 'Should Paul's thought still be a major source of inspiration for contemporary theological discussion? Or should it be rejected as a cul-de-sac, and should one seek inspiration elsewhere?'[2] The sociological relevance of Paul proposed by those on this side of the debate simply lacks the power of the profound 'theological' insights of the Lutheran position, at least in the estimation of those on the dominant side of the debate.[3] The strength of this minority position is its historical legitimacy, but the weakness is its failure to make Paul the omniscient physician of the human condition with both a correct theological diagnosis and an exclusive theological remedy.[4]

Identifying 'works of the law' with the Jewish ceremonial law places Bucer on the minority side of this debate in Pauline studies, and Tait appropriately perceives affinities between Bucer and the 'new perspective' (pp. 59,64-65). Bucer resembles those on this side of the debate in portraying Paul's critique of 'works of the law' as 'focusing on the ceremonial law because this was the part of the law in which his opponents were trusting' (pp. 62-63). Bucer's description of the bondage of the law as 'far less severe and less universal than that portrayed by Augustine' (p. 64) and Luther is characteristic of this minority side of the debate as is Bucer's denial of the necessity of the law to prepare all humanity for the reception of the Gospel (p. 61). Bucer may contend that his interpretation does not restrict 'Paul's critique of the law' to Jewish ceremonies only (p. 62) and that 'whether "works of the law" are ceremonies or moral precepts is not of ultimate importance' (pp. 64–65), but such contentions are largely lost on the other side once Bucer commits the fundamental error of identifying 'works of the law' with Jewish ceremonies.

In response to Tait's question of why Bucer's Romans commentary is neglected, therefore, I would emphasize Bucer's participation in the process of 'delutheranizing'

Paul by interpreting 'works of the law' in Rom 3:20 as the Jewish ceremonial law rather than law as a whole. Until recently, the direction of the subsequent debate belonged to those who were willing to extend and expand Luther's insights rather than to those who challenged or opposed them. The future belonged to those who were willing to universalize Paul's encounter with Judaism to encompass the entire human condition rather than to those who attempted to see Paul's encounter as temporally conditioned by salvation history or dispensationalism. Bucer was on the wrong side of this debate to enjoy much favor until the shift in the debate toward the minority position of 'delutheranizing' Paul in the past twenty years, during which time Bucer himself has experienced a 'resurgence of interest' (p. 59). Descriptions of this debate in Pauline Studies rarely if ever mention Bucer so I am grateful to Tait for connecting Bucer with this debate. I think that locating Bucer in this debate may perhaps shed some light not only on Bucer's past neglect but also on the recent resurgence of interest in him and his Romans commentary.

In response to Tait's 'single interpretive question', I accept his description of Bucer's theology and understanding of works of the law, but other questions about Bucer's theology interest me. One exegetical issue in Pauline Studies is whether to read Romans in the light of the more negative assessment of the law in Galatians or to read Galatians in the light of the more positive assessment of the law in Romans. A case can be made that Luther does the former, and Tait states, 'Bucer interprets Romans through the lens of Galatians' in reading the works of the law in Rom 3:20 as ceremonies (p. 61 n. 30). I wonder if a case can be made, however, that Bucer reads both Galatians and then Romans through the much more positive assessment of law in the Gospels.[5]

As I read Tait's paper, I also could also not help considering how Bucer's understanding of law relates to the various taxonomies of Paul's view of law. Veronica Koperski, for example, structures her taxonomy by asking what is wrong with the law.[6] She categorizes Pauline scholars by the answers they give to this question. Some answer quantitatively that the law cannot be kept in all its commandments. Others answer qualitatively that the very attempt to keep the law condemns humans who attempt to establish their own righteousness apart from the righteousness of God. Still others answer restrictively that the Law limits God's redemptive activity to Jews, and others even answer Christologically that the law is not Christ. What is Bucer's answer to the question of what is wrong with the law and how would he fit in this taxonomy? Perhaps Bucer belongs in the last category, but I would be interested in Tait's explicit placement of Bucer in this taxonomy.

Tait's placement of Bucer in one other taxonomy would also be of interest. Klein Snodgrass lists nine solutions to the problem of Paul's inconsistent statements about the law.[7] The solutions are of course quite diverse, and some are more interesting than others when considering Bucer. One solution asserts that 'there were two ways of salvation, an earlier way based on the law and a new way based on faith'. Paul's statements only appear inconsistent because sometimes he refers to the former and at other times to the latter. Another solution proposes that the ritual and civil elements of the law were annulled for Paul but the moral law remains in force. Distinguishing between the ritual and moral law resolves Paul's seemingly inconsistent statements. Still another solution posits 'that the law of God in Paul refers to more than the Torah since it includes the teaching of Jesus'. Paul's negative comments about the law refer to the former; his positive comments to the latter. Snodgrass himself proposes distinguishing different spheres of influence as a solution. Paul's negative and positive comments pertain to the law in the spheres of sin and

Spirit respectively. Tait's description of Bucer's understanding of law as divine teaching that is essentially consistent in both covenants (pp. 59-60) indicates that Bucer may have some value in resolving Paul's inconsistent statements about the law.[8] I would be interested to know how Tait would integrate Bucer into this taxonomy.

In response to Tait's final question of Bucer's significance among the Reformers and in contemporary scholarship, I cannot add to Tait's polemic of the advantages of Bucer's ideas over the positions of other Reformers. However, much more can be said about Bucer's merits 'in the light of modern Pauline scholarship' than is envisioned in Tait's brief suggestion at the end of his paper (p. 64). As I read Tait's description of Bucer, I kept thinking how contemporary Bucer seems, and I could not help considering how Bucer fits in recent discussions in Pauline studies. Bucer's refusal to make justification by faith the focus and his attempt to integrate this doctrine into his broader theology qualify Bucer as a participant in the search for the center or 'fulcrum or pivot point' of Paul's thought.[9] A comparison of Bucer with others who reject the Lutheran center of Paul's thought might be instructive, in particular with Herman Ridderbos, who sees a 'point of departure for an adequate approach to the whole in the *redemptive-historical, eschatological character of Paul's proclamation*', and J. Christiaan Beker, who posits the coherent center of Paul's thought as 'the apocalyptic coordinates of the Christ-event that focus on the imminent triumph of God'.[10] In spite of differences that most certainly exist between Bucer and these other scholars, Bucer's willingness to define a non-Lutheran center of Paul's thought increases his significance for this search.

Conclusion

Many other questions come to my mind as I read Tait's thought-provoking paper. I would especially like to have considered the question of the relationship of exegesis to theological reflection in Bucer's Romans commentary, but I realize that I have already exceeded the questions Tait addresses in his paper.[11] In posing these additional questions, I do not intend any criticism of Tait. All of us know that a short paper cannot address every issue. I would only point out that the reception of Tait's paper by someone in Pauline studies raises questions other than those posed by a Reformation scholar. Had his paper been written by a Pauline scholar, different questions would likely have been asked of Bucer's Romans commentary. Nevertheless, I would not even presume to rewrite Tait's fine and competent paper from which I have learned much not only about Bucer but also about Tait and not a little about myself as well.

Notes

1 Martin Luther, 'The Bondage of the Will', *Luther's Works* 33, ed. Philip S. Watson (Philadelphia: Fortress, 1972), pp. 258–260.

2 Francis Watson, *Paul, Judaism and the Gentiles: A Sociological Approach* (SNTSMS 56; Cambridge: Cambridge University Press, 1986), p. 181.

3 For an example of the sociological approach, see, Frank J. Matera, *Galatians*, Sacra Pagina 9 (Collegeville, MN: Liturgical Press, 1992), pp. 28–32.

[4] Many of those holding the Lutheran position would not concede historical legitimacy to the other side so easily. Stephen Westerholm entitles the third section of his recent book *The Historical and 'Lutheran' Paul*. See *Perspectives Old and New on Paul: The 'Lutheran' Paul and His Critics* (Grand Rapids: Eerdmans, 2004), p. 259. For him, the Lutheran Paul is the historical Paul.

[5] W. P. Stephens, *The Holy Spirit in the Theology of Martin Bucer* (Cambridge: Cambridge University Press, 1970), p. 8. Stephens comments, 'Nevertheless, it may be expected that a theologian who concentrates on the exposition of the gospels in a given period will produce a theology that bears the stamp of the gospels. It is also clear that a theology that is drawn from commentaries on the gospels is likely to have different stresses from one drawn from commentaries on the epistles'.

[6] Veronica Koperski, *What Are They Saying About Paul and the Law?* (WATSA; Mahwah, NJ: Paulist Press, 2001), p. 4.

[7] Klein Snodgrass, 'Spheres of Influence: A Possible Solution to the Problem of Paul and the Law', in *The Pauline Writings* (ed. Stanley E. Porter and Craig A. Evans; London: T & T Clark, 2004), pp. 154–158; repr. from *JSNT*, 32 (1988), 93–113.

[8] For some specific examples of Bucer's attempts to reconcile Paul's inconsistent statements in his Romans commentary, see D. F. Wright, *Common Places of Martin Bucer* (The Courtenay Library of Reformation Classics; Great Britain: St. Stephen's Bristol Press, 1972), p. 159.

[9] James D. G. Dunn, *The Theology of Paul the Apostle* (Grand Rapids: Eerdmans, 1998), pp. 722–723. See Ralph P. Martin, 'Center of Paul's Theology', pp. 92–95 in *Dictionary of Paul and His Letters*, ed. Gerald F. Hawthorne and Ralph P. Martin (Downers Grove, IL: InterVarsity Press, 1993). See also the more recent discussion by Koperski, *What Are They Saying*, pp. 93–103, 131.

[10] Herman N. Ridderbos, *Paul: An Outline of His Theology* (Grand Rapids: Eerdmans, 1975), p. 39; Johan Christiaan Beker, *Paul the Apostle: The Triumph of God in Life and Thought* (Philadelphia: Fortress, 1984), p. 58.

[11] Hastings Eells, *Martin Bucer* (New Haven: Yale University Press, 1931), p. 66. Eells asserts, 'Bucer's commentaries … were not so much exegetical works as theological treatises'. In the structure of Bucer's Romans commentary, however, Edwin describes explicit sections of '*expositio* – a discussion of the author's intention' (p. 4).

— FIVE —

Door and Passageway: Calvin's Use of Romans as Hermeneutical and Theological Guide

Gary Neal Hansen

◆

Introduction

John Calvin (1509–1564), Protestant reformer of Geneva and theological leader of the Reformed movement as a whole, was long known best as the writer of the *Institutes of the Christian Religion.* In recent decades, however, scholars have drawn more attention to Calvin's work as a biblical commentator. From 1540 to the end of his life in 1564 Calvin produced commentaries in a variety of forms on 24 books of the Old Testament and all but three books of the New. Biblical interpretation was a major focus of Calvin's publishing career, and he saw his commentaries as a full theological partner with the *Institutes.* In the *Institutes*, he developed a synthesis of the consistent teachings of Scripture, supported with references to individual texts, but without extensive commentary on the texts. This synthesis was intended to guide students to what they should look for when they study the Bible. In the commentaries, Calvin gave students a thorough discussion of individual texts in conversation with the teachings of Scripture as a whole, especially as he had synthesized them in the *Institutes*, without extensive excurses on points of doctrine. They were equally important genres, and were intended to be read together. This was Calvin's plan as he laid it out in the 'letter to the reader' from the 1539 second edition of the *Institutes.*[1]

This chapter will argue that Calvin's work on exegesis and doctrinal synthesis meet at Paul's letter to the Romans. It will begin by showing that this ought to be so: **H** Calvin's statements about Romans indicate its central role for hermeneutics and theology. Then it will attempt to show two ways that it really is so. First, Romans functioned as Calvin's guide in developing the theological synthesis in the *Institutes.* Second, much as Calvin intended the *Institutes* to be a hermeneutical guide to Scripture,[2] Romans functioned as a hermeneutical guide in interpreting passages of Scripture.

H Hermeneutical significance of Romans.

Calvin's Presentation of Romans as 'Door' and 'Passageway'

Calvin was working on the above-mentioned second edition of the *Institutes* at the same time as he was writing his first biblical commentary.[3] Calvin dated his dedicatory letter to the Romans commentary October 18, 1539, and the second edition of the *Institutes* had been published only two months before, in August.[4] So, just after completing a work intended to guide students into the meaning of Scripture, Calvin described his new work on the letter to the Romans in a very significant way. In Calvin's words in his dedicatory letter, '... if we understand this Epistle, we have a passage opened to us to the understanding of the whole of scripture'.[5] He says much the same thing a few pages later in the *Argumentum* or summary preface to the epistle. The supreme virtue of Paul's letter to the Romans is that 'if we have gained a true understanding of this Epistle, we have an open door to all the most profound treasures of Scripture'.[6] Romans is the door, and Romans is the passageway. When one travels through that metaphorical opening, according to Calvin, one can explore both breadth and depth: the passage leads broadly into the meaning of the whole of Scripture, and the door opens as if at the top of a staircase descending to the depths of Scripture's profound treasures.

Calvin's words about the *Institutes* were at times quite similar. In the 1560 French edition of the *Institutes* his prefatory note said of the work, '... I can at least promise that it can be a key to open a way for all children of God into a good and right understanding of Holy Scripture'.[7] His emphasis on this role of the Institutes was more emphatic in the letter to the reader in the Latin editions from 1539 onward where he went so far as to refer to his book as a 'necessary tool' for the interpretation of Scripture.[8] It is not only that the *Institutes*, the Commentaries are to be read together. Romans has a central place in the process: **H** The *Institutes* is intended as a guide to the whole of Scripture, and a proper understanding of Romans will do the same thing. Romans is the door and passageway to Scripture, and the *Institutes* provides the key to unlock it. One should expect there to be a very close relationship between Paul's letter to the Romans and the *Institutes* and, and between Romans and Calvin's practice of biblical interpretation elsewhere.

For Calvin, Romans is the door and passageway to the heart and breadth of biblical teaching because it is an exposition of the central Reformation doctrine of justification. When discussing what these 'most profound treasures of Scripture' are, he refers to 'the main subject of the whole epistle, which is that we are justified by faith'.[9] This epistle, more than any other book of Scripture, provides a thorough exposition of justification. This was the book about the doctrine which the Protestant reformers took to be the distinctly Pauline summary of the divine-human relationship, the foremost doctrine about which they were seeking to reform the Church. Calvin, like Luther, saw this doctrine as the central teaching of Scripture, and therefore of Christian theology. **H** Justification by faith is the deep treasure found in Romans, and it is also the meaning of the Bible as a whole.

Though today Calvin's view may appear to be bound up with the issues of his sixteenth-century context, he himself saw this doctrinal point as timeless. In the dedicatory letter to the Romans commentary, he notes that commentators of different eras and of his own era differ in their exposition of individual biblical texts.

H Role and function of the *Institutes* and of Romans are almost identical.

H Justification by faith as timeless doctrine, and as such the hermeneutical key for interpretation.

One ought not to expect unanimity in interpretation. In the same paragraph, the case is different for doctrine: '... but in the teachings of religion, in which God has particularly desired that the minds of his people should be in agreement, we are to take less liberty'.[10] Justification is a doctrinal matter and, as well as being the treasure found in Romans, it will appear centrally and consistently in his summary of biblical teaching in the *Institutes*. This is why, it seems, Calvin commented on Romans first among all books of Scripture, just when he was framing the *Institutes* as a hermeneutical guide. The subject matter of the two works is parallel, which should lead us to expect Romans to serve as a guide to his theology and hermeneutics.

The Book of Romans as the Passageway to the Contents of the Institutes

One can see the influence of the letter to the Romans in Calvin's *Institutes* in several ways. One is in the structure of the *Institutes*, or perhaps better to say the order of key topics. Another is in Calvin's selection of texts to buttress his theological points, both the distribution of citations of Romans and the amount of the letter to the Romans he cites relative to other books of the New Testament. There are also important matters to consider in the specific ways Romans is cited. In all these cases we will confine our study to the final 1559 version of the *Institutes*. Though this might seem methodologically problematic, since the structure of the *Institutes* shifted significantly over time,[11] it has advantages as well. First, one avoids the difficulties inherent in aiming at a moving target. The argument here is on the shape of the work as Calvin finally felt content with it – on its evolved form rather than its evolution. Also there is symmetry in comparing the first of Calvin's commentaries with the last reshaping of the *Institutes*, and any parallels in structure discerned can be thought of as an outgrowth of his mature thinking.

a. The Structure of the Institutes and the Letter to the Romans

To explore the issue of structure, one must compare the outline or order of topics in both Romans and the *Institutes*. The author suspects that any attempt of his own to discern an outline in the letter to the Romans would not meet with satisfaction among New Testament scholars. Calvin, however, discerned an outline in Paul's letter, and he recorded it in the *Argumentum* to his commentary on Romans, providing an accessible way to compare the order of topics dealt with in Romans with the order of the same topics in the *Institutes*. **A** Two observations can be made. First, a significant number of topics of Romans appear in the same relative order in the *Institutes*, although in Calvin's vastly larger work many other topics are woven in between. Second, the topics are important enough for Calvin that they comprise a kind of outline to his presentation, especially in the first three of the four books of the *Institutes*.

The topic of Rom. 1–5 is, according to Calvin, justification by faith, but he says the Apostle begins 'in the first place' by discussing human guilt 'because they do not recognize the Artificer in the great excellence of His works'. Though Calvin opens the *Institutes* with discussion of knowledge of God and ourselves, this matches up with the subsequent discussion in the opening chapters of God's revelation in nature

---

A Comparative analysis of the structure of Romans and the *Institutes*.

and human failure to perceive it.[12] In this section of the Institutes, Romans is cited only four times, but all four are of portions of Rom. 1:19–22. The key verses, Rom. 1:10–20, are cited nowhere else in the *Institutes*.

According to Calvin, Paul then turns to 'the foul and terrifying deeds' committed by all humanity, which are 'evidences of the divine wrath' in the ungodly. Though discussion of Scripture, idolatry, the Trinity, and human nature have intervened, in parallel relative order the second book of the *Institutes* begins with a thoroughgoing treatment of sin and its consequences.[13] Though Romans is by no means the only book cited, Calvin cites Romans 44 times in his five-chapter discussion of sin. Regarding the comparable sections in the outline of Romans, he cites Romans 2 once and Romans 3 eleven times, which is more than any other single chapter.

In the *Argumentum* to Romans, Calvin states that Paul 'now returns to his previous position that we are justified by faith', a reference to the beginning of Paul's main treatment of justification that appears to correspond with Rom. 3:21. Calvin portrays Romans 4 as the core of Paul's teaching on the topic, but his summaries of chapters 5, 6, and 8 all relate their topics to justification. In the *Institutes*, other topics have again intervened, including the law and Christology, faith, regeneration, and the Christian life, but justification by faith again comes in parallel relative order.[14] With 115 citations, there are more references to Romans in Calvin's discussion of justification than in any other single topic area. This mirrors Calvin's conviction that the book of Romans in essentially on the topic of justification. There are 42 citations of Rom. 3:21–4.25, and an additional 43 from chapters 5, 6, and 8. Thus 85 of Calvin's 115 citations of Romans in the discussion of justification in the *Institutes* come from the portions of that book that he specified as on the topic and which are structurally parallel to the section of the Institutes.

Chapter 9 of Romans, according to the *Argumentum*, '…refers us back here to the election of God …'. The text of Romans clearly begins to deal with election as early as 8.28 and Calvin's chapter summaries refer to predestination as part of the discussion up through chapter 11. This time only one topic, prayer, has intervened in the *Institutes* between the topics in parallel relative order.[15] In his discussion of election in the *Institutes*, citations of Romans number 63. Of these the largest number, 30, are from Romans 9, true to Calvin's view in the *Argumentum*. In fact, only seven references to Romans in this section come from outside the range of Rom. 8.28–11.36, further emphasizing Calvin's emphasis on the parallel section of Romans.

Calvin's *Argumentum* portrays Rom. 12–14 as 'exhortatory' with ch. 13 dealing '… for the most part with the authority of magistrates'. Though chapters on the Church and the sacraments have intervened, this is in relative parallel order with the final chapter of the *Institutes* on Civil Government.[16] Of the 16 citations of Romans in the chapter, 11 are from Romans 13, the remainder being from Romans 12. In the fourth section Calvin provides a brief exegesis of Rom. 13:1–4, and each of these verses is cited at least one more time during the chapter.

There are other places where other kinds of symmetry can be discerned. For instance, Calvin discusses idolatry in the *Institutes* after natural revelation and before the general treatment of sin. In the *Argumentum* to the Romans commentary idolatry is not mentioned at the same point, but he does deal with this issue in the commentary proper on Rom. 1:23. The topic of prayer, which comes between the topics of faith and justification in the *Institutes*, is not mentioned in the *Argumentum*, but Romans ch. 8, which concludes the discussion of justification issues according to

Calvin contains a notable passage on prayer, Rom. 8:26–27. Calvin cites Romans 21 times in his lengthy chapter on prayer in the Institutes, 10 of which are from Romans ch. 8, with four on Rom. 8:26–27. These are subtler evidences of structural parallels, but they do show more pieces of Romans in the same relative order as the Institutes.

On the other hand, when reading the references to Romans in the *Institutes* one can suspect other places of matching structure and emphasis on Romans and find that the evidence does not support it. The *Argument* refers to Rom. 12–14 as exhortations, and in the *Institutes* it can appear as if these chapters, and Romans 12 in particular, have special emphasis in the section of the *Institutes* on the Church (4:1–13). This is not observable, however, by a count of the references. While Romans is cited 32 times, the chapters 12–14 are cited approximately the same number of times as other chapters.

Without a comparative tally of citations from other books of Scripture this evidence does not quite make the case that Romans is dominant in Calvin's thinking on these important topics. Several things have become clear, however: Key topics in the structure of Calvin's theology occur in the same relative order in the *Institutes* as they do in the letter to the Romans. Revelation in nature, sin, justification by faith, and election are all crucial to his theology, and they unfold in a meaningful order in the *Institutes* – which happens to be the same order they occur in Romans. In most of these there is an abundant presence of citations from Romans. In all of these, citations from the structurally parallel sections of Romans play a significant or even dominant role relative to other references to Romans.

One must admit that there are also major sections in the *Institutes* that are not discussed in the book of Romans at all: as well as Calvin's extensive polemical discussions with opponents in his own day, this includes extensive discussion of Scripture as clearer revelation, the Trinity, God's providence, human nature before the fall, and the Lord's Supper (though Calvin does cite Romans to some degree in most of these topics too). Still, the overall ordering of Calvin's theology in the *Institutes* has parallels to Romans that are somewhere between suggestive and striking. Calvin was very intentional about his selection and ordering of topics in the *Institutes*, and it seems most likely that these parallels express his stated understanding that Romans is the passageway through which one finds an understanding of Scripture as a whole.

b. The Distribution of Romans Citations in the Institutes

A When one examines the distribution of citations of Romans in the 1559 *Institutes* (Figures 1a and 1b),[17] the pattern shows a relationship between the structure of the *Institutes* and the letter to the Romans. By visual observation the chart shows that Calvin tended somewhat to cite sections of Romans more in the corresponding zone of the Institutes. Earlier chapters of Romans are cited more early on in the *Institutes*, and later chapters are cited more later on. That is, Book 1 cites the first chapter of Romans relatively often, and cites later chapters very little. Book 2 cites Romans most from chapters 3–8, a range encompassing the second quarter of the letter, and cites the last half of Romans rather seldom. Book 3 cites Romans over a broad swath of the middle, from chapters 3–11, but with an

A Analysis of frequency of citations of Romans in *Institutes*.

enormous number of citations from chapter 8 and with over half of the total citations from chapters 8–11, which encompasses most of the third quarter of the book. Book 4 has its greatest number of citations from the chapters just at the beginning of the fourth quarter of the letter, the biggest group being from chapters 12 and 13 which it cites more than any other book does.

Within this pattern there are more citations where one expects them because the topic of Romans matches that of the *Institutes*. **H** However, some places one might expect citations one does not find them, and in many places one finds citations the larger structure of topics could not have predicted. For instance, in Book 1 one might expect Romans chapter 1 to be most heavily cited where natural theology and idolatry are discussed. However, while there are citations of Romans chapter 1 in the discussion of natural revelation, there are none in the discussion of idolatry. There are, though, a number of citations of Roman chapter 1 in Book 1 in the discussion of the Trinity and providence, and even more in Book 2 supporting the discussion of the law and Christology, topics which the central argument of Romans does not emphasize. Unlike certain sections of the *Institutes* that match the topic of a key passage of Romans and discuss it in some detail, such references tend to be citations in passing of evidence for theological points within the topic at hand, collections of evidence from a variety of texts to assemble a biblical view of a topic, or parts of responses to theological opponents.

c. The Proportion of the Letter to the Romans cited relative to Other Books

A third type of observation which lends support to this sense that Romans shapes Calvin's theological work in the *Institutes* is the relative proportion of Romans citations in comparison with his citations of other books. When one examines the citations of New Testament books in the *Institutes*, as found in the McNeill-Battles index, Roman continues to show its prominent place.

A Some basic quantitative observations are instructive. First one should note that with 575 citations in the index to the McNeill-Battles edition of the *Institutes* (figure 1b) there are more citations of Romans than of any other book of Scripture except the Psalms. When one keeps in mind the far shorter length of Romans than the 150 Psalms the importance of Romans becomes evident. The sheer volume of citations relative to other books shows something of the importance of Romans in Calvin's theological work.

When one calculates the number of verses of particular biblical books Calvin cites in the *Institutes* (figure 2), again Romans is dominant among the Pauline letters. When one examines all of Calvin's citations of verses of Pauline epistles, excluding from the count the places where he cites a full chapter or more, Calvin cites an average of 48% of the verses in each letter. In the case of Romans, Calvin cites 296 verses, or 68% of the 433 verses in the letter. This is the second highest percentage of verses cited for any of Paul's epistles, slightly behind Ephesians, of which he cites 72% of the verses. However, in that case he is citing a much fewer 112 verses of Ephesians out of a possible 155. He cites more verses of Romans than there are verses in Ephesians.

H Hermeneutical expectations not matched by thorough analysis.

A Analysis of quantity of Romans citations demonstrates the importance of the letter for Calvin.

In the *Institutes* Calvin also cites whole chapters or ranges of chapters of some books, including Romans, 1 Corinthians, 1 Timothy and 2 Timothy among the Paulines, and the non-Pauline letter to the Hebrews. When one includes all the verses in these chapter ranges, Romans is in the lead among the Pauline letters, with 338 verses cited, or 78% of the verses in the book. When Hebrews is included in this comparison, since it has comparable theological importance to Calvin, it pulls slightly ahead of Romans, with 247 verses cited, or 82% of the 303 verses in the letter. However, one such citation in Hebrews refers the reader to a full seven chapters, making this figure a misrepresentation of the degree to which Calvin is drawing on Hebrews in detail. When one counts only the more ordinary references of less than a chapter, Calvin cites only 134 verses or 44% of the total, far less than the 68% figure for Romans.

H Again, this is not conclusive evidence that Romans served as Calvin's theological guide in the Institutes, but one can say that he used Romans heavily in explaining and supporting his points, explicitly citing around seven out of every ten verses.

d. Observations on the specific ways Romans is cited

Calvin cites Romans with what often sounds like a peculiar confidence and authority. Sometimes it is a matter of proportion, as when discussing the law and human capacity he cites Romans once for each of the three other books by Paul cited.[18] Often, though, he will cite Paul as the one who sets principles and guidelines for all manner of things. Thus, in the first section of his exposition of prayer, he says 'the apostle ... has laid down this order' followed by no less than four citations of Romans, weaving three passages together as a kind of summary of doctrine.[19] Sometimes a passage of Romans can function as a rule even when neither Romans nor Paul is named in the text, but rather a clear allusion is made. Thus Calvin can cite a 'universal rule, not to pass over in ungrateful thoughtlessness or forgetfulness those conspicuous powers which God shows forth in his creatures...', which is a clear reference to Romans 1:19–21.[20]

Paul's dominance in general, and the dominance of Romans in particular, can be seen more plainly in other cases. For instance, one first encounters Romans in the Prefatory Address: 'When Paul wished all prophecy to be made to accord with the analogy of faith [Rom. 12:6], he set forth a very clear rule to test all interpretation of Scripture. Now if our interpretation be measured by this rule of faith, victory is in our hands'.[21] This assertion gives more authority to Paul than it gives clarity about interpretation, even when one looks closely at the verse in question. Nevertheless, it is an important rule for Calvin, and he cites it as a rule for all scriptural interpretation two times in Book 4, first on interpreting the relation of circumcision and baptism, and then on the Lord's Supper.[22] In other passages he gives a glowing testimony to Paul's clarity on various topics: 'This appears in many passages, but nowhere more clearly than in chapter 8 of Romans ...'.[23] Examples of such open-hearted admiration might perhaps be found in reference to other biblical authors, but they are quite prominent with reference to Paul. This attitude seems particularly focused on Romans, which could be a function either of the subject matter of the

---

H Quantitive analysis as indication of hermeneutical significance of Romans.

letter or of the sheer number of citations – though the number of citations is large because of Calvin's sense of the importance and clarity of the letter's subject matter.

Proving this point in a more detailed way is beyond the scope of this chapter, but the picture emerging from these examples, along with the parallels in the structure between Romans and the *Institutes* and the distribution of citations of Romans, should give a sense of how this particular book of Paul was indeed Calvin's guide in his theological work.

The Theology of Romans as the Door to the True Meaning of Other Texts

When one considers how the book of Romans functioned in the writing of Calvin's commentaries, the picture is somewhat different. There are several aspects to consider, **H** but all are implications of the idea that Romans is the clearest book of Scripture on the most important topics in Scripture. As a brief case study we will look at a few of Calvin's many citations of Romans in his commentary on Genesis. Genesis is useful in this, both because Romans refers to passages in that book quite prominently, and because the stories of the ancient forebears of the faith there raise ethical problems.

a. Quantitative Observations on Biblical Citations in the Genesis Commentary

Having examined all the New Testament citations in the Genesis commentary, I can say a number of things.[24] There are 153 citations of the New Testament in the 50 chapters of the Genesis commentary (Table 3). Interestingly, there are also 153 citations of the Old Testament if one excludes cross references to Genesis (Table 4), and a total of 44 books of Scripture are cited, not including Genesis, indicating something the breadth and balance in the way Calvin seeks to interpret Scripture with Scripture. However, Paul's letters account for 63% of the New Testament citations, indicating something of the dominance of Paul in Calvin's biblical interpretation. Among Paul's letters, 43% of the citations are to Romans, indicating something of the dominance of Romans in particular. Citations of Romans account for 27% of all New Testament citations, and 13% of all biblical citations. With 41 total citations of Romans, there are more citations of Romans than of any other book of the New Testament, and the only book of the Old Testament cited more than Romans is the book of Psalms with 48 citations. This is parallel to the proportion of biblical citations in the *Institutes*, as seen in the index to the McNeill-Battles translation, and indicates something of where Calvin's biblical imagination dwelt. **AH** In total number of citations, Calvin seems to have had Romans very much on his mind as he commented on Genesis.[25]

I have divided the citations into two groups: The first is those in which Calvin cites New Testament texts because they in turn cite the pertinent text of Genesis. In many of these Paul is declared to be the authoritative interpreter when some tensions must be resolved between accounts of history or on theological points.[26] The second group is those texts which are cited for other reasons, which I am calling

---

H Calvin's presupposition concerning Romans.

AH Analysis of Genesis commentary's citations of Romans confirms that the latter served as Calvin's hermeneutical guide.

'theological interpretation'. These may be ethical norms or doctrinal statements that guide his interpretation, apparent tensions with a New Testament text, or fragments pieced together to show a biblical viewpoint on an issue.

In both categories Romans is again in the lead numerically: Romans accounts for 17 of Calvin's 51 citations of New Testament texts which had made use of Genesis, more than any other New Testament book. The closest competitor is Hebrews with thirteen.

If one looks only at texts used for theological interpretation, removing Old Testament use of the New Testament, the percentage of citations of Romans is again strikingly large: In Calvin's 102 citations of New Testament texts for purposes of theological interpretation, texts by Paul account for 68 such references, two-thirds of the total. With 24 citations, Romans accounts for 35% of the Pauline references, and 24% of all such citations. This is significantly more than other books by Paul: First Corinthians comes next with 16, a third less than Romans. These figures seem particularly significant, because they indicate the frequency with which Calvin's interpretation was guided by Romans when the text did not strictly require it: A quarter of his theological use of New Testament texts is guided by the letter to the Romans.

b. Examination of Calvin's Interpretive Practice in the Genesis Commentary

A less quantitative case can be made by examining the ways Calvin cites Romans in comments on specific texts of Genesis. Certainly the most important case is that of Abraham's faith, which Genesis says was counted as righteousness, and on which Paul bases much of his doctrine of justification. Calvin's initial comment shows clearly his views on Paul and Romans: 'None of us would be able to conceive the rich and hidden doctrine which this passage contains, unless Paul had borne his torch before us'. (Rom. 4:3). Paul is the 'luminous expositor' who 'leads us to the celestial tribunal of God'.[27] The discussion that follows runs to three and a half columns in the *Corpus Reformatorum*, and at times it seems that Calvin is more intent on discussing the fine points of the Romans text than the Genesis text he has at hand. Here Romans clearly has led Calvin to what he thinks of as the profound treasure of Scripture.

The dominance of Romans on theological topics is seen in a variety of ways in other passages of the Genesis commentary. On the question of who is guilty for the sin in the garden, Calvin must decide between Paul in First Timothy, who says the woman, and Paul in Romans who says the man. Against other interpreters, Calvin interprets the Genesis text in harmony with the Romans text.[28] A little later on the same passage, in discussing the pervasiveness of original sin, Calvin refers the reader to the *Institutes*, but summarizes his point with two passages from Romans.[29] Commenting on an obscure reference to King Chedorlaomer who quelled a rebellion, Calvin affirms his right to do so based on the teaching of Romans 13:1 that civil authorities are put in place by God.[30] His comments on the story of Jacob and Esau, which weighs so heavily in his discussion of predestination in Romans, lead to another lengthy discussion dealing heavily with the Romans text.[31]

Calvin also is guided by Romans on ethical issues, first around food and drink. When in Gen. 1:28 God grants all plants but one for human food, Calvin, rather than emphasizing this early call to vegetarianism, uses the text to illustrate an ethical teaching from Romans:

> For it is of great importance that we touch nothing of God's bounty but what we know he has permitted us to do; since we cannot enjoy anything with a good conscience, except we receive it as from the hand of God. And therefore Paul teaches us that, in eating and drinking we always sin, unless faith be present (Rom. 14:23.)[32]

When, after the flood, animals too are given for human food, Calvin disagrees with other interpreters that this is, in fact, a change. His own opinion is guided by Romans: 'We have heard what Paul says, that we are at liberty to eat what we please, only we do it with the assurance of conscience, but that he who imagines anything to be unclean, to him it is unclean (Rom. 14:14).'[33]

Calvin also makes a number of ethical judgments on characters in Genesis, grounding his judgments in Romans. For instance, Jacob is judged on standards from Romans. When he tries to trick his father into granting him the blessing belonging to Esau, Calvin tells us his behavior is problematic because it is '... very contrary to faith. For when the Apostle teaches, that "whatsoever is not of faith is sin" (Rom. 14:23), he trains the sons of God to this sobriety, that they may not permit themselves to undertake anything with a doubtful and perplexed conscience'. Lest we miss the fact that an ethical precept is being offered, he tells us that this is 'the only rule of right conduct' for such circumstances.[34] Here Calvin is citing the same passage which he was seen to quote on Genesis 1:28 to explain the ethics of eating, and one sees that certain passages of Romans emerge as ethical principles, which in turn shape his interpretations.

Calvin is equally unimpressed by Jacob's clever strategy to produce sheep and goats in particular colors and patterns by putting sticks in their watering troughs. He is troubled not by the magic trick but by the motive:

> Therefore Jacob ought not to have resorted to this stratagem, for the purpose of producing degenerate cattle, but rather to have followed the rule which the Lord delivers by the mouth of Paul, that the faithful should study to overcome evil with good (Rom. 12:21). This simplicity, I confess, ought to have been cultivated by Jacob, unless the Lord from heaven had commanded otherwise.[35]

Calvin's ethical standard is a text from Romans, and it is a prominent one for him: Rom. 12:21 will appear twice more in the examples that follow. What is really surprising here is that he seems to expect that Jacob should have known this standard and taken it as an order from God. Paul's voice in Romans is not merely clear but functions as a kind of reverse prophecy.

Calvin also makes positive ethical judgments on biblical characters based on passages in Romans. Through the testimony of Romans, Calvin is so sure of the solidity of Abraham's earlier faith that when Genesis says that he fell down and laughed at the promise of a son, Calvin judges even this as an expression of faith.[36] Commenting on the scene where Joseph and his brothers feasted and drank, Calvin is careful to argue that it is not implied that they drank to excess. God gives such gifts liberally, beyond meeting mere needs, but still we must exercise restraint. The definition of this restraint comes from Romans: 'And, truly, I confess, we must diligently attend to what Paul prescribes (Rom. 13:14), "Make not provision for the flesh to fulfill the lusts thereof"'.[37] On Joseph's forgiveness and generosity to his brothers, Calvin notes that 'It was a token of a solid and not a feigned reconciliation, not only to abstain from malice and injury, but also to "overcome evil with good," as Paul teaches, (Rom. 12:21)'.[38]

Conclusion

There are interesting and similar cases of the dominant role of Romans in Calvin's interpretation in his New Testament commentaries. This is so even in the Gospels, regarding the words of Christ. When Jesus says not to resist evil, which seems plain enough, Calvin will say that 'Paul is our best interpreter of this passage, at Rom. 12:17 (and 21), where he tells us rather to overcome evil with good than to struggle with those who wish us harm'.[39] Paul seems almost superior to the incarnate Word in Calvin's comments when Christ raised a dead man to life: the Reformer writes, 'In these words, Christ testifies to the truth of Paul's teaching (Rom. 4:17), "God…calleth the things that are not, as though they were"'.[40] Similarly on the Lord's Prayer, when we are told to pray for forgiveness, Calvin writes that 'Thus is fulfilled the teaching of Paul (Rom. 3:19, 23), "For all have sinned, and fall short of the glory of God …"'.[41] Calvin interprets Scripture with Scripture as constantly in the New Testament Commentaries as in the Old, and he makes use of the whole of the Bible in doing so. Still, Paul is presented as the voice in Scripture who really must be heard to make sense of the words of others, and in such cases Romans appears with particular prominence.

Further study is needed to clarify similarities and differences between Calvin's citations of Romans and other Pauline works, and between his citations of Paul and other biblical authors and speakers. This would help to discern how often Calvin is simply using Romans as he might use any passage of Scripture to resolve a difficulty, and cases where Romans has a distinctive role shaping the theology he is willing to draw from other texts. One would need to develop a further classification of particular types of citations, and look at the proportion of different types of citations.

One sees in the citations of Romans, whether in the Genesis commentary or elsewhere, that this epistle does indeed function as Calvin's passageway to the whole of scripture. All of Paul, but Romans in particular, creates a theological substructure, an invisible system of theological and ethical ideas, which guides Calvin to clarity in the interpretation of both plain and obscure passages. As the outline and details of Romans shaped Calvin's *Institutes*, providing a passageway into the whole of scripture, the fully digested contents of Romans served as a door through which Calvin traveled as he mined the treasure in the individual books of the Bible.

There has long been debate about what the central doctrine or organizing idea is in Calvin's theology, and indeed whether there is one at all. R. Ward Holder has done an admirable job of summarizing this debate, from the older view that predestination is central, through denial of a central doctrine or system, to attempts to find a center in Christology, faith, sacramental word, or union with Christ. He offers a helpful new paradigm linking Calvin's theology to his pastoral work: Calvin was concerned with useful edifying doctrine for ministry and reform of the Church.[42] As useful as this is in linking the whole of Calvin's life's work into a unity, this author believes more can be said about the unity of Calvin's theology as found in the two major theological genres in which he wrote. That unity is found at the letter to the Romans, which Calvin portrays as the book which guided him, and should guide all Christians, into the meaning of the whole of Scripture. Though there may not be one doctrine which functions as systematically central, it is the doctrines presented by Paul in Romans, most crucially but not solely the stream of teachings that flow into and out of the doctrine of justification, which one finds repeatedly shaping his theology and his biblical interpretation. Whether one is reading the *Institutes* or the biblical commentaries, as Calvin hints that one will, one finds a distinctly Romans-shaped theology.

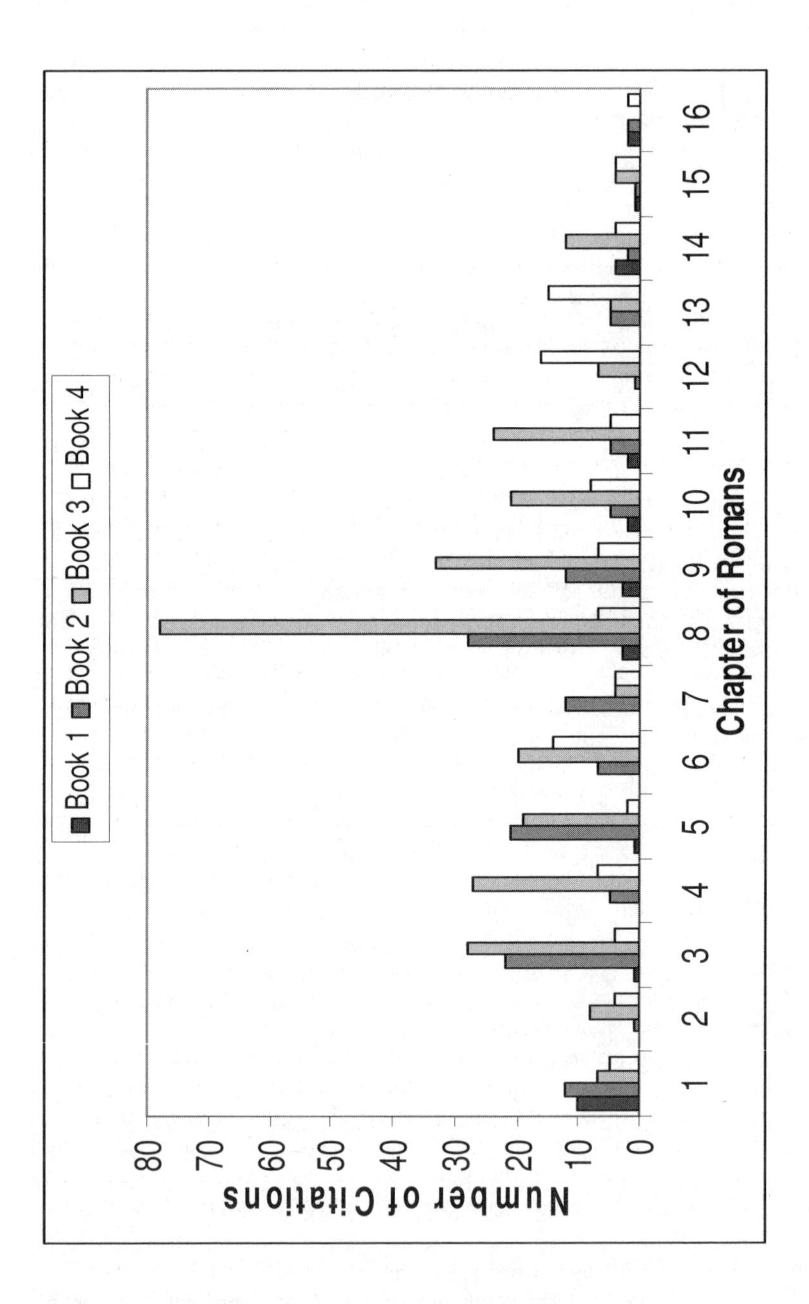

Figure 1a: Number of citations of each chapter of Romans in each book of the *Institutes*.

Chapter of Romans	Book 1	Book 2	Book 3	Book 4	Total
1	10	12	7	5	**34**
2	0	1	8	4	**13**
3	1	22	28	4	**55**
4	0	5	27	7	**39**
5	1	21	19	2	**43**
6	0	7	20	14	**41**
7	0	12	4	4	**20**
8	3	28	78	7	**116**
9	3	12	33	7	**55**
10	2	5	21	8	**36**
11	2	5	24	5	**36**
12	0	1	7	16	**24**
13	0	5	5	15	**25**
14	4	2	12	4	**22**
15	1	1	4	4	**10**
16	2	2	0	2	**6**
Total	**29**	**141**	**297**	**108**	**575**

Figure 1b: Data table of citations of each chapter of Romans in each book of the *Institutes*.

	Rom.	1 Cor.	2 Cor.	Gal.	Eph.	Phil.	Col.	1Thess.	2Thess.	1 Tim.	2 Tim.	Tit.	Phlm.	Heb.
Total verses	433	436	256	149	155	104	95	89	47	113	83	46	25	303
Verses cited	296	226	89	98	112	46	64	25	22	56	31	21	2	134
Percent of total book	68%	52%	35%	66%	72%	44%	67%	28%	47%	49.6%	37%	46%	8%	44%
Verses & chapters cited	338	246								57	64			134
Percent of total book	78%	56%								50.4%	77%			82%

Figure 2: Percentage of verses of Pauline Epistles and Hebrews cited in the *Institutes*.

	All NT	All Paul	Rom	I Cor.	Gal.	Other Paul	Heb.	Other NT
Total Citations in Gen.	153	96	41	19	11	25	23	34
OT used in NT	51	28	17	3	7	1	13	10
Theological Interp.	102	68	24	16	4	24	10	24

Figure 3: Citations of New Testament texts in the Genesis commentary.

	Exod-Deut.	Josh.-I Sam.	Job-Song*	Isa.-Mal.	*Ps. Alone
Citations	28	22	56	47	48

Figure 4: Distribution of citations of Old Testament books in the Genesis Commentary.

Notes

[1] 'John Calvin to the Reader', in *Calvin: Institutes of the Christian Religion,* ed. John T. McNeill, trans. Ford Lewis Battles (Louisville: Westminster John Knox Press, 1960) pp. 4–5. Hereinafter, *Institutes,* with citations to book, chapter, and section. Joannis Calvini, *Opera Selecta* vol. 3, ed. Petrus Barth (Monachii: Chr. Kaiser, 1928) p. 6. Hereinafter, OS 3.6.

[2] To use the phrase of R. Ward Holder, 'Calvin as Commentator on the Pauline Epistles', in *Calvin and the Bible,* ed. Donald K. McKim (Cambridge: Cambridge University Press, 2006) p. 235.

[3] On this and the changes to later editions, and to place this commentary in the context of all of Calvin's commentaries on Paul, see Holder, Calvin as 'Commentator on the Pauline Epistles', especially pp. 226–28, and 231-–32.

[4] For the 1539 *Institutes,* OS 3.7: 'Calend. August. Anno 1539'. For the Romans Commentary, *Calvin's [New Testament] Commentaries,* vol. 8, trans. Ross Mackenzie, ed. David W. Torrance and Thomas F. Torrance (Grand Rapids: Wm. B. Eerdmans Publishing Company, repr., 1991), p. 4. Hereinafter CNTC 8.4. *Ioannis Calvini Opera Exegetica,* vol. 13, T. H. L. Parker

and D. C. Parker (Genève: Librairie Droz, 1999) p. 6. Hereinafter OE 13.6: 'XV Calend. Novemb. M. D. XXXIX.'

[5] CNTC 8.2. OE13.4: 'quando siquis eam intelligat, aditum sibi quendam patefactum habet ad totius Scripturae intelligentiam'.

[6] CNTC 8.5, OE 13.7: 'quod siquis veram eius intelligentiam sit assequutus, ad reconditissimos quosque Scripturae thesauros adeundos habeat apertas fores'.

[7] Institutes, 7. OS 3.8. 'toutesfois ie puis bien promettre cela, que ce pourra estre comme une clef et ouverture, pour donner acces a tous enfans de Dieu, a bien et droictement entendre l'Escriture saincte'.

[8] 'John Calvin to the Reader,' *Institutes*, 5. OS 3.6: 'necessario instrumento'.

[9] CNTC 8.5, OE 13.7. 'Atque ita ingreditur principalem totius epistolae quaestionem, Fide nos iustificari'.

[10] 'John Calvin to Simon Grynaeus', CNTC 8.4, OE 13.6: 'in religionis autem dogmatibus, in quibus praecipue voluit Dominus consentaneas esse suorum mentes, minus sumatur libertatis'.

[11] See the diagrams in Ford Lewis Battles assisted by John R. Walchenbach, *Analysis of the Institutes of the Christian Religion,* reprint edition (Phillipsburg, NJ: R & R Publishing, 1980) 15-16, and Battles 'Calculus Fidei', in *Calvinus Ecclesiae Doctor* (Kampen, Netherlands : J H Kok, 1979) 85–110.

[12] 'Argumentum' CNTC 8.5, OE 13.7. *Institutes* 1.3–5, OS 3.37–60.

[13] 'Argumentum' CNTC 8.6, OE 13.7–8. *Institutes* 2.1–5, OS 3.228–320.

[14] 'Argumentum' CNTC 8.6–9, OE 13.8–10. *Institutes* 3.11–19, OS 4.181–296.

[15] 'Argumentum' CNTC 8.9, OE 13.11. *Institutes* 3.21–24, OS 4.368–432.

[16] 'Argumentum' CNTC 10, OE 13.11. *Institutes* 4.20, OS 5.471–02.

[17] The data being analyzed in these figures and observations is found in the scripture index from the McNeill-Battles English edition of the 1559 *Institutes* (pp. 1577–1580), the fullest listing of Calvin's biblical citations the author knows. The author wishes to thank Jeffrey Warrick for his gracious help with data entry on this part of the project.

[18] *Institutes* 2.5.6, OS 3.304.

[19] *Institutes* 3.20.1, OS 4.297.

[20] Institutes 1.14.21, OS 3.171–172. '... si illam primum universalem regulam sequantur, ut quas in suis creaturis Deus exhibet conspicuas virtutes, non ingrata vel incogitantia vel oblivione transeant ...'.

[21] *Institutes*, 'Prefatory Address to King Francis' 2, p. 12, CO 3.12. 'Paulus, quum ad fidei analogiam omnem prophetiam formatam esse voluit [Rom. 12.b.6], certissimam amussim posuit qua probari Scripturae interpretatio debeat. Ad hanc itaque fidei regulam si nostra exigantur, in manibus est victoria'.

[22] *Institutes* 4.16.4, 4.17.32, OS 5.308, 5.391. OS 5.391 cites Rom. 12.3 without Rom. 12.6, though it is clearly a reference to the same rule.

[23] *Institutes* 1.13.18, OS 3.132. 'multis id quidem locis, sed nusquam clarius quam cap. 8. ad Romanos ...'.

[24] The numbers are as complete as possible, without claiming perfect precision. I have sought to include all citations from the *Corpus Reformatorum*. In addition, if Paul is named but no text is cited, whenever the context makes it clear what text is being alluded to, I have

sought to include it. I have not made similar efforts to see if other New Testament authors or Old Testament authors are named without chapter and verse citations. The citations are somewhat different from those in the index to the Calvin Studies Society English translation. That Victorian era text does not translate some sections of the commentary (to wit, Gen. 17:31–37), presumably lest they cause the youth to blush. It also is idiosyncratic regarding citation of allusions the CR did not include, and omission of some citations the CR did.

25 The same can be said of the Psalms, and it would be useful to compare the ways the two books are cited.

26 For example, see his use of Rom. 5.12 at Gen. 3.6. *Calvin's Commentaries*, vol. 1, trans. John King (Grand Rapids: Baker Book House, repr. 1993) 155. Hereinafter CC 1.155. *Ioannis Calvini Opera quae Supersunt Omnia*, ed. Guilielmus Baum et al., (Brunsvigae: C.A. Schwetschke et filium, 1882) col. 60. Hereinafter CO 23.60. Or with more explicit praise of Calvin's authority, see his use of Rom. 4.3 at Genesis 15.6, CC 1.404, CO 23.211.

27 Genesis 15.6, CC 1.404–405, CO 23.211–212. 'Quam uberem et reconditam doctrinam contineat hic locus nemo nostrum coniiceret, nisi facem nobis praetulisset Paulus' (Rom. 4,3). 'Sed qui Paulum habebant dilucidum interpretem …'. 'Paulus … deducit nos ad coeleste Dei tribunal'.

28 Genesis 3.6, CC 1.152, CO 23.60.

29 Genesis 3.6, CC 1.155, CO 23.62.

30 Genesis 14.1, CC 1.382, CO 23.382.

31 Genesis 25.23, CC 1.45–46, CO 23.350.

32 Genesis 1.28, CC 1.99, CO 23.29. 'Atque ideo docet Paulus (Rom. 14.23) edendo et bibendo nos semper peccare, nisi adsit fides'.

33 Genesis 9.3, CC 1.292, CO 23.144. 'Audivimus quid Paulus dicat (Rom. 14,14), liberum esse vesci quibuslibet, modo adsit conscientiae certitudo: immundum autem esse quidquid sibi quisque immundum fingit.'

34 Genesis 27.11, CC 1.85, CO 23.374. 'Nam quum docet apostolus (Rom. 14.23) peccatum esse quidquid ex fide non est, ad hanc sobrietatem instituit filios Dei, ne quid dubia et perplexa conscientia aggredi sibi permittant. Haec certitudo unica est bene agenda regula …'.

35 Genesis 30.37, CC 1.155, CO 23.417. 'Non debuit igitur Iacob ad hanc versutiam confugere, ut degeneres haberet foetus, sed regulam potius sequi, quam Dominus per os Pauli tradit, ut studeant fideles bono malum vincere (Röm. [sic] 12.21). Haec simplicitas, fateor, colenda fuit ipsi Iacob, nisi Dominus e coelo aliud mandasset'.

36 Genesis 17.17, CC 1.459–460, CO 23.245.

37 Genesis 43.33, CC 1. 363, CO 23.545. 'Et certe fateor, sedulo quod praescribit Paulus Rom. 13.14. servandum esse ne illius curam agamus ad concupiscentias'.

38 Genesis 50.21, CC 1.489, CO 23.620. 'Hoc vero solidae ac non fucatae reconciliationis signum fuit, non modo abstinere a maleficio et noxa, sed etiam vincere bono malum sicuti, Paulus praecipit' (Rom. 12.11).

39 Matt. 5.39, CNTC 1.193, CO 45.184. 'Atque huius loci Paulus nobis optimus esse potest interpres, dum iubet potius vincere malum bono quam ut maleficiis certemus, ad Romanos cap. 12.47 [sic]'.

40 On Luke 7.14, CNTC 1.252, CO 45.239. 'Hac voce testatus est Christus, quam vere doceat Paulus (Rom. 4.17), Deum vocare ea quae non sunt, tanquam sint'.

41 CNTC 1.211, CO 45.200-201. 'Ita impletur quod docet Paulus (Rom. 3.23), Reos esse omnes, et destitui Dei Gloria …'.

42 R. Ward Holder, *John Calvin and the Grounding of Interpretation: Calvin's First Commentaries* (Leiden and Boson: Brill, 2006), pp. 163–168.

Structure or Door: Romans as Key to Reading Scripture
Response to Gary Neal Hansen

Kathy Ehrensperger

In this interesting and stimulating article, Hansen draws attention to Calvin's awareness of hermeneutical presuppositions in reading Scripture: the *Institutes* are perceived as a 'necessary tool' for the study of Scripture, and thus as the hermeneutical frame from which Scripture is interpreted. Hansen takes Calvin's appreciation of Romans as indicative of the role Romans played for Calvin in relation to the *Institutes*: the understanding of this letter provides the door and passageway to the 'treasures of Scripture'. The question arising from this is – How do Romans and the *Institutes* relate to each other since Calvin perceives both as hermeneutical guides for reading the Scriptures? What then is the relationship between the two – are there two distinct hermeneutical frameworks for interpretation and if so which is the primary or dominating one? Or to put it another way: in relation to these two, which is providing the hermeneutical frame for which Romans for the *Institutes,* or the *Institutes* for Romans?

Hansen's analysis suggests that Romans provides the template for the *Institutes*. No doubt Romans is of primary significance for the *Institutes*. As Hansen notes, there are significant differences in the frequency of the references to particular chapters – which to me seems indicative of the hermeneutical choices made by Calvin. But prior to looking at this in more detail I would like to raise another issue.

The question that needs to be addressed is: what are the hermeneutical presuppositions on which the prioritizing of Romans is based? If Romans provides the template for the *Institutes* this role cannot be attributed to them. The prioritizing of Romans obviously is influenced by 'outside' contextual factors. These outside factors are the church-related and political conflicts of sixteenth century Western Europe. Part of the movement of those who questioned and eventually challenged the dominating power of the Roman Catholic church focussed theologically on the doctrine of 'justification by faith'. But this focus, far from being purely theological, is driven by other interests and agendas beyond pure theology (if such ever existed). Romans was perceived as providing an elaborate exposition of the doctrine of justification by faith. But this perception, rather than representing the teaching of the first century apostle, is a focus on a particular aspect of Romans shaped by certain Reformers' agenda and thus by a particular context. Whether this is 'the distinctly Pauline summary of divine human relationship' as Hansen claims is a matter of lively debate, certainly after Krister Stendahl's famous lecture on 'Paul and the Introspective Conscience of the West'. Thus it is the Reformers' agenda, rather than Paul, that provides the hermeneutical frame for prioritizing Romans and this agenda is not shaped exclusively by so-called theological issues. Calvin's perception of Romans should be viewed then in light of this – it is a perception of Romans read in light of, and framed by, hermeneutical presuppositions of the Reformers' agenda. Framed as such, Romans then is taken as 'an exposition of the central doctrine of justification'. It is thus hermeneutical presuppositions which lead to the prioritizing of Romans. In this Calvin is not different from contemporary interpreters; the priorities in reading, the choices in relation to hermeneutical frameworks cannot be based on something like a plain text, however faithful to Scripture we perceive ourselves to be. The reader interprets from a specific perspective which is shaped by what Bourdieu called 'habitus' – the conglomerate of cultural, etc., contexts which shape us and influence our particular choices. I thus would raise a critical voice against Calvin's stance that 'the Church's teaching needs to be clear and unchanging'.

The frequency of references to Romans is striking and the case argued by Hansen is on solid ground here. I am not entirely convinced by the argument advocated that the *Institutes* are actually structured in accordance with the structure of Romans. The frequency of certain chapters of the letter does not as neatly cohere with the structure of the *Institutes* as Hansen sees it. There are more exceptions to the rule than a coherent structure in my view would allow. Thus to remove certain chapters from the discussion of structural correspondence, especially chapters 9–11, that is three chapters at the heart of the letter, weakens the argument for structural analogy between the letter and the *Institutes* significantly. I find Calvin's metaphor of door and passageway actually more convincing than structural analogies, since door and passageway provide more open and flexible images than the more static concept of 'structure' in light of which the links between Romans and the *Institutes* can be analyzed.

These more open images allow for more than seeing mere structural analogies or differences between the two. In particular, the increased references to certain chapters and the omission or rare references to others may reveal aspects of Calvin's specific hermeneutical choices. Thus, e.g., chapters 12–16 play a minor role in the *Institutes* with the exception of chapter 13. We find a significant focus on chapters 3-6 and 8 which coheres precisely with the hermeneutical presupposition of an agenda shaped as described above. Chapters 9–11 are in view in the *Institutes*, but not with the significance that recent interpretations often attribute to these in conjunction with the following chapters (12–16). The issue of chapters 9–11 tells us something about the context of Paul as well as that of Calvin. Thus, as in contemporary interpretation, the hermeneutical presuppositions obviously determined the interpretative choices of Calvin's perception of 'his door and passageway'. This comes to the fore again in Calvin's interpretation of 13:1–8 which he deems as emphasizing that all state authority is subordinate to God. The tune Calvin hears here is that of a relativization of any state authority, a tune which in the Reformed tradition led to the formulation of the right of resistance to state authorities who trespassed the limitations to which they were subject. This critical dimension over against state authorities is not present in the same way in Lutheran tradition, since Luther's interpretation of Romans 13:1–8, differed from Calvin's. The context of Calvin differed from that of Luther, who was protected by German princes. I cannot elaborate on this here, but Heiko Oberman, amongst others, has drawn attention to significant contextual issues which contributed to the specifically Calvinist perception of pilgrimage, etc. One influence which decisively shaped Calvin's thinking concerning the role of state authorities was the fate of the Huguenot refugees he pastored during his time in Strasbourg before being called back to Geneva.

Concerning the issue of Scripture interpreting Scripture, Calvin seems to be an interesting practitioner of inter-textual interpretation. He does interpret Scripture in light of Scripture, but the guiding principle seems to be Romans as read from with the Reformers' hermeneutical framework of the centrality of the doctrine of justification by faith. This framework was perceived as scriptural – it was what Scripture told them. But it is not 'Scripture' as such but 'Scripture' read in light of tradition, the very thing the Reformers thought to have left behind. But what this actually involved was not merely a return to 'Scripture' but a turn to 'Scripture' read in a different light, based on different hermeneutical presuppositions for contextual purposes. Thus Calvin read Romans in light of specific hermeneutical presuppositions and perceived 'this' Romans as his hermeneutical and theological guide. His principle of Scripture interpreting Scripture has a slight slant in that not all of Scripture is given the same weight or significance. Within this principle choices are made, as in the case mentioned concerning the agent of sin: the choice is based on the hermeneutical presupposition that Romans has more significance than I Timothy, and thus man is to be blamed rather than Eve. Whether Calvin decided on this purely on hermeneutical grounds or maybe also influenced by 'real' life experience must remain open! Maybe the Spirit guided him.

— SIX —

Calvin's Hermeneutic and Tradition: An Augustinian Reception of Romans 7

R. Ward Holder

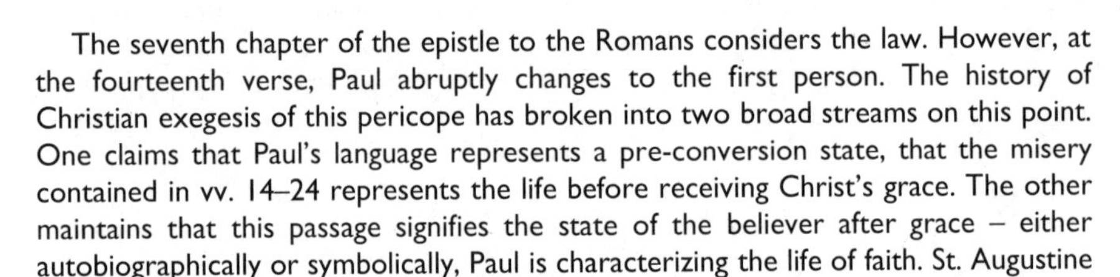

The seventh chapter of the epistle to the Romans considers the law. However, at the fourteenth verse, Paul abruptly changes to the first person. The history of Christian exegesis of this pericope has broken into two broad streams on this point. One claims that Paul's language represents a pre-conversion state, that the misery contained in vv. 14–24 represents the life before receiving Christ's grace. The other maintains that this passage signifies the state of the believer after grace – either autobiographically or symbolically, Paul is characterizing the life of faith. St. Augustine even defended both positions at different times in his life.

John Calvin, in his *Commentary on the Epistle of Paul to the Romans*, noted this change. He wrote that though Augustine had at first chosen the first option, he later righted himself. Calvin claimed that Augustine's second position was correct, and that in fact this passage could not be referred to anything but the regenerate (*non aliter quam de renatis posse exponi*)[1]. Thus, Calvin cited Augustine's later position as authority for his own stance, that the divided self of Romans 7 can only be referred to the regenerate believer. **H** But why did Calvin make this choice?[2] David Steinmetz has pointed out that this was hardly a 'Protestant' choice in the early modern period, as Cardinal Cajetan made the same choice.[3] Steinmetz makes clear that this choice was quite mainstream in the sixteenth century and did not represent a confessional identity issue.[4]

With the confessional rationale gone, we may ask why Calvin did choose Augustine's later position. The reasons are not yet clear. The medieval tradition of interpreting this text did not support the later Augustine. In Calvin's time this option was mainstream, but not a universal choice.[5] Even in our own day, the sense of the text is unclear enough that general agreement has not been reached.[6] Calvin had to abandon the medieval tradition that accepted Romans 7 as a description of life under the law, and Calvin was not an interpreter who lightly discarded the Church's exegetical traditions.[7] Finally and most curiously, Calvin's interpretive choice rejects the implicit solution that his favorite exegete, Chrysostom, had offered. Why did he make these choices? In this study, I will demonstrate that this is a particular case of Calvin's hermeneutical principles overriding his exegetical rules. We will see that though Calvin had strong exegetical reasons to follow the earlier tradition, his grasp of the Christian *religio* more urgently pointed him toward the later Augustine.

H A Question of Hermeneutics.

Calvin's Interpretation

Calvin argued that v. 14 is about the nature of the law and the nature of human beings.[8] The law is wholly spiritual, wholly good. **A** The law's purity is balanced by the wickedness of sinful human nature. Calvin poked fun at those who would speak of the glories of human nature by asking what agreement might exist between the purity of the law and the decadence of human nature. He answered, 'None – just as exists between light and darkness'.[9] Verse 15, on the other hand, describes the regenerate believer, who has different existential possibilities.[10] When he turns to v. 15, Calvin expressed the difficulty of the teaching which Paul gives. For Calvin, v. 15 represented two important themes. First, it is about the difference that exists between the wholly pure law and polluted human nature. Secondly, it teaches that it is impossible to state that the law actually causes death.[11] Calvin began his explanation by tracing and refuting popular opinions about the freedom of the unregenerate will. He wrote:

> Since carnal man rushes with the whole predilection of his mind into sinning, he appears to be sinning by free choice, as if it were his power to govern himself. And this most pernicious opinion has become valued among almost all people, that man is able by his natural faculties to freely choose what he pleases without the support of Divine grace. Yet though the will of the faithful man is moved to good by the Spirit of God, it is in him that the depravity of human nature becomes most conspicuous, because it resists obstinately and leads away from where it is led.[12]

Calvin saw that it is only the converted believer who experiences the conflict that Paul describes. David Steinmetz has noted in Calvin's interpretation that 'There is, therefore, a perverse sense in which sinners may be regarded as integrated personalities, at least on the level of the will's affections. If the ungodly are not free from a sometimes troubled conscience, they are at least free from the inner conflict that marks the life of faith.... But this freedom is deceptive, a mark of a subtler and deeper bondage'.[13]

Thus Calvin stated that v. 15 is an example of a believer who has been regenerated. He regarded this as an opportunity to consider the difference between the character of sin in the believer and in those who have not been regenerated. For Calvin, that difference has to do with the will rather than the intellect. Unbelievers, when they receive the pangs of conscience, do so because they experience a contradiction in their judgment rather than in their will.[14] For this reason v. 15 can only speak about the regenerate, who still bear the remains of flesh within them. Verse 15 is about a conflict of the will, not the intellect.

Augustine's Interpretations

Augustine interpreted the book of Romans frequently. Informally, he was concerned with its interpretation for years as a Manichaean hearer and a lover of philosophy.[15] Formally, he produced his *Propositions from the Epistle to the Romans* and his *Unfinished Commentary on the Epistle to the Romans* between 392 and around 400.

A Analysis of Calvin's views on the nature of the law and the nature of humans beings.

In the *Propositions from the Epistle to the Romans*, we see his early position. Commenting upon vv. 15–16, Augustine asserted:

> For I do not want to do what I do; but what I hate, this I do. If, moreover, I do what I do not want to do, I agree that the Law is good (7:15-16). This is the Law sufficiently defended from every accusation. But one must take care lest he think that these words deny our free will, for it is not so. (2) The man described here is under the Law, prior to grace; sin overcomes him when by his own strength he attempts to live righteously without the aid of God's liberating grace. (3) For by his free will man has a means to believe in the Liberator and to receive grace so that, with the liberating assistance of him who gives it, he might cease to sin. Thus might man cease to be under the Law, but rather be with or within it, fulfilling it by the love of God, which he could not do through fear.[16]

A Augustine noted clearly that the person under discussion in v. 15 is one who is under the law before the reception of grace (*sub lege positus ante gratiam*). Two concerns drove Augustine's interpretation. First is the protection of the goodness of the law; the second is the freedom of the will. The vindication of the law Augustine took from v. 14, where he wrote: '"We know that the Law is spiritual, but I am carnal" (7:14), indicates clearly that the Law cannot be fulfilled except by spiritual men, who are made such by the grace of God. (2) For he who has become spiritual like the Law will easily fulfill what it prescribes; nor will he be under the Law, but with it. He is one, moreover, whom temporal goods do not seduce nor temporal evils terrify'.[17] The law here functions as a code for those to whom God has given grace. Such spiritual people easily fulfill the demands of the law. In fact, their release from the bondage to the law is a comment about their motivation. They are not under the law, they are with the law (*nec erit sub illa sed cum illa*). They do not seem actually to have been released from the requirements of the law, they simply now have been changed so that they see the requirements as desirable, rather than onerous.

Around 396, Augustine composed his *Ad Simplicianum de Diversis Quaestionibus*.[18] This was Augustine's set of answers to the questions of interpretation that Romans 7 and 9 raise for believers. The first question concerned Romans 7:7–25. In the fourth paragraph, Augustine wrote, 'But sin was dead, that is, hidden, all the time that men were born mortal and lived without the commandment of the law, following the desires of the flesh in ignorance because there was no prohibition. Therefore he says, "I lived without the law once". Thereby he shows that he is not speaking in his own person but generally in the person of "the old man"'.[19] Augustine still held that earlier position, that Paul was not speaking autobiographically. Nor was Paul speaking of believers in general, rather he considered those who had not yet received grace. Clearly, in the 390's, Augustine interpreted this passage to safeguard free will and the goodness of the law.

C By 420, however, Augustine had experienced a change of heart about this passage. He had been embroiled in considering Pelagian issues since at least 411, when Marcellinus sent him a letter reporting that Pelagian views were expanding in

---

A Author's analysis of Augustine's perception of the 'I' in Romans.

C Pelagian issues are the contextual factors which lead Augustine to change his interpretation.

Carthage.[20] This dispute seems to have affected his understanding of the passage. In 420 and 421, Augustine provided a number of arguments against the idea that this passage refers to those before grace in his *Contra Duas Epistolas Pelagianorum*.[21]

Calvin noted this text by name, but does not quote the arguments.[22] In 426, Augustine again repudiated his earlier teaching, specifically. In his *Retractationes*, II, i, Augustine wrote concerning this that 'Whereas the apostle says, "The law is spiritual but I am carnal etc.", showing that the flesh wars against the spirit, I have expounded his words as if he were describing the man who is still under the law and not yet under grace. Long afterwards I learned that these words could also describe the spiritual man and in all probability do so'.[23]

In his own examination of the text, it was natural for Calvin to turn to Augustine, because Augustine was Calvin's favorite patristic source.[24]As he turned to Augustine, Calvin had to choose between the young Augustine and the late Augustine. Because the exegetical tradition is divided, Calvin's choice must reflect his theological convictions. Calvin's choice of the late Augustine, however, raises as many exegetical questions as it seems to answer. Steinmetz points out the difficulties which this position seems to create for Calvin. He writes

> On the other hand, Calvin's position is not without its exegetical difficulties. Paul's description of life in the Spirit is difficult to reconcile with Calvin's characterization of the Christian life as an existence marked by inner conflict and repeated failure. If the person described in Romans 7:14 as 'carnal, sold under sin' is a believer, then Calvin must explain how the same person can elsewhere be described as 'set free from sin' (6:18) and 'not in the flesh' (8:9). The exegetical data seems far easier to account for if, as the young Augustine argued, 7:14 refers to life under the law and the contradictory texts to life under grace.[25]

Calvin created an exegetical problem for himself by accepting Augustine's second solution. The unanswered question is why did he choose to do so? To answer this question, we must turn to Chrysostom.

Calvin and Chrysostom

C Chrysostom is the un-named figure lurking in the background in Calvin's consideration of Romans. In this section, we shall see that Calvin claimed Chrysostom's exegesis was undeniably better than that of Augustine. We shall demonstrate that Calvin knew of Chrysostom's homily on this text, which conflicted with the position taken by the mature Augustine. Finally, we shall see that Calvin turned away from Chrysostom for doctrinal concerns, rather than exegetical reasoning.

Augustine was not the only Father who influenced Calvin. Especially in his exegetical writings, Calvin frequently considered the opinions of Ambrose, Origen, and Jerome, among others.[26] But the citations of Chrysostom far outstripped these.[27] In fact, based on the named citations within his Pauline commentaries, we can see that Chrysostom was Calvin's favorite patristic exegete to consider, surpassing even Augustine. With one exception, Calvin never cited Augustine more than

---

C Significance of earlier interpreters as contextual factors.

Chrysostom, and frequently his citations to Chrysostom doubled or even trebled the number of citations to Augustine.[28] In the most remarkable difference, in the commentary on II Corinthians, Calvin only named Augustine five times, while he cited Chrysostom twenty-one times.[29]

But what was that one exception? The commentary on Romans. It cannot be that Calvin did not know of Chrysostom's sermons upon this text. The 1536 Paris edition of Chrysostom's works included these homilies, and Calvin had underlined one of them in his own copy.[30] Further, Calvin accepted Chrysostom as a model for both exegesis and practical application of the scripture to Christian life.[31] Our best evidence for this is Calvin's Latin preface to a proposed French edition of Chrysostom's homilies.[32] The original manuscript exists in Calvin's own handwriting, and forensic and paleographical evidence date it conclusively between 1538 and 1540.[33] This is significant for several reasons. First, this time is at the very beginning of Calvin's commenting upon scripture, by 1540 he would publish only the Romans commentary, and his next commentary, on I Corinthians, would not appear until 1546.[34] Secondly, the preparation of the preface to the planned Chrysostom edition would have been simultaneous with the preparation of the first edition of the commentary on Romans.

A What was the substance of Calvin's preface to Chrysostom? First, Calvin pointed out the reasons for producing aids for the reading and understanding of scripture for ordinary Christians, those who could not read classical languages. He did so by noting that it is important when reading the scripture to know '... what one ought to look for there, to have some sort of goal towards which we may be guided', in order to avoid wandering aimlessly.[35] The Holy Spirit enables the mind of believers to grasp the goal (*scopus*) of scripture, but once believers have received that power, they should also avail themselves of aids to understanding.

> Since, however, the Lord, with the same consideration by which he illuminates us through his Spirit, has, in addition, granted us aids, which he intends to be of assistance in our labour of investigating his truth, there is no reason for us either to neglect them as superfluous, or even to care less about them as if irrelevant. For what Paul said ought to be borne in mind, that though everything belongs to us, we however belong to Christ. Therefore, let those things which the Lord has provided for our use be of service to us.
>
> The point is, if it is right that ordinary Christians not be deprived of the Word of their God, neither should they be denied prospective resources, which may be of use for its true understanding. Besides, [ordinary Christians] do not have the educational attainment. As this in itself is a considerable privilege, so it is not granted to everyone. It is obvious, therefore, that they should be assisted by the work of interpreters, who have advanced in the knowledge of God to a level that they can guide others to as well. ... All I have had in mind with this is to facilitate the reading of Holy Scripture for those who are humble and uneducated.
>
> I am certainly well aware of what objection can be made to me in this business. This is that Chrysostom, whom I am undertaking to make known to the public, aimed his studies at the intelligentsia only. But yet, unless both the

---

A Analysis of the reasons which rendered Chrysostom so significant for Calvin.

> title [of his work] and [its] style of language deceive, this man specialized in sermons which he delivered to a wide public. Accordingly, he plainly adjusts both [his] approach and language as if he had the instruction of common people in mind. This being the case, anyone maintaining that he ought to be kept in seclusion among the academics has got it wrong, seeing that he did go out of his way to cultivate a popular appeal.[36]

Calvin set out the necessity of the laity reading the scriptures, and the concomitant essential of aids to understanding. Calvin himself would later follow this pattern by translating his own commentaries into French. Chrysostom was his choice, in part, because of Chrysostom's ability to accommodate his wisdom and understanding to the abilities of the common people.

Secondly, Calvin defended his choice of Chrysostom. He wrote:

> My reason for selecting Chrysostom as the most preferable needs likewise to be dealt with in passing. From the outset, the reader ought to bear in mind the kind of literary genre it is in which I prefer him to others. Although homilies are something which consist of a variety of elements, the interpretation of Scripture is, however, their priority. In this area, no one of sound judgement would deny that our Chrysostom excels all the ancient writers currently extant. This is especially true when he deals with the New Testament.[37]

Chrysostom was Calvin's ideal. We learn much about Calvin's own ideal of interpretation when we read his understanding of Chrysostom's principal significance. 'The chief merit of our Chrysostom is this: he took great pains everywhere not to deviate in the slightest from the genuine plain meaning of Scripture, and not to indulge in any license of twisting the straightforward sense of the words'.[38]

The comparison between Calvin's opinions of Augustine and Chrysostom is underscored when we compare Calvin's estimation of the two in the Chrysostom preface. Calvin lauded Chrysostom for avoiding any deviation 'from the genuine plain meaning of Scripture'. Directly before that in his text, Calvin considered Augustine. 'It is beyond dispute that Augustine does surpass everyone in dogmatics. He is also a very scrupulous biblical commentator of the first rank. But he is far too ingenious. This results in his being less sound and reliable'.[39] Augustine was without parallel in doctrine. His commenting, though voluminous, was however unsound and unreliable because of his ingenuity.

What of Chrysostom's doctrine? Calvin sought, without much success, to rescue the Greek father from his dependence on human freedom. Calvin wrote of Chrysostom that:

> By being unrestrained in asserting human free will, and in claiming the merits of works, he obscures somewhat the grace of God in our election and calling, and thereby the gratuitous mercy which accompanies us from our calling right up to death. Firstly, he attempts to link election to some consideration of our works. Scripture, though, proclaims everywhere that there is nothing by which God may be moved to elect us except our pathetic condition, and that he does not base his decision to come to our aid on anything except his own goodness. Secondly, to some extent [Chrysostom] divides the credit for our calling between God and ourselves, though scripture consistently ascribes the whole of it to God without qualification.[40]

Calvin attempted to reclaim Chrysostom from his errors about the freedom of the human will and the partial credit for human calling.[41] **AC** Calvin endeavored to do so by contextualizing Chrysostom. In Calvin's re-construction of the historical circumstances of this, he states two reasons the Greek father left the 'Christian teaching'. Both reasons were 'forced' upon Chrysostom. First, Chrysostom modified his own opinion so as not to be too different from public opinion, avoiding an opening for scorn from 'Sophist' slanderers.[42] Secondly, Calvin noted that many members of the church were living dissolute lives, and would take any opportunity presented to shift blame from themselves to another agency.[43] Therefore Chrysostom defended free will almost against his own will![44] Calvin's effort reminds the reader of the preacher whose sermon text bore the marginal note, 'Weak point – pound pulpit!' Calvin was unable to find a textual instance where Chrysostom agreed with the 'Christian teaching' that Calvin knew he must have held. By 1543, in his reply to Pighius, Calvin will not even make the effort to recover Chrysostom from his incorrect doctrine of free will.[45]

Calvin followed Augustine's doctrine. With Richard Muller, it is probably fairer to say that Calvin believed that he was finding in Augustine a particularly fruitful presentation of the Church's doctrine.[46] We can firmly establish that Calvin was thinking about Chrysostom's exegesis of Paul at the very time that he was avoiding the Greek father in his interpretation of Romans. Chrysostom did not slip from Calvin's mind; the evidence points instead to the conclusion that Calvin rejected Chrysostom.

Let us examine the evidence from the beginning of Chrysostom's Homily XIII on Romans 7:14.[47] Chrysostom, considering this passage, wrote:

ROM. VII:14 – 'For we know that the Law is spiritual: but I am carnal, sold under sin'.

> After having said that great evils had taken place, and that sin, taking occasion by the commandment, had grown stronger, and the opposite of what the Law mainly aimed at had been the result, and after having thrown the hearer into a great deal of perplexity, he goes on next to give the rationale of these events, after first clearing the Law of any ill suspicion. For lest – upon hearing that it was through the commandment that sin took that occasion, and that it was when it came that sin revived, and through it deceived and killed – any one should suppose the Law to be the source of these evils, he first sets forth its defence with considerable advantage, not clearing it from accusation only, but encircling it also with the utmost praise. And this he lays down, not as granting it for his own part, but as declaring a universal judgment. 'For we know', he says, 'that the Law is spiritual'. As if he had said, This is an allowed thing, and self-evident, that it 'is spiritual', so far is it from being the cause of sin, or to blame for the evils that have happened. And observe, that he not only clears it of accusation, but bestows exceeding great praise upon it. For by calling it spiritual, he shows it to be a teacher of virtue and hostile to vice; for this is what being spiritual means, leading off from sin of every kind. And this the Law did do, by frightening, admonishing, chastening, correcting, recommending every kind of virtue. Whence then, was sin produced, if the teacher was so admirable? It was from the listlessness of its disciples. Wherefore he went on

AC Analysis of Calvin's contextualizing of Chrysostom.

> to say, 'but I am carnal'; giving us a sketch now of man, as comporting himself in the Law, and before the Law.[48]

Chrysostom concerned himself in the interpretation of this passage with the defense of the law. **H** For him, this was not about anthropology *per se*, nor about the place of the sinner before God. The question which this pericope posed was how Paul would rescue the law from the confusion into which his rhetoric had led. The law was a good teacher and corrector of humans. The fault lay not with the law, but with the disciples, who were listless or sluggish (*segnitie*). Only in the very last phrase did Chrysostom mention anything about the issue which Calvin had quoted Augustine to support. Chrysostom did not take the time to consider the issue of whether the subject is before grace, before the law, or in any other condition. For Chrysostom, the question to answer was the character of the law itself. Finally he stated simply and in passing that Paul had indicated humans in the law, and before the law (*eum qui in lege et ante legem vixerat hominem indicans*).

Let us consider then what Calvin's choice among the fathers did for him. **H** On the positive side, his denial of human activity and merit in the process of salvation was safeguarded. Calvin achieved a proof text to buttress his claims about the conflicted character of the life under faith. However, on the negative side, he relinquished some flexibility in dealing with other passages from Romans, such as 6:16 and 8:9. Further, the whole tenor of the second half of chapter 8 seems incompatible with Calvin's divided believing self. If his theology was simply to be an exposition of scripture, these were serious drawbacks.

Calvin and Scripture, 1537–1540

When we look historically at what Calvin wrote during the time leading up to the publication of the first edition of the Romans commentary, we can discern a cluster of texts gathered around the issue of scriptural interpretation. This suggests that this issue was never far from Calvin's mind in the later period of his first stay in Geneva, and his entire time in Strasbourg.[49] We see this most clearly in the prefaces to the 1539 *Institutes*, to the edition of Chrysostom, and to the Romans commentary.

The 1539 edition of the *Institutes* was a fundamental change from the first edition of 1536. In 1536, the *Institutes* was a handbook for Christians, written with an added apologetic aim.[50] In the preface to the 1539 edition, Calvin makes it clear that he now has directed his work to the preparation of candidates in theology.[51] More importantly, Calvin made it clear at that point that scripture reading required a kind of hermeneutical framework, which he believed he was providing.

> It has been my purpose in this labor to prepare and furnish candidates in sacred theology for the reading of the divine Word, that they might be able both to have easy entrance into it and to advance in it unhindered. For it seems to me that I have provided a summary of religion in all its parts, and have arranged it in such an order so that should anyone rightly grasp it, it will not be difficult for him to establish what he ought particularly to seek in Scripture, and also to what goal he ought to refer its contents.[52]

H Hermeneutical presupposition guiding Chrysostom's interpretation.
H Calvin's choice guides and limits his interpretation of Romans.

Calvin supplied the summary of religion in all its parts which allowed the mysteries of the scriptures to be opened. This summary guided the choice of any interpreter's grasp of the meaning of the scriptures.

We have already considered the preface to Chrysostom at some length. What we must grasp is the number of parallel issues that Calvin also notes in his preface to the 1539 *Institutes*, stated either explicitly or implicitly. Explicitly, this is about scriptural interpretation. It appears to be a different level of interpretation, aimed at the common folk rather than learned candidates in theology. But Calvin's experience and wording gives that appearance the lie; many preachers would have needed any aids to scriptural interpretation and church history they could find, especially those written in vulgar languages.[53]

Implicitly, this work is about how one should handle biblical texts, and the relation of that to doctrine. Calvin set out Chrysostom as the exemplar for handling the scriptural texts. He does not deviate from the plain genuine meaning of scripture, and does not twist the straightforward sense of the words. This should have been enough had this preface really been only about exegesis. **H** But for Calvin, the relationship of exegesis and doctrine could never be denied. That is the reason for the excursus on Chrysostom's failings as a theologian, and Calvin's attempted rescue.

The dedicatory epistle for the Romans commentary that Calvin wrote to Simon Grynaeus also demonstrates Calvin's concern for right biblical interpretation.[54] Calvin recorded his 'interpretive' model, stating,

> I remember that three years ago we had a friendly conversation about the best manner of explaining Scripture. The way that pleased you best was also that which seemed best to me at that time. Both of us realized that the principal virtue of the interpreter was in lucid brevity. Because it is almost his [the interpreter's] only responsibility to make accessible the mind of the writer whom he has undertaken to explicate, he wanders away from that aim, or at least strays outside his goals, by the extent to which he leads his readers away from that meaning. We desired that from the number of those who at this day seek to assist the cause of theology in this task, one could be found who would study not only to be straightforward, but would also at the same time try to avoid detaining his readers with too much wordiness. I know, however, that this opinion is not received by all, and that those who do not accept this nevertheless have their own reasons, I however cannot be moved from a love of abbreviation.[55]

The letter is dated October 18, 1539. Calvin noted that since 1536 he had been considering the correct manner of interpreting scripture. Further, he began his career commenting upon scripture with Romans. This was not a necessary choice, for Calvin could have chosen the gospels as his starting place, following the order of the canon of the New Testament. **H** But his choice of the Pauline literature in general, and of Romans in particular, tells us something about his ideals for understanding the scriptures.[56] For Calvin, Romans solved the mysteries of the meaning of the scriptures. He wrote

---

H Calvin's implicit hermeneutical presupposition.

H Calvin's choice to start his interpretation of scripture with Romans is an indication of his pre-understanding of the letter.

> In considering the value of this Epistle, I doubt whether it would be worthwhile to spend much time on it, because I fear that as my recommendation of it will fall far short of its magnitude, everything I say might do nothing but obscure the Epistle. Further, at its very beginning the Epistle explains itself in a much better way than any words can describe. It will, therefore, be better for me to pass on to the argument itself. This will prove to us beyond any controversy that among many other exceptional virtues it has one in particular which can never be sufficiently appreciated. If someone gains a true understanding of it, that one has an entrance to all the most hidden (*reconditissimos*) treasures of Scripture.[57]

The charge of a 'canon within the canon' is not without merit when we consider Calvin's theology. He believed that Romans and its message of the centrality of justification by faith was the narrow gate by which one came to true understandings of scripture.[58] Scholars have pointed this out as the Pauline character of Calvin's thought, but it might perhaps be seen as the Augustinian-Pauline synthesis.[59]

What these texts demonstrate is that in 1540, Calvin had been considering the proper way to interpret scripture for a number of years. We can look at prefaces attached (or planned to be attached!) to three different genres – a summary of doctrine, a commentary, and an edition of a Greek Father. In each case, Calvin made the same point. Good biblical interpretation must be controlled by correct doctrine. The Preface to the 1539 *Institutes* claimed it to be a summary of doctrine, so that one reading scripture will know how to understand it. **H** The *Argument* to the Romans commentary claimed that the doctrine of the epistle to the Romans was the key to opening the most hidden or profound treasures in all the scriptures. The preface to Chrysostom argues the need for helps for ordinary people to read scripture, and carefully corrects the doctrine of the selected Father where he went astray. Calvin demanded that scripture be read with a proper doctrinal hermeneutic.

Calvin, Hermeneutics, and Exegesis

In examining Calvin's choices in Romans 7, modern analysts are faced with a question. After we sort through the possible options which Calvin received from the prior interpretive tradition, can we straightforwardly state why Calvin took certain positions? The question is too complicated for a simple 'influence' paradigm. Calvin was influenced by Augustine <u>and</u> by Chrysostom. Further, he had to choose between two options produced by Augustine!

Given the nature of the problem, we must use a different tool. In this study, we see the usefulness of a division between principles of hermeneutics and rules or practices of exegesis. This differentiation comes from the work of Karlfried Froehlich. In 1984, Froehlich wrote:

> Patristic hermeneutics (from the Greek *hermeneuein*, to explain, interpret) concerns itself with the developing principles and rules for a proper understanding of the Bible in the early Christian church. The *principles* reflect the theological framework in which the Biblical writings were interpreted by different groups and individuals at various times; they always included the basic

---

H Calvin's perception of Romans as the key to interpreting scripture raises questions: what then guides his perception of Romans?

> conviction that God's revelation in Jesus Christ was central to God's plan of salvation (*oikonomia*) but they left room for different readings of major themes, such as Israel and the church, eschatology, ethics, even, anthropology, and soteriology. The *rules* reflect the methodology by which the language of Biblical revelation was scrutinized so that it would yield insight into God's *oikonomia* and its ramifications for the life of the community; they were often taken over from the literary culture of the surrounding world but were then developed into new, creative paradigms of literary analysis.[60]

In this division between hermeneutic principles and exegetical rules, principles are the deeper term. These are the foundational ideas which an interpreter brings to interpretation; these are so basic to the interpreter that they form the lenses which clarify the text. Thus, they judge the text, rather than normally being judged by the text.[61] As well, hermeneutic principles tend to act subconsciously in the interpreter, being part of the worldview or 'structure of reality' for that person.

Exegetical practices are about the method of extricating meaning from a text. These are chosen by the interpreter. Frequently the history of interpretation has only dealt with exegetical practices. Terms such as allegory, *sensus germanus,* literal sense, historical-critical, typology, ἀναγωγή, and philological normally belong to this division. These are tools, the choice of which is almost as culturally conditioned as the choice of clothing.[62] Biblical interpreters chose various rules or practices so as to be understood and appealing to various audiences, and because they found those practices most useful.[63]

Finally, theologians in general, and Calvin in particular, allow hermeneutic principles to overwhelm exegetical rules in cases of disagreement. **A** Calvin noted that Augustine was the truest teacher of doctrine but from the very first verse of the Romans commentary chided his biblical interpretation by deriding his love of philosophical argumentation.[64] This is what we would expect, given what Calvin wrote about Augustine in the Chrysostom preface. We have already discussed that Calvin held out Chrysostom as the best exegete among the fathers. But at a key point in commenting upon Romans, Calvin turns away from the interpretation of Chrysostom, toward that of Augustine. In the 1540 edition, he does so without noting either father by name.[65] Calvin did so at the very point of difference between his theological hermeneutic and Chrysostom's own doctrinal failing. For Calvin, these stirrings of conscience cannot be infecting the will of the human who has not received the grace of regeneration, because that would suggest that pre-grace humans have the will to do something that Calvin claims they cannot do – turn to God.

If we accept this model of differentiating between hermeneutics and exegesis, we can begin to examine the problem before us by application of this division. Calvin 'knew' that the bondage of the will in matters of salvation was part and parcel of the Christian religion.[66] The doctrine of the bondage of the choice of the will was not only correct and factual, but to the advantage of the believer.[67] This acted as a hermeneutical principle. For Calvin, this was not a choice which he was making from a range of acceptable options. It was simple Christianity, right teaching would have to defend it, and that which did not could not be correct.

This model also helps to explain the expansion of the text at this point. It is likely that Calvin knew both the Augustine text against the Pelagians and the Chrysostom

---

A Author's analysis of hermeneutical principles which guided Calvin.

sermons prior to the publication of the first edition of the Romans commentary.[68] Though Calvin frequently expanded his works when he edited them (!), the addition of Augustine's name in the later editions can be taken as a grasping of authority. In adding the material from Augustine, Calvin in no way changed his earlier substance.[69] He did, however, add the weight of a significant doctrinal authority to his own position.

H Finally, Calvin believed that the correct teaching of religion took priority, in some manner, over the correct interpretation of scripture. In the dedicatory epistle to Grynaeus, he had finished with a brief acknowledgement of the difficulty of finding complete agreement in biblical interpretation, while noting that less room for discrepancy is given to the teaching of religion. He wrote:

> We have always observed, however, even among those who have not lacked in their zeal for piety, or in sobriety in handling the things of God, even among them there has not been consensus [concerning the interpretation of scripture]. God has never so dignified his servants with the blessing that each possessed a full and perfect understanding of every part of their subject. Without a doubt, his plan was first that we would be kept humble, and also that we should continue to have communication with our brothers. Therefore that which we most hope for in the present life, even though it were otherwise highly hoped for, we are not to seek in the present life for perpetual consensus among us on the exposition of passages of scripture. When, therefore, we depart from the views of our predecessors, we are not to be stimulated by any lust for innovation, not to be impelled by any desire to slander others, not to be aroused by any hatred, and not to be prompted by any ambition. Only necessity should force us, and we are to have no other object than that of doing good. We are to try to do the same also in expounding Scripture, but in the teachings of religion, in which God has particularly desired that the minds of his people should be in agreement, we are to take less liberty. I have studied both of these, as my readers will easily grasp.[70]

For Calvin, the teaching of religion and scriptural interpretation were indissolubly linked. But less liberty was allowed in religion! Calvin believed that scriptural interpretation must find its true goal (*scopus*) in Christ, and that only doctrines which edified the Church were true. **C** In Calvin's mind, his own time most closely approximated that of Augustine. Both were faced with the same doctrinal problem. Their opponents depended too much upon human merit and human freedom. Calvin followed Augustine's doctrinal authority, not because it necessarily made the most exegetical sense to him, but because the teaching of religion required it. In fact, Calvin consistently advanced the exegetical rule of following the simple or straightforward (*germanus*) meaning throughout his Pauline commentaries.[71]

Why did Calvin accept the solution of the older Augustine? **A** Because he recognized Augustine, somewhat uncritically, as the chief representative of orthodox doctrine. In examining the theological challenges of his own day, Calvin drew strong links between his own time and Augustine's struggle with the Pelagian heresy. The issue of the will was central to this question, and Calvin's own definition of the

---

H Calvin's hermeneutical principle: doctrine overrules correct biblical interpretation.
C Factors perceived as contextual determine Calvin's choice.
A Analysis of reasons for and difficulties resulting from hermeneutical choice.

Christian religion denied the possibility of tolerance on this point. To take this position, Calvin had to turn his back on the simple plain-sense exegesis of Chrysostom, the Father whom he identified as the best patristic exegete. Augustine's early interpretation of Romans 7:14–15 was too close to that of Chrysostom. In doing so, Calvin accepted the difficulties of making coherent sense of Paul's teaching in chapter 7 against the background of Romans 6 and Romans 8.[72]

Conclusion

To understand a theologian's conception of particular biblical passages or teachings is always devilishly difficult. It has not been my purpose in this study to argue that hermeneutics must be given pride of place and displace historical-exegetical work from the set of tools that analysts bring to the task of understanding. Indeed, many of the issues which I sought to consider are impossible to conceive without the insights which can only come from historical-exegetical work. My point in this study is to illustrate the complexity of the analytical task in considering theological interpretations of scripture, and to urge the use of an added investigative instrument to complement others.

Let us recount then what we have gathered. At the time of the publication of his first commentary on scripture, Calvin had been intensely considering the relationship of doctrine and exegesis for years. By this time, he had already determined his guiding lights for both efforts. Augustine was the teacher of religion, Chrysostom the guide to exegesis. Calvin almost certainly knew of Chrysostom's interpretation of Romans 7, but eschewed it in favor of the position which is represented in Augustine's later explanation. He did not cite Augustine at the time of the first edition, but did add the allusion to him in later editions of the Romans commentary.[73] Further, he added Augustine's material and influence at the very point at which his own theology differed most greatly with that of his favorite New Testament exegete – Chrysostom. The evidence collected suggests strongly that this is a test case for Calvin's hermeneutical principles overwhelming his exegetical sensibility. Calvin could not follow the early Augustine, for that position allows too great an opportunity for the mischief concerning the freedom of the wili to creep into the minds of believers. In the final analysis for Calvin, correct religion must take pride of place over the freedom of the exegete.

Texts Used:

Iohannis Calvini Commentarius in Epistolam Pauli ad Romanos, ed. T. H. L. Parker (Leiden: E. J. Brill, 1981).

Ioannis Calvini Opera Exegetica, Commentarii in Pauli Epistolas ad Galatas, ad Ephesios, ad Philippenses, ad Colossenses, ed. Helmut Feld (Geneva: Droz, 1992).

Ioannis Calvini Opera Exegetica, Commentarii in Secundum Pauli Epistolam ad Corinthios, ed. Helmut Feld (Geneva: Droz, 1994).

Ioannis Calvini Opera Exegetica, Commentarius in Epistolam ad Hebraeos, ed. T. H. L. Parker (Geneva: Droz, 1996).

Calvin's New Testament Commentaries. 12 volumes, eds. David W. Torrance and Thomas F. Torrance (Grand Rapids: Eerdmans, 1960. vv. 8–12).

Notes

[1] Comm. Romans 7.15, *Iohannis Calvini Commentarius in Epistolam Pauli ad Romanos*, T. H. L. Parker, ed., (Leiden: E. J. Brill, 1981), 149.31–37. 'Atqui Paulus, ut iam dixi, non hic proponit nudam hominis naturam: verum qualis et quanta sit fidelium infirmitas, sub persona sua describit. In communi errore aliquandiu versatus est Augustinus: verum loco propius excusso, non tantum retractavit quod male docuerat, sed libro ad Bonifacium primo, multis validis rationibus contendit, non aliter quam de renatis posse exponi'. All translations, unless otherwise noted, are my own. 'And Paul, as I have already said, does not at this point propose the simple natural man, but in his own person describes the infirmities of the faithful, and how great they are. Augustine was involved in the common error for a while; but after more clearly examining the passage, he not only retracted what he had badly taught, but in his first book to Boniface, he asserts, by many valid reasons, that it cannot possibly be understood as referring to anyone but the regenerate'.

[2] Actually, Calvin did not include this material until later editions of the commentary. Parker's text makes clear that this material was not in the 1540 edition. However, though it only achieved this form in 1556, the stance is unchanged, as other passages which are in the 1540 text give the same point. *Ad Romanos*, 149.31–37.

[3] David Steinmetz, 'Calvin and the Divided Self of Romans 7', In *Calvin in Context* (Oxford: Oxford University Press, 1995), pp. 110–121.

[4] Steinmetz, p. 117. 'What this brief history of the exegesis of Rom. 7:14–25 in the sixteenth century makes clear is that the division between exegetical schools does not correspond in any way to the division between the competing confessional families'.

[5] Steinmetz examines the interpretations of fifteen sixteenth century exegetes, finding three who preferred the earlier option. These were Bernardino Ochino, Fausto Sozzini, and Jacopo Sadoleto. Steinmetz, pp. 111–112.

[6] Although Joseph Fitzmyer only deals with this question in passing, perhaps signifying that it is a settled question (476), C. E. B. Cranfield took the opposite approach with considerable effort (p. 356ff.). Fitzmyer is supported by Achtemeier and Käsemann. Joseph Fitzmyer, S. J., *Romans: A New Translation with Introduction and Commentary* (New York: Doubleday, 1993); C. E. B. Cranfield, *A Critical and Exegetical Commentary on the Epistle to the Romans* (Edinburgh: T. & T. Clark, 1975); Ernst Käsemann, *Commentary on Romans*, trans. Geoffrey Bromiley (Grand Rapids: Eerdmans, 1980); Paul J. Achtemeier, *Romans* (Louisville: John Knox Press, 1985).

[7] Steinmetz, p. 118.

[8] Comm. Romans 7.14, Ad Romanos 146.39–41. 'Nunc propius committere inter se Legem et hominis naturam incipit, ut clarius intelligatur unde mortis vitium emergat'. 'He now begins to compare the Law with human nature, in order more clearly to understand whence the corruption leading to death comes'.

[9] Comm. Romans 7.14, Ad Romanos 146.45–46. 'Quae igitur convenientia naturae hominis cum Lege? nempe quae luci cum tenebris'.

[10] Comm. Romans 7.14, Ad Romanos 146.41-43. 'Deinde exemplum proponit hominis regenerati: in quo sic carnis reliquiae cum Lege Domini dissident, ut spiritus ei libenter obtemperet'.

[11] Comm. Romans 7.15, Ad Romanos 146.77–80.

[12] Comm. Romans 7.15, Ad Romanos 146.81–87. 'Siquidem quum homo carnalis tota animi propensione in libidinem peccandi ruat: videtur ita libera electione peccare, ut sit in potestate eius moderari sibi: ut haec opinio perniciosissima apud omnes fere invaluit, hominem naturali facultate posse utrumlibet eligere, citra Divinae gratiae auxilium. at vero dum voluntas fidelis hominis Spiritu Dei ad bonus agitur, illic perspicue patet naturae pravitas quae obstinate resistit, et nititur in adversum'.

[13] Steinmetz, p. 116.

[14] Comm. Romans 7.15, Ad Romanos 148.10–12. 'Illi enim conscientiae aculei, quibus punguntur, potius ex iudicii contradictione nascuntur, quam ex contrario voluntatis affectu'.

[15] Paula Fredriksen Landes, *Augustine on Romans: Propositions from the Epistle to the Romans, Unfinished Commentary on the Epistle to the Romans* (Chico: Scholars Press, 1982), p. ix.

[16] Landes, 16. 'Quod autem ait: Non enim quod volo, hoc ago, sed quod odi, illud facio. Si autem quod nolo, hoc facio, consentio legi, quoniam bona est, satis quidem lex ab omni criminatione defenditur, sed cavendum, ne quis arbitretur his verbis auferri nobis liberum voluntatis arbitrium, quod non ita est. (2) Nunc enim homo describitur sub lege positus ante gratiam. Tunc enim peccatis vincitur, dum viribus suis iuste vivere conatur sine adiutorio liberantis gratiae dei. (3) In libero autem arbitrio habet, ut credat liberatori et accipiat gratiam, ut iam illo, qui eam donat, liberante et adiuvante non peccet atque ita desinat esse sub lege, sed cum lege vel in lege implens eam caritate dei, quod timore non poterat'.

[17] Landes, p. 16. 'Quod autem ait: Scimus quia lex spiritualis est, ego autem carnalis sum, satis ostendit non posse impleri legem nisi a spiritualibus, quales facit gratia dei. (2) Similis enim quisque factus ipsi legi facile implet, quod praecipit, nec erit sub illa sed cum illa; is est autem, qui iam non capitur temporalibus bonis nec terretur temporalibus malis'.

[18] Peter Brown notes it in 396, in his Chronological Table C. *Augustine of Hippo: A New Edition with an Epilogue* (Berkeley: University of California Press, 2000), p. 178. This fits with John S. Burleigh's reconstruction in *Augustine: Earlier Writings* (Philadelphia: Westerminster Press, 1953), p. 372.

[19] Augustine, *To Simplician – On Various Questions*, In *Augustine: Later Writings*, edited by J. H. S. Burleigh (Philadelphia: Westminster Press, 1958), pp. 377–378. Augustine, *Ad Simplicianum de Diversis Quaestionibus* I.i.4. 'Sed mortuum fuerat, id est occultatum, cum mortales nati sine mandato legis homines uiuerent sequentes concupiscentias carnis sine ulla cognitione, quia sine ulla prohibitione. Ergo EGO, inquit, VIVEBAM ALIQVANDO SINE LEGE, unde manifestat non ex persona sua proprie, sed generaliter ex persona hominis se loqui'. *Corpus Christianorum* XLIV (Turnholt: Brepols, 1970), 10.

[20] Brown, p. 344.

[21] Migne, 44.549–638, esp. 560–562. Peter Brown notes that this was composed in 420–421, Chronological Table D, 282–283. Calvin certainly knew this text by 1543, when he quoted it against Pighius. Lane traces his knowledge of it to Erasmus' edition of Augustine, the text appeared in the seventh volume. By the 1559 *Institutes*, he was using it frequently, quoting the work twenty-two times, across eighteen distinct sections of the *Institutes*. See A. N. S. Lane, 'Calvin's Use of the Fathers and Medievals', and 'Calvin and the Fathers in his *Bondage and Liberation of the Will*', In *John Calvin: Student of the Church Fathers* (Edinburgh: T. & T. Clark, 1999), pp. 55, 176.

[22] *Ad Romanos*, 149.135–136.

[23] Burleigh, 370. Augustine, *Retractationes* II.1 'In qua illa apostoli uerba: Lex spiritalis est, ego autem carnalis sum et cetera, quibus caro contra spiritum confligere ostenditur, eo modo exposui, tamquam homo describatur adhuc sub lege nondum sub gratia constitutus. Longe enim postea etiam spiritalis hominis – et hoc probabilius – esse posse illa uerba cognoui'. *Corpus Christianorum* LVII (Turnholt: Brepols, 1984), 89. Brown dates this to 426–427, Chronological Table E, 380–381.

[24] See Johannes van Oort, 'John Calvin and the Church Fathers', In *The Reception of the Church Fathers in the West: From the Carolingians to the Maurists*, 2 vol., ed. Irena Backus (Leiden: Brill, 1997), v. 2, esp. pp. 689–690.

[25] Steinmetz, p. 111.

[26] Frequently, Calvin's citations of Ambrose are actually of Ambrosiaster.

[27] Irena Backus commented that Calvin used Chrysostom as a source for discipline and the use of scripture. 'Chrysostom was to Calvin a source of extremely useful information about the discipline of the Early Church, and as such could be adopted wholesale. Moreover, Chrysostom's way of using the Bible held great attraction for the Genevan Reformer. ... the Genevan Reformer's use of Chrysostom is remarkably coherent and, in contrast to his use of many other Church Fathers, not primarily oriented by the demands of inter-confessional polemics'. Backus, 'Calvin and the Greek Fathers', In *Continuity and Change: The Harvest of Late-Medieval and Reformation History: Essays Presented to Heiko A. Oberman on his 70th Birthday* (Leiden: Brill, 2000), p. 263. Further, A. N. S. Lane has noted that in the totality of his works, Calvin cited Chrysostom more than any other father, with the two exceptions of Augustine and Jerome. Lane, 'Calvin's Knowledge of the Greek Fathers', In *John Calvin: Student of the Church Fathers* (Edinburgh: T. & T. Clark, 1999), p. 72. Richard Gamble observed that Augustine could not be Calvin's model for exegesis, and that Chrysostom probably provides a source for Calvin's exegetical method. Gamble, '*Brevitas et Facilitas*: Toward an Understanding of Calvin's Hermeneutic', *Westminster Theological Journal*, 47 (1985), 8–9.

[28] Based on the indices supplied by Feld and the CNTC.

[29] See Appendix.

[30] Alexandre Ganoczy and Klaus Müller, *Calvins Handschriftliche Annotationen zu Chrysostomus: Ein Beitrag zur Hermeneutik Calvins* (Wiesbaden: Franz Steiner Verlag GMBH, 1981), p. 111.

[31] Ganoczy and Müller, 19–20. 'Mit dieser Beobachtung stossen wir auf ein eigenartiges Phänomen der Chrysostomusrezeption durch den französischen Reformator. Denn das anhand seiner eigenen Bearbeitung festgestellte paränetische Interesse scheint im Widerspruch zu stehen zu der von ihm ausdrücklich formulierten exegetischen Intention, mit der er dem Kirchenvater begegnet'.

[32] Two English translations exist. John H. McIndoe provided 'John Calvin: Preface to the Homilies of Chrysostom', *Hartford Quarterly*, 5, 2, (1965), 19–26. This version supplies little in the way of commentary or critical apparatus. The preferred translation is that of Ian P. Hazlett, 'Calvin's Latin Preface to his Proposed French Edition of Chrysostom's Homilies: Translation and Commentary', *Humanism and Reform: The Church in Europe, England and Scotland, 1400–1643: Essays in Honour of James K. Cameron*, edited by James Kirk (Oxford: Blackwell, 1991), pp. 129–150. I will offer the Hazlett translation because he had access to manuscripts which supplement the version available in the *Calvini Opera*.

[33] Hazlett, 133. Irena Backus notes Hazlett, and adds that '...given Calvin's insistence in the preface on the organisation of the Early Church as model for the Church of his own day, it is not unlikely that it was written in Strasbourg under the influence of Bucer'. 'Calvin and the Greek Fathers', p. 254.

[34] T. H. L. Parker, *Calvin's New Testament Commentaries*. 2nd ed. (Louisville: Westminster John Knox Press, 1993), pp. 17–19. See also Rodolphe Peter, *Bibliotheca Calviniana: Les Oevres de Jean Calvin publiées au xvi*[e] *siècle* (Geneva: Librairie Droz, 1991), Vol. I, 214–216.

[35] Hazlett, 141. Ioannis Calvini, *Opera Quae Supersunt Omnia*. 59 volumes, edited by Wilhelm Baum, Edward Cunitz, & Edward Reuss (Brunswick: Schwetschke and Sons, 1895). Hereafter CO. CO 9.832. '…scire quid illic quaerere oporteat, scopumque aliquem habere ad quem dirigamur'. This concern mirrors those which Calvin notes in his prefaces to the *Institutes*. See especially his 'John Calvin to the Reader', appended to the 1539 edition of the *Institutes*. Joannis Calvini, *Opera Selecta*, 5 volumes, 3rd ed., edited by Peter Barth and Wilhelm Niesel (Munich: Christian Kaiser, 1967). Vol. 3.6.18–31.

[36] Hazlett, 141–142. CO 9.832-833. 'Quum tamen Dominus eadem, qua nos per spiritum suum illuminat, benignitate adminicula quoque nobis contulerit, quibus voluit studium nostrum in veritatis suae investigatione adiuvari, non est cur ea vel negligamus quasi supervacua, vel etiam quasi non adeo necessaria minus curemus. Obversari enim animis nostris debet quod ait Paulus, omnia nostra esse, nos autem Christi. Serviant ergo nobis quae in usum nostrum Dominus destinavit.

Iam vero, si aequum est plebem christianam non spoliari Dei sui verbo, neque deneganda sunt ei instrumenta quae ad veram eius intelligentiam usui sint futura. Artes porro et disciplinas non habet: quae ut sunt alioqui non minima subsidia, ita non omnibus conceduntur. Superest ergo ut interpretum opera adiuvetur, qui sic in Dei cognitione profecerunt, ut alios quoque manuducere ad eam possint. … quo nihil aliud mihi propositum fuit quam ad scripturae sacrae lectionem rudibus ac illiteratis viam sternere.

Equidem non me fugit quid hic obiectari mihi queat: Chrysostomum, quem vulgo hominum publicare instituo, doctis tantum et literarum peritis lucubrationes suas destinasse. At vero, nisi et titulus et orationis compositio mentitur, quos ad universum populum sermones habuit hic complexus est. Ita certe et rerum tractationem et dictionem attemperat, quasi hominum multitudinem instituere velit. Proinde frustra quis contendat, eum inter doctos reconditum esse oportere, quum data opera studuerit esse popularis'.

[37] Hazlett, 144. CO 9.834. 'Cur autem Chrysostomum ex omnibus potissimum delegerim, eius quoque rei obiter ostendenda ratio est. Ac primum quidem meminisse lectorem oportet, quale sit scripti genus in quo ipsum aliis praetulerim. Sunt autem homiliae, quae quum variis partibus constent, primum tamen in illis locum tenet scripturae interpretatio, in qua Chrysostomum nostrum vetustos omnes scriptores qui hodie exstant antecedere nemo sani iudicii negaverit. Praesertim ubi novum testamentum tractat'.

[38] Hazlett, 145–146. CO 9.835. 'Chrysostomi autem nostri haec prima laus est quod ubique illi summo studio fuit a germana scripturae sinceritate ne minimum quidem deflectere, ac nullam sibi licentiam sumere in simplici verborum sense contorquendo'.

[39] Hazlett, 145. CO 9.835. 'Augustinus citra controversiam in fidei dogmatibus omnes superat. Religiosus quoque imprimis scripturae interpres, sed ultra modum argutus. Quo fit ut minus firmus sit ac solidus'.

[40] Hazlett, 146–147. CO 9.835. 'In praedicando hominis libero arbitrio, in meritis operum efferendis immodicus, gratiam Dei in electione ac vocatione nostra, gratuitam deinde misericordiam, qua nos a vocatione ad mortem usque prosequitur, sic nonnihil obscurat. Primum electionem cum aliquo operum nostrorum respectu implicare nititur: quum scriptura passim reclamet nihil esse quo ad nos eligendos provocetur Deus nisi extremam miseriam, nec aliunde ipsum sumere quo nobis opem ferat, quam a sua ipsius bonitate. Deinde laudem vocationis nostrae inter Deum et nos quodammodo partitur, quum scriptura constanter solidum eius complementum Deo assignet'.

[41] Hazlett's note at this point is helpful. In note 50, he writes 'Calvin can do no other than to distance himself from Chrysostom's views on grace, works, merit, election, justification, etc.

Standing firmly within the Reformation version of the radical Pauline and Augustinian revival, he could have little sympathy with a theology which, in fact, represents the entire Greek patristic tradition. The latter proceeded on the basis of the semi-Pelagian notion of a mutual approximation between God and humanity, whereas the former posited a chasm and polarity between God and humanity, which can only be bridged by divine initiative and operation'. 146–147.

[42] Hazlett, 147–149. CO 9.836.

[43] Hazlett, 149. CO 9.836. Calvin's reconstruction sounds as if he has the Empress Eudoxia in mind, a person who frequently took Chrysostom's moral teachings as a personal affront. If that is the case, he is placing the Romans homilies and their semi-Pelagian stance too late in Chrysostom's career. See J. N. D. Kelly, *Golden Mouth: The Story of John Chrysostom – Ascetic, Preacher, Bishop* (Grand Rapids: Baker, 1995), pp. 90–91.

[44] Hazlett,149. CO 9.836.

[45] John Calvin, *The Bondage and Liberation of the Will*, edited by A. N. S. Lane, translated by G. I. Davies (Grand Rapids: Baker, 1996), 79ff. CO 9.287–288.

[46] 'What Calvin intended to teach was the church's doctrine, not his own doctrine. To the extent that he was successful, his originality must be sought more in his manner of presenting Christian doctrine, in the way he received, incorporated, or modified forms and arguments of patristic and medieval theology, in his particular fusion of older theological substance either with his own exegetical results or with Renaissance rhetorical forms, and in the nuances that he gave to the elements of extant tradition'. Richard A. Muller, *The Unaccommodated Calvin: Studies in the Foundation of a Theological Tradition* (Oxford: Oxford University Press, 2000), p. 7.

[47] David Steinmetz has also considered this in his 'Calvin and the Patristic Exegesis of Paul', *The Bible in the 16th Century*, David Steinmetz, ed., (Durham: Duke University Press, 1990), pp. 100–118.

[48] Philip Schaff, NPNF vol. 11, Chrysostom, Hom. XIII. Migne, Patrologia Graeca, v. 60, 507. Homilia XIII. '*Cap. 7. v. 14. Scimus autem, quia lex spiritualis est: ego autem carnalis sum, venumdatus sub peccato.* 1. Postquam dixerat magna fuisse mala, et peccatum admissum potentius fuisse lege, et contra quam lex satagebat accidisse, et cum in magnam dubitationem auditorem conjecisset; rationem postea dicit, per quam haec advenere, cum prius legem a prava suspicione vindicasset. Etenim ne quis audiens, peccatum occasionem per mandatum accepisse, et quod eodem mandato accedente peccatum revixit, et quod per illud decepit atque interfecit; ne quis, inquam, legem horum malorum causam putaret esse, primo illius defensionem affert uberrimam; non modo illam ab accusatione liberans, sed laudem ipsi maximam texens. Hocque adhibet non quasi ipse in ejus gratiam loquatur, sed quasi communem omnium sententiam exponens. *Scimus enim*, inquit, *quod lex spritualis sit*. Ac si diceret, hoc in confesso et manifestum est, quod sit spiritualis: tantum abest, ut sit causa peccati, et malis quae advenerunt obnoxia. Et vide quo pacto non modo illam abaccusatione liberet, sed etiam supra modum laudet. Nam cum spiritualem illam dicit, magistram virtutis ostendit esse, et nequitiae adversariam: hoc est enim esse spiritualem, et ab omni peccato abducere; quod lex faciebat, terrens, admonens, puniens, corrigens, quae ad justitiam pertinent omnia consulens. Unde ergo, inquit, peccatum exstitit, si tam admirabilis sit praeceptor? A discipulorum segnitie. Quapropter haec subjunxit: *Ego autem carnalis sum*, eum qui in lege et ante legem vixerat hominem indicans'.

[49] Calvin was exiled from Geneva in April of 1538. He returned in September of 1541. In the interim, he ministered in Strasbourg, being surrounded by learned colleagues, and mentored by Martin Bucer. Cornelis Augustijn has written on this period in his 'Calvin in Strasbourg', In *Calvinus Sacrae Scripturae Professor: Calvin as Confessor of Holy Scripture*, ed.

Wilhelm Neuser (Grand Rapids: Eerdmans, 1994), pp. 166–177. Augustijn provides a helpful summary of the literature on this period, and notes four aspects of Calvin's stay in Strasbourg which he sees as insufficiently researched. He does not list Calvin's maturing sense of the interpretation of scripture and its relationship to doctrine.

[50] François Wendel noted this in his summary of the changing purposes of the *Institutes* as it matured. See his *Calvin: Origins and Development of His Religious Thought*, originally 1950, translated by Philip Mairet (Durham, NC: Labyrinth Press, 1987), pp. 145–146.

[51] Wendel, 146.

[52] Joannis Calvini, *Opera Selecta*, in 5 volumes, 3rd ed., edited by Peter Barth and Wilhelm Niesel (Munich: Christian Kaiser, 1967). Vol. 3.6.18–31. 'Porro hoc mihi in isto labore propositum fuit, sacrae Theologiae candidatos ad divini verbi lectionem ita praeparare et instruere, ut et facilem ad eam aditum habere, et inoffenso in ea gradu pergere queant; siquidem religionis summam omnibus partibus sic mihi complexus esse videor, et eo quoque ordine digessisse, ut siquis eam recte tenuerit, ei non sit difficile statuere et quid potissimum quaerere in Scriptura, et quem in scopum quicquid in ea continetur referre debeat'.

[53] Calvin attempted to spare the feelings of ministers who lacked facility in languages. 'In addition to this point, there is a further consideration: among us it does not always happen that those charged with the ministry of the churches are sufficiently versed in Greek and Latin as to be able to understand the ancient writers in the original. Yet I think it is widely recognized how important it is that a pastor of the Church knows what the nature of the ancient form of the Church was, and that he is equipped with at least some knowledge of Antiquity. And so in this respect, too, this work of mine could be fruitful, as everyone may admit; for no one denies that it is proper for all those responsible for Christian education to be familiar with this kind of writing. Yet there will maybe be some people around who will only manage with the help of a translation'. Hazlett, 143. CO 9.833. 'Huc etiam accedit quod non semper ita bene nobiscum agitur, ut qui ecclesiarum administrationi praesunt ita sint in graeca latinaque lingua exercitati ut veteres illos scriptores sua lingua loquentes audire queant. Quantopere autem referat, ecclesiasticum pastorem tenere qualis fuerit vetusta ecclesiae facies, et aliqua saltem antiquitatis notitia esse praeditum, palam esse existimo. Itaque hac quoque parte fructuosus esse poterit meus iste labor, vel omnium confessione, quia nemo negat utile esse versari in hoc scripti genere omnes eos qui docendi provinciam in christiano populo sustinent. Reperientur autem forte nonnulli qui hoc non consequentur nisi interpretationis beneficio'.

[54] An interesting point is that in March of 1538, Grynaeus had written a critical letter to Calvin, chastising him for arrogance about intellectual superiority. See Cornelis Augustijn, 175–176.

[55] Comm. Romans, Dedicatory epistle. *Ad Romanos*, 1. 'Memini, quum ante triennium de optimo enarrandae Scripturae genere inter nos familiariter commentaremur, eam quae plurimum tibi placebat, rationem mihi quoque prae aliis probatam tunc fuisse. Sentiebat enim uterque nostrum, praecipuam interpretis virtutem in perspicua brevitate esse positam. Et sane quum hoc sit prope unicum illius officium, mentem scriptoris, quem explicandum sumpsit, patefacere: quantum ab ea lectores abducit, tantundem a scopo suo aberrat, vel certe a suis finibus quodammodo evagatur. Itaque cupiebamus ex eorum numero, quibus in hoc laboris genere theologiam iuvare hodie propositum est, unum aliquem extare qui et facilitati studeret, et simul daret operam ne prolixis commentariis studiosos ultramodum detineret. Quanquam autem scio sententiam hanc non apud omnes receptam esse: et eos qui non recipiunt, nonnullis quoque argumentis adduci ut ita iudicent: ego tamen dimoveri non possum ab amore compendii'.

[56] T. H. L. Parker has suggested that this choice was a '…deliberate theological policy which Calvin believed was demanded by the New Testament itself'. *Calvin's New Testament Commentaries*, 2nd ed. (Edinburgh: T. & T. Clark, 1993), p. 31.

[57] Comm. Romans, *Iohannis Calvini Commentarius in Epistolam Pauli ad Romanos*, edited by T. H. L. Parker (Leiden: E.J. Brill, 1981), *Argumentum in Epistolam Ad Romanos*, 5.1–11. 'In praedicanda Epistolae huius utilitate, nescio an operae pretium sit diutius immorari, tum quod vereor ne meis elogiis haud dubie infra eius magnitudinem longe subsidentibus, nihil quam obscuretur: tum etiam quod multo magis ipsa primo statim se proferat, et vera specie melius se explicet, quam ullis verbis enarrari queat. Ergo iam ad argumentum ipsum transire satius fuerit: unde citra controversiam protinus constabit, praeter plurimus alias, et eas eximias dotes, hanc ei proprie competere, quae nunquam pro dignitate satis aestimetur: quod siquis veram eius intelligentiam sit assequutus, ad reconditissimos quosque Scripturae thesauros adeundos habeat apertas fores'.

[58] Comm. Romans, *Ad Romanos*, Argumentum, 5.18–19. 'Atque ita ingreditur principalem totius epistolae quaestionem, Fide nos justificari'.

[59] See for instance Alexandre Ganoczy's 'Forschungsansatze zur Hermeneutik Calvins: Calvin als paulinischer Theologe'. Lecture given at the Europaischer Kongress für Calvinforschung, Amsterdam, Sept. 16–19, 1974; or Barbara Pitkin's *What Pure Eyes Could See: Calvin's Doctrine of Faith in Its Exegetical Context* (Oxford: Oxford University Press, 1999), esp. pp. 82–83.

[60] *Biblical Interpretation in the Early Church*, translated and edited by Karlfried Froehlich (Philadelphia: Fortress Press, 1984), p. 1.

[61] It would be incorrect to say that the biblical text can never change an interpreter's hermeneutic. However, when it does in a significant manner, the event will have seismic consequences for the interpreter. Perhaps the best case in point is Luther's transformation through a herneneutical discovery in Romans 1:16.

[62] I have covered this at greater length in my book, *John Calvin and the Grounding of Interpretation: Calvin's First Commentaries* (Leiden: Brill, 2006).

[63] One normally does not think about interpreters "choosing" their rules of exegesis. But see M. L. Monheit's 'Young Calvin, Textual Interpretation and Roman Law', *Bibliothèque d'Humanisme et Renaissance: Travaux et Documents*. 59, No. 2, (1997), 263–82; Monheit demonstrates various models of interpretation taught to Calvin, and his subsequent use of them.

[64] Comm. Romans 1.1, *Ad Romanos*, 11.22–23. 'Quod Augustino placuisse hoc tantum nomine puto, ut argute philosophandi occasionem arriperet'. This follows the version of 1540, not the later additions.

[65] *Ad Romanos*, 149.30–38.

[66] Even when Calvin attempted to defend Chrysostom's defense of free will by historically contextualizing him, Calvin's own incredulity about the Greek father's choices crept into his text. He wrote, 'Yet it is hard to believe that [Chrysostom] was so naïve about Christian teaching as not to be aware either of the afflicted condition of humanity or of the grace of God, which is the sole remedy for its distress'. Hazlett, 147. CO 9.835–836. 'Neque tamen christianae doctrinae sic fuisse imperitum ac rudem credibile est, ut vel miseram hominis conditionem, vel Dei gratiam, quae unicum est eius miseriae remedium, ignoraret'.

[67] See *Institutes* II.ii.1, almost all of which came from the 1539 *Institutes*. *Opera Selecta,* in 5 vol., 3rd ed., Peter Barth and Wilhelm Niesel, ed. (Munich: Christian Kaiser, 1967), OS 3.241–242.

[68] The Chrysostom evidence is given above. The McNeill-Battles edition of the *Institutes* gives a citation to Augustine that Calvin does not name as being to this text, and coming from the

1539 edition. See *Institutes of the Christian Religion*, in 2 vols, translated by Ford Lewis Battles, edited by John T. McNeill (Philadelphia: Westminster Press, 1960), II.ii.8, n. 44.

69 I agree here with T.H.L. Parker's analysis, *Calvin's New Testament Commentaries,* 2nd ed. (Louisville: Westminster/John Knox Press, 1993), pp. 36–59.

70 Comm. Romans, Dedicatory Epistle to Grynaeus, *Ad Romanos* 3.110–4.19. 'Verum animadvertere semper licuit, illos ipsos quibus nec pietatis studium deesset, nec in tractandis Dei religio ac sobrietas, nequaquam ubique inter se consensisse. Nunquam enim tanto beneficio servos suos dignatus est Deus, ut singuli plena perfectaque omni ex parte intelligentia praediti essent. Nec dubium quin eo consilio, ut nos in humilitate primum, deinde communicationis fraternae studio retineret. Ergo quum sperandum in praesenti vita non sit, quod maxime alioqui optandum esset, ut in locis Scripturae intelligendis perpetua sit inter nos consensio: danda est opera ut nulla novandi libidine incitati, nulla suggillandi alios cupiditate impulsi, nullo instigati odio, nulla ambitione titillati: sed sola necessitate coacti, nec aliud quaerentes quam prodesse, a superiorum sententiis discedamus: deinde ut id fiat in Scripturae expositione: in religionis autem dogmatibus, in quibus praecipue voluit Dominus consentaneas esse suorum mentes, minus sumatur libertatis. Utriusque studium mihi fuisse, facile deprehendent lectores'.

71 See his comment on I Cor. 6.18, CO 49.399; II Cor. 1.17, Secundam ad Corinthios 27.13–14; Galatians 1.15, Ad Galatas 26.21–23. This last is instructive, because Calvin is critiquing Chrysostom. Olivier Millet has written: 'Nous avons d'ailleurs vu qu'il reproche à saint Augustin sa "prolixité", évidemment opposée à sa propre briéveté. Mais cela ne veut pas dire que Calvin n'a pas trouvé chez les Pères des modèles d'éloquence. ... Enfin, si notre auteur a pu de fait trouver dans la littérature patristique des formes d'expression et de style, cet intérêt littéraire, tel que nous pouvons le saisir chez Calvin, relève principalement des attitudes et des stratégies de l'orateur: nous rencontrerons Tertullien pour l'apologète, Augustin pour le 'défenseur infatigable de la foi', et nous allons ici nous intéresser à Chrysostome comme théologien vulgarisateur et prédicateur, car c'est notamment à travers Chrysostome que Calvin réfléchit sur la mission et les formes du '*munus docendi*'. *Calvin et la Dynamique de la Parole: Etude de Rhétorique Réformée* (Paris: Librairie Honoré Champion, 1992), p. 169.

72 Here, Calvin breaks another of his exegetical rules. For him, the context of the particular book of scripture was a guideline to the mind of the author. He uses this clearly in his interpretation of Colossians 2.13, *Ad Colossenses* 429.13–24; I Thessalonians 2.7, CO 52.148; and I Corinthians 11.3, CO 49.474. This last is particularly instructive, as it is a case of Calvin using context to determine that Paul had not contradicted himself between I Corinthians and Galatians.

73 T. H. L. Parker makes it clear that of the Pauline group of commentaries, Romans receives the greatest amount of revision. See his *Calvin's New Testament Commentaries,* 2nd ed. (Louisville: Westminster/John Knox Press, 1993), pp. 36–59.

Appendix

Comparison of Citations to Augustine and Chrysostom

	Parker/Feld		CNTC	
Romans	A-13	C-5	A-14	C-4
I Corinthians			A-11	C-25
II Corinthians	A-5	C-21	A-4	C-21
Galatians Group	A-9	C-16	A-10	C-16
I Thessalonians			A-1	C-4
II Thessalonians			A-1	C-4
Timothy			A-4	C-8
Titus			A-2	C-2
Philemon			A-0	C-1
Hebrews	A-4	C-6	A-4	C-4

A – Augustine; C – Chrysostom

Response to R. Ward Holder

David M. Whitford

Academic presentations often begin with a conundrum that teases at the scholar's curiosity until it finally demands the attention necessary to solve the question. Professor Holder begins his essay with not just one conundrum but three. The first question concerns the history of exegetical opinion regarding Romans 7. We know that Paul suddenly changes to the first person half-way through the chapter. Professor Holder wants to know how exegetes in the past understood the chapter. This question led him not so much to an answer as to a new question. There are two traditions for the text, one that sees Paul's language in terms of a Christian's pre-conversion state while the other saw it as Paul's admission that even after conversion the Christian continues to struggle with the demands of the law. Why then, Holder asks, did exegetes choose one line of interpretation versus another. This leads almost inevitability to his third conundrum. Holder's main focus in this essay is a close examination of John Calvin's decision. Holder recognizes that Calvin made the latter choice – Paul is speaking of the struggles still faced by the regenerate (*non aliter quam de renatis posse exponi*).[1] The reason for this choice is what teases at Holder. David Steinmetz has noted that the 'regenerate believer' choice was hardly a Protestant verses Catholic decision. Some Protestants chose the first opinion that Paul was speaking of the believer before conversion while some Catholics, including Cardinal Cajetan (Thomasso de Vio, 1469–1534), who was both a Humanist and a harsh critic of Protestantism, chose the second. Holder writes, 'With the confessional rationale gone, we may ask why Calvin did choose [the second] position?' His answer to this conundrum drives the paper.

John Calvin had many options open to him when attempting to exegete Romans 7, including two opposing positions, both argued with some verve and persuasiveness by Augustine. Holder notes that Calvin sides with the later Augustine in choosing the 'regenerate' option. Holder also notes that in doing so, he rejected the opinion the one Patristic Father he holds in almost as high opinion as Augustine – Chrysostom. The answer to this conundrum, Holder argues, lies in Calvin's decision to 'override' his normal exegetical standards and rules and turn instead to hermeneutical considerations. Thus, while 'Calvin had strong exegetical reasons to follow the earlier tradition, his grasp of the Christian *religio* more urgently pointed him toward the later Augustine'.

Holder then demonstrates that Calvin's theological understanding of the Law and the bondage versus freedom of the will led him to reject the first interpretation of Romans 7 and endorse the 'regenerate' position. To choose the first option would require Calvin to 'suggest that pre-grace humans have the will to do something which Calvin claims they cannot – turn to God'. This theological and hermeneutical presupposition overrode Calvin's dedication to Chrysostom and the exegetical tradition that chose the first option.

Thus, when one returns to Holder's conundrum of why Calvin chose the second option, what one discovers is that confessional identity did indeed determine Calvin's exegetical decision. David Steinmetz has argued that 'what has already been written on a passage of scripture is far more important and exercises more influence on subsequent exegesis than the hermeneutical theory of any would-be interpreter'.[2] However, Calvin could not depend upon a single line of exegetical tradition. He was forced to choose, and his choice – opting for the bound and deficient will – was, most categorically, a Protestant decision.

Throughout the sixteenth century, Protestant exegetes were forced to make decisions about the importance and value of the Tradition. The mantra *sola scriptura* could only take one so far, and as Calvin discovered when he arrived at Romans 7, *sola scriptura* could not help his solve the question whether Paul was speaking of the pre-converted or regenerate individual. Each and every Protestant exegete of the sixteenth century looked to the Tradition. Steinmetz is certainly correct that oftentimes they followed the Tradition, but what Holder has demonstrated –hereby moving the scholarship on this topic in a new direction from Steinmetz – is what happened when the Tradition was in conflict with their new-found theological convictions. At times, they could find a Patristic – or even Scholastic – source that agreed with them, as Luther did when he cited Augustine in his debate with Erasmus over the bondage of will. At other times, Protestants were forced, like Calvin here, to pick between competing claims to authority. In those cases, theological and hermeneutical presuppositions dominated.

The interplay between the authority of scripture, theological presupposition, and the Tradition has always been more complicated than either the Protestant mantra of *sola scriptura* or the Tridentine retort of 'scripture *and* tradition'. Even those who firmly held to the position codified at Trent – such as Cajetan – were forced to make decisions between conflicting traditions. What Holder demonstrates is that to properly understand the history of exegetical interpretation we must understand *why* exegetes made the decisions they made. Calvin, by framing the discussion around the will, made a Protestant choice. Cardinal Cajetan arrived at the same decision as did Calvin – viewing the discussion at hand to be about the regenerate individual. The conundrum of why he made that choice remains. Perhaps this is a question that shall tease at Professor Holder in the future.

Notes

[1]Comm. Romans 7.15, *Iohannis Calvini Commentarius in Epistolam Pauli ad Romanos*, T. H. L. Parker, ed. (Leiden: E. J. Brill, 1981), 149.

[2] David Steinmetz, 'Divided by a Common Past: The Reshaping of the Christian Exegetical Tradition in the Sixteenth Century', in *Journal of Medieval and Early Modern Studies*, 27/2 (1997): 245–64; here 251.

— SEVEN —

Luther, Melanchthon, and Calvin on Romans 5 and 13: Three Reformation Approaches to Reading Romans

G. Sujin Pak

◆

Introduction

Martin Luther, Philip Melanchthon and John Calvin unanimously esteemed Paul's Epistle to the Romans as providing the clearest teaching of the central messages of the Gospel, namely correct understandings of justification, grace, faith, sin, Law, and good works. In Luther's 1522 preface to Romans, he writes, 'This epistle is in truth the most important document in the New Testament, the gospel in its purest expression … it is a brilliant light, almost enough to illumine the whole Bible'.[1] Melanchthon wrote in a letter to a colleague that Romans is 'by far the deepest of all the letters and [serves] as the *scopus* in the entire Holy Scripture'.[2] Similarly, Calvin proclaimed concerning this Pauline epistle: 'If we have gained a true understanding of this epistle, we have an open door to all the most profound treasures of Scripture'.[3]

After having begun his career at Wittenberg University with a set of lectures on the Psalms (1513–1515), Luther turned to lecture on Romans in 1515–1516. **C** Thus, one must note that Luther's lectures on Romans came very early in his career and were central to the shaping of his emerging reformation concerns. While Romans remained a crucial touchstone for much of his theological writing to come, he never returned to lecture upon it a second time.[4] Indeed, Philip Melanchthon took over these lectures on Romans and lectured on this Pauline epistle periodically from 1519, continuing at least as late as 1552. Melanchthon's initial work on Romans was published in 1519, entitled 'A Theological Introduction to Paul's Letter to the Romans'. The following year his students published his arrangement of Romans according to its theological themes, which Melanchthon revised in 1521 into his famous *Loci communes theologici*.[5] Furthermore, Luther had Melanchthon's lectures on Romans and Corinthians published in 1522.[6] In 1532, Melanchthon published his own commentary on Romans, which he revised and expanded in 1540.[7]

John Calvin's commentary on Romans was also published in 1540, based upon lectures he had given in Geneva around 1536–1537/38. This Latin 1540 commentary was expanded and translated into French in 1550.[8] Calvin specifically names his reasons for writing a commentary on Romans in his dedication of the work to Simon Grynaeus. Calvin notes that several significant reformers had already written

---

C Context of Luther's lectures on Romans.

commentaries on Romans, such as Philip Melanchthon, Heinrich Bullinger, and Martin Bucer. Though he esteems these commentaries highly, Calvin concludes that Melanchthon's topical approach leads him to neglect many important points, while Bucer's verbosity does not lend itself to clear and simple instruction of Christians. Hence, Calvin writes that he has undertaken this work 'for no other reason than the common good of the Church' in order that he might 'treat every point with brevity' and point his Christian readers to the best interpretation of Romans.[9]

This essay examines the commentaries of Martin Luther, Philip Melanchthon, and John Calvin on chapters 5 and 13 of Paul's Epistle to the Romans as lenses to compare and contrast their theological emphases and interpretive methods. Romans 5 provides a picture of their views on the fruits of justification, the role of suffering in the Christian life, and their definitions of sin, Law, and grace. Romans 13 reflects these three reformers' teachings concerning the Christian's relationship to governing authorities and the fulfillment of the Law through love of neighbor. While many common correlations are found in their readings of Romans 5 and 13, there are also some significant differences that speak to their particular theological emphases and exegetical strategies. This essay aims to demonstrate that three different general approaches may be discerned in these interpretations of Romans. Namely, Luther's approach to Romans is primarily contextual, while Melanchthon's method may be characterized as principally theological and Calvin's as chiefly analytical.[10] In addition to setting forth these differing approaches to Paul's Epistle to the Romans, this essay also argues that while there are many doctrinal agreements on the theological content of Romans amongst Luther, Calvin and Melanchthon, their doctrinal differences on this theological content point to the potential use of exegesis for the formation of separate confessional identities.[11] We turn first to a discussion of Luther's, Melanchthon's and Calvin's exegetical method in their interpretations of Romans 5 and 13 and then to a study of the theological content of their exegeses of these two chapters.

Luther's, Melanchthon's, and Calvin's Exegetical Methods

Luther, as a Catholic monk trained in scholastic method, writes his commentary according to the expected scholastic schema of glosses and scholia.[12] In his comments on Romans 5 and 13, however, he does not employ the medieval fourfold senses of Scripture (historical, allegorical, tropological, and anagogical readings).[13] Luther's own context is very important for the exegetical moves he makes; his situation as a Catholic monk starting to question ecclesiastical authorities and their practices and teachings greatly shapes his reading of Romans. **CA** Thus, one sees a monk-like emphasis on the good of suffering and devotion to ascetic practices, while also seeing challenges to and criticisms of ecclesiastical authorities.[14]

In terms of practice, Luther comments verse by verse, but he has no problem with skipping over several verses with little to no comment. What is very evident in Luther's Romans commentary – and indeed in all of his biblical exegesis – is his principle of Scripture interpreting Scripture. He brings in many other scriptural passages to highlight, expand, supplement, or explain a biblical verse. And when he wants to focus upon a specific theological theme, such as suffering and original sin in

---

CA Analysis of contextual dimension in Luther's specific emphasis.

Romans 5 or freedom and slavery in Romans 13, Luther writes an extended commentary devoted to the explication of just those few verses. Moreover, in his Romans commentary he refers fairly often and usually positively to church fathers' readings of certain verses, particularly to Augustine and sometimes Chrysostom, Bernard, Ambrose, Lombard, and Lefèvre.[15] In addition to other biblical passages and the church fathers, at other points Luther gives reference to philosophers, historians and poets, such as Aristotle, Vergil, Suetonius, Juvenal, and Catullus, in order to highlight or explain a point.[16]

While Melanchthon also uses Scripture to interpret Scripture, he does this on a much smaller scale than Luther. Melanchthon comments on the text verse by verse, but also displays a more explicit didactic method by setting forth lists of key theological teachings from particular passages.[17] His *loci* method – the method of drawing out theological themes – is most evident in his use of the lens of the distinction between Law and Gospel throughout his exegesis of both Romans 5 and 13, but it can also be seen in the accent he places upon describing the theological virtues of faith and hope and defining what he understands to be the correct doctrines of justification by faith alone, original sin, Law, and grace. At least in his exegesis of Romans 5 and 13, Melanchthon rarely refers to church fathers; when he does, it is negative and often targeted at a general group (such as the scholastic theologians).[18] On the other hand, in his comments on Romans 13, Melanchthon refers to Greek philosophers and Greek history to highlight the meaning of the text.[19]

Calvin's exegetical method in his commentary on Romans is different from those of Luther and Melanchthon in significant ways. Calvin also gives a verse by verse exposition, but he leaves no part of a verse uncommented upon. At least in his Romans commentary, Calvin employs the principle of Scripture interpreting Scripture on a vastly lesser scale than Melanchthon, let alone Luther.[20] **H** Most importantly, a key governing principle of Calvin's exegesis is his concern for authorial intention. This concern can be seen frequently in his comments on Romans 5 and on nearly every page of his comments on Romans 13. Often Calvin will write 'Paul intends' or refer to what Paul 'means to do'. For example, after citing Augustine's reading of Rom. 5:5, he comments that Augustine's interpretation 'is a devout sentiment but not what Paul means'.[21] Indeed, Calvin will even supply his own words and explanation in addition to those of Paul, if he deems that Paul's text does not sufficiently or clearly express what Calvin knows to be his intention. For example, on Rom. 5:17 he adds to the words of Paul in order to demonstrate that Paul does not mean universal salvation.[22] Similarly, on Rom. 13:9 Calvin writes that one must 'supply what [Paul] has passed over in silence' – namely, that obedience to civil authorities is part of love of neighbor.[23] As part of his concern for authorial intention, Calvin also makes a point to put the biblical text in its original social setting and context. For example, he begins his comments on Romans 13 with the conviction that some social situation necessarily led Paul to write on the subject of the proper relationship of Christians to civil authorities. Likewise, at the end of his comments on Romans 13, Calvin simply interprets Paul's words that 'salvation is nearer to us now' from the perspective of the recipients of the letter.[24]

In addition to his focus on authorial intention, another interesting difference between Calvin's method and those of Melanchthon and Luther is his greater

---

H Hermeneutical framework of Calvin's exegesis.

attention to philology and grammar. He often refers to points of grammar in order to support his reading of the passage.[25] Furthermore, at least in his comments on Romans 5 and 13, Calvin makes no explicit reference to Greek philosophers, historians, or poets. He does refer to Augustine and Origen in a few of his comments on Romans 5, but, like Melanchthon, his references to the church fathers are mostly negative.[26]

It should be cautioned that some of the nuances and differences between Luther, Melanchthon, and Calvin's exegesis and interpretative method should not be generalized as a definite rule, such as how well they attend to philology and grammar. Yet, some attributes are distinctive and characteristic for each, such as Melanchthon's *loci* method, Calvin's concern for authorial intention, and the importance of context and the prevalent use of supplementary Scripture in Luther's exegesis. Thus, one may discern three general Reformation approaches to Paul's Epistle to the Romans: Luther's contextual approach, Melanchthon's theological approach, and Calvin's analytical approach. Though Melanchthon's approach is more explicitly theological in method, of course all three focus upon particular theological teachings and themes in their interpretations of Romans 5 and 13, to which we now turn.

Luther, Melanchthon, and Calvin on Romans 5

C Luther, at the time of his Romans commentary, writes as a Catholic monk concerned with pious practices and disillusioned with the church leaders of his day. In this context, he focuses upon aspects of monastic piety, such as the role of suffering in the Christian life, while pointing to the promise of a pacified conscience and the freedom of the Christian. Melanchthon, in writing his commentary with several years' hindsight after the emergence of Luther's reformation, portrays a theological/doctrinal approach in which he more explicitly takes up the theological themes of the distinction between Law and Gospel and justification by faith alone. Calvin's approach to Romans reveals itself as more analytical in method; yet he also sets forth in his reading of Romans his own distinctive theological emphases upon the doctrines of providence and election. A study of Luther's, Melanchthon's and Calvin's interpretations of the various pericopes of Romans 5 and 13 help to unveil the details of the similarities and differences of their theological emphases and themes.

Rom 5:1–2: Fruits of Justification by Faith Alone

In their opening comments on Romans 5, Luther, Melanchthon, and Calvin all emphasize that the fruits of justification by faith alone are peace and a pacified conscience.[27] Luther focuses upon the spiritual peace that comes only through the inseparable connection between Christ and faith – though many in his day try to separate these two aspects of 'through Christ' and 'by faith'.[28] **H** Melanchthon reiterates this teaching of Luther; however, he explicitly places the conversation

---

C Luther reads Romans while still a monk.

H Melanchthon's interpretation is framed according to law/gospel dichotomy.

within the framework of Law versus Gospel. More than talking about the inseparable connection between Christ and faith, Melanchthon heavily emphasizes that justification by faith alone does not come by fulfillment of the Law but through the actions of Christ the Mediator. He seethes against the scholastic theologians of his day 'who suppose that the regenerate are thereafter righteous on account of the fulfillment of the Law', an idea that destroys faith and makes no need for Christ.[29]

A In addition to his emphasis on Law versus Gospel, Melanchthon adds two more aspects not touched upon by Luther. He affirms that this peace and pacified conscience are bulwarks against doubt, henceforth providing a kind of certainty of salvation and remission of sins.[30] Yet, Melanchthon, unlike Luther, does not end the conversation with the peace of salvation but extends this peace to the ongoing process of *sanctification*. He writes that Christians can have peace and confidence even though they still struggle with sin. This is the 'hope of sharing the glory of God' (Rom. 5:2), for this glory is not yet attained perfectly. Thus, Melanchthon concludes, 'Although we are still unclean, we are pleasing by faith and await perfect newness'.[31]

John Calvin also affirms that peace and a serenity of conscience are the fruits of justification by faith alone. The weight of his exegesis, however, falls upon the *certainty* of salvation that he finds taught in Rom. 5:1–2. His criticism of Catholic theologians is less about the inseparable connection between faith and Christ or their lack of distinction between Law and Gospel and more about their teaching that Christians are always in a state of uncertainty concerning their salvation. Paul, says Calvin, has set forth in these verses the 'sure pledge in Christ of the grace of God'.[32] Implicit within this emphasis is Calvin's doctrine of election: the foundation of this certainty is that salvation is based not upon our works but upon the grace of God and that this same grace continues to be given to [elect] Christians so that they may persevere in their salvation and be certain of it.[33]

Rom. 5:3–5: Role of Suffering in the Christian Life

Martin Luther spends a significant amount of time in his exegesis on Rom. 5:3–5 to talk about the role of suffering in the Christian life. Indeed, this emphasis is only second to his teaching concerning original sin, which is the focus of the remainder of his interpretation of Romans 5. He stresses that suffering reveals the true character of a person.[34] A true Christian, writes Luther, accepts suffering willingly and bears it with patience.[35] Moreover, he connects the need for these trials and tribulations to two factors: the fact of original sin and the need to direct one's hope properly:

> If God did not test us by tribulation, it would be impossible for any [person] to be saved. The reason is that our nature has been so deeply curved in upon itself because of the viciousness of original sin ... Therefore our good God, after [God] has justified us and give us [God's] spiritual gifts, quickly brings tribulation upon us, exercises us, and tests us so that this godless nature of ours does not rush in upon these enjoyable sins, lest in [one's] ignorance [a person] should die the eternal death.[36]

Paul, says Luther, teaches that suffering ultimately leads to hope (Rom. 5:3–4) because it instructs Christians to despair of the created things in which they place

A Analysis of Melanchthon's interpretation in comparison with Luther's.

their hope and trust in God alone.[37] Finally, based upon Rom. 5:5, he concludes that the strength to bear suffering comes not from human effort but as a gift of God's love given through the Holy Spirit. Here, Luther adopts the language of freedom versus slavery to teach that this love of God given by the Spirit into human hearts is a sign of the distinction between the free sons of God and bondservants. Free sons of God accept suffering willingly and persevere in hope, while bondservants run away in fear.[38]

Melanchthon is much less concerned with the question of the role of suffering in the Christian life per se; rather, his primary aim is to argue that suffering needs to be understood not under Law but under Gospel. Afflictions, insists Melanchthon, are not signs of God's wrath but exercises allowed by God to strengthen faith, patience, obedience, and hope. Indeed, afflictions belong to Gospel, for they are not intended as punishment (Law) but as a means to bring about repentance, obedience, and faith.[39] Moreover, rather than emphasizing the contrast between free sons and bondservants as Luther does, Melanchthon concludes by declaring that Rom. 5:5 announces the very message of the Gospel: the love of God given on account of Christ by grace and not on account of merit (i.e., Law). He concludes with an emphasis upon the certainty that a Christian may have based upon the statement 'hope does not confound' (Rom. 5:5a), which is the surety of God's promise that 'God's love has been poured out' on account of Christ (Rom. 5:5b).[40]

Calvin, unlike Luther, does not assert that Christians should seek suffering; rather, he admits that saints bitterly dread adversity. Instead, he points to the *providential* character of suffering for a Christian. He writes that Christians can be "greatly consoled by the thought that all their sufferings are dispensed for their good by the hand of a most benevolent Father."[41] Hence, Calvin teaches that ultimately sufferings contribute to one's salvation and final good, and this is why one may glory in afflictions. Furthermore, unlike Luther and Melanchthon, Calvin feels compelled to reconcile the teaching of Rom. 5:3–5 with that of James 1:2–4 to show that they are not contradictory: Paul speaks of patient endurance through sure trust in God's protection, while James 'uses the same word to mean tribulation itself'.[42] Finally, Calvin is even more intent than Melanchthon to accentuate the certainty Christians may have as expressed in Rom. 5:5. Patience in afflictions, writes Calvin, is proof of God's help. The ability to endure afflictions confirms one's hope and election and shows salvation to be most certain, for it demonstrates the presence of the Spirit in one's life and the pouring of God's love into one's heart (Rom. 5:5b).[43]

Rom. 5:6–11: Certainty of Salvation and God's Love

Luther actually spends little to no space commenting on Rom. 5:6–11. His main objective is to set forth varying interpretations of Rom. 5:6, 'For while we were still weak, at the right time Christ died for the ungodly'.[44] Melanchthon, on the other hand, interprets Rom. 5:6–11 as an amplification of the signs and testimonies of the love of God already set forth in Rom. 5:5. He uses this pericope in Romans 5, particularly verse 11, to continue to teach through the language of Law versus Gospel about the certainty of salvation a Christian may have; it is a certainty that rests upon the fact that one's salvation is based not upon Law but upon Gospel. Thus, this certainty is founded not upon human worthiness or the keeping of the

Law but upon the surety of God's promise in Christ.[45] **H** While not using the lens of Law versus Gospel, Calvin also reads Rom. 5:6–11 concerning Christian certainty of salvation and emphasizes that this confidence rests upon the work of Christ alone and is nothing of our own doing.[46] Yet, unlike Melanchthon, he sets forth here his distinctive teaching that Christ not only procures salvation for the elect, he provides the perseverance to preserve it 'safe and secure to the end'.[47]

Rom. 5:12–21: Sin, Grace, and the Law

For Luther, the subject matter of the remainder of Romans 5 is original sin. This includes statements about the proper definition of original sin, the relationship between the Law and sin, and an explanation concerning in what ways Adam is and is not a type of Christ. Among the ten reasons Luther gives for why original sin is the correct subject matter of the last half of Romans 5 are the arguments that sin is spoken of in the singular (while actual sins would have to be spoken of in the plural), that the passage speaks of a sin 'in which all sinned' (which can only mean original sin), and that the result of this sin is death for all humanity (whereas personal sins do not result in death for all).[48]

A Thus, concerning the proper definition of original sin, Luther contends against the scholastic definition as a 'lack of original righteousness' and offers what he considers to be a more accurate and biblical definition that points to total depravity:

> [I]t is not only a lack of a certain quality in the will, nor even only a lack of light in the mind or of power in the memory, but particularly it is a total lack of uprightness and of the power of all the faculties both of body and soul and of the whole [person]. On top of this it is a propensity toward evil. It is a nausea toward the good, a loathing of light and wisdom, and a delight in error and darkness ...[49]

Concerning the relationship between Law and sin, Luther wants his readers to understand that the Law can never take away sin; it only serves to enable the recognition of sin. More importantly, the Law reveals the need for grace and faith. It is neither a help nor a cure, asserts Luther, but it reveals that one can never fully keep the Law and is thus in the bonds of sin.[50] As to the ways in which Adam both is and is not a type of Christ, Luther asserts that Adam is a type of Christ in that 'the likeness of Adam's transgression is in us', while the 'likeness of Christ's justification is in us'. Yet, he more strongly emphasizes the differences between Adam and Christ. Adam brought death to all, while Christ brought life 'to those who belong to him'.[51] He concludes with a focus upon Rom. 5:15 ('but the free gift is not like the trespass') to argue that if the sin of one man has so much power, how much more powerful is the grace of God.[52]

Melanchthon reiterates all of these points made by Luther and then takes the discussion in a different direction.[53] He once more sets forth the teachings of this passage through the trope of Law versus Gospel. It is a doctrine of Law, asserts Melanchthon, to believe that some quality in ourselves can make us righteous or not.

H Calvin's interpretation shaped by hermeneutical framework which differs from Melanchthon's.

A Analysis of Luther's definition of sin and its relation to the law.

But the remission of sins and the imputation of righteousness are completely gratuitous. The Word of God, proclaims Melanchthon, does not teach Law but declares the promises of the Gospel. Thus, he contrasts the effects of grace from the effects of the Law. Yet, this discussion of the effects of the Law leads Melanchthon, unlike Luther, to expound on the usefulness of the Law not just to lead to salvation (i.e., reveal sin), but its ongoing usefulness in the Christian's process of sanctification.[54] Finally, Melanchthon explicitly emphasizes that God's offer of grace is universal.[55]

Calvin also maintains that the subject matter of Rom. 5:12–21 is original sin, which includes a definition of original sin as total depravity and a description of the role of the Law to reveal sin.[56] The weight of Calvin's exegesis, though, is very different from that of Luther or Melanchthon. Calvin does not want this passage read as affirming in any remote way the concept of universal salvation – a possibility that Melanchthon's reading of this passage opens up. Thus, he spends much time arguing that a central difference between Adam and Christ is that while Adam's sin extends to all, Christ's salvation only extends to the *elect*.[57] He stresses that one of the main differences between Adam and Christ is that 'Christ's benefit does not come to all [people] in the manner in which Adam involved his whole race in condemnation'.[58] Thus, Calvin contends that in Rom. 5:15 ('much more surely have the grace of God and the free gift in the grace of the one man, Jesus Christ, abounded for the many') Paul does not speak of all humanity, but only of the believing elect, for faith is necessary in order to participate in the grace of Christ.[59]

Theological Similarities and Differences in the Three Approaches to Romans 5

Luther's interpretation of Romans 5 in his *Lectures* is very clearly shaped by his particular historical context of 1515–1516. He is still very much writing as a Catholic monk, as can be seen in prominence the teachings upon the role of suffering in the Christian life occupy in his exegesis of Romans 5. **A** In this early commentary on Romans, one does not find a substantial or explicit stress upon the doctrine of justification by faith alone per se. Instead one sees more of an emphasis upon the role of tribulation in a Christian's life to exercise and test the Christian in order to overcome the power of original sin and to teach the Christian to rely upon the love God freely gives through the Spirit. Yet, it is in these two latter teachings – the emphasis upon the power and bondage of original sin and upon the love freely given by God – one can discern the seeds that will later grow into his fuller doctrine of justification by faith alone.

There are a couple of significant points of theological agreement between Melanchthon and Calvin. While all three of these interpreters agree on a definition of original sin as total depravity and the role of the Law to reveal sin, Melanchthon and Calvin both want to focus on the certainty of salvation that a Christian may have. Moreover, Melanchthon makes some exegetical moves that could be viewed as ventures towards further theological agreement with Calvin. Of considerable note is his emphasis that the Law is not only useful for salvation by revealing sin, but that it possesses an ongoing usefulness in Christian sanctification – a teaching often referred

A Analysis of Luther's specific emphasis in the light of his own context.

to as the 'third use of the Law', for which Calvin is well known. **C** Indeed, around the year 1540, when both Melanchthon and Calvin published commentaries on Romans, there are indications that Melanchthon and Calvin were seeking areas of agreement between them. For example, in 1540 Melanchthon produced a revised version of the Augsburg Confession, called the *Variata*, which Calvin himself signed.[60] Calvin also displays indications of his concern for Protestant agreement, as can be seen precisely in a letter he wrote in 1540 to Heinrich Bullinger: 'What ... should more anxiously occupy us in our letters than to keep up brotherly friendship among us by all possible means.... It is therefore our duty to cherish true friendship for all preachers of the word and to keep the churches at peace with one another. As far as in me lies, I will always labor to do so'.[61]

While such points of agreement between Melanchthon and Calvin cannot be ignored, neither should the confessional interests influencing the different nuances of their interpretations of Romans be overlooked. Throughout his exegesis of Romans 5, Melanchthon emphatically employs the characteristically *Lutheran* interpretive tool of the contrast between the Law and the Gospel.[62] Calvin, on the other hand, displays his own confessional theological concerns in the prominence of the doctrines of election and providence in his exegesis. Thus, Calvin's particularly Reformed theology leads him to underscore the evidences of election and providence that he finds in Romans 5 and clearly to deny the doctrine of universal salvation.

Luther, Melanchthon and Calvin on Romans 13

Rom. 13:1–7: Submission to Authorities

For Melanchthon, Paul in Rom. 13:1–7 writes very clearly about the Christian's proper relationship to civil society and civil authorities. Later in his commentary, however, Melanchthon extends this discussion of authority to questions of church authority – and this only to demonstrate the ways that civil law is more binding than ecclesiastical law.[63] **HC** Calvin also reads the text as addressing the Christian's proper response to civil authorities; yet, Calvin does not extend the discussion to ecclesiastical authority.[64] Luther, on the other hand, while acknowledging in his gloss that the text is about civil authorities, prefers to read it as concerning the spiritual realm. In this way, Luther uses Rom. 13:1–7 to criticize church leaders, rather than to address the Christian's relationship to the state.[65]

Both Melanchthon and Calvin find in Romans 13 the teaching that governments and their officials are ordained and preserved by God and given for the common good. Hence, together they emphasize obedience to civil authorities as part of a Christian's obedience to God.[66] Calvin and Melanchthon also address, each in his own way, the problem of tyrannical governments and corrupt magistrates. Melanchthon leaves little to no room for resisting tyrannical governments. Rather, he addresses this problem merely by arguing that a true magistrate should understand that this authority is given to him by God for the common good; thus magistrates

---

C Contextual factors contribute to some theological agreement concerning the role of the law.
HC Hermeneutical choices influenced by contextual factors shape interpretation.

who become tyrants and abuse this power for their own desires destroy the ordinance of God and are themselves guilty.[67] Moreover, Melanchthon sternly warns that disobedience of the government is a mortal sin and that the overthrowing of governments is the work of the devil.[68]

Like Melanchthon, Calvin says that any who strive to overturn God's ordained order – i.e., state governments – are in effect resisting God and waging war against God. More pointedly, such persons despise God's *providence*. Yet, Calvin concedes, 'dictatorships and unjust authorities are not ordained governments'; they are not God's original intention. Nonetheless, *the right of government* is ordained by God for the common good.[69] Hence, Calvin argues, 'no tyranny can exist that does not in some respect assist in protecting human society'.[70] **H** Even tyrannies serve their purpose and are not outside of God's sovereignty, asserts Calvin; thus, the proper response of a Christian to *any* government is obedience. Like Melanchthon, he simply deals with unjust rulers by saying that they are answerable to God. Even more explicitly than Melanchthon, Calvin advocates obedience to wicked rulers, for that ruler acts as scourge to punish sin.[71]

Though in his later applications of Romans 13 Luther iterates these same emphases of Melanchthon and Calvin concerning a Christian's proper relationship of obedience to civil authorities,[72] in the early years of his commentary on Romans he does something completely different. **C** First, he uses Rom. 13:1–7 to criticize the church leaders of his day. These priests, says Luther, 'are only shadows of what they should be'.[73] He accuses current church leaders of encouraging vices (pride, ambition, prodigality) and placing unfit, unholy and unlearned men in positions of power. They do not practice love of neighbor but, rather, love themselves too much. Indeed, says Luther, the secular authorities are fulfilling their duties more effectively than the ecclesiastical rulers.[74]

Next, Luther makes a surprising move. On the basis of the wording in Rom. 13:1 ('Let every *soul* be subject to the governing authorities'), he launches into a discussion of the three elements of the human – body, soul, spirit – in order to focus upon teachings concerning slavery and freedom. The body, says Luther, is subject to the state. The spirit, however, is completely free and subject to no one but God. The soul, on the other hand, is that midpoint between body and spirit. The soul, Luther writes, is the spirit 'insofar as it lives and works and is occupied with visible and temporal matters'. Thus, the soul is subject to every human institution 'for the Lord's sake'.[75] Yet, Luther focuses upon a discussion of freedom and slavery in order to emphasize the Christian's freedom from slavery to the Law and from preoccupations with temporal matters. Furthermore, he sets forth the true 'slavery' to which a Christian is called; namely, Christians are to be servants to one another through love (Gal. 5:13). Luther avows that this is both the highest form of freedom of a Christian and also the proper kind of servitude of a Christian. The absolute wrong kind of servitude for the Christian is slavery to the Law.[76]

If Luther finds theological instruction concerning freedom and slavery in Romans 13, Melanchthon and Calvin find very different theological teachings. Melanchthon uses Rom. 13:1–7 to discuss the relation of the Gospel to civil society, teach about God's institution and preservation of governments, and contrast civil law and Mosaic Law. While state governments do not belong to Gospel but to reason, these

---

H Hermeneutical presuppositions of the author have an impact on her interpretation.
C Interpretation is directly related to context.

governments are supposed to serve the purposes of the Gospel and, therefore, are not opposed to Gospel. Melanchthon repeats several times the point that God ordained governments in order that 'God might become known in society and in order that [Christians] might have exercises of confession, patience, faith, and love'.[77] Hence, Melanchthon concludes that the Gospel affirms temporal forms of government because ultimately the purpose of these governments is to preserve and protect civil matters so that spiritual matters may flourish.[78]

Melanchthon also maintains that the fact that God is the one who is ultimately in control of all authorities is a source of comfort.[79] More so, though, Melanchthon focuses upon the contrast between civil law and Mosaic Law. Here he addresses a seeming contradiction that Christians are free from the Law and yet are commanded by Paul to be subject to the laws of the government. Melanchthon explains that this spiritual freedom (i.e., freedom from the Law of Moses) does not exclude the requirement of obedience to the laws of the government, which is part of one's *bodily* obedience. Hence the spirit is free from Mosaic Law, but the body remains subject to those laws that concern the body (i.e., civil laws).[80] Indeed, Melanchthon goes so far as to proclaim, 'Civil laws obligate more than ecclesiastical laws', by which he means that disobedience to civil laws is a mortal sin, whereas Christ wants freedom to reign in the church.[81]

More than just the emphasis upon governments as ordained, instituted and preserved by God, Calvin uses Rom. 13:1–7 explicitly to emphasize God's *sovereignty*, particularly God's *providence*. Governments are under the sovereignty and providence of God. This means that civil rulers are ultimately answerable to God and all of their power ultimately remains under God's sovereignty. This also includes the fact that governmental rulers can have the authority to implement God's wrath in punishing the wicked, putting the guilty to death, and exercising God's vengeance.[82]

Rom. 13:8–10: Fulfilling the Law through Love

Luther uses Rom. 13:8–10 to teach the true love of neighbor, to warn against the pretense of love, and to urge a practice of love that is not self-seeking but truly seeks the good of the neighbor.[83] On the other hand, Melanchthon's and Calvin's exegeses of these verses focus upon the proper relationship between faith and works so that they both find the need to qualify Paul's statement that the Law can be fulfilled through love (Rom. 13:8). They stress that everyone is justified by faith alone and not by works. **H** Thus, Melanchthon argues that it is more accurate to say that faith is the true fulfillment of the Law.[84] Calvin, on the other hand, places the emphasis upon justification by faith alone via a different route. Calvin argues that when Paul writes that love fulfills the Law, he does not refer to the whole Law but only to the Second Table of the Law, since the commandments of the Decalogue cited by Paul are from the Second Table (Rom. 13:9). Thus, the First Table of the Law, which concerns humans' relationship to God, can only be fulfilled through faith (i.e., justification by faith alone), while the Second Table concerns one's relationship to one's neighbor and is fulfilled by love. Furthermore, in keeping with his concern for authorial intention, Calvin ties this teaching to the previous section of Romans 13 concerning

H Both Melanchthon and Calvin clarify their interpretation according to their hermeneutical presuppositions.

obedience to civil authorities. One's obedience to the government is part of one's love of neighbor.[85]

Rom. 13:11–14: Closing Exhortations

Luther believes that Paul writes the final verses of Romans 13 to lukewarm Christians. Thus, he exhorts these Christians to arise from their lukewarm lives and lay aside their wrong, superficial penitential practices. Indeed, these lukewarm Christians sound very much like the ecclesiastical leaders he has been criticizing previously. Through the warning against vices in Rom. 13:13, Luther exhorts people to flee vices such as gluttony and devote themselves to fasting and temperance.[86]

Melanchthon, on the other hand, thinks these final verses are written to those ignorant of true doctrine. Those who 'sleep' (Rom. 13:11) are persons ignorant of true doctrine, while the 'armor of light' (Rom. 13:12) is the knowledge of God's Word and the 'works of darkness' (Rom. 13:12) are the works resulting from ignorance of God.[87] Similarly, Calvin reads 'sleep' in reference to those in need of the revelation of divine truth. 'Night' and 'sleep', then, also refer to the ignorance of God, and 'light' indicates the revelation of God's truth.[88]

Both Melanchthon and Calvin want to explain why Paul says 'salvation is nearer to us now', but they do so differently. Melanchthon writes that believers now have the revealed Christ, whereas the Old Testament patriarchs only had the promised Christ; hence, believers have a clearer, closer revelation. Calvin, on the other hand, in keeping with his concern for authorial intention, simply explains the nearness of salvation in reference to the Romans themselves: now that they have faith, their salvation is nearer.[89]

Finally, Melanchthon and Calvin provide different interpretations of Paul's command to 'put on the Lord Jesus Christ' (Rom.13:14), while Luther does not deal with this command at all. Melanchthon emphasizes that Christ is not merely an example to be imitated; the proper response to Christ is faith. Calvin, alternatively, reads this verse in reference to the cloak of the Holy Spirit given for the believer's protection. Furthermore, 'putting on Christ' signifies the renewal of God's image in the Christian soul and the calling of the believer to be engrafted into the Body of Christ.[90]

Theological Similarities and Differences in the Three Approaches to Romans 13

In his 1515–1516 Romans commentary, Luther employs chapter 13 to criticize the church leaders of his day. This criticism continues throughout his exegesis of Romans 13 from Paul's statements about obedience to governing authorities to the call to love of neighbor to the concluding exhortations of the chapter. In each case, Luther finds reason to rebuke the attitudes and practices of current church leaders. 'How can one expect laypersons to obey the hypocritical ecclesiastical rulers, who love themselves more than they love their neighbors and who are "sleeping in their smugness?"' asks Luther.[91] **C** One can see that Luther's immediate historical context and, more specifically, the pressing needs of the church, shape his reading of the text.

C Context directly shaping interpretation.

In a context in which he has become increasingly disillusioned with church leaders, Luther finds the opportunity to voice his concerns and criticisms.[92] Moreover, his context as a Catholic monk is once more apparent in his exhortations to his readers to pursue practices of fasting, temperance, sobriety, and chastity with all devotion and seriousness.[93] Finally, Luther's theme of freedom versus slavery, seen briefly in Romans 5 and more explicitly in Romans 13, reveals itself as the very heart of his early understanding of Romans and should be understood as the groundwork of his later doctrine of justification by faith alone.[94]

Both Melanchthon and Calvin interpret Romans 13 primarily concerning the Christian's relationship to civil governments and their authorities. They both see civil governments as ordained by God and, thus, deserving Christian obedience even in cases of unjust rulers. **C** Indeed, it should be remembered that both Melanchthon and Calvin write their commentaries on Romans after the historical event of the German Peasants' Revolt in 1524–1525, during which Luther himself issued stern statements about the Christian's duty to obey governmental authorities out of love of neighbor, even if those authorities are unjust and corrupt.[95]

Though there are significant theological parallels between Melanchthon's and Calvin's readings of Romans 13 concerning the obedience due to civil governments and authorities, one can discern the nuances of the different theological foundations of this doctrine for Lutherans as opposed to Calvinists. Melanchthon appeals to the purpose and usefulness of civil governments for the flourishing of the Gospel. Again he uses the trope of Law and Gospel to demonstrate how the civil law differs from Mosaic Law and how civil law functions to serve the Gospel. Melanchthon also wants to draw a clear contrast between the type of obedience required by civil laws as opposed to ecclesiastical laws.[96] Rather than through the lens of Law and Gospel, Calvin, on the other hand, explains the foundation of a Christian's obedience to the state in the very Reformed terms of God's sovereignty and providence. Through the recognition of the state as part of God's sovereignty and providence, the proper response of a Christian to any government (whether just or unjust) is obedience.

As to the subject of the fulfillment of the Law through love in Rom. 13:8–10, both Melanchthon and Calvin are concerned to explain how this is not contrary to a doctrine of justification by faith alone. Yet, subtle differences in exegetical method may also point to slightly differing confessional emphases. In very Lutheran form, Melanchthon's main argument is that it would have been better and clearer to say that *faith* is the true fulfillment of the Law. Calvin, alternatively, again in keeping with his principle of the importance of authorial intention, prefers to keep Paul's actual language of 'love' by explaining that Paul is speaking only about the Second Table of the Law (i.e., one's relationship to neighbor), which is indeed fulfilled by love.[97]

Finally, both Melanchthon and Calvin reveal their commonly held pedagogical focus in their interpretation of the closing exhortations of Romans 13 as concerning the need for the teaching of correct doctrine. However, again the differing nuances of their interpretations reveal confessional assumptions. While Melanchthon interprets 'put on the Lord Jesus Christ' as referring to that exchange of properties that occurs through faith (i.e., the very Lutheran emphasis upon the *communicatio idiomatum*), Calvin uses the language of the cloak of the Holy Spirit, the renewal of

---

C Contextual factors influence the readings of Melanchthon and Calvin in a way which differs from Luther.

God's image in the Christian, and the calling to be engrafted into the Body of Christ, which are clear aspects of Calvin's theology of Christian election.[98]

Conclusion

This essay has emphasized the primacy in interpreting Romans of the contextual approach for Luther, the theological approach for Melanchthon, and the analytical approach for Calvin; however, a word of caution must be said here. Just as the editors of a previous volume of the Romans through History and Culture project have pointed out, rarely is just one approach being used at one time and, indeed, it is desirable that scriptural readers recognize the tripolarity of the interpretive process.[99] Likewise, Luther, Melanchthon and Calvin are each employing all three of these approaches to one degree or another: they all interpret within their own contexts, they all seek key theological teachings from Romans, and they all understand themselves to be attending to the words of the text. Yet, I hope, that through the analysis presented here of their interpretations of chapters 5 and 13 of Romans, one can identify how the primacy given to a particular approach does greatly guide their emphases, conclusions and readings of Romans.

This essay has also argued that, whether intentional on Luther's, Melanchthon's, or Calvin's part or not, biblical exegesis is not only shaped by the primacy of the approach the interpreter takes but also the distinctive theological emphases of their own confessional identities. Biblical exegesis has been and continues to be used to set forth particular confessional teachings and emphases (here, Lutheran versus Reformed) that – whether inadvertently or intentionally – advance the development and consolidation of separate confessional identities. Even in a biblical epistle such as Romans, where so many of the centrally shared Reformation teachings may be found, the differences in both approach and theological emphases amongst these key Protestant reformers are both remarkable and revealing.

Notes

[1] Martin Luther, *Preface to the Epistle of St. Paul to the Romans* (1522) in John Dillenberger, *Martin Luther: Selections from his Writings* (New York: Doubleday, 1962), 19. For the original German version see *D. Martin Luthers Werke* in Weimarer Ausgabe, *Die Deutsche Bibel*, volume 7, page 3 [herafter cited as WADB].

[2] H. Scheible, ed., *Melanchthons Breifwechsel: Kritische und Kommentierte Gesamtausgabe* (Stuttgart: Frommann, 1977–) 68 (*T*1.159, 7–9), dated 11 December 1519. Heretofore, *Melanchthons Breifwechsel* will be referred to by *MBW*. See also a similar statement by Melanchthon in *MBW* 47 (*T*1.112, 32–33), dated 27 March 1519.

[3] John Calvin, *The Epistles of Paul the Apostle to the Romans and to the Thessalonians*, trans. by Ross Mackenzie, ed. by David W. Torrance and Thomas F. Torrance (Grand Rapids, MI: William B. Eerdmans, 1960), 5. The Latin text of Calvin's commentary on Romans may be found in *Ioannis Calvini Opera Quae Supersunt Omnia* [hereforth referred to by CO], Vol 49 (Brunsvigae: C. A. Schwetschke and Sons, 1892), 1–292; here, 1.

[4] For example, much later in his life, in his 1545 preface to his Latin writings, Luther gives an account of the radical change in his understanding of the 'righteousness of God' upon his rereading of Rom. 1:17. See WA 54:185–85; Dillenberger, 10–11. Though scholars debate the reliability of this account for providing an accurate date of his 'breakthrough', it is agreed that Romans played a large role in the shaping of Luther's reformation concerns. There is a potential problem with my choice of studying only Luther's 1515–16 lectures on Romans, rather than tracing the use of Romans throughout his theological thought. The problem is one of reception: how widely available were Luther's lectures on Romans? I am contending that due to the number of very close parallels between Luther's and Melanchthon's comments on Romans, I can be reasonably sure that Luther shared his lectures with Melanchthon. Secondly, I chose to stay with Luther's lectures on Romans rather than tracing the use of separate verses of Romans in his theology because I am primarily interested in his exegetical method and approach to Romans as a whole. The use of separate citations of Romans in his theology – much of it as a kind of proof-texting – does not get at this concern nearly as clearly, nor is it parallel to the form of texts that I use for Melanchthon and Calvin (i.e., their commentaries on Romans). To keep some parallelism of form, then, I have chosen to stay with each of their commentaries on Romans, though I acknowledge that this means we do not get Luther's later, more developed theological thought on Romans.

[5] The work published by his students was entitled 'Themes and Topics of Theological Matters' (*Rerum Theologicorum Capita seu Loci*). Notably, Melanchthon's *Loci Communes Theologici* comes out of his work on Paul's Epistle to the Romans.

[6] Luther published this under the title of 'Annotations' (*Annotationes Phil. Melanchthonis in Epistolas Pauli ad Romanos et ad Corinthios*).

[7] It is this latter 1540 commentary that is used in the writing of this essay.

[8] T. H. L. Parker, *Calvin's New Testament Commentaries*, 2d ed (Louisville, KY: Westminster/John Knox, 1993), pp. 15, 206–207. This essay uses Calvin's 1540 Latin commentary, however.

[9] See CO 10:403–405 and the English translation, 'John Calvin to Simon Grynaeus' in his dedication of his commentary on Romans in *The Epistles of Paul the Apostle to the Romans and to the Thessalonians*, pp. 2–3.

[10] In the introduction to *Reading Israel in Romans: Legitimacy and Plausibility of Divergent Interpretations* (ed. by Cristina Grenholm and Daniel Patte, Harrisburg, PA: Trinity Press, International, 2000), the editors of this volume map out precisely these three general approaches to reading Romans: analytical, hermeneutical (which I have called 'theological'), and contextual. See especially pp. 34–42.

[11] By this I mean theological themes that point to denominational differences. I want to argue for a greater recognition of the role of biblical exegesis as a key tool to promote what Reformation historians call 'confessional formation' – the ways in which Lutherans, Reformed, Anabaptists, and Catholics began to differentiate themselves. Ernst Walter Zeeden first coined this term in his book *Die Entstehung der Konfessionen: Grundlagen und Formen der Konfessionsbildung* (Munich, 1965).

[12] Glosses are short interlinear comments, while scholia are the longer, marginal comments that are gathered together as his commentary on the biblical text.

[13] Indeed, throughout his Romans commentary he only refers to these senses individually a handful of times. On the allegorical sense, see WA 56:162, 165, 408–409; and the English translation may be found in *Luther's Works*, Vol 25: *Lectures on Romans*, ed by Hilton C. Oswald, trans by Jacob A. O. Preus (St. Louis: Concordia, 1972), pp. 141, 144, 398 [hereafter, *Luther's Works* will be referred to by LW]. On the literal sense, see WA 56:224, 230, 408; LW 25:209, 214, 398. On the tropological sense, see WA 56:162, 228, 408; LW 25:141, 212, 398.

[14] Eric W. Gritsch argues precisely this point that Luther's cultural and historical contexts greatly shape his exegesis. See his article 'The Cultural Context of Luther's Interpretation', *Interpretation*, 37 (1983), 266–76. See also Scott H. Hendrix, 'Luther Against the Background of the History of Biblical Interpretation', *Interpretation*, 37 (1983), 229–39.

[15] In his comments on Romans 5, Luther refers to Augustine eleven times and all positively. See WA 56:309, 310, 314, 315, 316, 317, 319; LW 25:296, 297, 302, 303, 304, 305, 307. He refers to Chrysostom five times (WA 56:310, 317; LW 25:297, 304, 305) and Lefévre (WA 56:316; LW 25:304), Lombard (WA 56:305; LW 25:292), and Ambrose once (WA 56:317; LW 25:304). In his comments on Romans 13, Luther refers to Bernard of Clairvaux twice positively. See WA 56:480, 486; LW 25:472, 478.

[16] At least in his comments on Romans 5 and 13 these are used positively and informationally. For example, on Romans 5 Luther uses Vergil's mythological monsters (Hydra, Cerberus, and Antaeus) to describe the power of original sin (WA 56:313; LW 25:300). On Romans 13, he uses the testimonies of Suetonius, Juvenal, and Catullus to describe the vices of Rome (WA 56:488; LW 25: 481).

[17] For example, on Rom. 5:3 Melanchthon gives a list of four teachings concerning afflictions. See *Corpus Reformatorum*, ed by Carolus Gottlieb Bretschneider, *Philippi Melanthonis Opera Quae Supersunt Omnia*, Volume 15, pages 615-16 [herafter referred to by CR]. The English translation may be found in Philip Melanchthon, *Commentary on Romans*, trans by Fred Kramer (St. Louis, MO: Concordia, 1992), 126. Likewise, he lists four key teachings Paul gives in Romans 13 concerning the Christian and civil governments. See CR 15:712; Melanchthon, 218.

[18] In his comments on Romans 5 and 13, Melanchthon only names one church father explicitly: he argues against Origen's reading of Rom. 5:1. See CR 15:611; Melanchthon, 122. He also rants against the scholastic theologians' definition of original sin, as do Luther and Calvin. CR 15:628; Melanchthon, 137–38. WA 56:312; LW 25:299. CO 49:99; Calvin, 115.

[19] Melanchthon exalts Paul's definition of government as superior to Aristotle's (CR 15:713; Melanchthon, 219), and he refers to Clodius, Catiline, and Mark Antony as examples of scornful persons who stirred up rebellion against governments and incur eternal punishments for doing so. See CR 15:715; Melanchthon, 221. For a few studies on Melanchthon's exegetical method in his commentary on Romans, see Rolf Schäfer, 'Melanchthon's Interpretation of Romans 5.15: His Departure from the Augustinian Concept of Grace Compared to Luther's', in *Philip Melanchthon (1497–1560) and the Commentary*, ed. by Timothy J. Wengert and M. Patrick Graham (Sheffield: Sheffield Academic, 1997), pp. 79–104; Richard Muller, '"*Scimus enim quod lex spiritualis est*": Melanchthon and Calvin on the Interpretation of Romans 7.14–23', in ibid., pp. 216–37; and Timothy J. Wengert, 'Philip Melanchthon's 1522 Annotations on Romans and the Lutheran Origins of Rhetorical

Criticism', in *Biblical Interpretation in the Era of the Reformation*, ed. by Richard A. Muller and John L. Thompson (Grand Rapids, MI: William B. Eerdmans, 1996), pp. 118–40.

[20] One should keep in mind that Calvin always intended for his commentaries to be read alongside his *Institutes*. In *Institutes* one finds Calvin drawing many biblical passages together in order to interpret one another and provide a clear teaching of a doctrine or theological theme.

[21] CO 49:92; Calvin, 108.

[22] See CO 49:100; Calvin, 116–17.

[23] CO 49:253; Calvin, 285.

[24] CO 49:248-49, 255; Calvin, 280, 287.

[25] See, for examples, CO 49:93, 97, 101, 255; Calvin, 109, 113, 117, 287. Melanchthon is a Greek scholar, but he gives little explicit attention to Greek grammar in his commentary on Romans. Luther does give attention to grammar in many of his other commentaries, but not at all in his comments on Romans 5 and 13 and hardly at all in Romans in general.

[26] CO 49:92, 97; Calvin, 108,114. For significant studies on Calvin's exegetical method, see Hans-Joachim Kraus, 'Calvin's Exegetical Principles', *Interpretation*, 31 (1977), 8–18; Richard C. Gamble, '*Brevitas et Facilitas*: Toward an Understanding of Calvin's Hermeneutic', *Westminster Theological Journal*, 47 (1985), 1–17; and T. H. L. Parker, *Calvin's New Testament Commentaries*, 2d ed (Louisville, KY: Westminster John Knox Press, 1993), pp. 85–108. For more recent studies, see David Steinmetz, 'John Calvin as an Interpreter of the Bible', in *Calvin and the Bible*, ed. by Donald K. McKim (New York: Cambridge University Press, 2006), pp. 282–91 and R. Ward Holder, 'Calvin as Commentator on the Pauline Epistles', in ibid., pp. 224–56. All of these scholars point to Calvin's concern for authorial intention and find its roots in his humanism. Holder particularly cautions against giving too modern a reading of Calvin's concern for authorial intention.

[27] WA 56:297; LW 25: 285. CR 15:611; Melanchthon, 122. CO 49:88–89; Calvin, 104.

[28] WA 56:298; LW 25:286.

[29] CR 15:611–13, here 611; Melanchthon, 122–24, here 122.

[30] CR 15:612; Melanchthon, 123.

[31] CR 15:613-14, here 614; Melanchthon, 124, here 125.

[32] CO 49:88, 89, here 89; Calvin, 104, 105, here 105.

[33] CO 49:89; Calvin, 105.

[34] WA 56:301; LW 25:288.

[35] Here Luther asserts that the 'impatient [person] is not yet a Christian' (WA 56:303; LW 25:290). He continues by naming different kinds of persons based upon their degrees of impatience and patience. The lowest degree bears suffering impatiently and seeks a quick release from it; persons in the middle willingly bear suffering but do not seek it; and the highest grade seek suffering 'like a treasure' (WA 56:303–304; LW 25:290–91).

[36] WA 56:304, 305; LW 25:291, 292.

[37] WA 56:305; LW 25:292.

[38] WA 56:308; LW 25:294–9. This theme of freedom and slavery appears more strongly in his comments on Romans 13.

[39] CR 15:615-16, 614-15; Melanchthon, 126–27, 125–26.

[40] CR 15:617, 618; Melanchthon, 127, 128.

[41] CO 49:90; Calvin, 106.

[42] CO 49:91; Calvin, 107.

[43] CO 49:91-92; Calvin, 107–108.

[44] According to Luther, one interpretation teaches that Christ according to his humanity died in time but is alive forever according to his divinity. Another interpretation asserts that Christians are 'weak' according to time but already righteous according to God's predestination. The reading that Luther prefers is simply that Christ died 'when we were not righteous and whole, but rather weak and sickly', and he leaves it at that with no other comments on these verses. See WA 56:309; LW 25:296.

[45] CR 15:619–21; Melanchthon, 129–31.

[46] CO 49:93–94; Calvin, 109–11. For example, Calvin proclaims that if reconciliation is accomplished through Christ's death, how much more will Christ's life sustain the lives of Christians and 'strengthen [their] minds with confidence in [their] salvation' (CO 49:94; Calvin, 110). Likewise, he writes that the whole purpose of the Apostle Paul is to 'establish the confidence and security of our souls' (CO 49:93; Calvin, 109).

[47] CO 49:93; Calvin, 109. The whole purpose of the Apostle Paul, writes Calvin, is to 'establish the confidence and security of our souls' (CO 49:93; Calvin, 109).

[48] WA 56:309-11; LW 25:296–98.

[49] WA 56:312; LW 25:299.

[50] WA 56:315–16, 319; LW 25:302–304, 307.

[51] WA 56:317; LW 25:305. This statement could be seen as an assertion concerning predestination and an implicit denial of a doctrine of universal salvation.

[52] WA 56:318; LW 25:305.

[53] Melanchthon writes that the passage concerns original sin, not actual sins, and he defines original sin much like Luther. He also affirms that the Law cannot take away sin, only reveal it. He concludes, like Luther, that the differences between Christ and Adam are greater than their similarities. See CR 15:622–23, 624–25, 626; Melanchthon, 132–33, 134–35, 136.

[54] CR 15:627, 630–31; Melanchthon, 137–38, 140–42.

[55] CR 15:630; Melanchthon, 139. Melanchthon writes that grace is offered to all, for it is God's will that all be saved; yet, he does add that not everyone will accept this grace.

[56] CO 49:95–97, 102–103; Calvin, 111, 112–13, 119–20.

[57] CO 49:92–93, 98–100; Calvin, 108–109, 115–17. Calvin is clear that neither Rom. 5:6 nor Rom. 5:15–19 speak of universal salvation. On Rom. 5:6 Calvin argues that 'at the right time Christ died for the ungodly' means that Christ died for believers at a time before their actual reconciliation to God. Namely, according to Calvin, Christ dies for the elect, but he does so while they are still ungodly. See CO 49:92–93; Calvin, 108–109.

[58] CO 49:100; Calvin, 117.

[59] CO 49:98, 101; Calvin, 115, 117. Calvin writes, 'In order, however, that we may participate in the grace of Christ, we must be ingrafted into Him by faith. The mere fact of being a man, therefore, is enough to entail participation in the wretched inheritance of sin, for it dwells in human flesh and blood. It is necessary, however, to be a believer in order to enjoy the righteousness of Christ, for we attain to fellowship with Him by faith' (CO 49:100; Calvin, 117).

[60] To be clear: the more 'pro-Calvinist' elements in this revision of the Augsburg Confession have to do with Melanchthon's views on the Lord's Supper.

[61] CR 39:27. For more conversation on Melanchthon's and Calvin's attempts at agreement, see portions of an article by John T. McNeill, 'Calvin's Efforts Toward the Consolidation of Protestantism', *Journal of Religion*, 8 (1928), 414–18. Randall Zachman has more recently argued for a greater emphasis on Calvin's attempts to lessen the differences between himself and Melanchthon. For example, Zachman highlights the friendship between Calvin and Melanchthon and their common interests in the teaching and encouragement of piety. See chapter two in his book, *John Calvin as Teacher, Pastor, and Theologian: The Shape of His Writings and Thought* (Grand Rapids, MI: Baker Academic, 2006), pp. 29–53. Similarly, Zachman emphasizes Calvin's conciliating efforts in his essay, 'The Conciliating Theology of John Calvin: Dialogue among Friends', in *Conciliation and Confession: The Struggle for Unity in the Age of Reform, 1415–1658*, ed. by Howard P. Louthan and Randall C. Zachman (Notre Dame, IN: University of Notre Dame Press, 2004), pp. 89–105. I do not disagree with Zachman's emphasis on Calvin's willingness to find areas of agreement and unity, especially in his relationship with Melanchthon. However, I do not think such an understanding of Calvin and Melanchthon necessarily undermines the point I am trying to make here: namely, that biblical exegesis can be and was used for confessional formation. I am not trying to argue that Calvin and Melanchthon explicitly set out from day one to use biblical exegesis for confessional formation; I am arguing that their particular confessional emphases are evident in their exegesis from very early on and throughout and that this has clear ramifications for

the development and consolidation of the confessions, whether they intended it originally or explicitly or not.

[62] The exegetical tool of Law versus Gospel comes from Luther himself. For a study of the centrality of Law and Gospel in Luther's exegetical method, see Gerhard O. Forde, 'Law and Gospel in Luther's Hermeneutic', *Interpretation*, 37 (1983), 240–52.

[63] CR 15:709–10, 716–17; Melanchthon, 216–17, 222.

[64] CO 49:248–49; Calvin, 280–81.

[65] WA 56:123, 476–77, 478–79, 480; LW 25:109, 468, 469, 471, 473.

[66] CR 15:711–12; Melanchthon, 217–18. CO 49:249, 251; Calvin, 281, 283.

[67] CR 15:713, 715; Melanchthon, 219, 221.

[68] CR 15:714, 712; Melanchthon, 220, 218. This language of insurrection as the work of the devil was used previously by Luther in his treatises against the German Peasants' Revolt. For examples, see WA 18:301, 308, 316, 357, 359–61, 387–88; LW 46:24, 28, 33, 49, 51–55, 67–68.

[69] CO 49:249–50; Calvin, 281.

[70] CO 49:250; Calvin, 282

[71] Ibid. Calvin writes, 'If a wicked ruler is the Lord's scourge to punish the sins of the people, let us reflect that it is our own fault that this excellent blessing of God is turned into a curse'.

[72] For example, this can be seen in his 1522 preface to Romans where Luther writes, 'In chapter 13, [Paul] teaches us to respect and obey the secular authorities' (Dillenberger, 33; WADB 7:25). More pointedly, in his 1523 treatise *Temporal Authority: To What Extent It Should Be Obeyed*, Luther repeatedly refers to Romans 13 in order to argue that the state is ordained by God and should be obeyed out of love of neighbor. See WA 11: 247, 251, 253, 257, 265–66; LW 45: 91, 93, 99, 110. Yet, secular authority does not have the right to command in the area of faith. See WA 11:265–66; LW 45:110.

[73] WA 56:478; LW 25:470.

[74] WA 56:478–79; LW 25:471–72.

[75] WA 56:476–77, there 477; LW 25:468–69, there 469. See also WA 56:480–81; LW 25:473. It is only in these brief statements ('the body is subject to the state' and the 'soul is subject to every human institution') that Luther touches upon obedience to the state. He does acknowledge in his interlinear glosses that Romans 13 concerns civil authorities, and he comments that Paul teaches obedience even to evil rulers. He also affirms that governments are ordained by God for the common good and therefore should be preserved. See WA 56:123; LW 25:109.

[76] Luther adds in his comments on this passage in Romans 13 statements that in respect to secular authorities, Paul does not address the question of freedom and that obedience to governments is neither a matter of freedom nor a matter of servitude. WA 56:480–82; LW 25:473–75. Later Luther will clarify this to argue that a Christian is ultimately free, but out of love of neighbor should obey secular authorities and civil laws. See *Temporal Authority* (1523) in WA 11:250, 253, 254; LW 45: 89, 94, 96.

[77] CR 15:709–12, here 711; Melanchthon, 216–18, here 217.

[78] For example, Melanchthon writes, 'The Gospel does not set up any kind of worldly government, but approves the forms of government ... In public it wants our bodies to be engaged in this civil society and to make sure of the common bonds of this society with decisions about properties, contracts, laws, judgments, magistrates and other things. These external matters do not hinder the knowledge of God ... In fact, God put forth these external matters as opportunities in which faith, calling on God, fear of God, patience, and love might be exercised ... [God] wanted all offices of society to be exercises in confession and, at the same time, exercises of our faith and love' (CR 15:710; Melanchthon, 216).

[79] CR 15:711–12; Melanchthon, 218. This is also the foundation of Melanchthon's reasoning that one should never aim to overthrow governments, since they ultimately belong to God's sovereignty.

[80] CR 15: 714–15; Melanchthon, 220-21. Note that Melanchthon is very much echoing Luther's own alignment of the body's obedience to the state in contrast to the spirit's freedom.

[81] CR 15:716; Melanchthon, 222. The consequence of this teaching of both Luther and Melanchthon is that there is more room to challenge ecclesiastical authority than state authority.

[82] CO 49:249–51; Calvin, 281–83. Calvin particularly sets up the discussion of civil government as part of God's *providence*. See CO 49:249; Calvin, 281. For another study comparing Melanchthon and Calvin's exegeses of Romans 13, see David Steinmetz, 'Calvin and the Civil Magistrate', in *Calvin in Context* by David Steinmetz (New York: Oxford University Press, 1995), pp. 199–211.

[83] WA 56:483–84; LW 25:475–77. One should note that this commentary comes upon the heels of his previous emphasis upon the freedom of a Christian and the proper servitude of being servants to one another through love.

[84] CR 15:718; Melanchthon, 223–24.

[85] CO 49:252–54; Calvin, 284–86. By the time of Calvin's commentary, Luther has already set forth the theology that obedience to secular authorities is part of love of neighbor. Calvin writes that 'to introduce anarchy, therefore, is to violate charity' (CO 49:253; Calvin, 284). The attempt to overthrow governments, then, is in violation of love of neighbor.

[86] WA 56:485–91; LW 25:478–84.

[87] CR 15:718–19; Melanchthon, 224.

[88] CO 49:254–55; Calvin, 286–87.

[89] CR 15:719; Melanchthon, 224–25. CO 49:255; Calvin, 287. In addition, Melanchthon does not comment on the list of vices (Rom. 13:13) at all, whereas Calvin deals with this list by dividing them up into three general kinds of vices: intemperance, carnal lust, and envious and contentious conduct (Calvin, 288; CO 49:256).

[90] CR 15:719; Melanchthon, 225. CO 49:256; Calvin, 288.

[91] See WA 56:477–80, 485–87; LW 25:470–72, 478–79.

[92] Scholars particularly point to his visit to Rome in 1511 as a significant starting point of his disillusionment with Catholic leadership. See, for example, Martin Brecht, *Martin Luther: His Road to Reformation, 1483–1521* (Minneapolis: Fortress, 1985), pp. 73, 98–105.

[93] See his comments on Rom. 13:11–14 in WA 56:487–91;j LW 25:481–84. Martin Brecht points out the importance of Luther's life as a monk in his early years as a scholar and his early biblical exegesis in particular. See Brecht, 46–70, 144–50.

[94] In his comments on love of neighbor (Rom. 13:8–10), Luther does not yet express the clear distinction that faith is the right response to God while works belong to love of neighbor. This is later clearly set forth in his 1520 treatise *The Freedom of a Christian*. See WA 7:49–73, esp 51–53, 64–66, 69; LW 31:343–77, esp. 346–49, 364–67, 371.

[95] See Luther's *Admonition to Peace, A Reply to the Twelve Articles of the Peasants in Swabia* (1525); *Against the Robbing and Murdering Hordes of Peasants* (1525); and *An Open Letter on the Harsh Book against the Peasants* (1525) in WA 18:303–304, 313–14, 357–58, 360–61, 386, 387–88, 389, 391–92; LW 46:25, 31–32, 49, 50, 52–53, 66, 67–68, 70, 73, 74. Luther appeals to verses in Romans 13 several times in each of these documents.

[96] Melanchthon states, 'civil laws obligate more than ecclesiastical laws' (CR 15:716; Melanchthon, 222).

[97] Whereas, the First Table of the Law is fulfilled by faith, but for Calvin, Paul is not here talking about the First Table of the Law. See CO 49:253–54; Calvin, 284–86.

[98] For example, in Calvin's explanation of election as occurring through Christ alone, he writes, 'For since it is into his [Christ's] body the Father has destined those to be engrafted whom he has willed from eternity to be his own, that he may hold as sons all whom he acknowledges to be among his members, we have a sufficiently clear and firm testimony that we have been inscribed in the book of life if we are in communion with Christ' (*Institutes* 3.24.5). Likewise, Calvin writes, 'Christ, when he illumines us into faith by the power of his Spirit, at the same time so engrafts us into his body that we become partakers of every good' (*Institutes* 3.2.35). Moreover, election for Calvin involves regeneration, which is the restoration of the original image of God. Calvin proclaims, 'Therefore, in a word, I interpret repentance as regeneration, whose sole end is to restore in us the image of God that had been disfigured and all but obliterated through Adam's transgression' (*Institutes* 3.3.9).

[99] See Cristina Grenholm and Daniel Patte, 'Receptions, Critical Interpretations, and Scriptural Criticism', in *Reading Israel in Romans*, pp. 19, 19–34.

Response to G. Sujin Pak

David M. Whitford

Professor Pak is to be thanked for taking seriously a task that would make many shudder – comparing Luther, Melanchthon, and Calvin on, of all things, Romans. Further, Professor Pak has chosen two of the most significant chapters out of that weighty book – Romans 5 and 13.

In the Spring of 1515, Luther placed an order with Wittenberg's printer – Johann Grunenberg – for a copy of Romans for himself and his students for an upcoming course. The text contained Jerome's Vulgate version printed down the middle of the page with wide spaces between the lines of text. Likewise the margins were very wide. This allowed Luther to follow a typical Late Medieval lecture format of Glosses and Scholia. It is from these Scholia, largely, that Professor Pak has taken her work. As Pak notes, Luther never returned to lecture on Romans in a formal manner; though he repeatedly returned to themes expressed in Romans. Luther did, however, preserve his copy of the lectures and some of his students from those days did as well. Following his death, his son Paul inherited much of his corpus and the lectures were sold off in the 1590s. For the most part, they were thought lost and as a consequence were never published. A copy of the lectures appeared in the Vatican in the nineteenth century, apparently having arrived there during the Thirty Years' War. The Romans Lectures were first published in 1908 and revised in 1938 in WA 56.[1]

Thus, Professor Pak rightly notes, Martin Luther (unlike Melanchthon and Calvin) never wrote a formal commentary on Romans. What we have, instead, are lecture notes prepared for a class on Romans. This raises a problem when attempting to use these lectures to assess the reception of Romans because we have little knowledge about the degree to which Luther felt free to represent his own opinion in the lectures. As he was a newly appointed professor, we are unable to grasp from this distance how much of what he said was truly his own opinion or the opinions operational around him. Might he, for example, have felt the need to make his dean happy by noting this particular point or that? These things happen every day today; they might very well have happened then as well. Thus, Professor Pak is to be encouraged for delving into this work because it can help us assess what themes might be emerging in Luther; but we cannot ever, I would argue, assume that what we read in public lecture notes represents absolutely his own opinion. Her contention that Melanchthon's lectures represent a continuation of Luther's thought is intriguing and will require further examination before one can conclusively argue for Luther's positive role in Melanchthon's lectures. I would welcome further study by Dr. Pak on this issue because it will not only elucidate the early life of the Reformation in Wittenberg but further our understanding of the complex relationship between Luther and Melanchthon. Using the Lectures on Romans as an avenue for examining Luther's development of theological concerns that will emerge during the Reformation is also very helpful because compared to other early writings of Luther, the Lectures on Romans have received relatively little attention.

To that end, then, it would be helpful to have Professor Pak delve further into the themes that she has explored as Luther's theology develops. For example, she states that Luther cites Patristic writers and other church fathers with both regularity and admiration in the Romans lectures. Does his use of the Fathers in Romans represent an emerging pattern in Luther's exegetical method or a pre-Reformation methodology that is abandoned later? Does his use of scripture to interpret scripture diminish or increase during the 1520s and 30s? Finally, the focus on Law and Gospel is especially interesting and as Professor Pak continues her work in this area I would encourage her to examine the relationship between Luther's understanding of Law and Gospel and that of Melanchthon. This would provide important insights into the relationship between Luther's thoughts on Romans and Melanchthon's. Professor Pak argues, in perhaps the most important thesis of the work, that 'due to the number of very close parallels between Luther and Melanchthon's comments on Romans, I can be reasonably sure that Luther shared his lectures with Melanchthon'.[2] Examining Romans 5:15 in greater detail can provide a small glimpse into the possibilities of this line of research.

In commenting on Romans 15:5, Professor Pak notes that Luther views the pericope largely in terms of original sin and salvation, with a decided bent towards God's grace as a gift. In the Scholia to 5:15, Luther writes:

> The apostle joins together grace and the gift, as if they were different, but he does so in order that he may clearly demonstrate the type of the One who was to come which he has mentioned, namely, that although we are justified by God and receive His grace, yet we do not receive it by our own merit, but it is His gift, which the Father gave to Christ to give to men, according to the statement in Eph. 4:8, 'When He ascended on high, He led a host of captives, and He gave gifts to men'. Therefore these are the gifts of God's grace, which Christ received from the Father through His merit and His personal grace, in order that He might give them to us, as we read in Acts 2:33: 'Having received from the Father the promise of the Holy Spirit, He has poured out this gift which you see'. Thus the meaning is: 'the grace of God' (by which He justifies us, which actually is in Christ as in its origin, just as the sin of man is in Adam) 'and the free gift', namely, that which Christ pours out from His Father upon those who believe in Him. This gift is 'by the grace of that one Man', that is, by the personal merit and grace of Christ, by which He was pleasing to God, so that He might give this gift to us.[3]

In 1515, then, Luther sees the grace of God spoken of by Paul in Romans 5 as a free gift given to humanity by God without merit. Pak is right, therefore, to note that we can begin to see here even as early as 1515 glimpses of what will become a major theological theme in Luther. When she turns to discuss Melanchthon, she writes, 'Melanchthon reiterates this teaching of Luther; however, he explicitly places the conversation within the framework of Law versus Gospel'. This framework emerges after the 1521 edition of Melanchthon's Commentary, however.[4] Thus, it is important to examine what Luther wrote on this text during the 1520s in order to assess Pak's important question about Luther-Melanchthon reciprocity and influence. For example, in 1521, in his passionate diatribe *Against Latomus*, Luther began to explore the ramifications of his new appreciation of the works of the Law versus the Gospel as it relates to Romans 5. In a long discourse, coming near the end of the work, Luther turns to discuss the distinction between the Law and the Gospel. He writes,

> The gospel, on the contrary, deals with sin so as to remove it, and thus most beautifully follows the law. The law introduces us to sin and overwhelms us with the knowledge of it. It does this so that we may seek to be freed and to sigh after grace, for the gospel also teaches and preaches two things, namely, the righteousness and the grace of God.[5]

Following a discussion of the works of the Law and the Gospel, Luther then offers a completely different understanding of Romans 5:15 based on his new understanding of the proper distinction between Law and Gospel. Where before Luther saw the 'Grace of God and the free gift of grace' as synonymous – note that he thought they were the same in 1515 – he now sees them as distinct. Again, Luther writes:

> Faith is the gift and inward good which purges the sin to which it is opposed. It is that leaven which is described in the gospel as wholly hidden under three measures of meal [Matt. 13:33]. The grace of God, on the other hand, is an outward good, God's favor, the opposite of wrath. These two things are distinguished in Rom. 5[:15]: 'For if many died through one man's trespass, much more have the grace of God and the free gift in the grace of that one man Jesus Christ abounded for many'. He calls faith in Christ – which he more often calls a gift – the gift in the grace of one man, for it is given to us through the grace of Christ, because he alone among all men is beloved and accepted and has a kind and gentle God so that he might merit for us this gift and even this grace.[6]

Thus, Luther's new paradigm of Law and Gospel required him to reinterpret 5:15. The 'Grace of God' is now understood as the favor of God that accepts sinful humanity. It is an 'outward good' that forgives us and justifies us freely. It is, he will write even later, based on the relationship established in Christ between God and humanity, not on merit or works. Here we see Luther's understanding of theology as testament. We are saved not because of what we do, but because of who we are. The 'gift of grace' is now distinguished from the 'grace of God'; Luther now understands it to be the gift that follows justification. It is the fruit of the Spirit and the gift that enables us to begin our journey towards sanctification. Thus, when we look at other places in the Luther corpus where he returns to themes arising in Romans 5, we find that he has begun to explore the implications of Law and Gospel. It would be very fruitful to track the similarities between Luther's thought on this and Melanchthon's expressions in his 1532 Commentary.[7]

Professor Pak has provided us with a stimulating and thought-provoking essay that highlights the fruits that can be harvested by looking at the ways in which theologians who share similar (and not so similar) positions exegete scriptural texts for theological reflection.

Notes

[1] This paragraph is dependent upon the Introduction to Volume 25 of the American Edition of Luther's Works.

[2] Pak, n. 4.

[3]Martin Luther (1999, c1972). *Vol. 25: Luther's works, vol. 25: Lectures on Romans* (J. J. Pelikan, H. C. Oswald & H. T. Lehmann, ed.). *Luther's Works* (Saint Louis: Concordia Publishing House).

[4] See CR 15: 456–460 for the 1521 text of Melanchthon's Commentary on Romans. While the Law and the Gospel are discussed, they do not provide the framework for the chapter's discussion. That framework appears in the 1532 edition, which is substantially longer and more in-depth.

[5] LW 32.227.

[6] LW 32.227.

[7] See Luther's Lectures on Psalm 51, LW 12.376. See also, F. Edward Cranz, *Luther's Thought on Justice, Law and Society* (Cambridge, HUP, 1959) for a discussion of this very point (pp. 40–50).

— EIGHT —

Bullinger on Romans[1]

Peter Opitz

◆

Introduction

The commentary on Romans of Heinrich Bullinger (1504–1575), Reformer of Zürich and successor of Zwingli, which was first printed in 1533[2], has so far not gained adequate recognition of its significance and rightful place in the history of Protestant interpretation of Romans.[3] This is despite the fact that this is the commentary of a Reformer whose influence exceeded the influence of Calvin in Upper Germany and in European Protestantism in general in many aspects.[4] The period of Bullinger's activity spans half a century. **C** The 'fathers' of the Swiss Reformation Zwingli and Oecolampadius, important German 'humanist reformers' like Bucer and Melanchthon, and leading exegetes of the incipient 'Reformed Orthodoxy' like Vermigli and Beza, were among his personal conversation partners even when it came to discussions concerning exegesis[5]. However, Bullinger's humanist formation and his aversion against 'scholastic theology'[6] created a lifelong reticence toward 'Aristotelian' methods which seemed to him inadequate to the living language of biblical texts. As a consequence his exegetical method always remained close to Zwingli, Oecolampadius, and Erasmus in particular.

As first pastor of the Zürich church, Bullinger decisively contributed to the development and sustainability of the Zürich 'Hohen Schule'. **H** In this 'School' of higher theological education the aim was to apply thoroughly the best humanist methods for the exegesis of written texts to the exegesis of the Old and the New Testament and thereby put these in the service of Reformation theology and preaching. It is self-evident that in this early modern humanist-reformed exegesis, significant 'modern' aspects can be discovered, but there are also strong continuities with medieval exegetical practice. This holds true also for Bullinger's interpretation of Romans.[7] This bears witness to his significant participation in the process of hermeneutical reflection[8] which became necessary since the programmatically declared Scripture principle had to be applied to concrete exegesis in order to prove its value.

C Theological conversation partners as context of Bullinger's writing.

H Hermeneutical presupposition that humanist methods are the best to serve exegetical task in relation to reformation theology.

Bullinger's Lectures on Romans in Kappel 1525

After the completion of his Master's studies in Cologne, Bullinger worked as a public teacher between 1523 and 1529 at the convent of the Cistercians in Kappel, which was under the jurisdiction of Zürich. The abbot of the convent, Wolfgang Joner, who was favorably disposed toward the Reformation movement, had appointed Bullinger on the 17th January 1523 when he was only 19 years of age. Bullinger made full use of his time there to clarify his own theology and also lectured regularly in public on the exegesis of books of the New Testament. In 1525 he reached Romans – this was the year when Zwingli initiated the Zürich *Prophezei* and 14 years prior to Calvin's commentary on Romans. Bullinger's handwritten notes of his lectures on Romans 1–5 have now been made available in a published edition. [9] Doubtless these formed the core of the later Latin commentary which appeared in print in 1533. In her analysis of these early Bullinger lectures, Susi Hausmann[10] discerned the following sources and exegetical tools: the Vulgate, Erasmus's edition and annotations, the annotations of Faber Stapulensis, and a German translation, most likely a reprint of Luther's September Testament (with linguistic variations).[11] In addition Bullinger mentions in his *Diarium* that he also consulted the commentaries of Origen, Ambrosiaster, Theophylactus and Melanchthon (probably the latter's 1522 annotations to the letter to the Romans). He particularly praises Erasmus as the king of the Graecists.[12] Even after the final theological and ecclesial separation between Humanism and the Reformation, Bullinger continued to adhere to Erasmus as his teacher in philological matters.[13]

Already during his Kappel lectureship and in conjunction with his lecturing in exegesis, Bullinger took detailed account of the exegetical methods of the Bible. An account of these can be found in his unpublished *De Propheta Libri Duo*, the core of which was incorporated in his Zürich inaugural lecture of 1532.[14] A more comprehensive account is found in his *Studiorum ratio,* originally a study guide in the manner of the humanist tradition, which he had formulated as a guide to practice.[15] Dealing with such themes as organizing your daily study time, and questions relating to the exegesis of particular biblical books, the work came to completion in 1528 when Bullinger was 24 years of age; but it was never published during his life-time.

The Romans Commentary of 1533: Context, Purpose and Method

Context and Purpose

Information concerning the context, purpose and method of the 1533 Romans commentary, which we will now consider, is provided by two Prefaces from Bullinger. The first is the Preface to the 1533[16] Romans commentary itself, and the second is the Preface to the 1537[17] composite edition of the commentaries on all the New Testament Epistles.

A In the latter Bullinger locates his enterprise within the context of the whole of church history perceived as the history of the exegesis of the Bible, and thus within the Reformation's rediscovery of the priority of the Scriptures. As a result of the deterioration of biblical exegesis and the direct study of Scripture since Augustine and Jerome, the scholarly world was preoccupied with speculative questions

---

A Bullinger's analysis of the state of biblical interpretation prior to the Reformation.

emerging, for example, with Thomas Aquinas and Duns Scotus. In parallel to this, the practice of preaching was based on collections of sermons of doubtful origin and quality with the result that the majority of pastors had no first-hand knowledge of the Bible.[18]

It is directly from this perception of the church in history that Bullinger's goal proceeded. **H** The purpose of his commentary cannot therefore be to lead away from the biblical Scriptures but exactly the opposite – to provide entrance into them and thus provide ways to their understanding, with the sole purpose of serving the honor and truth of Christ.[19] Accordingly his exegesis, as he stresses already in the first sentence of his Preface, must not be viewed as divine command but rather as exegetical possibility.[20] Bullinger views himself as part of a community of exegetes who offered their interpretations as a basis for discussion, which also had a diachronic dimension. Time and again he refers to examples of exegesis from the tradition, in particular from the Ancient Church, especially when he agrees with them. Beside Ambrosiaster and Jerome as exegetes, among many others the overall presence of Augustine needs to be noted here.[21] Ultimately the concern is to open the biblical text, not with one's own originality. Thus a lenient attitude towards the errors of previous scriptural exegetes is more appropriate than harsh criticism. [22]

The specific occasion for the working out and printing of a complete commentary on Romans came from the request of Berchtold Haller, his colleague from Bern. The latter had asked him for his exegetical notes on Romans so that he could use them in his preparation for sermons on Romans. This is the reason Bullinger dedicated to Haller his Romans commentary which appeared in print in 1533, a few months after the latter's request,[23] and why the most significant themes in the exegesis of Romans were summarized in the Preface.[24]

It follows from this that Bullinger's Romans commentary must be viewed as a development in Latin of his original German series of lectures of 1525. This was completed in the shortest possible time and at a critical phase of the Reformation in the Swiss Federation. **C** Bullinger had not yet completed his first year in office as the successor of Zwingli. After the latter's sudden death and the resultant political crisis for the Reformation in Zürich and also in Bern a clear and decisive stance for the reformed cause was absolutely essential. Already in his Karlstag Address printed in 1532 Bullinger had laid out programmatically his understanding of the office of ministry.[25] Decisive for this office is that, being perceived as a prophetic office, its essence is the exegesis of Scripture in the service of and for the upbuilding of the congregation:

> the task of a true prophet is none other than ... to exegete the Holy Scriptures, to oppose errors and evils, to further the fear of God and truth, and finally not only to offer righteousness, faith and mutual love to the hearts of men with full eagerness and zeal, but to heavily press these upon them. It is also his task to strengthen the faint, to comfort the sad, and encourage and exhort those failing or falling behind in the way of the Lord. [26]

Basic to this is Bullinger's understanding of Paul, particularly his exegesis of 1 Cor. 14:3. Bullinger's Romans commentary, published a little later, was thus conceived as a

---

H Presupposition of the role of reading: interpretation is not divine command but suggests an exegetical possibility.

C Context of Bullinger's commentary.

help in the practice of such a prophetic office in the reformed pulpits in his sphere of influence. As a consequence, Bullinger's main intention was not to write a commentary dealing with every philological detail. Instead the practical goal, to give a concise overview over the main topics of the Pauline letter which should be dealt with in the pulpit, prevailed. That Bullinger regularly clarifies Greek words and sentences by 'German' or 'Swiss' expressions is only one of several indications of this intention.[27]

Exegetical Methods

Bullinger's exegetical method, as set out in his 1537 Preface, springs from his preparatory hermeneutical works from the time in Kappel and should be understood in the light of this background. In order to unfold the 'meaning' of the text certain specific methodological steps must be observed. **H** It is above all a matter of being true to the Greek text. In view of his own abilities in the philological sphere, which he himself perceived as limited, Bullinger relied primarily on the works of Erasmus, and he only adds to these minor points through his own study of the Greek vocabulary.[28] Rare words must be clarified, linguistic unevenness must be smoothed out and Hebraisms explained. Bullinger put much weight on the rhetorical analysis of the epistle. The line of thought and the scope of the text must be worked out and the differing parts of the text organized in relation to this.[29] Thus the loci[30] to which the pericope is related, are only noted, not actually dealt with. Further, what appears foreign within the text must be translated into one's own time and context. Finally, 'heretical' exegeses must be contradicted, and this in simple, understandable speech. All of these steps can be found again in the Romans commentary but they are not developed in relation to every single pericope.[31] The discrepancy between Bullinger's exegetical theory, laid out in his prefaces, and his practice has certainly to do with his office as first pastor of Zürich. As the leading figure of the Swiss Reformation after Zwingli's death, it was his responsibility to meet the practical needs of the Swiss Protestant churches of his time, among them to help the Protestant pastors, most of them educated in the Roman Catholic tradition, to interpret the Bible in the pulpit.[32]

The theological foundation which guides and legitimates this approach is spelt out in the 1533 dedication address to Berchtold Haller. **H** Above all, Bullinger takes up a position against the obscurity of Scripture, and thereby promotes the Reformation stance of the perspicuity of Scripture. He does this by means of an argument concerning the doctrine of God: God who is truth and himself brightest of all light cannot be the origin of obscurity.[33] The darkness of failure in understanding is for this reason on the human side. But this theological argument in no way means that Bullinger glosses over problems and difficulties in the exegesis of Scripture.[34] This is rather the starting point that sets in motion his hermeneutical thinking. Thus it follows that Paul, and through his message God himself, should be read as a rhetorician who intends to make himself intelligible. This means moreover paying attention to the language, its peculiarity, its rhetorical figures and its character as address, its contexts and its flow. Even the specific rhetorical style of Paul must be

---

H The emphasis on philology is due to the Humanist presupposition that return to 'origins' serves the purpose of getting closer to the truth.

H Theological foundation that Scripture is meant to be understood.

taken into account. Decisive above all is that Paul, speaking in normal human manner, does so with the intention to be understood.[35]

Through this, Bullinger campaigns against a dialectial-logical use of isolated biblical sentences like that in medieval theological *summae*, and simultaneously against seeking after an intrinsic hidden meaning of the text. The traditional medieval hermeneutical movement, we might say, is thus reversed. In opposition to what Bullinger calls a *superstitious* treatment of the biblical text, he promotes the use of the rhetorical method as the tool which enables the Pauline letters to be interpreted as living human language and likewise as goal-directed speech.[36] The obscurities in the Scripture are not due the hiddenness of divine truth; they arise on the contrary from the ambivalences of human speech. [37]

In the 1537 Preface, Bullinger eventually addresses the scope of the entire biblical message. This consists in the proclamation of the one and only true, living and eternal God in Christ. For in Christ God offers human beings *omnis plenitudo*, in him to us is all fullness given and transmitted to us.[38] In accordance with this stands the motto from Matt 17:5 which Bullinger put on the cover of almost all his writings, and also on the title page of the commentary on all the apostolic letters.[39] By means of this the covenant concept which Bullinger often used, especially in view of the Old Testament, is not displaced but explicitly formulated in its Christological dimension. In what follows some of the fundamental emphases of Bullinger's exegesis of Romans will be highlighted.

The Pauline Message to the Romans

The Occasion and the Structure of Romans

Bullinger perceives the letter to the Romans not as a decontextualized theological treatise, and also not as a timeless presentation of the pure gospel, but as the proclamation of the gospel in a specific historical situation by Paul, who was called to be apostle to the Gentiles (Rom. 1:1f.). Already when in Kappel Bullinger had devoted detailed attention to the historical background of the letter to the Romans.[40] He sought to find information about the time of composition from Rom. 15:25 f.[41], along with Acts 11:27–30. He also drew in all available extra-biblical material, including information from Suetonius, Josephus and Eusebius. [42]

HC Decisive for the understanding of the letter is its occasion. This consists in the threat of 'false prophets'[43] who stress that human beings can achieve righteousness from the doing of the law. In support of this Bullinger refers to Rom. 16:17–20. Following Jerome, Bullinger calls them *Nazarenes*. They are the same group who also cause confusion for the congregations in Galatia, Corinth and elsewhere.[44] Characteristic for their doctrine is that they are not consistent in holding fast to *solus Christus*, but add to their confession of Christ the demand to do the works of law. [45]

In Romans Paul expounds the gospel in the face of this obscuring of its message. From this arises the rhetorical character of the letter: in as much as Paul sets out the gospel in Romans in a didactic style which takes up the greatest part of the letter, this is in the pattern of the *genus demonstrativum*. But also in so far as Paul accuses and convicts of sin, as he does in Romans 1–3, he uses the *genus iudiciale*. The

---

HC Contextual dimension as hermeneutical guide for reading.

comforting passages, such as are found in Romans 7 and 8, should be reckoned on the other hand as in the *genus deliberativum*.[46]

According to Bullinger's *argumentum* to Romans the letter consists of three parts: In the first part (chapters 1–8) the topic is, as demonstrated by his marginal notes, 'true righteousness' and 'the essence of the gospel'. In the second part (chapters 9–11) the issue is 'the rejection of the Jews and the call of the Gentiles', and finally in the third part (chapters 12–16) paraenesis on various topics.[47]

On the Exegesis of Romans 1–8

As the first eight chapters of Romans entail all the main points of the gospel[48] Bullinger dedicates 74 pages to this first part, compared to 19 pages dedicated to Romans 9–11 and 25 pages dedicated to Romans 12–16. Only some of the most important aspects of his exegesis can be mentioned here.

Bullinger's structuring of Romans 1–8

It is worth paying some detailed attention to Bullinger's differentiated structuring of Romans 1–8. **A** The core doctrine of Romans, as presented by Bullinger in the *argumentum*, is that righteousness is given to us neither on the basis of works of merit nor through observance of religious laws but only through faith.[49] This is what Paul means when he summarizes the scope at the beginning of his argumentation as follows: *the righteous one lives by faith* (Rom. 1:17).[50]

In teaching this thesis and elaborating it in detail, Paul addresses at the same time the current dispute between Jewish and Gentile Christians concerning the meaning of the law and demolishes its cause.[51]

Thus Paul sets out in the first five chapters through differing lines of argumentation that nothing but sin emerges from human beings themselves. Righteousness on the other hand comes from God, and this alone through Christ, and is acknowledged through faith alone as illustrated in the case of Abraham.[52] This theme is further developed and deepened in chapters 6–8. As a whole, chapters 1–8 follow the line of argument of John 16:8–11[53]: Paul first convicts Jews as well as Gentiles of sin (Rom. 1:18–3.20; cf. John 16:9). Sin consists ultimately not in specific deeds but in lack of faith, in the failure to recognize the never-ending kindness of God as the sole source and author of all good.[54] This failure, which in fact is a refusal out of human arrogance, inevitably leads to idolatry. Romans 2 gives Bullinger the opportunity to outline the history of idolatry, which comprises pagan and Jewish forms as well as idolatry and the cult of images in the Christian Church. Even Gregory's claim that the pictures are the Bible for the illiterate is challenged here.[55] Paul's overall distinction according to Bullinger is the distinction between 'false' and 'true' religion.[56]

Secondarily, Paul elaborates on the nature of the 'righteousness' which consists in 'iustificatio', based on the death of Christ on the cross and his resurrection (Rom. 3:21–5:21; cf. John 16:10f). This is what is meant when Christ according to John 16:11 combines the 'iustitia' with his 'going to the Father' (i.e. the death, resurrection and ascension of Christ).[57] And thirdly the topic is the 'sentence' (Rom. 6–8; cf. John

---

A Analysis of Bullinger's structuring of Romans 1–8.

16:11). This means the devil and his claim over humans through the power of sin has been annulled and justly judged through the death of Christ, as Romans 6 demonstrates. Since the power and claim of sin is 'judged', the Christians are freed, which means awakened to a life of 'piety ... faith, innocence and love'.[58]

The subject matter of Romans 1–8 therefore is the constitution and creation of righteousness, the creation of new life, and also the practicing and outworking of the new created life of freedom.[59] What the departing Christ had promised concerning the Spirit of truth now takes concrete form in the proclamation of Paul the apostle to the nations (Rom. 1:1). His message is not difficult to grasp. All 'the mysteries of the gospel' are according to Bullinger set forth in the first chapters of Romans. They consist simply in the forgiveness of sins and life restored through Christ.[60]

Christ as Omnis Plentitudo

The material above already indicates that Bullinger aims at interpreting what he calls the scope of Romans, 'iustum ex fide vivere' (Rom. 1:17), ultimately not as a doctrine about the way to 'justification' but as witnessing to Christ himself, the only source and fullness of all good. The 'forgiveness of sins' and the 'restored life', 'righteousness', and 'sanctification' are achieved through the death and resurrection of Christ, and participation in both is possible only through faith in Christ. For it is faith in Christ through which 'all fullness is given' to us, and as spirit-created faith it is simultaneously participation in the Spirit of the resurrected Christ himself, that is, in the Spirit promised in John 16:8–11, which is also at work in the Pauline proclamation. According to Bullinger, the Pauline and the Johannine witness mutually interpret each other.

In Romans, as likewise in Galatians and Hebrews,[61] Paul unfolds this message of Christ as *omnis plenitudo* in particular ways in relation to the righteousness of human beings in dispute with *judaizing* Christians. Whereas Hebrews deals primarily with the assertion of the *lex ceremonialis* as the way to salvation, Romans unfolds the message of Christ above all in opposition to the assertion of attending to the *lex moralis* as the way to righteousness – and demonstrates at the same time where the true source of life in accordance with the divine and permanently valid *lex moralis* lies. The fact that 'all fullness' is both contained and revealed in Christ, means that the righteousness of man is available in him alone and through him:

> The most important principle of Christian faith on which all others depend is this, that in Christ the entire fullness is contained (cf. Col. 1:19), and that therefore all who are justified are justified only and exclusively through faith in him and on no other ground. For this is the essence of the entire gospel. This is the theme of all the letters of Paul, but especially of those written to the Romans, the Galatians, and the Hebrews.[62]

As far as Romans is concerned, the matter, though not the expression, is according to Bullinger always present. When for example Paul in Romans 10:3–10 contrasts the 'righteousness through the law' (*iustitia legis*) and the 'righteousness through faith' (*iustitia fidei*), he contrasts all kinds of fictitious ways to righteousness with the 'righteousness of God' (*dei iustitia*), which is nothing else than Christ himself, apprehended by faith. For Christ has 'reconciled' us with the Father and 'fulfilled' the law.[63] Paul's reference to Dt. 30:14 in Rom. 10:6–8 issues a call to hear the 'near' word of the proclamation of Christ, which means the message of the 'fullness of Christ',[64] as Bullinger formulates it and explains by a brief excursus on the 'essence of faith' (*summa fidei*). Thus the call to 'listen to Christ' is addressed to both, the Jews who are familiar with the law and all those who have lost their way in philosophical traditions or theological speculation.[65] **AH** Bullinger's motto from Mt. 17:5 characterizes also his exegesis of Romans. But listening to Christ means having faith in Christ, which is possible only in pneumatological union with Christ, i.e., in participation in Christ's spirit of love.[66] Again Bullinger connects Paul with John: the 'closeness' of God's word (Rom. 10:8; Dt. 30:14) is interpreted by John 6.[67]

This is also confirmed by a glance at Bullinger's exegesis of Rom. 1:16ff. where Paul explains the essence of the gospel.[68] The *dynamis theou*, which Paul addresses, is ultimately nothing else than Christ in person, 'in whom God grants the whole world all fullness',[69] and calls to nothing else than to 'faith'.

On the interpretation of the quotation from Habakkuk 2:4 (*ex fide in fidem)* to which Paul refers, Bullinger rejects any solution which question the *sola fide*: it means neither the transition from *fides informis* to *fides formata*,[70] nor the transition from Old Testament to New Testament faith,[71] nor an individual growth in faith. Not only is any human work excluded from the perspective of justification by faith, but even faith itself may in no way be perceived as a work, as Bullinger emphasizes following Oecolampadius.[72] Over against this he proposes two interpretive options: The phrase can simply be understood as a pleonastic form of speech as is often encountered in the Bible and elsewhere. It serves here to underline the meaning of faith.[73] Alternatively the expression can be understood in the sense of trust in God's faithfulness (*ex fide*) and steadfastness (*in fidem*), thus taking into account the fact that the Hebrew *emet* encompasses both, as Bullinger had learnt from Luther.[74] With this second option Bullinger links back to his lectures of 1525. That *fides* encompasses the element of *faithfulness* both on the part of human beings as well as God is always emphasized by Bullinger. Thus as an illustration of human *fides* he refers also to Heb. 10:38 , where Habakkuk 2:4 is also in view, and at the same time to the concept of faith in Hebrews 11.[75] The divine *fides* is on the other hand identical with God's *faithfulness*, his *fidelitas* and *veritas*, as Bullinger says in his explication of Rom 3:7, and there also with reference to the Hebrew *emet*.[76]

Christ as God's Son and Messiah

With this a further significant aspect of Bullinger's interpretation of Romans comes in view, which provides also the background of his exegesis of Rom. 10:4: the significance of the Hebraic-biblical tradition. **H** For Bullinger in the Pauline proclamation of Christ two trajectories of thought must be noted: on the one hand the theology of incarnation, which confesses Christ as the place of God becoming human, and on the other hand the history of tradition which sees Christ as the Messiah, the fulfiller of salvation history. Thus Paul immediately in Rom. 1:1 confesses Christ as the 'Son of God' and as the 'Christ' from the seed of David promised by the prophets. For the New Testament message of Paul as well as other New Testament writers is strengthened by the Hebrew Bible and it is in fact derived from it.[77]

Accordingly Bullinger finds at the beginning of Romans a biblical precedent for the 'divinity' of Christ and thus for the appropriateness of the Christological dogma.[78]

AH Analysis of the role of one of Bullinger's guiding principles.
H Bullinger's dual hermeneutical presupposition.

On the other hand he always pays close attention to the Pauline argumentation from the Old Testament. Although Paul, as the Pharisaic Jew from the school of Gamaliel,[79] has been called to become apostle to the nations according to God's will, he has, because of his education, a special ability to argue from 'Law and the Prophets' in relation to the Jews for the Messiahship of Jesus,[80] and he actually does so in diverse ways in his letters. The Pauline gospel is not new but links back to the prophetic promises and the Davidic royal tradition of the Hebrew Bible. From this ancient tradition Paul derives a good part of his authority.[81]

C A significant historical background for Bullinger's emphasis is the dispute with the Anabaptists, who negated the validity of the Old Testament. Over against these Bullinger emphasized always the continuity of the Old and New Testaments and did this by means of countless references from the Pauline writings, which explicitly refer to the Hebrew biblical tradition. From Romans, alongside Rom. 1:1, one can also mention Rom. 4:23.[82] Bullinger understands the principle that the Scripture interprets itself in such a way that the New Testament must be read within the faith tradition of the Hebrew Bible, and he holds that such a reading can act as a corrective to the subjectivity of biblical interpretation. [83]

On the Exegesis of Romans 9–11

Bullinger's emphasis on the Hebrew biblical tradition also has implications for his doctrine of God. Here he specifically emphasizes God's 'community faithfulness'. The gospel as the fulfillment of the ancient promises (Rom. 1:1) or the Pauline emphasis on *pistis* in its Hebrew meaning make this clear: faithfulness, truth and righteousness according to the Hebrew are different sides of same divine favour to humans. It is God's faithfulness to his promises, to his covenant and thus to humans as his creation, that motivates and determines his action and word.[84] Accordingly Bullinger underlines again and again the divine patience with his rebellious creatures, God's *longanimitas*.[85] But faithfulness also means that God does not get into conflict with himself; but rather he pursues and executes his one purpose of salvation despite human opposition without distraction. From this presupposition Bullinger also reads Romans 9–11. In distinction from other Reformation contemporaries who interpret this passage more or less directly in relation to the individual believer and who view Paul as being concerned with the mysterious depth of divine election and rejection, Bullinger proceeds on the basis that Paul even here is not presenting an abstract doctrine of God but rather writes concretely as a proclaimer of the gospel in its kerygmatic and paraenetic dimension. And he does this in the light of the historical situation in which it is obvious that the Jews in their majority have rejected Christ and still do so. According to the witness of Acts (Acts 13:46) it was this that led to the mission of Paul to the Gentiles. Therefore Romans 9–11 is interpreted by Bullinger not as a doctrine of a divine decree which precedes the divine universal purpose of salvation revealed in Christ, leaving it open to question. God is not the author of malice and evil, and wants 'all humans to be saved and to come to the knowledge of the truth.'[86] **H** Romans 9–11 should rather be read as address, as a warning against continuing in unbelief, and at the same time as comfort.

C Contextual factor which leads to such strong emphasis on the significance of the Hebrew Bible.

H Theological supposition shapes Bullinger's interpretation of Romans 9–11.

Unlike the interpretations of contemporaries like Beza, for Bullinger Romans 9–11 does not constitute the theological foundation of Romans 1–8. Paul's line of thought is rather the other way round. He sees himself in need of addressing the call of the Gentiles because of the rejection of the gospel by those Jews who look to their tradition and to works, as well as by those Gentiles who want to adhere to their ignorance. The question of 'predestination' is thereby dealt with only incidentally.[87] Thus chapters 9 and 10 are essentially to be interpreted as Paul's admonishments to the Jews to submit in faith to the gospel.[88] Chapter 11 according to Bullinger is a chapter of comfort: the issue here is to soften the terror which the thought of the rejection of Israel causes, and to warn Jews as well as Gentiles not to boast over and despise the other.[89] Thus Bullinger entitles chapter 11 'The restoration of Israel'[90] and he understands the Pauline phrases in Rom. 11:25–32 in such a way that the Jews' coming to faith in the Messiah is promised.[91]

Bullinger remains coherent in his adherence to his basic/foundational thought: God's essence is unchangeable and so is his will. However, God's will is this: He does not want injustice and he does not want the death of the sinner but, his repentance and his life. He pursues this goal with impressive *longanimitas*. That the latter at some time will come to an end renders the proclamation of grace its serenity, since this is the living God rather than a metaphysical principle. It is not our business to ask what God's intention was prior to the foundation of the world.[92] But this is certain: God does not act in the manner of a tyrant, according to the motto 'Sic volo, sic iubeo'.[93]

In relation to the hardening of Pharaoh (Rom. 9:17f), according to Bullinger, the kindness of God, expressed in scholastic terms, is the 'causa sine qua non', but not the 'causa efficiens'.[94] The emphasis for Bullinger lies also here on the proclamation of God's *longanimitas*. Bullinger can thus present Pharaoh as an example for all humans. He is able to do this only because also he views the second part of Romans and its doctrine of God in the light of the first part. So therefore the hardening of the heart of Pharaoh must be understood not as an inexplicable arbitrary act of God through which he rejects individual humans so that they shut themselves out of his favor, but rather as the divine reaction to Pharaoh's lack of repentance and insistence in the face of God's *longanimitas*, in analogy to Rom. 1:18–3.20. Bullinger can connect God's decision to reject Pharaoh with the divine foreknowledge of Pharaoh's future failure to repent. However, he does not draw metaphysical consequences from that. Instead his sole intention is to remain faithful to his theological concept that God is the source of all good and his will is expressed by 1Tim 2:4.[95] It is part of God's nature that all whom he saves he saves by pure grace, but at the same time he does not condemn anyone except as a consequence of the sinner's own guilt.[96]

Also the 'unsearchability' of the divine decisions which Paul recalls with reference to Isa. 45:9 and Jer. 18:6 are put more precisely by Bullinger: it is valid in relation to God's activity in history but not in relation to the divine will for humans. This is known in Christ and stands fast as his will for salvation.[97] **H** The divine will for salvation as manifested in Christ, combined with the call to faith for everyone, as explained in Romans 1–8, stands also as the theological criterion for the interpretation of Romans 9–11 and should not be restricted or questioned by this second part.

H What is identified as theological focus of Romans 1–8 is also the hermeneutical framework for reading Romans 9–11, according to Bullinger.

On the Exegesis of Romans 12–16

The third part of Romans consists, according to Bullinger, of various kinds of paraenesis, which address actual questions in the Romans community, questions, however, that are later asked again in the life of the Christian community. These present Bullinger in various ways with the occasion to relate the Pauline guidance to his own time and to apply these moments of guidance in controversial theological disputes against 'heretical' and otherwise inappropriate exegeses. With reference to Melanchthon, Bullinger sees Romans 12 as dealing with 'private' matters and Romans 13 with the 'public' sphere.[98] The main topic of Romans 14, however, is not, as Melanchthon had claimed, the 'ceremonies', but 'scandals' and the appropriate use of Christian freedom.[99] Zwingli's 'theology of freedom'[100] seems to be reflected here.

Paul's paraenesis in Romans 12 according to Bullinger explains what it means that 'God is spirit and want to be adored spiritually'.[101] Christian worship is not a matter of religious ceremonies but rather of the Christian 'person', and thus it is a matter of ethics and conduct of individual and social life.[102]

A As far as political life is concerned, Bullinger takes Romans 13 as an occasion to outline briefly the principles of his understanding of Christian government, and to refer to the distinction between legitimate power in the public-political sphere on the one hand and the prohibition of private revenge as formulated in the Sermon on the Mount on the other.[103] Bullinger's emphasis beyond the biblical text consists in his stress on the responsibility of Christian rulers for their actions before God. He refers to the limits of their commission and asserts that one must obey God more than humans.[104] The Pauline summons of Romans 13:1–7 is for Bullinger simultaneously an opportunity for a polemic against the Anabaptists, who without cause resist the political order.[105]

The passage concerning the 'weak and the strong' in Rom. 14:1–15:6 provides Bullinger with the opportunity to argue pointedly against any form of outward cultic religiosity, be it monastic food laws or generally the religious exploitation of the people by the Roman church, the 'tyrants of our time'.[106] Paul according to Bullinger intends specifically (again) to indicate that God is spirit and that he must be revered 'in spirit and in truth'.[107] This means ultimately nothing other than: through faith and love in the form of 'repentance and blamelessness of life'.[108] Even in the exegesis of varied Pauline paraeneses Bullinger always tries to understand these within the scope of the entire letter to the Romans: 'iustum ex fide vivere', which means linking them back to the life-giving spirit of Christ himself, the source of all good.[109]

Conclusion

Bullinger's interpretation of Romans is characterized by a high hermeneutical consciousness, which had emerged already in the mid-20's, at the peak of the activity of the first generation of Reformers. His intent to make fruitful application of humanist exegetical methods, especially rhetoric, for a Reformed exegesis of Romans is, however, never an end in itself but stands very concretely in the service of the proclamation of the central Reformed insights during a critical phase of the Reformation. These insights are quite simple. Although presented in flexible forms of speech and not in fixed theological terminology, Romans according to Bullinger is

---

A Bullinger's emphasis on Romans 13 is analyzed.

ultimately to be understood in all its parts as proclamation of 'solus Christus' and 'sola fide', both being interpreted against the Hebrew biblical tradition of promise. On the basis of these two axioms he views Paul as arguing in relation to the Roman community and their questions, and both of these should consequently be brought to expression in the interpretation of Romans in the pulpits of the present time. Faith, to which Paul, invites, is simply to let Christ be what he is: the living and life-giving center in which all of God's fullness dwells ('omnis plenitudo'; Col. 1:19). Bullinger's interpretation of Romans corresponds to his understanding of the scope of the entire biblical message.

Translation by Kathy Ehrensperger

Notes

[1] In accordance with the concept of this volume the focus here is on central aspects of Bullinger's exegesis of Romans. For a more detailed analysis of Bullinger's Paulinism, see Peter Opitz, 'Bullinger and Paul', in *Paul in the Reformation*, R. Ward Holder (ed.), (Leiden: Brill, 2008).

[2] Bullinger, *In Omnes Apostolicas Epistolas Commentarii, HBBibl* 1, Nr 84–89 9 quoted, as *In epistolas*.

[3] The work of the recognized Calvin scholar T. H. L. Parker is in this respect unsatisfactory (*Commentaries on the Epistle to the Romans 1532–1542* [Edinburgh 1986], quoted asParker, *Romans*). Without any reference to historical embeddedness, Calvin is here not only at the center of attention but at the same time is taken to be the criterion of evaluation. Bullinger's significance for Calvin's Romans commentary, which Calvin himself explicitly acknowledges (cf. COR II.XIII, p. 4 = CO 10b, p. 404), has been decisively outlined by Fritz Büsser ('Bullinger as Calvin's Model in Biblical Exposition: An Examination of Calvin's Preface to the Epistle to the Romans', in *In Honor of John Calvin 1509–1564: Papers from the 1986 International Calvin Symposium*, E. J. Furcha (ed.) [Montreal 1987], pp. 64–95). Other impulses, above all from Bucer, but also Calvin's humanist education as is already evident in his *De Clementia* commentary von 1532 (CO 5, p. 5–162), need not be designated as being of secondary importance. See also J. E. Kok, 'Heinrich Bullinger's Exegetical Method: The Model for Calvin?', *Biblical Interpretation in the Era of Reformation: Essays Presented to David C. Steinmetz in Honor of His Sixtieth Birthday*, Richard A. Muller and John L. Thompson (eds.) (Grand Rapids: Eerdmans, 1996), pp. 241–254.

[4] Some results of the recent research on Heinrich Bullinger: Fritz Büsser, *Heinrich Bullinger. Leben, Werk und Wirkung*, 2 vols. (Zürich 2004) [quoted as Büsser, *Bullinger*]; Peter Opitz, *Heinrich Bullinger als Theologe. Studien zu den* Dekaden (Zurich, 2004); Emidio Campi and Peter Opitz, *Heinrich Bullinger: Life – Thought – Influence. Zurich, Aug. 25–29, 2004. International Congress Heinrich Bullinger (1504–1575)* (Zurich, 2007) (with extensive bibliography).

[5] Oecolampadius and Melanchthon are also explicitly referred to several times in the 1533 Commentary on Romans; see e.g. Bullinger, *In Epistolas* p. 4.9.16.81.83.96.105. On the other hand, Zwingli's name occurs not often, possibly out of 'political' reasons one year after his death. However, his importance is not suppressed: 'Zvinglius acerrimi in sacris iudicii vir', Bullinger, *In Epistolas*, p. 63. A few indications to Zwingli will be made at crucial points.

[6] 'Seneca plus syncerioris theologiae posteritati reliquit quam omnes fere omnium scholasticorum libri', Bullinger, *In Epistolas*, p.10.

[7] Cf. the short but essentially very appropriate note by Richard Muller: *Biblical Interpretation in the Era of Reformation: Essays Presented to David C. Steinmetz in Honor of His Sixtieth Birthday*, Richard A. Muller and John L. Thompson (eds.) (Grand Rapids: Eerdmans 1996), p. 16.

[8] Bullinger is the only one among the Reformers who regularly begins his catechetical writings (including his Confessio Helvetica posterior) with a doctrine of the 'word' of God in the scriptures and its interpretation.

[9] Heinrich Bullinger *Werke. Dritte Abteilung: Theologische Schriften* Band 1, edited by Hans-Georg vom Berg and Susanna Hausammann (Zurich 1983) (quoted as *HBTS* 1).

[10] Susi Hausammann, *Römerbriefauslegung zwischen Humanismus und Reformation. Eine Studie zu Heinrich Bullingers Römerbriefauslegung von 1525*, (Zürich/Stuttgart 1970).

[11] Cf. Hausammann, *Römerbriefauslegung,* p. 50f.53f.59.

[12] Heinrich Bullinger Diarium (QSRG II), E. *Egli* (ed.), Basel 1904, p. 10, 8–11 [quoted: HBD]. Cf. Hausammann, *Römerbriefauslegung*, p. 53f., 59. Also in the 'Studiorum ratio' Erasmus is referred to as authority in relation to the New Testament: 'in Graecanicis regnat Erasmus', *P. Stotz, Heinrich Bullinger, Studiorum ratio –Studienanleitung*, 2 Teilbände. Bd. 1 Edition, Bd. 2 Einleitung, Kommentar, Register, (Zürich, 1987) [quoted as *HBSR*], p. 74.

[13] Cf. Hausammann, *Römerbriefauslegung*, p. 55; 155ff.

[14] Cf. 'De prophetae officio, et quomodo digne administrari possit, oratio', Heinrycho Bullingero Authore, (Zürich: Christoph Froschauer, 1532) (HBBibl 1, Nr. 33) [quoted as De prophetae officio].

[15] See n. 9 above.

[16] Bullinger, *In Epistolas* p. a^{r-v}.

[17] Bullinger, *In Epistolas* p. $aaa2^{r}$-$aaa6^{v}$ (ad lectorem).

[18] Bullinger, *In Epistolas,* p. $aaa2^{v}$-$aaa3^{r}$.

[19] Bullinger, *In Epistolas,* p. $aaa3^{v}$.

[20] Bullinger, *In Epistolas,* p. aaa 2^{v} (Ad lectorem).

[21] On the importance of Augustine and the works regularly used and quoted by Bullinger cf. Opitz, *Bullinger.* See also the index of sources (Quellenverzeichnis) in *Heinrich Bullinger Werke.* 3. Abt. Theologische Schriften, ed. E. Campi, Bd. 3.1 und 3.2: Dekaden, ed. by Peter Opitz (Zürich: TVZ, 2008).

[22] Vgl. Bullinger, *HBSR,* p. 208.

[23] *HBD* 22,18f; *HBBibl* 1, Nr. 42.

[24] Cf. Berchtold Haller's letter to Bullinger of the 8. September 1532, *HBBW* 2, p. 234f. It was Haller who shortly after encouraged Bullinger to publish a commentary on the entire New Testament. (Letter of 2. October 1532, *HBBW* 2, p. 247 l. 43f). There had been ongoing discussions about specific exegetical questions for quite some time. Thus e.g.

Haller's question concerning Bullinger's understanding of the concept of *conscientia* in Rom. 2:15 (*HBBW* 2, p. 237, l. 29f).

[25] *De Prophetae Officio*, vgl. Anm. 11.

[26] *De Prophetae Officio*, fol. 3r. Cf. also Peter Opitz, 'Bullingers Lehre vom munus propheticum', in Emidio Campi and Peter Opitz (eds.), *Heinrich Bullinger: Life – Thought – Influence. Zurich, Aug. 25–29, 2004 International Congress Heinrich Bullinger (1504–1575)*, (Zurich: TVZ 2007), pp. 493–513.

[27] See e.g. Bullinger, *In Epistolas*, p. 4;8;22;29;33.100.101 and so forth.

[28] Bullinger, *In Epistolas*, p. aaa4.

[29] 'Rursus ostendi quae sit orationis series, quod filum, hoc est, quis scopus eorum de quibus disseritur, quae sententiarum et argumentorum iter sese connexio, quo referenda sint omnia, quid probent aut quid velint. Simul autem his rationibus indagavi, et pro gratia mihi a domino data, aperui sensum apostolicorum verborum', Bullinger, *In Epistolas*, p. aaa4.

[30] Concerning the special significance of the *loci* method and their use in relation to the Pauline epistles cf. Opitz, 'Bullinger on Paul', n.1 above.

[31] Bullinger, *In Epistolas*, p. aaa4^{r}-aaa4^{v}.

[32] Parker seems to neglect this context and purpose when he notes that Bullinger's 'accounts of the art or science of interpreting and expounding Scripture ... are certainly among the best and fullest statements of the sixteenth century evangelical position'. But 'It is disappointing to have to record that Bullinger's reach exceeded his grasp. His commentary is undoubtedly among the best in our group, but it falls short of Bucer in profundity and thoroughness, of Melanchthon in clarity, and of Calvin in penetration. When Calvin commended him, it must surely have been for his theory rather than his practice'. T. H. L. Parker, *Commentaries on the Epistle to the Romans 1532–1542* (Edinburgh 1986), p. 15.22. Bullinger concludes his commentary by pointing out '... utpote qui ex tempore intra certos dies scripserim haec omnia', Bullinger, *In Epistolas*, p. 121.

[33] Bullinger, *In Epistolas*, p. a^{r}.

[34] The marginal notes 'Difficultas scripturae', Bullinger, *In Epistolas*, p. a^{r}.

[35] 'obscuritas enim omnis et divinarum rerum difficultas e nobis, hoc est ex socordia nostra, deinde ex idiomatum et schematum neglectu, postremo ex non observato orationis contextu enascitur ... Caeterum si non teneatur orationis filum, nihil mirum est, si et prophetarum et apostolorum imo Rhetorum quoque disertissimorum scripta miscellaneae quaedam et phanaticorum hominum videantur esse commenta, ad quorum sensum nemo penetrare possit', Bullinger, *In Epistolas*, p. a^{r}.

[36] Accordingly he primarily asks or the 'Orationis dispositio et phrasis' (Marginal, a^{r}) of Romans. Cf. already *HBSR* 1, p. 106.

[37] 'Sed non vident superstitiosi, loquendi rationem et consuetudinem non esse petitam ex rhetorum praeceptis, sed praecepta ex diligenter observato naturali dicendi more. Id enim si viderent, mox intelligerent eos, qui in sacris contextum observant orationis, non Canones

observare, sed nativum loquendi morem sine quo nemo foeliciter in authoribus cum profanis tum sacris versabitur', Bullinger, *In Epistolas,* p. a[r].

[38] Bullinger, *In Epistolas, p. a*aa5[v].

[39] In a quite original translation which refers to the core motif of reconciliation, 'Hic est filius meus dilectus in quo placata est anima mea, ipsum audite', cover of Bullinger, *In Epistolas.*

[40] *HBTS* 1, p. 34–37.

[41] Bullinger, *In Epistolas*, p. 115f.

[42] Bullinger, *In Epistolas*, p. 116.

[43] *HBTS* 1, p. 34.

[44] Bullinger, *In Epistolas*, p. 2. Cf. Jdg. 13.7 and Num. 6.

[45] 'Ea prorsus de Christo dicebant et credebant quae nos, sed uni non omnia tribuebant ut nos', Bullinger, *In Epistolas*, p 2.

[46] Bullinger, *In Epistolas*, p a2[r].

[47] Bullinger, *In Epistolas*, p. a[v]-a2[r].

[48] 'potissimam evangelii summam', Bullinger, *In Epistolas,* p. 2.

[49] 'Iustitiam non deberi vel legalibus vel operum meritis, sed fidei Christianae', Bullinger, *In Epistolas*, p 2.

[50] 'Iustum ex fide vivere', Bullinger, *In Epistolas*, p. 2.

[51] Bullinger, *In Epistolas*, p 2.

[52] Bullinger, *In Epistolas*, p 2.

[53] 'si enim non abiero paracletus non veniet ad vos; si autem abiero mittam eum ad vos et cum venerit ille arguet mundum *de peccato* et *de iustitia* et *de iudicio*; *de peccato* quidem quia non credunt in me, *de iustitia* vero quia ad Patrem vado et iam non videbitis me, *de iudicio* autem quia princeps mundi huius iudicatus est; ...' (John 16.8–11, Vulgate). Explicit references in the Romans commentary: Bullinger, *In Epistolas*, pp. 9.32.54.76f.

[54] 'unicus fons et author boni', Bullinger, *In Epistolas*, p. 10–16, here 16.

[55] Bullinger, *In Epistolas*, p. 15.

[56] Cf. Bullinger, *In Epistolas*, p. 10–16.

[57] 'De iustitia vero quia ad patrem vado' (John 16.11), see: Bullinger, *In Epistolas,* p. 77.

[58] '... mentem legis, pietatem videlicet, fidem, innocentiam et charitatem ...' Bullinger, *In Epistolas,* p. 62.

[59] 'Liberati ergo a peccati, servi facti estis iustitiae', Rom 6.18, cf. Bullinger, *In Epistolas,* p. 59.

[60] 'peccatorum videlicet remissionem et vitam per Christum restitutam', Bullinger, *In Epistolas*, p. 2.

[61] For Bullinger's interpretation of Hebrews see Peter Opitz, 'Bullinger and Paul', cf. n.1 above.

[62] 'Primarium enim Christianae religionis dogma et cui omnia alia innituntur, hoc est, quod in Christo sit omnis plenitudo, et proinde omnes qui iustificantur, unica in illum fide, et nulla alia re, iustificari. Haec enim est summa totius Evangelii. Haec omnium Epistolarum Pauli materia est, maxime vero earum quas ad Romanos, Galatas et Hebraeos conscripsit', *In Acta*, p. 176f (on Acts 15.1).

[63] 'Quemadmodum vero paulo ante iustitiam aliam quidam fidei, aliam vero legis fecit; ita nunc aliam quidam vocat propriam, aliam vero dei iustitiam. Propria autem est quam nobis ipsi fingimus, vel ex scripturis sinistre intellectis, vel ex aliorum exemplis hypocrisique vel ex opinione quapiam carnali et intenzione ... bona, sed stulta et scripturis adversa. ... Sed quae nam est dei iustitia? Christus', Bullinger, *In Epistolas*, p. 86.

[64] 'in Christo omnem plenitudinem esse novit', Bullinger, *In Epistolas*, p. 87. Cf. e.g. Z II, p. 27–29.222 (Article 2 and 21) (Z = Huldreich Zwingli: *Sämtliche Werke*, [CR 88–101]; Berlin / Leipzig / Zürich 1905 - incomplete).

[65] Bullinger, *In Epistolas*, p. 87.

[66] Cf. Z II, p. 72 (Article 13).

[67] 'Atque ad hunc modum salus prope est in ore et corde cuiusvis. Haec fidei constantia ac certitudo est unde sursum deorsumque non voluitur, sed tranquilla apud se fruitur pane coelesti a quo quicumque aluntur non esuriunt in aeternum', Bullinger, *In Epistolas*, p. 87. Cf. e.g. Z II, p. 141f.

[68] Marginal: 'Evangelium, quid sit, et quae eius nobilitas', Bullinger, *In Epistolas*, p. 7f.

[69] 'Virtus itaque dei, ‚dynamis theou', potentia dei est, robur, maiestas, veritas, iustitia, misericordia, adeoque brachium illud dei ipse filius Iesus Christus dominus noster, per quem declaravit pater potentia, veritatem et iustitiam, denique et misericordiam suam mundo. Euangelium itaque illa est coelestis denunciatio, quam nobis potentiam dei Iesum Christum praedicat, in quo deus orbi omnem plenitudinem exhibuit, ut quisque illi fidit, non pereat, sed habeat vitam aeternam', Bullinger, *In Epistolas*, p. 8.

[70] Cf. Thomas Aquinas, *Summa Theologica* II–II q. 4a. 4–5.

[71] Thus the *Glossa ordinaria*, vgl. *HBTS* 1, p. 52.

[72] 'Iustitia fidei nostrae, si exacte loquaris, non ita tribui, quasi operi nostro; hoc enim foret abuti fide, si inquam fide mea videar fidere, quasi dignum aliquid in me sit quod deus remuneret', Bullinger, *In Epistolas*, p. 9.

[73] Bullinger, *In Epistolas*, p. 8. Bullinger thereby corrected in 1533 the 'over-interpretation' of his 1525 interpretation which had been criticized by Hausamann in accordance with her proposal. Cf. Hausammann, *Römerbriefauslegung*, p. 232f.

[74] Since the Hebrew expression 'emunah' means 'faithfulness and truth' according to Luther, Paul's statement 'The righteous will live by faith' does not mean anything else than 'Der, der in sinem hertzen und by imm gloubt, das imm Gott trüw sye, der ist grecht, er wirt ouch

leben ... das ist: Indem wir sehend trüw sein Gott in der gschrifft und in sinem Zusagen, in dem selbigen leerend wir imm glouben. Und der selbig gloub, das ich also Gott für wahrhafft und trüw hab, ist die fromgheit und ist das leben', *HBTS* I, p. 51. On this see Hausammann, *Römerbriefauslegung*, p. 229f.

[75] Bullinger, *In Epistolas*, p. 8f.

[76] Bullinger, *In Epistolas*, p. 29.

[77] '...Evangelium roborari propheticis scripturis, imo ex iis esse petitum ...', Bullinger, *In Epistolas*, p. 4f.

[78] Bullinger, *In Epistolas*, p. 4f.

[79] *HBTS* I,32.

[80] *In Acta*, p. 114v.

[81] Bullinger, *In Epistolas*, p. 4 (on Rom 1:11f.).

[82] Cf. Bullinger's letter to Berchtold Haller from the 4. June 1532 (*HBBW* 2, p. 129–134, here p. 132, Zl. 71. Zl. 84.

[83] Vgl. *HBBW* 2, p. 132, Zl. 86 – p. 133, Zl. 142.

[84] Cf. Bullinger, *In Epistolas*, p. 29 (on Rom. 3:1–8).

[85] Bullinger, *In Epistolas*, p. 21f (on Rom. 2:4); p. 81 (on Rom 9:17f).

[86] 1Tim. 2.4, one of Bullinger's favourite passages.

[87] 'Non enim crediderim ipsum nisi per occasionem, idque opido paucis de electione et praedestinatione disputare', Bullinger, *In Epistolas*, p. 77.

[88] 'monens ut iustitiae Christi se subdant per fidem; alias enim perituros id quod etiam Prophetae praedixerint', Bullinger, *In Epistolas*, p. 3.

[89] 'consolationem instituit ac mitigationem...', where he likewise warns the Gentiles not to despise the Jews. 'Siquidem iudicia dei ut nova et mirabilia, sic inscrutibilia esse', Bullinger, *In Epistolas*, p. 3.

[90] 'Restitutio Israelis', Bullinger, *In Epistolas*, p. 90–95.

[91] 'Mutabit deus mentem Iudaeorum ... non mittet novum liberatorem, sed semel missum Iesum Christum dominum nostrum illis reddet amabilem', Bullinger, *In Epistolas*, p. 94.

[92] Bullinger, *In Epistolas*, p. 82.

[93] Bullinger, *In Epistolas*, p. 81.

[94] 'Est igitur dei bonitas caussa sine qua non (ut more scholastico loquar) sed non est caussa efficiens. Nam deus non fecit malum seu indurationem illam in corde Pharaonis, interim vero malum illud et induratio non fuit sine deo'. Bullinger, *In Epistolas*, p. 81.

[95] Bullinger, *In Epistolas*, p. 81.

[96] Bullinger, *In Epistolas*, p. 81.

[97] Bullinger, *In Epistolas*, p. 82.

[98] See Melanchthon, 'Commentarii in epistolam Pauli ad Romanos' (1532) in *Melanchthons Werke V. Band. Römerbrief-Kommentar 1532*. ed. by Rolf Schäfer in conjunction with Gerhard Ebeling (Gütersloh 1965), p. 284f.330 (quoted: Melanchthon, *Ad Romanos*).

[99] Bullinger, *In Epistolas*, p. 96; see Melanchthon, *Ad Romanos*, p. 285.330.

[100] See Bernd Hamm, *Zwinglis Reformation der Freiheit* (Neukirchen1988).

[101] 'Siquidem deus non vult mortuas pecudes, sed hostiam vivam, ipsum inquam hominem, sanctum, id est, sanctificatum et a sceleribus repurgatum, purum et qui uni placere studeat. Is autem rationalis cultus est, illi gratus, fide constans et spiritu, non sanguine aut auro aut alia quapiam ex externa. Deus enim spiritus est, et spiritu coli vult' (John 4.24)' Bullinger, *In Epistolas*, p. 96. Cf. e.g. Z II, p. 348 (Article 44); Z VI.5, p. 79f (*Fidei expositio*.)

[102] 'ipsum ... hominem, sanctum, id est, sanctificatum', Bullinger, *In Epistolas*, p. 96.

[103] Bullinger, *In Epistolas*, p. 101–103.

[104] Bullinger, *In Epistolas*, p. 102.

[105] Bullinger, *In Epistolas*, p. 104.

[106] Bullinger, *In Epistolas*, p. 107.

[107] Bullinger, *In Epistolas*, p. 110.

[108] Bullinger, *In Epistolas*, p. 110. 'Omnia autem ad Charitatem refert; quasi dicat: Quid vero opus fuerit multa scribere de debito, de contractibus, de locatione et mutuo et hisce id genus aliis rebus? Charitas sit istorum omnium regula', Bullinger, *In Epistolas*, p. 105.

[109] 'Vera enim religio non est sita in cibo, potu, diebus aut vestibus, sed in spiritu et veritate. Ergo qui iustitiam coluerit, pacem sectatus fuerit, et gaudium quoque in adversis senserit, is Christo servit, acceptus quoque deo est et apud omnes pios boni nominis', Bullinger, *In Epistolas*, p. 111 (on Rom. 14:17f).

Built on Tradition but not Bound by Tradition:
Response to Peter Opitz

William S. Campbell

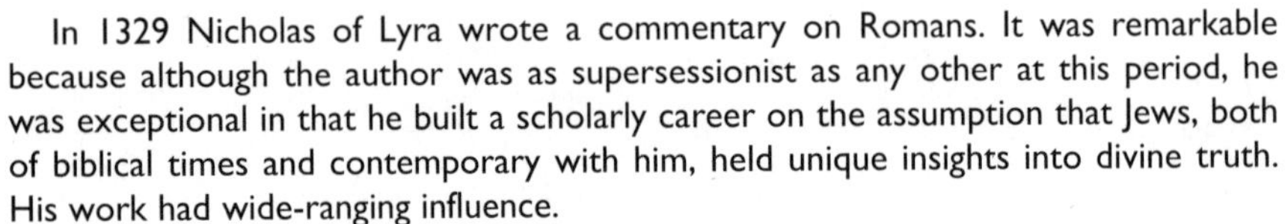

In 1329 Nicholas of Lyra wrote a commentary on Romans. It was remarkable because although the author was as supersessionist as any other at this period, he was exceptional in that he built a scholarly career on the assumption that Jews, both of biblical times and contemporary with him, held unique insights into divine truth. His work had wide-ranging influence.

Thus, surprisingly, the Hebrew text - and ancient and modern Rabbinic interpretation of it – stood at the heart of Nicholas's approach to the literal sense of Scripture. This approach to Scripture, influenced by the study of Hebrew and the use of literal exegesis, went back to the twelfth century, but it was to blossom once again at the Reformation in the region of Southern Germany, Strasbourg and Switzerland and Bullinger stands in this tradition.[1]

All the Reformers, however new their perspectives, still maintained solid links with the interpretive traditions prior to the Reformation. In this they had much in common with each other, differing slightly in individual preference in relation to specific topics. Thus Bulllinger uses Origen's commentary on Romans as well as Ambrosiaster. In his own time, as we have heard, he follows Erasmus closely and makes full use of Melanchthon's *Annotationes* and other works. But though indebted to Luther, he also differs from Luther and is more akin to modern scholars in his verse-by-verse continuous exegesis coupled with a humanistic-philological approach. As noted, this is most apparent when comparison is made with Luther's lectures on Romans delivered in 1415–16. Having worked a little on these lectures, I must say that my initial impression was that Luther was still very much part of the medieval tradition despite his new reformed stance, whereas Bullinger relates more easily to more modern approaches. In this Bullinger is indebted to Erasmus, whose influence in Switzerland was very strong.

It would appear that Bullinger also differed from other Reformers in the strong emphasis he placed upon history. This is apparent already in his view of Romans as written by Paul from a specific situation to a specific congregation. Peter Opitz has underlined the novelty of this position with regard to Luther, Melanchthon and Calvin. In my view the Reformation left a legacy in which theological emphases have tended to dominate exegetical and historical emphases in biblical interpretation. But for Bullinger the Bible should be read as any other document, that is, as far as is possible in its original languages and in relation to the genre of the text; thus historical books should be read historically, poetic books poetically, and so on. Most significantly, Paul should be read rhetorically in light of the structure of the letter as known from ancient rhetoric. By paying attention to the historical situation, Bullinger recognized the significance of contextual interpretation in a way that is also extremely modern. The differing style of each Pauline letter is determined by the specific needs of the addressees. Significantly, Bullinger's strong historical perspective led him also to stress the unity and continuity of both Testaments more than his contemporaries. But this continuity is not simply that of one era ending and giving way to another which in essence replaces it. Bullinger gives real value to the Old Testament in and of itself, and in its fulfillment in the New, which unlocks the sense and meaning of the Old Testament thus enabling it to realize its full potential.

This is not to deny a Christological interpretation of the Old Testament. Against Luther's view that Jewish exegesis had perverted the meaning of the Old Testament, Bullinger insisted that, since Christ himself was immersed in the Hebrew Bible traditions, then 'solus Christus' cannot be in opposition to the content of the Hebrew Bible, read in the original Hebrew. Christ himself is recognized through the Old Testament and the meaning of who Christ is is derived from it. For him, Christ is the compass or 'Richtungspunkt' to guide to a true understanding. But in keeping with a South German, Alsace and Swiss triangle of scholarship, Bullinger even stressed the necessity of Hebrew for a proper understanding of the New Testament since it is full of Hebraisms.

This appreciation of the New Testament as nothing less than an exegesis of the Old means that to understand the importance of significant Christian themes one has to begin with the text itself. This has, as Opitz notes, a significant outcome in Bullinger's exegesis of Romans, firstly in Paul's self-understanding of himself as called to be an apostle. Bullinger sees this as a link with the calling traditions of Israel, and with Amos and Isaiah in particular. This positive regard for continuity in Bullinger occurs, of course, in an era when scholars were not so aware of historical development as we are today. It was long after the Reformation before people in the theater thought it necessary to wear Roman dress in depicting the ancient world. On the other hand, Bullinger's interpretation escapes the influence of later developments in which history is seen from an evolutionary perspective, as in the nineteenth century, particularly in approaches influenced by Hegel and Baur. Nor is Bullinger prevented from giving due weight to previous history as he might have been in the twentieth century, as, for example, due to Bultmann's existentialist approach.

The place of the past and its significance appears most vividly in Bullinger's interpretation of Romans 9–11. With his historical emphasis, he is able to view these chapters as a new development which he entitles 'The Calling of the Gentiles'. It is noteworthy here that nothing negative is highlighted, such as the guilt of the Jews or their hardness of heart. This is partly a result of Bullinger's emphasis upon peoples rather than individuals, the latter emphasis being typical of most of the other Reformers except perhaps Zwingli. For these the case of Pharaoh led to the strange puzzle of a God who elects to life but also hardens whom He wills.

In the centuries following, and in Calvin in particular, the stress on the individual's election or damnation led to horrific incidents among the faithful, as well as to division in the church. The doctrine of double predestination was a *cul de sac* which was to lead eventually to a neglect of election as an element in the gospel. I think the last book in which an old-fashioned interpretation of election and predestination occurs was that of Bouttier in the 1930's. As Karl Barth famously noted in his *Dogmatics*, II/,2, 'if you start where Calvin started' – that is, as we have noted, in stressing the individual and the inscrutability of the divine decrees concerning election and predestination, 'you must, if you are logical, inevitably end up at the same conclusion as Calvin did'. The only solution was to start elsewhere as Barth did with Ephesians, where election is in Christ, and for Barth Christ himself the only elect individual.

So for Bullinger, Romans 9–11 is not about a supralapsarian divine decree but consists of words both of comfort and warning. Notably the warning is against boasting, but in contrast to many more modern commentators, the warning is addressed to both Gentiles and Jews alike against arrogance and scorn of each other. And again, there is not only warning; comfort also is offered in these chapters because Romans 11 is a chapter of comfort to help ease the fear caused by the thought of Israel's rejection. The overall positive emphasis of Bullinger in Romans 9–11 reflects the prophetic messages in the Old Testament, where there is judgment in plenty, but never without the promise of mercy. Thus Bullinger entitles Romans 11 'the Restoration of Israel'. The emphasis on continuity and the positive view of Israel emerges from Bullinger's conviction that the gospel which Paul proclaims is the message of loyalty to the covenant of the God of the Old Testament. This did lead to his being dubbed a 'Judaizer', but Bullinger's concept of covenant was not of some unhistorical or suprahistorical entity, but simply the symbol of the God of Israel's dynamic relation to the world of humankind, with all the diversity and contingencies of history.

In modern interpretation, particularly post-Stendahl and Sanders, opposition to individualistic understandings of Paul's gospel has clearly emerged. But this has in turn led to a reaction against continuity and against covenantal conceptions of theology in favor of what is perceived as 'personal' or individual salvation. The historical reservations arising from the dangers of a Heilsgeschichte that was designed to favor a certain people or kingdom, also led to a reaction toward a 'new creation' type of theology in which the past is deemed irrelevant, where there is no real earthly continuity in the church, and where the Almighty only occasionally and arbitrarily reveals himself existentially in revelation to individuals. The Bultmann, Käsemann and Louis Martyn strands of interpretation can in various ways be seen as anti-covenantal. But common to them all is the problem of history, not least the history of the church. Bullinger recognized that if God is faithful to his own character and to his commitments to his people, this faithfulness will have some visible continuity in history, at least within the church or the people of God. It is no exaggeration to claim that since the beginning of the nineteenth century at the time of F. C. Baur, biblical scholars have been struggling with the concept of history and of God's ongoing activity within it. Whatever the concept of history adhered to, without some such concept the faithfulness of God in and through history becomes virtually unintelligible.

Due to an emphasis upon predestination, Romans 9–11 were neglected chapters over a long period of history. Their interpretation since the Reformation is very diverse if not spasmodic. It is to Bullinger's credit that, of all the Reformers, he is closest to modern interpretation of the letter and that in relation to several major themes. How can we explain the fact that one person arrives at a specific interpretation which to us now seems so obvious but escaped many others? My answer is partly that his emphasis upon history and upon covenant and continuity assisted him toward what I perceive as an innovative overview of Romans. His emphasis upon the situation led him to find opponents in 16:17–20 whom he called Nazarene after Jerome, but even here he is not particularly biased against these opponents as related to Judaism.

To sum up those characteristics of Bullinger which are particularly significant:

1. Bullinger is open to insights from all points of view but remains independent: He sided with Luther and Zwingli on the question of free will, but he continues to use Erasmus and to use humanistic tools of interpretation for his Reformed commentary, admits to learning from Erasmus, and wishes to continue to do so.

2. Although he agrees with Luther in the adoption of Luther's concept of transference of the foreign righteousness of Christ to the believer, instead of following the emphasis of Luther and Melanchthon in interpreting Paul's teaching on justification in the context of a fundamental differentiation of law and gospel, Bullinger turns to the Gospel of John and interprets the forensic by means of the mystical. In my view this is a more profitable route for today, when there seems to be a return to abstract debates about law and works. Bullinger refused the faith/works dichotomy as the key to interpreting Paul, something that might be worth reconsidering today in the light of current unfruitful debates.

3. Bullinger is decidedly theocentric rather than Christocentric. That is, faith means not only taking up the promises of God, but faith in God himself, God's faithfulness as a whole. In this I find he has captured one of the dominant themes in Romans, 'this was to show that He Himself is faithful and he justifies the one who has faith in Jesus' (Rom 3:26).

4. Bullinger is significant especially for his understanding of unity and continuity between the Testaments. So often today we find a perfectly reasonable interpretation of a New Testament text by looking for echoes or parallels in the scriptures, something previously neglected.

5. His understanding of Romans as addressed to a particular context is something that has had to be fought for, because scholars demanded to have Romans as a useful summary of Paul's theology. Even today some scholars are reluctant to view the letter as a fully contextual document.

6. In his understanding of Romans 9–11, Bullinger stands in line with the prophetic insights of the OT and in relation to the covenant being opened up also to Gentiles. The negative effects of viewing Judaism as a particular and therefore tribal religion in antithesis to the universal religion of Christianity has caused huge deficits in our ability to understand these chapters, not evident in Bullinger.

7. Bullinger stressed the corporate dimension of Pauline and Old Testament thought so that he was saved from the general tendency to think only in terms of elect or righteous individuals. Until we learn afresh our corporate identity in Christ, there will be aspects of Paul which will remain hidden from our view.

Our conclusion must be that Bullinger is an excellent model for contemporary interpretation of Romans and of Paul. But how are we to explain his relative neglect in comparison with Luther or Calvin? This reminds us again of context and circumstance. If he had been born later or lived in a different place, might his influence have been so much greater? The context is much less limiting for us today – we have a world of interpretation at our fingertips. Bullinger appeals to us as a scholar among scholars who did not fear to follow or to disagree with his peers. The neglect over many years of emphases already highlighted in Bullinger's reading of Romans should alert us to widening our search for insights, and his independence should prevent us from claiming that we must follow the crowd wherever they may lead. If, as some would claim, there is a need today to de-Lutheranize Paul this could be done, not by bypassing the Reformation and its impact, but rather by returning to a scholar who, as a near contemporary of Luther, was original and independent enough to offer us a very different, and to my view, a more comprehensive and appealing view of the letter.

Notes

1 For more detail on this see Deeana C. Klepper's fine chapter 'First in Knowledge of Divine Law: The Jews and the Old Law in Nicholas of Lyra's Romans Commentary' in *Medieval Readings of Romans,* W. S. Campbell, P. S. Hawkins, B. D. Schildgen (eds.), (T&T Clark, 2007).

— NINE —

Romans 7 in the Reformation Century

Mark W. Elliott

In this paper, a review of treatments of Romans 7 *in commentaries,* twenty in all, will aim to show more clearly what was at issue between interpreters who wrote between 1500 and 1600.

I have used a translation of Colet and of Calvin, which may be viewed at http://www.ccel.org/c/calvin/comment3/comm_vol38/htm/_fnf3. The translations and paraphrases of the rest are my own.

I first proceed in roughly chronological order of first publication to give an account of each commentator on Romans 7, an account which is more descriptive than evaluative and which follows a mixed form of summary, paraphrase and quotation.

1. Colet, John, 1467–1519.

An Exposition of St Paul's Epistle to the Romans (Oxford, 1497); translated by J. H. Lupton (London: Bell & Daldy, 1873).

With Colet's sermon, there is something of a feel of the spiritual non-technical homiletical style of the *devotio moderna.* There is a very simple structure with a division of the chapter into two sections, concerning plight and solution respectively. The latter contains an emphasis on loving God, imitation of Christ and then waiting in turn for divine love which drives out fear. Law contributes to sin's sinfulness by making it a conscious matter and thus more culpable. It is clear that Colet's approach is homiletical and moral.

2. Erasmus, Desiderius, 1466–1536.

Annotations on the NT Acts-Romans-I and II Corinthians. A. Reeve and M. A. Screech (Leiden: Brill, 1990). *Paraphrases: in Collected works of Erasmus.* Vol. 41 – New Testament scholarship: Paraphrases on Romans and Galatians; edited by Robert D. Sider [et al.] (Toronto: University of Toronto Press, 1984).

By way of contrast, Erasmus's remarks are of a text-critical and grammatical nature. He is half-way through Romans 7 before he remarks on the theology of the chapter. Origen has said that up to this point of exclamation of thanks (v.25) Paul was speaking of his pre-Christian experience under the law. The joyful exclamation, Ambrose thought, was of one rejoicing that he had been freed from the law, not that

that freedom was yet to come ('*liberatum*', not '*liberandum*'). As Paul says, and it would be unworthy to think otherwise of such a great saint, Christ *has liberated* him from sin and death. In a later edition, marked by '[ ]', Erasmus considers that to answer the question 'who will liberate me from this body of death?' with 'the grace of God' would suggest that Paul is not yet liberated, while to read *charis theô* means to answer 'thanks be to God', which he takes to be the authentic reading at v. 25 is implying that this liberation has happened. He concedes that even if we take 'the body of death' to be that which is prone to sin, this need not make the passage inappropriate to Paul. For Augustine thinks it includes all Paul's human experience from boyhood onward, as a carnal person under the law as well as a person under grace: so it is not the case that he gave his assent to these carnal emotions, and it is better to see this as not about Paul *qua* Apostle, but *qua* representative of all states of human spirituality, all of which stand in need of liberation. A little later, in his *Paraphrases*, he writes that human beings, for all that they know the law, are nevertheless slaves to sin, with their inner mind which is our human identity totally at a loss in the struggle. V. 25 is paraphrased thus: 'He has snatched us from such great evils, not through the law of circumcision but through Jesus Christ our Lord. If this had not happened, I myself also, although I am one and the same man, would be torn apart in the same way, so that with my mind I would be a servant to the law of God insofar as I desire goodness, while with my flesh I would be a servant to the law of sin, insofar as the allurement of sin conquered me'. Immediately the paraphrase of Chapter 8 follows: 'But if there still remain some remnants of former servitude in some Christians, they will overcome these by a pious zeal and will not be dragged against their will into any serious sin for which those deserve to be condemned who, through faith and baptism, have once been incorporated into Jesus Christ'. Erasmus's position is one which will more or less be that vindicated by the Council of Trent (Decree on Original Sin, 17/6/1546; DS 1515).

3. Luther, Martin, 1483–1546.

D. Martin Luthers Werke Kritische Gesamtausgabe 56. Band. Der Brief an die Römer (1515–16) (Weimar: Herman Böhlhaus Nachfolger, 1938).

Luther (WA 56, 349) took delight in the Pauline phrase (v.17): 'Now it is not I who produces this but the sin which dwells in me'. Not surprisingly his view is at variance with that of Erasmus, although these Romans lectures (1515–16) were given almost a decade before their famous disagreement. He asks:

> Has not the fallacious metaphysics of Aristotle and the philosophy that follows human traditions deceived our theologians? As they do not know how to remove sin through baptism or penitence they think that it is absurd that the Apostle says: 'But what dwelled in me was sin'. So this phrase offends them most severely, so that they rush into the false opinion that the Apostle cannot have been speaking in his own person but in that of the carnal person. That he had no sin at all they contend at length in the face of many quite clear statements in many Epistles.

It seems crucial that Luther was elsewhere aware (WA 57, 184) that Augustine in *I Retractiones* 23 had said that these words can be understood as about the Apostle himself.

For Luther, the law brought about wrath. He follows Augustine at 7:4 in holding that not sin but the soul must die from sin for there to be liberation from the law. *We* do not *have* infirmity but we *are* infirmity. Sin is not something like a hole that we can work on to repair by grace and *ascesis*. Sin is left in the spiritual person for the exercise of grace, for the humbling of pride, for the repression of presumption.

> For whoever does not diligently endeavor to drive it out without doubt still has it even if he has not sinned and on its account he might be condemned. For we are not called to ease but to work against the passions. These are not without blame (for they are indeed sins and certainly damnable) unless the grace of God will not reckon them to us ...
>
> It is however to be observed that the Apostle did not wish that spirit and flesh be understood as two things but as one altogether, just as wound and flesh are one ... But flesh is its weakness or wound and in as much as he loves the law of God there he is Spirit; in as much as he lusts (*concupiscit*) there is the weakness of the spirit and the wound of sin which begins to be healed.

A slightly confusing metaphor! Luther drew heavily on Book 2 of Augustine's *Contra Iulianum* (5,12 and also III,20,29 and 26,62.) The division of the soul into parts which Luther opposed is found in Ockham (*Quodlibet* II q10&11), who had already been criticised on this matter by Gregory of Rimini and Biel. But Luther believed that the nominalist theologians were still prevalent in the Church, so he concludes by attacking them:

> The metaphysical theologians who ignore Scriptural warrant with their fine terminology forget that the flesh is its own weakness; it is just like a wound of the whole person who through grace has begun to be healed in reason or spirit.

4. Oecolampadius, Iohannes, 1482–1531.

In Epistolam B. Pauli Apost. ad Rhomanos adnotationes à Ioanne Oecolampadio Basileae praelectae (Basileae: apud Andream Cratandrum, 1525).

Oecolampadius was famous for being one of the first to combine Lutheranism with a respect for the ongoing usefulness of the law, spiritually understood, in the Christian life.

> The first husband is the old man and the tinder for sin, a man clearly base and who begets the foulest progeny, the works of the law. And through it we are said next to be impregnated with death. But the second husband is Christ.

He then takes the opportunity to lay out the gospel, showing how law opens our eyes to sin, where before we were ignorant.

> The law is given that when he saw that he could not fulfil it he then recognized that he was weak ... and so despairing of his own powers he sought help from the most excellent God, and with the spirit of divinity received he did what the weakness of the flesh denied.

This sounds as if law plays an important part of the process of becoming a Christian. Oecolampadius is confessing that he owes it to the law that he knows this and can confess his sin. **H** Oecolampadius, like others of the Swiss Reformation who had a high regard for the spiritual nature of the Old Testament, seems to interpret Paul as meaning that the law does nothing more sinister than reveal sin. Although the law's role is not a salvific one, since for Paul the law in its reporting of God's standards made things worse because it led to a hatred of the law-giver, nevertheless the law does not contribute to the amount of sin in Oecolampadius's view of Romans 7:7ff.

'Indeed without the law sin is "dead": this "to be dead" is not the same as not to be, or not to be reckoned as sin'. To paraphrase the rest of this section: in other words, Paul is not arguing that sin never existed without law, but that the sinful nature would not have been stirred up without the law. Paul writes that he did not know himself, and in that was like the Pharisees who felt secure and self-justifying because they did not know the power of the law due to their own filthiness. *Ego autem* – this refers to Paul's time as a Pharisee when he did not know the power of the law, which is ironic since the Pharisees made it their business to know the law. The law is good because it shows us what is owed to God. Sin increased in making me know I was a sinner – and that's a worse position to be in! And yet there is some spiritual progress in gaining awareness of one's plight. The law is called spiritual because it demands the spirit to be fulfilled, not that it needs spiritual understanding as per Origen or other allegorizers. When Paul says that the law 'delights' him he is speaking in his own person although he was justified, for only the justified like the law. Paul was used to glorying in his affliction, but he is quick to mourn his sins.

What we have in Oecolampadius is the view that Paul is describing the change of his attitude towards the law from his life as a Pharisee, when he did not know his sins, to his present situation when he is only too aware of its demands. The law has not caused but made sin known to the formerly self-deluded.

5. Melanchthon, Philipp., 1497–1560.

Melanchthons Werke in Auswahl. Band. 5., Römerbrief-Kommentar 1532; Herausgegeben von Rolf Schäfer (Gütersloh: Mohn, 1965).

H Melanchthon in his Romans commentary of 1532 does not dwell long on the issue and makes it seem like a very simple matter unworthy of controversy. 'In the rest of the account Paul describes how even now he battles with sin. For he wants to show that sin inheres in carnal nature so that the regenerate do not once put off all of sin'. One is outside the law if it does not terrify (blatant law-breakers, hypocrites). Being carnal is both seeking material things and trusting in one's own powers of wisdom and righteousness; there is an intermediate state of realizing one is condemned and a third state of feeling consoled. It is a demanding law of the inner conscience. There is no good thing within us and saints do not satisfy the law of God.

In other words it is a lifelong struggle with sin for believers. But there is a thankful trust which means believers are freed.

H Hermeneutical framework of Oecolampadius's reading.

H Melanchthon's hermeneutical framework renders the chapter non-controversial for him.

6. Vio, Tommaso de (Cardinal Cajetan), 1469–1534.
Epistolae Pauli et aliorum apostolorum ... per ... Dominum Thomam de Vio ... iuxta sensum literalem enarratae (Paris: Apud Iod. Badium Ascensium. & Ioan. Paruum. & Ioannem Roigny, Sub prelo Ascensiano, 1532).

Cajetan first establishes, on the basis of 7:1, that those to whom Paul is writing are no longer under the law, although the fact that they have once been legalists meant that Paul's employment of a legal metaphor would have been helpful to them! Cajetan takes delight in sketching the drama with the four actors – law, the baptized, Christ and death. Death had already inseminated the baptized [!] who were married to the law, and death duly sprouted. **A** In other words, there is some kind of nascent death at work even in the baptized. But to say 'you have been made dead to the law' is the conclusion Paul is trying to get to: the point is that Christians are exempt from the law. This takes place not through works [understand, of mortification] but through the body of Christ, that is 'through the death which the body of Christ sustains'. This seems a clear reference to the Eucharist in which receipt of the body of Christ works mortification in the sense of exemption from the law. Salvation requires that the baptized take hold of this means of grace. Where v. 5 holds that 'we were in the flesh', this means not that we were substantially in the flesh, which of course even the baptized are, but the state of being in the flesh, that is without a trace (*adminiculo*) of grace. V. 6 speaks of the new state of being in Christ, and this is a condition associated with eucharist, not baptism.

The law is not just good but spiritual and of spiritual use. V. 14 speaks of sin not being something of our foundation, of God's good creation, but of something into which we are sold: 'venundatus'.

> For anyone who wills or does not will according to this part of the mind is a slave of sin: in the case of a justified man to will according to it is said to be the *fomes* of sin ... For divine goodness dwells in the higher part of man through baptism.

In other words Cajetan thinks there is an area unaffected and unreachable by grace which simply needs to be kept in check by the higher part of the mind which can be renewed by that grace.

> Paul says he is a lover of the law according to the inner man, that is, according to the mind, according to hope. And he called the higher part of the soul the inner man, by which it completes its workings inside. In him it is apart from the physical organs, for the intellect and the will are raised above and separate from the whole body. And by contrast the man according to the sensory parts, whether internal or external, is called the external man, in that they are sunk in carnal duties.

One can see Cajetan trying to preserve the balance between a grace that is prevenient and is at work outside our understanding and a grace that requests our free will to engage it.

> In me as justified there are two principles inclining to the contrary, that is the mind and the flesh. And by this I am justified: in my mind I incline to the willing

A Analysis of how death is at work in the baptized.

service of the law of God, in the flesh, however, I incline to willing service of the law of sin.

7. Bullinger, Heinrich, 1504–1575.

In sanctissimam Pauli ad Romanos Epistolam Heinrychi Bullingeri commentarius (Tiguri: Apud Christoph. Frosch., mense Febr. anno 1533).

Bullinger uses the authority of no less a pagan than Cicero to show that law came about to check the wildness of human behavior. The same happened in the case of the Israelites who had become depraved through Egyptian slavery to the point that they did not know the difference between righteousness and sin; then the Lord acted. Since their laziness and blindness led to ignorance of the law of nature written on the heart, he wrote the law on stone tablets, wishing to assert and renew what was written on the heart. By the law sin was recognized, just as sin took its opportunity through the precept. Bullinger explains that some translate 'operatum est in me' ('worked in me') 'genuit in me' ('bore/begat in me'), others 'excitavit in me'. To translate the Greek κατειργάσατο ἐν ἐμοὶ πᾶσαν ἐπιθυμίαν in verse 8, Zwingli chose 'showed the measure' (of concupiscence in me). Bullinger himself goes further and ends his remarks on v.8 by saying that Paul thinks of human beings as personifications of concupiscence: 'That is, by the law it became clear that the whole of a human being is not only liable to (*obnoxiam*) concupiscence but is in fact concupiscence itself. For it has power to effect what he says: 'measured in me every concupiscence'. This concupiscence is serious sin (cf. Luther, against the dominant Roman Catholic baptismal theology), although for a time Paul did not know it. 'Without law sin is dead': this does not mean that sin did not exist but that it did and he just did not know it. Paul himself is the example here, who thought that as a Pharisee he was innocent. In other words, coming to know the law and his spiritual state was a step towards salvation. **H** The law which points out God's good will is spiritual, not because it has allegories in it but because it demands a spiritual fulfilment, not just in appearance, and because it requires righteousness and sanctity in the heart, not hypocrisy and mere external works. Paul as carnal even in his believing state is one who shrinks from spiritual things. Bullinger repeatedly insists on the absolute opposition between Spirit as God's Spirit and flesh in Paul, with reference to Galatians. The flesh ignores the call of the Spirit. By 'flesh' is meant the whole man which is prone to evil, and the soul is included in this. After all, *anima* (soul) is animal-like! Even the saints are vitiated and there is no such thing as free will, as Jeremiah had to insist against the 'free-willers' of his day! All the saints groan with Paul in this spiritual struggle. There are no higher and lower parts of a human being (despite what we just saw in Cajetan). The only way out is to bypass the flesh and walk in the Spirit.

H The law is understood as spiritual, which provides the guiding principle for reading Romans 7.

8. Sadoleto, Jacopo, 1477–1547.
Iacobi Sadoleti Episcopi Carpentoractis in Pauli Episolam [sic] ad Romanos Commentariorum Libri Tres (Venetijs,1536).

Sadoleto sees Paul as giving an account of the history of salvation in Romans 7. Paul depicts the original Jewish experience, a time of childhood in which there was little awareness of God's law and its demands, so that there was no power of sin in the people and no malicious intent to sin. But after the law, David is a good example of how aware they became of sin, writing that the law delivered him to death, and that the weapons intended for salvation and life brought death itself. Perhaps unhappy with that metaphor, Sadoleto turns to a medical one: as happens in the use of poultice (*cataplasmatis*), put on the body for the breaking out of pus; when they do not manage to take away all of the pus but try to repress its force in one part of the body they give cause and motion to the pus so that it erupts even more sharply and violently (96v). This is the effect of the law on sinful humanity.

> The Apostle is speaking for every person in his own person, as if each were speaking one minute on behalf of the flesh and the next on behalf of the Spirit ...The sin which dwells, he says, whose *fomes* is placed in us by nature, is a seed-bed of lusts and of all rebelliousness, which it is not in our power to remove from us, and the frequency and the repetition by the practice of persuasion is turned into a habit of behavior is opposed to the law and prevails against the reason of the mind.

A Sadoleto is starkly pessimistic about the human condition in a manner almost reminiscent of his soon-to-be adversary in his own diocese (Calvin). It is a supremely Augustinian account without the more 'mainstream Catholic' remedy to be found in the Church's sacraments, and this perhaps explains why he was for a time disgraced after his commentary's publication.

9. Brenz, Johannes, 1499–1570.
Explicatio Epistolae Pauli ad Romanos (Schwäbisch Hall, 1538), in S. Strohm (Hrsg.), *Johannes Brenz, Schriftauslegung: Teil 2* (Tübingen: Mohr Siebeck, 1986).

Brenz recounts how marriage to 'Moses' or the law was oppressive, expecting perfect righteousness, and like a tyrannical husband it repudiated the errant wife; the result was to become more aware of sin and also hate the law; thus the law handed man over to Satan. However Christ dissolved the law by his death so that it had no grounds for exercising tyranny over us. The image of head and body or man and wife best expresses the situation between Christ and the believer. The wife shares the honor and goods of the husband and his name, and even becomes queen; he gives her his righteousness and the Holy Spirit by whose power we can do good things (*cuius viribus possumus bona facere*). And if anyone sins from weakness he restores them, unlike the law; but to serve (in the sense of intentional persistence) the flesh or sin would be adultery.

Of course the law's demands excite sin but they do not cause it. But why did God give law in the first place? Well, for the purpose of giving a diagnosis before the cure

---

A Analysis of Sadoleto's perception of the human condition.

so that we would learn that there is a medicine we need. And since the law is necessary, then so are its punishments.

In vv. 7–8 Paul wants to show us the spiritual use of the law. Paul is not here speaking of the civil use of the law, but of the spiritual use of the law in conscience, which is more necessary for the *iustificandis* (an interesting gerundive!) The law does not cause sin to grow; the sins are already there full grown but latent and unknown. The law tells us of the grave seriousness of the situation; for our tendency is to restrict 'sin' to 'big' sins like murder and theft. It is original sin that makes us corrupt underneath. The sophists are simply wrong to say that not ceremonial but moral law does justify; it doesn't. Paul before his conversion was like a child. Children sin, but only with adolescence do they understand the weight of sin and feel the magnitude of God's wrath against sin.

Vv. 9–11 make us wonder 'how could Paul have lived without the law'? Well he was never lawless, but Paul before his conversion lived without law, in the sense that an external law-keeping which does not feel the enormity of sin is living without the law. We need to learn and recite the Decalogue so as to avoid the wretchedness of false security.

On v. 14, 'the law is spiritual', Paul includes himself in those who lack the Holy Spirit by nature. As 'venditus' he is a total slave; even saints like David had sins waiting to spring up. There is no justifying before God – Luke 17:10: 'when all is done, say "we are only servants"'. Job did well in saying 'The Lord giveth…', but he had execrations and blasphemies against God lurking within which came out later. 7:15 tells us that we do not sin unwillingly. To be sure, original sin does capture even our will, yet we will to sin.

In vv. 16–18 Paul had transferred blame from law to himself, and now on to sin. Paul is clearly speaking about the renewed in Christ and saintly people (*de renatis in Christo et sanctis*), and each of them is '*duplex*'. Anything done from flesh is ungodly and is the work of the external earthly man. The internal spiritual man is different since by faith he has accepted Christ to indwell him. For Christ is the treasury of heavenly goods and presents his whole treasury with himself to the one believing. There are two men who live in the saint: one from the first birth, the other from the second; each lives but with this qualification, that in the saints the one spiritual man dominates the old and does not allow him to exercise his lust but restrains his desires. The old can boss the new for a season, but normality will be restored.

So we should understand: *Ego vetus et carnalis homo facio, quod* ego spiritualis et novus homo *non volo*. It is the old man who *does*, but the new man who does *not* so desire. There might still be natural virtues in people but none that would please God or save them.

7:18b–20 recounts the example of Abraham who did obedient, good work but also omitted things he should have done, although David is an even better example of that. It is true that the righteous man sins in good work: not that the work itself is not good, but that we do it imperfectly because of 'the other man'. Paul concludes with the cry of v. 25, *Miser ergo homo, quis me liberabit?* Brenz comments: 'Now we are being liberated through Christ.' One should note the use of the present tense here ('*liberamur autem per Christum*').

10. Bucer, Martin, 1491–1551.
Metaphrasis et Enarratio in Epistolam D. Pauli Apostoli ad Romanos ... (Basileae, 1562).

Martin Bucer, as was his reputation, is prolix and exhausting, yet there is much of interest amid all the repetition and at times lack of clarity. Bucer from his paraphrase of v. 6 concludes that the law is useful for godliness and that the one who studies it is blessed, but since the law does not by itself promote godliness it is actually more blessed to be dead to the law. Indeed, although those such as Timothy were advised by Paul to grasp the law that has 'incubated' in him since his youth, for others whom the Spirit of Christ does not aid the Mosaic sacrifices get in the way of simple faith in Christ and ruin the majesty of the law. Therefore Paul encouraged Timothy to study the Law, for the law of God stirred up the sin that was still in him *ad Christum*: the believer is driven to penitence and to find Christ. The restitution of original righteousness by faith in Christ is not yet complete. The wound is deep. The law also works by terrifying us of God's judgment. The people of the old covenant were like children in the household of God, in that they knew nothing of the maturity that comes with the Spirit of Christ. The law is necessary for the Christian until the old Adam is totally remade and we are released from the law, which is all the while, with the Spirit's supervision, correcting us and driving us towards Christ, as we now no longer live ourselves but Christ lives in us. Thus the verses can be reconciled in which we are proclaimed to be dead to the law and yet are ordered to address ourselves to the law: the law is confirmed *both* to be harmful and to be of highest salvific import. This is not a contradiction; rather it corresponds with the contradiction of grace and sin or Christ and Adam in a believer. The law in itself is good, but *per accidens* it provokes sin in us. Law is properly that which is written – by Moses or others for other civilizations: all law which forbids evil and promotes the good is divine law. Any trace of natural law inside the human soul has been obliterated by sin, so that some external law is needed to tell us our plight, for the law of the mind of our nature is depravity. Here there is a definite preference for Augustine's anthropology over that of the Eastern fathers. To become 'dead' is to be conscious of wrongdoing, not unconscious of it, as Chrysostom thought. Only then do we sense the horror of God's wrath and hell, the despair of Cain and Judas. When sin was dead we were alive, when it revived we died – through the law. The law of course is holy, as Psalm 19 and other passages attest.

He then breaks off to give a summary: the only difference between Paul and Moses on the tenth commandment is that Moses commands that we should not covet certain things, Paul more radically that we should not covet. The tenth commandment tells us that it is not just about doing or abstaining from doing but having the right mind. The ten commandments are really ten words, and as such not 'legalistic', while from the Gospel we learn that we cannot please God from the heart unless we are first of all persuaded that he is propitious towards us. So it is important to take the first words of Exodus 20 as part of the whole: 'I am the Lord your God who brought you out of the land of Egypt'. At the end of the section he appends the thought that the Spirit is of the few, since to the few is it given to truly believe in Christ. The spiritual lesson that the law teaches is to have a living faith in God, and to be a sure lover of one's neighbor and all such things, and it shows the means, the Spirit who writes on the heart so that even the one who is not yet renewed by the Spirit of Christ can perceive it. The metaphor of being a slave to sin, thinks Bucer, might be slightly exaggerated in its imagery. Yet, as long as we are not totally renewed by Christ we are driven to evil, on the way toward the demon-possession Christ warns us about. We can thus speak of two causes of our sin, the emptiness of our human nature and the strong power of sin in all things. The Apostle in this chapter represents the person who loves the law, in other words, a believer. But because the normal Christian life is one in which the will is split (or rather *duplex*), the will, the controlling faculty loved by humanists, does not really do such a good job integrating the person. David in his adultery with Bathsheba is one example; although he loved the law and was taught in it, yet the violence of his desire carried him away. Bucer here seems almost to excuse David, as he does when he mentions that Peter was not even given time to consider that his fear of men should be outweighed by his fear of God and blind fear took over. It is the force of the evil thought which is often too strong for Christians in their 'middle state' of perfection. When he comes to the verse: 'But I am carnal' (v. 14), Paul is representative of 'us' who have such perversity of nature that we need to come running to Christ for his liberation. And whereas many ancient commentators thought 'I find this law in me' to mean the Torah, for Bucer it is clear that it means the wicked law of his members. In fact, Bucer reckons, there are five laws which Paul mentions: the law of the Spirit, the law of God, the law of the mind, the law of sin and the law of rebellion which is the law of Satan. The 'inner man' means not the inward part of a human being (mind, soul) but the renewed whole person. Right at the very end Paul seems to suggest that there is a better state of existence for mature Christians, that this state of losing a hard battle is for those who 'are not yet in the full freedom of the Spirit'. That possible state of Christian existence will be treated more fully in Ch 8. But in this seventh chapter he describes and explains the state of the man of God in his own example, one in whom the law is now known. This means that for Bucer, Romans 7 is about the post-conversion Paul but one who is on the way to a fuller belief in Christ and reception of his Spirit; thus the Romans 7 'Paul' is one who is more like a saint of the OT or like pre-Pentecost Peter.

11. Soto, Domingo de, 1494–1560.

In Epistolam Divi Pauli ad Romanos Commentarii (Antwerp, 1550).

H De Soto writes that the law is in itself good: hence the Manichaean and the Marcionite heresies openly are condemned as is their blaspheming about the law, since they defame the law and call it something evil. The law does give sin the opportunity for sinning. Sin itself is the cause of our troubles, given out dual nature. The law of the Spirit of life which is written in hearts is in continuity with the Mosaic or moral law. There is a superior part in us in which reason reigns, but also a sensual inferior part which is not so ruled but responds without reason's governance to material things. Now humans are *a priori* reasonable and only *a posteriori* sensual and carnal. For we were created free from servitude but sold ourselves into sin. Here Origen and Chrysostom may be followed. The later and the earlier Augustine are contrasted. In the 'late' *Two Letters against the Pelagians*, Augustine has recalled how many of the fathers, including Ambrose, Hilary and Gregory Nazianzen, believe that from v. 7 Paul is representing the groaning of believers who are wrestling with sin.. The law of God and the law of the mind coincide just as do the law of sin and the

---

H The law perceived as good guides the reading.

law of members, although the law of God is also the cause of the law of the mind. Against those who argue that being host to such a struggle would be unworthy of the great Saint Paul, we must remember that he was looking forward to a release from the body of sin, since it is not so much about release from guilt as release from the consequences of sin, something that is yet to come for the saintly believer. But, according to De Soto, the division here and now is one between mind and flesh, so that some of our actions will proceed from one, some from the other, but they cannot work together to produce some sort of neutral action.

12. Ochino, Bernardino, 1487–1564.
Bernhardini Ochini expositio Epistolæ diui Pauli ad Romanos / de Italico in Latinum translata [by S. Châteillon] (Augustæ Vindelicorum: P. Vilhardus, 1550).

Ochino writes in a loose, flowery style and in giving his opinion is more expansive on some verses than on others. It is only the Spirit or the interior breath of God, the living law and love marked on our souls through Christ, that can resist sin.

Paul, now regenerate, admits he was once blind, and unless the law inasmuch as it is righteous had declared these things to be sins to be avoided, he would not have recognized them as such.

> Paul is saying that once he slept in his sin, until he was reminded, or woken up to it. Here he is speaking in the person of the unregenerate man, earthly, so that I do not have it in my power not only to love God with my whole heart ...but not even to be restrained in one's emotions. Apart from God's help I would not be able not to love myself and human things beyond measure nor to love God above all nature of things, let alone with all my heart.

'In me, that is, in my flesh, there is no good thing'. In the corporeal human being, in whom the law fulfils its office, in whose person Paul speaks, there is all the same something good; for the knowledge of God's will is present, but this goodness is not located in *the flesh*. The contests of praiseworthy battles and the spark of will are within; but it is not in the flesh by which they show whatever in us strives for our cause. 'It is not I that do it but the sin with in me': Sin harshly orders the unregenerate so that I am compelled to do that which my mind illuminated by the divine law abhors. Ochino believes in 'higher' and 'lower' parts of the human being.

13. Alesius, Alexander, 1500–1565.
Omnes Disputationes D. Alexandri Alesij de Tota Epistola ad Romanos (Lipsiae: G. Hantzsch, 1553).

Alesius's commentary has a preface by Melanchthon. With this in mind perhaps it is not so surprising that Alesius insists that Romans 7 is about true penance as penitence of the heart. You are dead to the law if you are converted by the true mortification of sin in penitence (*per veram mortificationem peccati in poenitentia*) and believers are to obey their new husband, Christ. Alesius then suggests that there are three types of people. There are those who are smug Pharisee, or Epicurean, whose consciences seem clear; second, those oppressed by their consciences; and third and best, those whose conviction comes from the voice of the gospel (*pavoribus conscientiae eriguntur voce Evangelii*) that leads them to peace. There need be no worry about whether ascribing sin to himself is a problem for the saintliness of Paul: for he is doing just what the prophets in whose tradition he stands used to do, speaking of the sin of his people just as if it were his own. This counters the contention of those sophists who on account of Paul's saintliness hold that he was not writing about himself, or only of his pre-conversion state, or maintain that the law is just too hard to keep. Paul was not without sin, and only hypocrites think that such a state is possible. Melanchthon had already been clear about this, back in 1529. But Alesius's argument seems to be that Paul is perhaps exaggerating his sin in order to represent his (Christian) people, just as Bucer, with like sensitivity to Paul the rhetorician, had also suggested.

14. Musculus, Wolfgang, 1497–1563.

In Epistolam Apostoli Pauli ad Romanos: Commentarij (Basileae: per Ioannes Heruagios, 1555).

Musculus observes that it is indwelling sin, not the law or 'the opinion of my mind' that is responsible for captivity to sin which leads to death. It is interesting that he offers a tripartite typology of *Christians*. He then adds that there are three types of saints: (1) those who in the manner of drunkards are *sopitus* and live in sins and in whom the law of God is not at work. (2) Those who whenever they stop to consider the illumination by judgment of reason and the unshaken disposition, they then desire to do what is good and thus agree with and delight in the law of God and hate evil but are still under the tyranny of sin which is too strong for them, so that they are driven unwillingly to evil and the good which they approve desire and wish they do not do, but the evil which they hate and shun, that they do. To this category should be referred those things which Paul here discusses from his own example. In him the struggle of flesh and spirit went on. 'The flesh has not yet beaten the Lord and the spirit is fighting back but not yet winning ... And what I say here about the lustful sense of the flesh, the same can be maintained about the sense of fear, of which examples are David's adultery and Peter's denial'. These Anabaptist pretenders are to be dismissed who excusing their sins say, 'Not I but my flesh did it', while all the time are judges of everyone, looking down on them. (3) The third type are those in whom the force and wickedness of sin are controlled and overcome through the Holy Spirit. Set in the freedom of righteousness, they obey not the law of sin but rather the law of the Spirit reigning in their members, and they have the faculty of willing and also the faculty of accomplishing. This category we find treated in the next chapter in which the power and grace of Christ will be set forth along with the action and work of the Holy Spirit in believers, about which the prophets looking forward to the New Testament foretold many things.

So Musculus, like Bucer, thinks that there is a Christian perfection which lies ahead.

15. Calvin, John, 1509–1564.

Commentarius in Epistolam Pauli ad Romanos, edidit T. H. L. Parker (Leiden: Brill, 1981) (originally published posthumously in 1579).

Calvin likes the metaphor of the law putting pressure on sin, so that it erupts more violently. The important point for Reformed theology is that the Pharisees failed to live by the law in that they could not keep a commandment like 'do not covet' since they kept it only in an external way.

> Thus the eyes of hypocrites are covered with a veil, that they see not … We ought, at the same time, to remember the difference between evil lustings or covetings which gain consent, and the lusting which tempts and moves our hearts, but stops in the midst of its course.

Calvin having made this distinction does not seem to consider that 'the Papists' only mean that it is the latter (lusting which tempts) which is no sin. However the Calvinist position is that sin as evil consent is also present in the regenerate. On v. 14 he mentions that unlike 'some' who think that 'the law is spiritual' means that the law has to do with inward religion, Calvin prefers to see it as having to do with its being antipathetic to the flesh.

He demonstrates how human bondage is a chosen unfreedom:

> We are so entirely controlled by the power of sin, that the whole mind, the whole heart, and all our actions are under its influence. Compulsion I always except, for we sin spontaneously, as it would be no sin, were it not voluntary. But we are so given up to sin, that we can do willingly nothing but sin; for the corruption which bears rule within us thus drives us onward. Hence this comparison does not import, as they say, a forced service, but a voluntary obedience, which an inbred bondage inclines us to render.

The ungodly consent to and approve of sin, even while troubled by it at times.

> Hence the case of a regenerated man is the most suitable; for by this you may know how much is the contrariety between our nature and the righteousness of the law.

Calvin is thus happy to say that the believer is divided in the way an unbeliever is not, and the struggle leads him to rely more on the Spirit. Augustine was right to change his mind and in the letter to Boniface apply this to the regenerate.

The flesh is totally opposed to the Spirit, but Paul's soul does have room for the former. On v. 17 he writes:

> But Paul here denies that he is wholly possessed by sin; nay, he declares himself to be exempt from its bondage, as though he had said, that sin only dwelt in some part of his soul, while with an earnest feeling of heart he strove for and aspired after the righteousness of God, and clearly proved that he had the law of God engraved within him.

It seems that Calvin is clear that he wants to show that it is not all 'doom and gloom' in the state of a believer, through his attention to two little words from v.18 which probably had little such significance for Paul:

> Then *in me*, means the same as though he had said, 'So far as it regards myself'. In the first part he indeed arraigns himself as being wholly depraved, for he confesses that no good dwelt in him; and then he subjoins a modification, lest

> he should slight the grace of God which also dwelt in him, but was no part of his flesh … by the term *spirit*, which is commonly opposed to the flesh, he means that part of the soul which the Spirit of God has so re-formed, and purified from corruption, that God's image shines forth in it.

On v. 22 the anthropological statement is clearly made. **A** Calvin is somewhere between the anthropology of lower and higher parts (typically Catholic) and that of the Spirit and Flesh as opposing forces (typically Lutheran.)

> But we ought to notice carefully the meaning of the *inner man* and of the *members;* which many have not rightly understood, and have therefore stumbled at this stone. The inner man then is not simply the soul, but that spiritual part which has been regenerated by God; and the members signify the other remaining part; for as the soul is the superior, and the body the inferior part of man, so the spirit is superior to the flesh.

16. Vermigli, Pietro Martire, 1499–1562.

In Epistolam S. Pauli Apostoli ad Romanos, D. Petri Martyris Vermilii Florentini (Tiguri: apud A. Gesnerum, 1559).

Vermigli is clear about the indwelling of sin in believers, even while they despise it. The law by nature was good and intended to bring life, as Moses in Deuteronomy 30 said. Christ also taught that one should keep the commandments in order to enter life. The point is, however, that Christ is the only one who has ever been free from sin. The Apostle does indeed say that 'we have been liberated from sin through Christ: however not fully but only with an inchoate liberty'.

> The 'Pelagians' say that Paul called himself carnal because since he lived here he had not yet put on the spiritual flesh which we will have in the Resurrection. But he carries this around still, which with many troubles in the meantime is a harmful thing.

In other words they say he is just lamenting his mortal state: no, he is lamenting his inner corruption. And the devil gets even into our thoughts. Ambrose says this, but the 'Scholastici' don't like to admit this, just as they do not like to admit there is no place in Paul for free will. Such people like to think that 'I do not do what I want but what I hate' is to be referred only to the first motions (i.e. temptation). But, as Scripture clearly says, the righteous also fall and we all offend in many ways, so he does not see why the opinion of the Apostle has to be twisted so. He says that *he* did not do it in that he as a whole did not do it, since the regenerate part of him abhorred it.

> These things cannot be experienced by those who are distant from Christ and are godless and without a share in the Holy Spirit. Those who deny this are led very much by a logic that persuades them that sin has no place in saintly people.

So this passage is not just about the non-regenerate but believers. Paul to the Galatians does not say 'walk in the Spirit and you will not have desires of the flesh', but only that you will not carry out these desires. David laments his sin, Isaiah speaks

---

A Analysis of Calvin's anthropology.

of our filthy rags, I John says not to pretend we have no sin and James that we offend in many ways. There is also the witness of Augustine *Against Julian*, Book 6.

17. Viguerius, Joannes, fl. 1558.
D. Pauli epistolam ad Romanos ... (Parisiis: Vaeneunt apud Claudium Fremy, 1560).

Viguerius first treats the question of whether it is the natural law that Christians are not free from: 'some' think that given the mixed Gentile-Jewish congregation this would make sense. Others think it is the Jewish law of Moses which he means. *Scientibus legem loquor* is key here: for not all of them would have known the law of Moses, so it must be the Jews he is addressing. It is those converted from Judaism who were asserting that the law of Moses needed to be kept along with the Gospel since it was given by God; and so he is not addressing those converted from the Gentile world.

In the midst of representing Paul's 'pessimistic' outlook, Viguerius enjoys speaking brightly about bearing fruit for the glory of God. There is an assertion that the law can be kept through the help of the Spirit who writes the new law on the heart. The apostle despises those who blame the law, just as Ps 18 (19) praises the law's goodness. The law does a good job in that without it, one would not have known that sin was offensive to God and punishable. The mention of concupiscence in *Nam concupiscentiam nesciebam* means the root of all actual sins, '*generale peccatum*' (with a note in the margin; Aug 9!!) It is not the law, for Paul says the opportunity was taken, not that the opportunity was *given (occasione autem accepta)*.

Perhaps to be clear it is better to say that sin 'entered', to add a substance to the already existing *fomes* of original sin which in turn is nothing other than the sensory appetite deprived of original justice. **H** Paul then speaks *not* in his own person but in the person of the destitute humanity. What then happened is that sin grew out of the *fomes* and was something done wilfully and consciously after the law came; there is a change epistemologically in the awareness of sin, which even if not aware of guilt is aware of sin and under death's sway. Viguerius answers the question of the law's goodness by referring the mention of the law as spiritual to the new law of the spiritual gospel. He eventually addresses the key question: is this humanity without grace or with it? With it, he answers, because only one under grace would be able to admit he was carnal; this is when the mind is under attack from rather than subject to sin, a sin which has its base in the lower part. And so when Paul speaks of the regenerate person he can say he is sold under sin in the sense that there is original sin out of which fleshly activity arises in the lower part. It is an area hard to take control over, for even the will is divided.

> If this is to be understood about the just man, it should be taken to be about incomplete action, which consists in no more than concupiscence getting in the way of the judgement of reason and about a hate which is complete: such as in the Psalmist, I hated them with a perfect hate.

In other words as a believer one still has the passion of the sin, but it does not become sin through action because his hatred of sin is more comprehensive.

H The 'I' as corporate.

> And since the Lutherans and the innovating heretics have a crooked understanding of this phrase, they deny human free will, especially in the sinful human, saying that he is lame and is not even able to limp and do wrong.

Viguerius then insists that 'free' is that which is not determined, like fire, is fixed to ascend and stones to fall. For we choose which way to fall, and then we will be confirmed in our choice of good or evil (*firmatus in bonum/malum*). That we have free will can be seen from experience, reason and scripture as interpreted by the *Ecclesia Catholica*. Paul here is the natural man who wants to do good – that is, *secundum naturam vel gratiam*.

> For, as we said, if the Apostle is understood to be speaking about man as sinner, it is clear that he does not speak about a will and a hatred that is completed in particular action, but rather about will and hatred which is *not* completed and is general.

Viguerius mentions 'the *fomes peccati* which Apostle calls *peccatum*'(!!), Viguerius seem unaware that Paul's use of *peccatum* is an argument for the continuing indwelling of sin in believers; he tries to gloss *peccatum* so as to say 'when Paul writes "*peccatum*" he really means "*fomes peccati*"'. It is this which drives our reason to evil.

Just like Cajetan, so Viguerius concludes that the grace of God dwells not in the flesh but in the mind or heart (Ephesians 3:17). The struggler is indeed the regenerate Paul – this is not an unbeliever but one under the goodness of grace. At this point there is a disagreement with St Thomas's teaching that virtues can be infused into the lower part of the soul so as to counterbalance and sooth the ravings of vices. For the Apostle denies this, meaning to exclude any goodness alone which would be able to prevent totally the dominion of sin, or would totally subject the sensory appetite to the reason so it would in no way be able to lust against the spirit and in no way incline to evil, as it was in Adam and will be in the blessed (in heaven). It takes more than just human goodness.

18. Bèze, Théodore de, 1519–1605.

Cours sur les épitres aux Romains et aux Hébreux 1564–66, d'après les notes de Marcus Widler: Thèses disputes à l'Académie de Genève, 1564–67. Edités par Pierre Frankel et Luc Perrotet (Genève: Libraire Droz, 1988).

Beza establishes that Paul full of the Holy Spirit speaks in his Apostolic authority not as a man but as the *organon* and instrument of God. And if a regenerate person is lacking, how much more the unregenerate?! Of course the Apostle approved of much that he did: I Cor. 11:1, 'be imitators of me as I of Christ'. And of course he sins only unwillingly. Against the Catholic line of argument, Beza asserts: 'When we say that we are regenerate and that yet the Spirit fights with the flesh, do not imagine that the higher part is regenerate and the lower not. That is diabolical'. The intellect, will and the active faculties – all of these have regenerate and unregenerate parts. The fact is that the regenerating power is far more efficacious within than outward; there is more will than act – the latter has yet to strengthen; just as when an arrow is fired it slows down as it reaches its target. Sin remains intrinsic; however in the future it will be driven away.

'If the sophists wish to infer that our nature is harmed, I concede that we do not do well as mutilated, since our will is not strong enough to do well'. It seems harsh to say that there was nothing good in Paul, but it is in his flesh that we mean; he did not say that he didn't have the power to do good but to *perfect* the good. David was regenerate at the time he committed adultery and the killing that went with it. Of course drunken men have no sense of reason, yet all the same the soul remains in them without consenting. The vapors get in the way of the organs so that reason cannot work. So too it happens in the case of regenerate men: the Spirit is quenched (*suffocatur*). The law works in the unregenerate to beget (*gignere*) a sense of sin and that sin become more focused. But in the regenerate, it works so that that we know our weakness and leads us in the right way.

Interiorem hominem is what Paul calls the regenerate part. But one should not think that it denotes the intellect alone (as Catholics like Cajetan would have it). For if *interior* meant intellect then *membra* would be the body, which does not fit. The soul is meant to rule the whole person and so being within the person (homo) it is called *interior homo.*

19. Olevian, Caspar, 1536–1587.

In Epistolam D. Pauli Apostoli ad Romanos Notae, ex Gaspari Oleviani Concionibus excerptae, et a Theodoro Beza editae (Geneva, 1584).

Olevian writes that sin under the law increases, in the way that a natural force causes an opposing reaction. This has the result of making sin and evil within humans clearly recognizable, as an ulcer in those who are going to be healed has to come to the surface, driving us to seek the doctor and putting them on their guard. But its purpose is that they might know the extent of grace in Christ. **H** The law is spiritual: it is the revealing of eternal wisdom in God and of created wisdom in angels and humans, to which all persons want to be conformed. There is a state before conversion in which all are enslaved, after conversion, sin attacks a faithful person, yet he is not dominated by it and it does not so rule that the man obeys sin fully. So sin is unable to dominate faithful believers, since although they have the law, they are not under the law, that is, under the law's compulsion and curse, but are under grace. For the grace under which believers stand is twofold: 1. In that the believer has the law written by the Holy Spirit in his heart which is in part renewed, the law does not increase sin, nor hatred of the law and divine justice in him, for he loves it, that is the law. 2. The other particular grace is the imputation of free grace.

Believers walk not according to the flesh but according to the Spirit, since they are ruled by the Spirit of God in the special disposition of their heart, although they are attacked by the flesh. For the law produces death only in the non-reborn but performs a more positive function in the reborn: it brings forth salvific fruit of holiness. So that the recognition of sin might grow in believers, and they be truly humbly reformed to the image of God, the law of God is an instrument of the Holy Spirit for that end. Jeremiah 31 says not that he will give a new law, but that whereas he wrote on tables of stone he will write on their hearts. So Paul is the example of one who fights all his life to prove he is not the slave of sin.

H The law is seen as spiritual which guides its understanding.

20. Musso, Cornelius, 1511–1574.

In B. Pauli Apostou (sic) Epistolam ad Romanos absolutissima Commentaria (Venetiis, 1588).

Musso observes that the law is that which gives knowledge that sin is sin, but of course as a witness, as a sign towards sin, it does not itself work sin. In this chapter Paul is playing the role of universal humanity in its fallenness. While 'flesh' means not a part but the whole person in corruption, 'spirit' means the whole person according to the superior part of a person. What is remarkable is the proximity to Calvin on this.

Conclusion

What do these commentators contribute to a modern-day reading of Romans 7? Well, they take the Old Covenant very seriously and thus the OT is hardly left behind as 'the letter' but is read 'spiritually' in the light of Christ, to edify Christians. They see original sin not as something 'tragic' (as, say, does Krister Stendhal in his *Final Account: Paul's Letter to the Romans*), but as wilful, chosen, guilty and requiring radical help. They see the law and the spirit as not opposed but mutually reinforcing. As Volker Stolle has recently argued, Luther maintained against the dispensationalism of Agricola that the law set standards of good behavior or *Lebensordnung*. **C** Even Luther was more 'new perspective' than one might expect. The strong ecclesiological dimension to so many of these commentaries denies any accusation of early modern 'individualism'. The Reformation commentators are fiercely theological. For them Romans is not just about 'identity' but about deeper matters, even where they disagree on these. They differ on the extent to which God's grace builds on the spiritual desire of the 'inner person' and what the Church's sacramental activity contributes. But these disagreements cause us to read the text more carefully and to take Paul the Apostle and theologian at his word.

C Interpretation of the commentaries analyzed in the light of issues relevant in contemporary interpretation.

Issues Arising from the Comparison of Reformation Commentators

Response to Mark W. Elliott

William S. Campbell

As Mark Elliott's title suggests, there are obvious weaknesses in T. H. L. Parker's overview of Romans in the decade between 1532 and 1542. I have no real dispute with his three-point critique: that Parker's story of Reformation Romans in one decade is lacking in both beginning and resolution, that there is a lack of focus on major theological struggles, and that better passages could have been chosen from Romans by which to illustrate the stance of the commentaries.

But if we choose to concentrate on a different chapter of Romans, we must be careful not to lay ourselves open to similar criticisms. Any 'snapshot' of scholarship on a limited area of text in a limited historical period is necessarily a very tendentious enterprise, liable to misconception by its artificial and self-imposed boundaries. For example, if the exercise is to review the commentaries published in a given decade, the list should really only include those published for the first time within that period, or else only the additions or emendations should be noted since the other republished material from a previous version of the commentary rightly belongs to an earlier decade. Also, in order to avoid laying ourselves open to criticism, we need to be clear firstly as to what is the purpose of the exercise on which we are embarking, as well as from what perspective we are evaluating.

A synchronic reading is exceedingly useful for highlighting the *historical process* in a given decade by facilitating a close look at the forces for change, etc. But if the primary concern is to measure the overall contribution of a given commentator in order to demonstrate the *progress in exegesis* of Romans in a certain period, then a short period such as Parker has chosen is too limited. Also, from this perspective, it would be important to put most emphasis upon the final edition of an author's work, rather than those that had been later emended. Elliott rightly questions whether it is sensible to prefer the polemical use of Romans by Calvin in the early 1540's to his more mature and considered treatment of the 1550's. But if, on the other hand, our interest lies primarily in developments within the 1540's, then it would be legitimate, even essential, to use Calvin's 1540's commentary. Elliott's more extensive period of comparison is in this respect less problematic, more useful and therefore offers greater potential. His intention to 'aim to show more clearly what was at issue between the interpreters' is, however, not self-explanatory. I take it that by 'what was at issue between the interpreters' he means the points at which they disagreed concerning the interpretation of scriptural passages and, since he also takes some note of the *Tendenz* of the respective interpretations, I take this to mean that he is also concerned with the reasons which lead them to this choice. It is interesting in this respect that Elliott notes the more positive perception of the law as spiritual on the part of Swiss commentators such as Oecolampadius and Bullinger.

A useful point of comparison in both Parker and Elliott's work concerns how these commentators viewed their function in relation to their predecessors. Bullinger, for example, follows Luther rather than Erasmus with regard to the clarity of scripture. If the scripture is not clear, it is because of our spiritual dullness or to a failure to read in context. Bucer is explicit in his intentions: 'I am working hard to show the consent of the Church throughout all ages'. It is also of interest which of the fathers they follow and which they oppose. Luther complains of the 'metaphysical theologians who ignore scriptural warrant'. In general Augustine ranks high with most commentators but it is not safe to presume agreement on this - innovation and individuality are not completely lost in that scholars can choose one authority over another, or even a particular author's opinion, where it is clear that this opinion was later discarded or modified. It therefore tends to be a process of selection within a varied tradition of readings rather than simply a following of one author as it were *en bloc*. Despite this, it has to be recognized that the risk of having one's reading labelled Pelagian continued to exercise a strong negative influence. Most significant however is Bullinger's recognition ... 'I observed that Luther came closer to the theology of the fathers than the schoolmen. I observed also that, whereas the schoolmen deferred to the opinions of the fathers, the fathers themselves deferred to the opinions of the two Testaments'. It would appear that medieval tradition was beginning to lose its authority. As Bullinger diagnosed it, the problem was that 'Canonical scripture lies neglected and in its stead human inventions are accepted, which century after century have been increasingly cultivated and foisted on the Church as next door to divine oracles' (Parker, p.15).

Parker summarizes his findings on the Romans commentaries in relation to the significance of Erasmus by noting three lines of influence, even though the fifth edition of Erasmus's *Novum Testamentum* and *Annotationes* were largely written before the decade he was considering (p.89).

1. Many of these commentators must have used Erasmus's edition of the Greek New Testament. All the authors here will either treat the Greek as authoritative or as a subsidiary authority by correcting the Vulgate, usually in their notes, and so in the 1530's the stranglehold of the Vulgate was loosened.

2. Indebtedness to Erasmus was not limited to his New Testament but extended also to his *Annotationes*. These were used, whether acknowledged or not, and in this respect they were, in Parker's words, 'modern commentators'.

3. The third line of influence, according to Parker, was Erasmus's emphasis on observing the context; this he reinstated in such a manner that 'after him, its place in expounding a document was accepted'. Heinrich Bullinger is one example of a scholar learning the significance of this factor.

There can be no doubt that the influence of Erasmus was one of several factors that produced innovation at the commencement of the period we are considering. The change in the status of the Greek text and the bearing of this on that of the Vulgate was itself a powerful force. But there was more than this. A similar factor was the rediscovery of Hebrew, as for example, in the case of Conrad Pellican (born in 1478, started to learn Hebrew in 1499, published his Romans commentary in 1539, and also wrote the first Hebrew grammar by a Christian); or similarly in the case of Martin Bucer who asserts that 'even the holy fathers themselves failed, from ignorance of the Hebrew tongue, to understand a lot of the Pauline language',

(Parker, pp. 37–38). It would be beneficial for our wider understanding if some indication could be given of how biblical interpretation generally was influenced by those changes that led to the Renaissance and how the Renaissance itself in turn effected change.

I thought it would have been helpful to have some form of grid through which to compare the commentators in relation to their interest in what I have noted as recurring themes. These are as follows: the use of scripture, both OT and NT; the use of analogies in explanation; in particular, their understanding of the divided person, inner and outer man, etc; the use of the Pharisees or OT Israelites as a negative foil; the references to the Spirit and whether the role ascribed is positive or negative; the relation of the content of Romans 7 to Romans 8 within the context of the letter and how this affects the stance adopted. In addition, it would be useful to see whether Catholic commentators differed on these issues from Protestant, as Elliott specifically notes in relation to Cajetan and the means of grace.

I realise that to look at some twenty commentaries is a major task in itself, and the fact that most early modern commentators treat Romans chapter by chapter imposes certain limits and makes some other options very difficult. I am of the opinion, however, that to consider Romans 7 even in comparative isolation from Romans 8 is to somewhat distort our image of Paul. I would like to know to what extent the choice of Romans 7 as the focus of enquiry is itself determined by Reformation interests rather than our own. If it is the former, then I can appreciate that this is of value in itself, but if it is determined mainly by the latter, then I think it should not have been considered on its own. I view the two chapters, or at least the greater part of the same, to be quite inseparable in Paul's argument concerning both flesh and law. If we read chapter 7 on its own, it suggests a far greater anthropological interest on the part of Paul than is typified elsewhere in Romans and the other main epistles. It is artificial to discuss law and flesh without reference to the Spirit and to the redemption of the body and the whole of creation. I acknowledge that this is a contemporary perspective not necessarily shared by the commentators of the Reformation era; but should we, for the purposes of our own evaluation, not be guided by what we now consider as best practice?

On the other hand, the fact that the writers of this period did not always read Romans 7 and 8 in conjunction is a useful indicator that their primary agenda was different from ours. I suspect that it was the all pervading concern with human sinfulness and the extent of this that made Romans 7 particularly significant, and thus another reason for our selection of it as an area of comparison. The problem with this chapter for interpreters, both Reformation and modern, is that in it there appears to be some duplicity in Paul's statements. This is particularly significant when commentators acknowledge that to recognize that one is a sinner is an indication of grace already at work. But what is the status of the 'anthropos' thus described: is it Saul or is it Paul? I suspect that the focus on this issue at the Reformation had something to do with debates about the actual difference in life that justification by faith was supposed to produce, an issue between Catholic and Protestant interpreters of Romans 7.

One of the major differences between these commentators and contemporary scholars is their lack of detailed reference to the historical context of Paul's letters. Whilst they do react to the fathers and to each other, it is not always explicit to what in their contemporary social setting they are reacting to. And even if we were intending only to look at their work from the perspective of the history of ideas, it would still be most beneficial if something in more detail of their social contexts could be supplied.

— CONCLUSION —

Reformers in Conversation over Romans: Diversity in Renewal and Continuity

Kathy Ehrensperger

The significance of the interpretation of Romans during the sixteenth century may be unmatched but the conversations and controversies between theologians of that time have extended their influence beyond their particular contexts and their theological and ecclesiastical concerns. Although these conversations and controversies are as contextual as any reading of Scripture, the significance of interpretive choices by sixteenth-century theologians renders these powerful voices which can hardly be ignored in contemporary conversations over the interpretation of this Pauline letter. This is not only due to the fact that they were great interpreters and theologians who addressed issues which are still deemed to be of significance even in entirely different contexts, but it has as much to do with the political and ecclesiastical impacts some of their interpretations have had and to some extent still have.

The excellent collection of articles in this volume reflects on specific aspects of these conversations in either focussing on a particular theologian's interpretation (i.e., Opitz) on the interpretation of specific chapters by one or more interpreters (Carrington, Sujin Pak, Elliott), on specific topics in the letter (Tait, Thompson) or paradigms which guided a particular theologian's interpretation (Stegemann, Hansen, Holder) or a combination of two or more of these.

Interpretive Conversations – Diachronic and Synchronic

The topics dealt with in these articles and the particular foci chosen are in themselves the result of hermeneutical choices not only of the twenty-first century authors in their interpretations of sixteenth century interpretations of Romans but also of the predecessors of the latter. These are topics and focal points of interpretation which emerged and re-emerged over time and space in ongoing synchronic as well as diachronic conversations over this letter. This is not to say that there are timeless universal themes emerging from these conversations which can be discussed beyond and irrespective of specific contexts. But no interpreter of Scripture, however innovative he/she may be, is detached from his/her context. Part of the context of reading Scripture is the tradition of reading Scripture, and thus in the case of Romans, the conversations over the interpretation of the letter of previous times and contexts. The most innovative interpreters of the sixteenth century themselves are excellent examples of such conversations over the meaning of a text over time and space. None of these interpreters denied significance and indebtedness one way or another to previous and contemporary interpreters. They are aware that they are partners in a conversation in its diachronic dimension. All of the sixteenth century interpreters dealt with in this volume are engaging with previous interpreters and explicitly acknowledge this. As Holder in relation to Calvin notes there is no linear chain of influence of one particular ancient partner in the conversation which led to a specific sixteenth century interpretation. As Holder convincingly demonstrates, the interpretive choices emerged out of a non-linear net of numerous factors (p.107). But a common factor for all of them was their aim to be true to tradition.

Inasmuch as they were looking for ways of understanding Romans in a meaningful way, in and for their particular contexts, they did not perceive themselves as creating something new. The call to a return to Scripture (which was not unique to those who eventually broke with the Roman Catholic church; cf. Carrington, p.11) did not intend to bypass the interpretation of the Church Fathers, and the urge for translations of the Scripture from the original Hebrew and Greek was not a drive for innovation but rather a concern to return to the origins of the Gospel. It is significant to note here that, as is highlighted by contributions to the previous volume in this series, *Medieval Readings of Romans,*[1] most of the issues that became so prominent in sixteenth century interpretations and had decisive political and ecclesial consequences were already under way, even explicitly addressed in earlier interpretations. What the contributions of this volume in conjunction with the previous volume in particular demonstrate is that reading Scripture, including Romans, is a collaborative and certainly not an individualistic enterprise. Even interpreters who are perceived to have had revolutionary new insights have found these in conversation with, and are indebted to, partners in that conversation. Luther's indebtedness to Augustine has been praised and criticized but never put into question. Calvin considered Chrysostom an excellent exegete but Augustine the better theologian, etc.

The sixteenth century interpreters are aware of the fact they are in conversation with traditions and acknowledge this, as does, e.g., Bullinger who views himself as 'part of a community of scholars who offered their interpretations as a basis for discussion' (p. 150). In his case this notably led to an attitude of humility as an interpreter since he perceived his interpretation as 'exegetical suggestion'; and thus the view that 'a lenient attitude towards the errors of previous scriptural exegetes is more appropriate than harsh criticism' (p.150). Although this attitude is not found in all sixteenth century interpreters it may be a part of a scholarly tradition worth cherishing!

The emphasis on cherishing tradition and diachronic as well as synchronic conversation over the meaning of Romans sounds almost like the rationale of the Romans Through History and Cultures Seminar! It moreover resonates with approaches which, following notions of Derrida and Levinas, perceive the search for truth and meaning as an ongoing negotiation of meaning in conversation over texts.[2] Despite the male domination in sixteenth century interpretation, this emphasis on the dimension of conversation in interpretation may prove to be a trajectory of tradition which may provide some link to feminist approaches to interpretation.

Hermeneutical Presuppositions and Interpretive Choices

The impact which certain sixteenth century interpretations of Romans have had indicates that the significance of tradition and the perception of interpretation as conversation were combined with another aspect which is highly significant when viewed in light of contemporary Pauline interpretation. The sixteenth century interpreters dealt with in the articles of this volume were not bound by tradition nor did they perceive interpretive conversations as a kind of chat-room where conversation is an end in itself. These conversations were seen as serving a specific purpose – to contribute to the understanding of Scripture, that is, to serve the honour and truth of Christ. Thus, their respective contributions to the interpretive conversations were shaped by choices concerning their diachronic conversation partners from tradition as well as by choices concerning key theological factors which supposedly guided their interpretation. It is significant to note how explicitly aware many of the interpreters were concerning this aspect of interpretation. To me they seem to demonstrate more awareness of the significance of interpretive choices guided by the hermeneutical presuppositions of the interpreter than is sometimes found in contemporary interpretation. The pre-Enlightenment interpreters in this respect provide examples which are worth being seriously considered by post-Enlightenment interpreters

Thus although Chrysostom was clearly Calvin's exegetical champion among the church fathers, when it comes to the interpretation of a theologically sensitive passage of Romans, he decides not to follow him but the conversation partner he perceives to be the 'better' theologian, that is, Augustine. This is an illuminating example of the priority of hermeneutical presuppositions in relation to exegetical choices (Holder, p.109). This could be judged as 'bad' exegesis on the part of Calvin. But the openness with which Calvin refers to his interpretive choice and his explicit acknowledgement of the fact that this is a choice guided by his hermeneutical presupposition is actually a remarkable example of transparency in the process of interpretation.

Even when one does not follow his interpretive decision the clarity of the interpreter about his own hermeneutical, that is, theological presuppositions is exemplary. From the perspective of contemporary interpretation this could be viewed as an almost paradigmatic approach to scriptural interpretation. In a context where there now exists a wide scholarly consensus that there is no perspective from nowhere and that the notion of objectivity is fuelled as much by hermeneutical presuppositions as any other scholarly stance, the necessity to clarify hermeneutical presuppositions of any Scriptural interpretation of Scripture should be self-evident. Feminists as well as theologians who were not part of mainstream scholarship were among the first in the contemporary discourse of biblical interpretation to emphasize this.[3] Interpreters of the sixteenth century may not come to mind as partners in the conversation over hermeneutical presuppositions in the first instance, but the examples in this volume demonstrate that they have something significant to contribute. The issue is not whether it is appropriate that presuppositions influence or even determine interpretive decisions. The issue is whether this is recognized and consciously discussed as a significant aspect in the process of interpretation or not. Calvin went so far as to contend that reading Scripture must be guided reading, and he claimed that his *Institutes* provided that guidance (cf. Holder p. 107). Nevertheless Romans was perceived to provide *in nuce* that hermeneutical framework for understanding scripture, or as Hansen formulates, that door and passageway. The interdependence of hermeneutical presuppositions and the interpretation of Scripture become obvious here.

The Reformation principle of the priority of Scripture is not understood by any of the Reformers as nurturing the illusion that a perceived plain reading of the text was possible. In their application of methods of interpretation they were all more or less indebted to the Humanists and their tradition, and some of them, like Bullinger, kept close links with these even after the ecclesial rupture. The decisive difference between 'old' and 'new' faith was actually not the 'return' to Scripture but the divergent hermeneutical/theological presuppositions of interpretation. The priority of such hermeneutical presuppositions was not denied by the Reformers, as the explicit example of Calvin, Bullinger, but also of Luther demonstrates. At the heart of their interpretive activities was their theological insight concerning the centrality of the doctrine of justification by faith. The principle of 'sola scriptura' is never viewed as having any meaning without the principles of 'sola fide', 'solus Christus' and 'soli Deo gloria'. In their understanding of these the Reformers differed, but they agreed that their reading of Scripture was guided by doctrine, theological foundation, or whatever term was used for the description of what went prior to interpretation. Although this is certainly not identical with a contemporary awareness of hermeneutical presuppositions in interpretation, the issue of reading from somewhere and through a specific lens was clearly recognized. The transparency concerning hermeneutical presuppositions and interpretive choices highlighted in the analyses of sixteenth century interpreters of Romans could be seen as a factor which could encourage similar transparency in the contemporary conversation of interpreters, not in the first instance to settle disputes over controversial interpretations but to clarify in the first instance what the dispute is about. Is it a controversy concerning methodological issues, or are there other, i.e., hermeneutical, philosophical, theological, or other issues, behind an exegetical discussion or a combination of a number of factors?

Contextual Factors

The presuppositions and interpretive choices do not happen in a vacuum. This could not be more obvious than in the interpretation of Romans during the sixteenth century. Not all Reformers reflected as consciously on this aspect as they did on their hermeneutical presuppositions, but the significance of the contextual dimension for many of the interpretations is addressed in some of the contributions to this volume. It is beyond doubt that Luther's interpretation of Rom 1:16 was not merely a particular exegesis of a biblical text but had much to do with the ecclesio-political as well as his personal situation. The recognition of the contextuality of sixteenth century interpretations is of a significance on the same scale as the recognition of the contextuality of the letter to the Romans itself. The differentiation worked out by Stegemann between the apocalyptic reading of Romans by Luther and the apocalyptic perception of the world by Paul in Romans contributes to a move away from the question "Did Luther get Paul right or not? to the question How did Luther read and interpret Paul? What was the context within which his hermeneutical presuppositions emerged and his interpretive choices were determined? The question which follows from this is not so much whether a so-called Lutheran Paul is the real Paul, or whether the Lutheran Paul needs to be de-Lutheranized, but what is the contribution and relevance of Luther's reading of Romans for the contemporary conversation over the reading of Romans. Given that interpretations are not only contextual, driven by hermeneutical presuppositions and choices, but also have effects, impact and consequences, this is a dimension which, in the evaluation of previous interpretations for the contemporary conversation, cannot be ignored.

Thus the fact that Bucer's as well as Bullinger's interpretations of Romans did not get the same prominent recognition as e.g. Calvin's or Luther's may be due less to their theological or exegetical quality than to contextual factors which influenced either their approach or/and the impact these commentaries had. Bucer tried to interpret Romans in view of a reconciliation between the differing strands of the 'new' faith he had hoped and worked for. This ecclesial as well as political goal influenced his interpretation in many aspects; thus in a time when confessional boundaries and sharp distinctions determined the ecclesial and political fields, an interpretation which tried to reconcile and accommodate differing strands of interpretations and even hermeneutical presuppositions had not much chance of being heard or read.

I wonder how much Bullinger's context of living in a loose political federation where negotiation was part of daily political life, combined with the experience of disaster resulting from Zwingli's attempt to violently promote the cause of the Reformation, shaped his way of theologizing. Certainly he came into a position of high responsibility when the Reformation in Zürich was in a critical phase and his interpretation had clearly the goal to strengthen the proclamation of Reformed insights. A significant way of doing this was the education of preachers who should be given guidance to understand the Scriptures. Noteworthy here is that Bullinger at certain points sounds like a contemporary interpreter when he emphasizes that Romans is a contextual letter, not a theological treatise, a proclamation of the gospel in a specific historical situation; that rhetoric provides the most useful tool for understanding the drive of Romans. Moreover Paul is perceived as speaking in a normal human manner primarily with the aim of being understood! In addition there is a remarkable emphasis on the covenantal dimension of the gospel – a notion which acts as one of the theological foundations of his reading of Romans. Whether there is again a contextual factor which contributed to this emphasis is an open, but in my view not unreasonable, question since Bullinger lived in a political entity which was constituted by a more or less voluntary covenant (and Calvin lived in close vicinity to it!). I cannot pursue these thoughts any further here but the influence of context upon hermeneutical presuppositions and interpretive choices should not be underestimated. According to Bourdieu we incorporate much of our context physically, psychologically and intellectually to what he labelled the *habitus*. That political, ecclesial and personal events shaped sixteenth century interpreters' approaches can hardly be doubted. This is not to claim that they were wholly determined by these since the way humans incorporate and relate to contexts leaves open a wide range of options. But theologizing takes place in this world, and this world certainly plays a role in the formulation of interpretive insights inasmuch as interpretive insights are not mere thoughts, and especially not in the case of the Reformers, but have impacts on the lives of contemporaries and even future generations.

Diversity in and from Tradition

Contemporary interpretations of Romans are guided by different hermeneutical presuppositions emerging from different contexts; but they are still in one way or another influenced by, if not dependent upon, interpretive choices made by sixteenth century interpreters. The hermeneutical presupposition that the core of the gospel was justification by faith in distinction from works of the law became a dominant framework of reading Paul and Romans, in particular in Protestant interpretation. The advent of the 'New Perspective' in the 1970s which emerged as a paradigm shift in Pauline studies but has been perceived by some scholars rather as a paradigm shift in the perception of first-century Judaism nevertheless initiated a fresh wave of rethinking many hermeneutical and theological presuppositions and thus has led to a broadening of readings of Romans in a wide range of ways. It has also initiated a reaction against what is perceived to be a the paradigm of the 'New Perspective' in the emergence of so-called theological interpretations of Romans as well as readings which seek to establish the accuracy of pre-New Perspective readings. The necessity of rethinking hermeneutical presuppositions afresh, and of reflecting openly about them time and again, is one aspect of theologizing through scriptural interpretation which is shared by the Reformers dealt with in these articles.

However, there is one fascinating dimension unfolding through the contributions of this volume: despite the conviction, shared by all the Reformers, that justification by faith is the core theological presupposition from which to read Scripture, and Romans in particular, their actual interpretations of the letter differ and that sometimes significantly. The one shared conviction, even the shared goal to serve with their interpretation, the cause of the Reformation, apparently was not sufficient common ground to lead them to arrive at shared interpretive conclusions. This indicates that this core doctrine was not sufficient or precise enough to lead to identical interpretations of Scripture even among contemporaries during the sixteenth century.

There are other factors involved which influenced and guided the Reformers' interpretations. I have mentioned already the significance of the representatives of tradition, the church fathers, which each Reformer chose as his guiding diachronic conversation partner. The diversity of the latter's respective emphases in interpretation is one source for emerging differences in the Reformers interpretations. Their contemporary conversation partners, their own different contexts and positions, were other factors which must have had significant influence on divergent emphases. In addition to these the doctrine of justification by faith, although shared by them, was/is by no means self-explanatory. It was as much subject to interpretation as Scripture itself, and they interpreted it in light of the contextual factors noted above, and of their readings of Scripture in turn, in different ways.

They all aimed at being true to the message of the gospel and true to tradition. Those who decided to break away from the Roman Catholic church saw in the cause of the Reformation the fulfilment of this aim. But nevertheless they arrived at a wide variety of divergent interpretations of the letter to the Romans. Thus, as highlighted in the contributions of this volume, differing emphases witness to the richness of the fruits of interpretation: the word must run free, the Torah is not identical with the law, Reformed doctrine is superior to exegetical accuracy or/and the notion that faith includes the faithfulness of God to his promises and thus to the emphasis that the message of the gospel cannot be understood except when read in light of the Old Testament/Hebrew Scriptures.

In conjunction with clear hermeneutical presuppositions these Reformers were not exempt from the burden or joy of interpretive choices. They thus were also not exempt from responsibility in and for interpretation. The Reformers did not shy away from the notion of hermeneutical and interpretive choices. They communicated even openly about these in their written conversations. Whether they were always aware of the implications of their choices and whether they were always able to bear the responsibility for their decisions is an open question. But they contributed to the emergence one not of tradition in the wake of the Reformation but a rich diversity of traditions. They can be exemplary for contemporary interpretation not in the sense of being copied but rather in their openness concerning presuppositions and choices, in their awareness that interpreting Scripture means to be part of an ongoing diachronic and synchronic conversation in which no issue will ever be finally settled; they can be exemplary also in their courage to be open about the fact that interpretation has also something to do with making choices. This transparency is a tradition with which contemporary scholarship must interact in open and creative conversation, thus aiming at being true to tradition in the fullest possible sense.

To be true to tradition thus cannot settle any debate over the interpretation of Scripture. Reading Romans in the wake of the tradition of the Reformation cannot but result in diversity - which is at the heart of any lively conversation over interpretation. That ethical responsibility is inherently part of that conversation[4], and part of that dimension which influences hermeneutical presuppositions and interpretive choices is an insight gained from the privileged position of hindsight. If certain interpretive choices are, upon hindsight, seen as having contributed to, or even caused effects upon others which are in contradiction to the message of the gospel, then such choices have disqualified themselves through the actual effects on the lives of real men, women, and children. This is not to judge those who at that time made such choices but to learn from what has happened in order to contribute responsibly to the interpretive conversation today. The contributions of this volume demonstrate that if we are really to be in conversation with the Reformers' readings of Romans, we must remember them not as exegetes who were in reaction against tradition, but as those who selectively chose within and in conversation with the diversity of earlier interpretations.[5]

Notes

[1] W. S. Campbell, P. S. Hawkins, B. D. Schildgen (eds.), *Medieval Readings of Romans* (London, New York: T.&T. Clark, 2007).

[2] See my 'Levinas, the Jewish Philosopher meets Paul, the Jewish Apostle: Reading Romans in the Face of the Other', in D. Odell-Scott (ed.) *Reading Romans with Contemporary Philosophers and Theologians* (London, New York: T.&T. Clark, 2007).

[3] Cf. my *That We May Be Mutually Encouraged: Feminism and the New Perspective in Pauline Studies* (London, New York, 2004), pp. 5–27.

[4] See D. Patte, *Ethics of Biblical Interpretation.* (Louisville,KY: Westminster/John Knox Press, 1995, and E. Schüssler Fiorenza, 'The Ethics of Interpretation: De-Centering Biblical Scholarship', *JBL*, 107 (1988), pp. 3–17.

[5] I wish to thank Carol Dery for her expertise in getting this book into camera-ready format and the department of Theology, Religious Studies and Islamic Studies, University of Wales Lampeter, UK for support for this project.

Contributors

WILLIAM S. CAMPBELL is Reader in Biblical Theology at the University of Wales, Lampeter, and editor of the *Journal of Beliefs and Values.* He has published widely on Paul and Christian Origins including *Paul's Gospel in an Intercultural Context: Jew and Gentile in the Letter to the Romans* (1992), *Paul and the Creation of Christian Identity* (2006), and he is co-editor with Peter S. Hawkins and Brenda Deen Schildgen of *Medieval Readings of Romans* (2007).

LAUREL CARRINGTON is Professor of History at St. Olaf College, Northfield, MN. Her publications include 'Calvin and Erasmus on Pastoral Formation', *Calvin and the Company of Pastors* (2004), 'Impiety Compounded: Scaliger's Double-Edged Critique of Erasmus', *Erasmus of Rotterdam Society Yearbook*, 22 (2002), 'Desiderius Erasmus', in *Reformation Theologians: An Introduction to Theology in the Early Modern Period,* Carter Lindberg, ed. (2002).

KATHY EHRENSPERGER is Senior Lecturer in New Testament Studies at the University of Wales, Lampeter. Her publications include *Paul and the Dynamics of Power: Communication and Interaction in the Early Christ-Movement* (2007), *That We May Be Mutually Encouraged: Feminism and the New Perspective in Pauline Studies* (2004), and 'Levinas, the Jewish Philosopher meets Paul, the Jewish Apostle: Reading Romans in the Face of the Other', in *Reading Romans with Contemporary Philosophers and Theologians* ed. by D. Odell-Scott (2007).

MARK W. ELLIOTT is Lecturer in Church History at the University of St. Andrews. He teaches in the areas of Early and Medieval Church, pre-Enlightenment Theology, and Christian life and thought since Reformation times, with a special interest in the history of biblical interpretation and theology. His publications include *The Song of Songs and Christology in the Early Church* (2000) ,*The Dynamics of Human Life*, ed. and contributor (2002), *Ancient Christian Commentary Series: Old Testament XI: Isaiah 40–66* , ed. (2007).

GARY NEAL HANSEN is Assistant Professor of Church History at University of Dubuque Theological Seminary. Among his recent and forthcoming publications are 'Traktate [Tracts and Treatises]', in *Calvin Handbuch*, ed. Herman Selderhuis; 'Calvin as Commentator on Hebrews and the Catholic Epistles', in *Calvin and the Bible*, ed. Donald K. McKim (2006); 'John Calvin's Non-Literal Exegesis', *Proceedings of the Ninth International Congress on Calvin Research, August 21–27, 2006* (Emden, Germany, forthcoming); 'John Calvin's Non-Literal Interpretation of Scripture: On Allegory', in *John Calvin and the Interpretation of Scripture*: Calvin Studies X and XI: Papers Presented at the 10th and 11th Colloquiums of the Calvin Studies Society at Columbia Theological Seminary January 28–29, 2000 and March 1–2, 2002 (2006).

R. WARD HOLDER is Associate Professor of Theology at Saint Anselm College, Manchester, NH. His Publications include *John Calvin and the Grounding of Biblical Interpretation: Calvin's First Commentaries* (2006); 'Calvin as Commentator on the Pauline Letters', Chapter 9 in *Calvin and the Bible*, Donald McKim (ed.) (2006); 'Paul as Calvin's (Ambivalent) Pastoral Model', in *Dutch Review of Church History* (2004); 'Calvin's Heritage', Chapter 14 in *The Cambridge Companion to John Calvin*, Donald McKim (ed.) (2004).

CYNTHIA BRIGGS KITTTREDGE is Associate Professor of New Testament at the Episcopal Theological Seminary of the Southwest, Austin, TX. Her publications include *Community and Authority: The Rhetoric of Obedience in the Pauline Tradition* (1998); 'Rethinking Authorship in the Letters of Paul: Elisabeth Schüssler Fiorenza's Model of Pauline Theology', in Kittredge, C. B, Matthews, S., Johnson-Debaufre, M. (eds.) *Walk in the Ways of Wisdom: Essays in Honor of Elisabeth Schüssler Fiorenza* (2003).

TROY W. MARTIN is Professor of Biblical Studies at Saint Xavier University, Chicago. Among his publications are *Metaphor and Composition in I Peter* (1992); *By Philosophy and Empty Deceit: Colossians as Response to a Cynic Critique* (1996); 'Covenant of Circumcision (Gen 17:9–14) and the Situational Antitheses in Gal 3:28', in *JBL* (2003); 'Paul's Argument from Nature for the Veil in 1 Corinthians 11:13–15: A Testicle instead of a Head-Covering', in *JBL* 2004.

PETER OPITZ is Privatdozent in Church History at the University of Zürich, Oberassistent at the Institut for Swiss Reformation, Zürich. Among his publications are *Calvins theologische Hermeneutik* (1994); *Heinrich Bullinger als Theologe* (2004); 'The Exegetical and Hermeneutical Work of John Oecolampadius, Huldrych Zwingli and John Calvin', in: *Hebrew Bible/Old Testament: The History of its Interpretation (HBOT), vol. II, From the Renaissance to the Enlightenment, B Reformation*, ed. by Magne Saebø (2007).

G. SUJIN PAK is Assistant Professor of the History of Christianity at Garrett-Evangelical Theological Seminary Evanston, IL. Her publications include 'Luther, Bucer, and Calvin on Psalms 8 and 16: Confessional Formation and the Question of Jewish Exegesis', in *The Formation of Clerical and Confessional Identities in Early Modern Europe*, ed. by Wim Janse and Barbara Pitkin, (2006); *The Judaizing Calvin: Sixteenth-Century Debates over the Messianic Psalms* (forthcoming).

KURT A. RICHARDSON is Professor in the Faculty of Theology, Department of Philosophy, McMaster University Hamilton, ON. Among his publications are *Commentary on the Epistle of James* (1997); *Reading Karl Barth: New Directions in North American Theology* (2004); *Nicea Scripturally Reasoned: Foundational Christian Theology* (2007); *Leviticus. Septuagint Commentary Series* (forthcoming).

EKKEHARD W. STEGEMANN is Professor of New Testament at the Theologische Fakultät, University of Basel. Among his publications are ed. with W. Stegemann, *The Jesus Movement: A Social History of its First Century* (1999); ed. with G. Pfleiderer, *Politische Religion. Geschichte und Gegenwart eines Problemfeldes* (2004) *Paulus und die Welt. Aufsätze*. ed. by Christina Tuor and Peter Wick (2005).

STANLEY K. STOWERS is Professor of Religious Studies at Brown University Providence, RI. Among his publications are *A Rereading of Romans: Justice, Jews and Gentiles* (1994); *Letter Writing in Greco-Roman Antiquity* (1986); *The Diatribe and Paul's Letter to the Romans* (1981). He has published more than thirty articles in books and peer reviewed journals, including a commentary on Fourth Maccabees (Harper's Bible Commentary).

EDWIN W. TAIT is Assistant Professor of Bible and Religion at Huntington University. His publications include 'The Regensburg Colloquy' and 'The Geneva Catechism', for the *Encyclopedia of Protestantism* (2004).

DEANNA A. THOMPSON is Chair and Associate Professor of Religion at Hamline University St. Paul, MN. Her publications include *Crossing the Divide: Luther, Feminism, and the Cross* (2004); 'Becoming a Feminist Theologian of the Cross', in *Cross Examinations: Readings on the Meaning of the Cross Today*, (ed.) Marit Trelstad (2006); 'Jesus Loved Her More Than the Rest: Mary Magdalene, The Sacred Feminine, and What's Really Been Covered Up', in *The Da Vinci Code in the Academy* (ed.) Bradley Bowers (2006); The Chapter on Martin Luther in *Empire and the Christian Tradition: New Readings of Classical Theologians*, (eds.) Don H. Compier, Kwok Pui-lan, Joerg Rieger (2007).

DAVID M. WHITFORD is Associate Professor of the History of Christianity at United Theological Seminary, Trotwood, OH. Among his publications are *Tyranny and Resistance: The Magdeburg Confession and the Lutheran Tradition* (2001); 'From Speyer to Magdeburg: The Development and Maturation of a Hybrid Theory of Resistance', *Archiv für Reformationsgeschichte*, 96 (2005); '*Cura Religionis* or Two Kingdoms: The Late Luther on Religion and the State', *Church History*, 73/1 (2004); 'Martin Luther's Political Encounters', in *The Cambridge Companion to Martin Luther*, (ed.) Donald K. McKim (2003). He is associate editor of *The Sixteenth Century Journal* and the editor of *Reformation and Early Modern Europe: A Guide to Research* (2007).

Bibliography

Primary Texts

Bibles

The New Oxford Annotated Bible, New Revised Standard Version with the Apocrypha. New York: Oxford University Press, 2001.

The New Oxford Annotated Bible, Revised Standard Version. New York: Oxford University Press, 1977.

Ancient, Medieval and Reformation Era Primary Texts

Alesius, Alexander. *Omnes Disputationes D. Alexandri Alesij de Tota Epistola ad Romanos.* (Lipsiae: G. Hantzsch, 1553).

Augustine. *De Sermone Domini.* Corpus Christianorum. Series Latina, v. 35. (Turnholt: Brepols, 1967).

Augustine. *Augustine: Earlier Writings.* Ed. J. H. S. Burleigh. (Philadelphia: Westminster Press, 1953).

Augustine. *Augustine: Later Writings.* Ed. J. H. S. Burleigh. (Philadelphia: Westminster Press, 1958).

Augustine. *Ad Simplicianum de Diversis Quaestionibus.* Corpus Christianorum Series Latina, v. 44. (Turnholt: Brepols, 1970).

Augustine. *Retractationes.* Corpus Christianorum Series Latina, v. 57. (Turnholt: Brepols, 1984).

Bèze, Théodore de. *Cours sur les épitres aux Romains et aux Hébreux 1564–66, d'après les notes de Marcus Widler: Thèses disputes à l'Académie de Genève, 15674–67.* (Ed. Pierre Frankel and Luc Perrotet. Genève: Libraire Droz, 1988).

Brenz, Johannes. *Explicatio Epistolae Pauli ad Romanos* (Schwäbisch Hall, 1538), in S. Strohm (Hrsg.), *Johannes Brenz, Schriftauslegung: Teil 2.* (Tübingen: Mohr Siebeck, 1986).

Bucer, Martin. *Metaphrasis et Enarratio in Epist. D. Pauli ad Romanos.* (Basel, 1562).

Bucer, Martin. *In Sacra Quatuor Evangelia Enarationes Perpetuae.* (Strasbourg, 1527, 1530, 1536).

Bucer, Martin. *Correspondance, jusqu'en1524.* Jean Rott (ed.) *Martini Buceri Opera Omnia*, series 3: *Correspondance*, vol. 1. (Leiden: Brill, 1979).

Bullinger, Heinrich. *In Omnes Apostolicas Epistolas Commentarii, HBBibl* 1, Nr 84–89.

Heinrich *Bullinger Werke. Dritte Abteilung: Theologische Schriften* Band 1, ed. by Hans-Georg vom Berg and Susanna Hausammann. (Zurich, 1983).

Bullinger, Heinrich. *In Sanctissimam Pauli ad Romanos Epistolam Heinrychi Bullingeri commentarius.* (Tiguri: Apud Christoph. Froschauer, mense Febr. anno 1533).

Calvin, John. *Opera Quae Supersunt Omnia.* 59 volumes. Ed. Wilhelm Baum, Edward Cunitz, & Edward Reuss. (Brunswick: Schwetschke and Sons, 1895).

Calvin, John. *Opera Selecta.* 5 volumes. 3rd ed. Ed. Peter Barth and Wilhelm Niesel. (Munich: Christian Kaiser, 1967).

Calvin, John. *Institutes of the Christian Religion.* Ed. John T. McNeill, Trans. Ford Lewis Battles. (Louisville: Westminster John Knox Press, 1960).

Calvin, John. *Ioannis Calvini Opera Exegetica,* vol. 13. Eds. T. H. L. Parker and D. C. Parker. (Genève: Librairie Droz, 1999).

Calvin, John. *The Bondage and Liberation of the Will.* Ed. A. N. S. Lane, Trans. G. I. Davies. (Grand Rapids: Baker, 1996).

Colet, John. *An Exposition of St Paul's Epistle to the Romans.* (Oxford, 1497). Trans. J. H. Lupton. (London: Bell & Daldy, 1873).

Erasmus, Desidirius. *Annotations on the New Testament Acts-Romans-I and II Corinthians.* Eds. A. Reeve and M. A. Screech. (Leiden: Brill, 1990).

Erasmus, Desidirius. *Paraphrases on Romans and Galatians.* Ed. Robert D. Sider ... [et al.] (Toronto: University of Toronto Press, 1984).

Erasmus von Rotterdam. *Ausgewählte Schriften.* Vierter Band. Ed. Winfried Lesowsky. (Darmstadt, 1969).

Luther, Martin. *Luther's Works.* Ed. Jaroslav Pelikan. (Philadelphia: Fortress Press, 1955–1986).

Luther, Martin. *D. Martin Luthers Werke: Kritische Gesamtausgaber.* 65 vols. in 127. (H. Böhlau, 1883–1993).

Luther, Martin. *Martin Luther: Selections from his Writings.* Ed. John Dillenberger. (New York: Doubleday, 1962).

Luther, Martin. *The Bondage of the Will*. Trans. J. I. Packer and O. R. Johnston. (Old Tappan, New Jersey: Revell, 1957).

Melanchthon, Philip. *Melanchthons Breifwechsel: Kritische und Kommentierte Gesamtausgabe*. Ed. H. Scheible. (Stuttgart: Frommann, 1977-).

Melanchthon, Philip. *Corpus Reformatorum. Philippi Melanchthonis Opera quae supersunt Omnia*. Ed. Karl Bretschneider and Heinrich Bindseil. (Halle: A. Schwetschke & Sons, 1834–1860).

Melanchthon, Philip. *Commentary on Romans*. Trans. Fred Kramer. (St. Louis: Concordia, 1992).

Musculus, Wolfgang. *In Epistolam Apostoli Pauli ad Romanos: Commentarij*. (Basileae: per Ioannes Heruagios, 1555).

Musso, Cornelius. *In B. Pauli Apostoli Epistolam ad Romanos Absolutissima Commentaria*. (Venetiis, 1588).

Oecolampadius, Johannes. *In Epistolam B. Pauli Apost. ad Rhomanos adnotationes à Ioanne Oecolampadio Basileae praelectae*. (Basileae: apud Andream Cratandrum, 1525).

Ochino, Bernardino. *Bernhardini Ochini expositio Epistolæ diui Pauli ad Romanos*. De Italico in Latinum translate (S. Châteillon). (Augustæ Vindelicorum: P. Vilhardus, 1550).

Olevian, Caspar. *In Epistolam D. Pauli Apostoli ad Romanos Notae, ex Gaspari Oleviani concionibus excerptae, et a Theodoro Beza editae*. (Geneva, 1584).

Sadoleto, Jacopo. *Iacobi Sadoleti Episcopi Carpentoractis in Pauli Epistolam ad Romanos Commentariorum Libri Tres*. (Venetijs, 1536).

Soto, Domingo de. *In Epistolam divi Pauli ad Romanos Commentarii*. (Antwerp, 1550).

Viguerius, Joannes. *In D. Pauli Epistolam ad Romanos*. (Parisiis: Vaeneunt apud Claudium Fremy, 1560).

Vio, Tommaso de (Cardina Cajetan). *Epistolae Pauli et Aliorum Apostolorum ... per ... Dominum Thomam de Vio... iuxta sensum Literalem Enarratae*. (Paris: Apud Iod. Badium Ascensium. & Ioan. Paruum. & Ioannem Roigny, Sub prelo Ascensiano, 1532).

Vermigli, Pietro Martire. *In Epistolam S. Pauli Apostoli ad Romanos, D. Petri Martyris Vermilii Florentini*. (Tiguri: apud A. Gesnerum, 1559).

Abbreviations

CWE: *The Collected Works of Erasmus*. (Toronto: University of Toronto Press, 1974).

CO: John Calvin, *Opera Quae Supersunt Omnia*. 59 volumes. Ed. Wilhelm Baum, Edward Cunitz, & Edward Reuss. (Brunswick: Schwetschke and Sons, 1895).

LB: Jean Leclerc, ed., *Desiderii Erasmi Roterodami opera omnia.* (Leiden, 1703; repr. Hildesheim: Georg Olms Verlagsbuchhandlung, 1962).

LW: *Luther's Works*. (Philadelphia: Fortress Press, 1955–1986).

OS: John Calvin, *Opera Selecta*. Ed. Peter Barth and Wilhelm Niesel. (Munich: Christian Kaiser, 1967).

WA: *Martin Luthers Werke, Kritische Gesamtausgabe*. (Weimar, 1883–1993).

Secondary Texts

Abray, Lorna Jane. *The People's Reformation: Magistrates, Clergy, and Commons in Strasbourg, 1500–1599*. (New Haven: Yale University Press, 1985).

Achtemeier, Paul J. *Romans*. (Louisville: Westminster John Knox Press, 1985).

Augustijn, Cornelis. 'Calvin in Strasbourg', in *Calvinus Sacrae Scripturae Professor: Calvin as Confessor of Holy Scripture*. Ed. Wilhelm Neuser. (Grand Rapids: Eerdmans, 1994, 166–177).

Backus, Irena. *Historical Method and Confessional Identity in the Era of the Reformation (1378–1615)*. (Leiden: Brill, 2003).

Backus, Irena. 'Calvin and the Greek Fathers', in *Continuity and Change: The Harvest of Late-Medieval and Reformation History: Essays Presented to Heiko A. Oberman on his 70th Birthday*. (Leiden: Brill, 2000).

Backus, Irena. 'Ulrich Zwingli, Martin Bucer and the Church Fathers', in *The Reception of the Church Fathers in the West*, vol. 2, *From the Carolingians to the Maurists*. Ed. Irena Backus. (Leiden: Brill, 1997), pp. 627–660.

Battles, Ford Lewis and John R. Walchenbach, *Analysis of the Institutes of the Christian Religion*. Reprint edition. (Phillipsburg, NJ: Presbyterian & Reformed Publishing, 1980).

Battles, Ford Lewis. 'Calculus Fidei', in *Calvinus Ecclesiae Doctor*. (Kampen, Netherlands: J H Kok, 1979), pp. 85–110.

Bhabha, Homi K. *The Location of Culture*. (London: Routledge, 1994).

Beker, Johan Christiaan. *Paul the Apostle: The Triumph of God in Life and Thought.* (Philadelphia: Fortress, 1984).

Bendemann, Reinhard von. 'Die kritische Distanz von Wissen, Wollen und Handeln. Traditionsgeschichtliche Spurensuche eines hellenistischen Topos in Römer 7', *Zeitschrift für Neutestamentliche Wissenschaft*, 95 (2004), 35–63.

Bentley, Jerry. *Humanists and Holy Writ: New Testament Scholarship in the Renaissance.* (Princeton, N.J.: Princeton University Press, 1983).

Betz, Hans Dieter. 'The concept of the "Inner Human Being", ὁ ἔσω ἄνθροπος in the Anthropology of Paul', *New Testament Studies*, 46, (2000), 315–341.

Bornkamm, Heinrich. *Das Jahrhundert der Reformation. Gestalten und Kräfte*, 2. (Auflage, Göttingen: Vandenhoeck & Ruprecht, 1961).

Boyle, Marjorie O'Rourke. *Erasmus on Language and Method in Theology.* (Toronto: University of Toronto Press, 1977).

Brecht, Martin. *Martin Luther: Shaping and Defining the Reformation: 1521–1532.* Trans. James Schaaf. (Minneapolis: Fortress Press, 1990).

Brecht, Martin. *Martin Luther: His Road to Reformation, 1483–1521.* Trans. James L. Schaaf. (Philadelphia: Fortress Press, 1985).

Brown, Peter. *Augustine of Hippo: A New Edition with an Epilogue.* (Berkeley: University of California Press, 2000).

Büsser, Fritz. *Heinrich Bullinger. Leben, Werk und Wirkung*, 2 vols. (Zürich: Theologischer Verlag, 2004).

Büsser, Fritz. 'Bullinger as Calvin's Model in Biblical Exposition: An Examination of Calvin's Preface to the Epistle to the Romans', in *In Honor of John Calvin, 1509–1564: Papers from the 1986 International Calvin Symposium.* Ed. E. J. Furcha. (Montreal, 1987), pp. 64–95.

Campbell, W. S., Hawkins, P. S., and Schildgen, B. D., eds. *Medieval Readings of Romans.* (London, New York: T & T Clark 2007).

Campi, Emidio and Peter Opitz. *Heinrich Bullinger: Life – Thought – Influence. Zurich, Aug. 25–29, 2004. International Congress Heinrich Bullinger (1504–1575).* (Zurich: Theologischer Verlag Zurich, 2007).

Carey, Phillip. *Augustine's Invention of the Inner Self.* (New York: Oxford University Press, 2000).

Coogan, Robert. 'The Pharisee Against the Hellenist: Edward Lee Versus Erasmus', in *Renaissance Quarterly*, 39.3 (Autumn, 1986), 476–506.

Cranfield, C. E. B. *A Critical and Exegetical Commentary on the Epistle to the Romans.* (Edinburgh: T & T Clark, 1975).

Cranz, F. Edward. *Luther's Thought on Justice, Law and Society*. (Cambridge, Harvard University Press, 1959).

Das, Andrew. *Solving the Romans Debate*. (Minneapolis: Fortress Press, 2007).

Dunn, James D. G. *The Theology of Paul the Apostle.* (Grand Rapids: Eerdmans, 1998).

Ebeling, Gerhard. 'Luthers Kampf gegen die Moralisierung des Christlichen', in *Lutherstudien III*. Ed. Gerhard Ebeling. (Tübingen: Mohr, 1985).

Ebeling, Gerhard. *Luther: An Introduction to His Thought.* Trans. R. A. Wilson. (Philadelphia: Fortress Press, 1970).

Eells, Hastings. *Martin Bucer.* (New Haven: Yale University Press, 1931).

Ehrensperger, Kathy. 'Levinas, the Jewish Philosopher meets Paul, the Jewish Apostle: Reading Romans in the Face of the Other', in *Reading Romans with Contemporary Philosophers and Theologians.* Ed. D. Odell-Scott. (London, New York: T & T Clark, 2007).

Ehrensperger, Kathy. *That We May Be Mutually Encouraged: Feminism and the New Perspective in Pauline Studies.* (London, New York: T & T Clark, 2004).

Engberg-Pedersen, Troels. *Paul and the Stoics.* (Louisville, Kentucky: Westminster John Knox Press, 2000).

Fitzmyer, Joseph, S.J. *Romans: A New Translation with Introduction and Commentary.* (New York: Doubleday, 1993).

Forde, Gerhard O. 'Law and Gospel in Luther's Hermeneutic', *Interpretation*, 37 (1983), 240–52.

Fredriksen, Paula. *Augustine on Romans: Propositions from the Epistle to the Romans Unfinished Commentary on the Epistle to the Romans.* (Chico: Scholars Press, 1982).

Froehlich, Karlfried. *Biblical Interpretation in the Early Church*. (Philadelphia: Fortress Press, 1984).

Gadamer, Hans-Georg. *Truth and Method*, 2nd rev. ed., Trans. Joel Weinsheimer and Donald G. Marshall. (New York: Crossroad Publishing, 1989).

Gamble, Richard. '*Brevitas et Facilitas*: Toward an Understanding of Calvin's Hermeneutic', *Westminster Theological Journal*, 47 (1985), 1–17.

Ganoczy, Alexandre and Klaus Müller. *Calvins Handschriftliche Annotationen zu Chrysostomus: Ein Beitrag zur Hermeneutik Calvins.* (Wiesbaden: Franz Steiner Verlag GMBH, 1981).

George,Timothy. 'Modernizing Luther, Domesticating Paul: Another Perspective', in *Justification and Variegated Nomism,* Wissenschaftliche Untersuchungen zum Neuen Testament, 181. Eds. D. A. Carson, Peter T. O'Brien and Mark A. Seifrid. (Tübingen, Mohr Siebeck, 2004).

Gill, Christopher. *The Structured Self in Hellenistic and Roman Thought.* (Oxford: Oxford University Press, 2006).

Grenholm, Cristina and Patte, Daniel, eds. *Gender, Tradition and Romans: Shared Ground, Uncertain Borders,* Romans Through History and Cultures. (T & T Clark, 2005).

Grenholm, Cristina and Patte, Daniel, eds. *Reading Israel in Romans: Legitimacy and Plausibility of Divergent Interpretations.* (Harrisburg, Pennsylvania: Trinity Press International, 2000).

Grenholm, Christina and Patte, Daniel. 'Receptions, Critical Interpretations, and Scriptural Criticism', in *Reading Israel in Romans: Legitimacy and Plausibility of Divergent Interpretations.* Eds. Christina Grenholm and Daniel Patte. (Harrisburg, Pennsylvania: Trinity Press International, 2000), pp. 19–34.

Greschat, Martin. *Martin Bucer: A Reformer and His Times* (Munich: Beck, 1990); Trans. Stephen Buckwalter. (Louisville: Westminster John Knox, 2004).

Gritsch, Eric. 'The Cultural Context of Luther's Interpretation', *Interpretation,* 37 (1983), 266–76.

Hausammann, Susi. *Römerbriefauslegung zwischen Humanismus und Reformation. Eine Studie zu Heinrich Bullingers Römerbriefauslegung von 1525.* (Zürich/Stuttgart: Zwingli Verlag, 1970).

Hazlett, Ian P. 'Calvin's Latin Preface to his Proposed French Edition of Chrysostom's Homilies: Translation and Commentary', *Humanism and Reform. The Church in Europe, England and Scotland, 1400–1643. Essays in Honour of James K. Cameron.* Ed. James Kirk. (Oxford: Blackwell, 1991), pp. 129–150.

Heckel, Theo. *Der Innere Mensch: Der Paulinische Verarbeitung eines Platonischen Motivs.* (Tübingen: Mohr Siebeck, 1993).

Hendrix, Scott H. 'Luther Against the Background of the History of Biblical Interpretation', *Interpretation,* 37 (1983), 229–39.

Holder, R. Ward. 'Calvin as Commentator on the Pauline Epistles', in *Calvin and the Bible.* Ed. Donald K. McKim. (Cambridge: Cambridge University Press, 2006), pp. 224–256.

Holder, R. Ward. *John Calvin and the Grounding of Interpretation: Calvin's First Commentaries.* (Leiden and Boston: Brill, 2006).

Hultgren, Arland. *Paul's Gospel and Mission.* (Philadelphia: Fortress Press, 1980).

Jasper, David. *A Short Introduction to Hermeneutics.* (Louisville: Westminster John Knox Press, 1989).

Käsemann, Ernst. *Commentary on Romans.* Trans. Geoffrey Bromiley. (Grand Rapids: Eerdmans, 1980).

Kaufmann, Thomas. 'Bucers Bericht von der Heidelberger Disputation', *Archiv für Reformationsgeschichte*, 82 (1991), 147–70.

Kelly, J. N. D. *Golden Mouth: The Story of John Chrysostom – Ascetic, Preacher, Bishop.* (Grand Rapids: Baker, 1995).

Kittelson, James. *Toward an Established Church: Strasbourg from 1500 to the Dawn of the Seventeenth Century.* Veröffentlichungen des Instituts für Europäische Geschichte Mainz, Abteilung abendländische Religionsgeschichte 182. (Mainz: Von Zabern, 2000).

Klepper, Deeana C. 'First in Knowledge of Divine Law: The Jews and the Old Law in Nicholas of Lyra's Romans Commentary', in *Medieval Readings of Romans.* Eds. W. S. Campbell, P. S. Hawkins, B. D. Schildgen. (New York: T & T Clark, 2007).

Koch, Karl. *Studium Pietatis: Martin Bucer als Ethiker.* (Neukirchen-Vluyn: Neukirchener Verlag, 1962).

Kok, Joel. 'Heinrich Bullinger's Exegetical Method: The Model for Calvin?', in *Biblical Interpretation in the Era of Reformation. Essays Presented to David C. Steinmetz in Honor of His Sixtieth Birthday*, Eds. Richard A. Muller and John L. Thompson. (Grand Rapids: Eerdmans 1996), pp. 241–254.

Kok, Joel. *The Influence of Martin Bucer on John Calvin's Interpretation of Romans: A Comparative Case Study* (unpublished doctoral dissertation). (Duke University, 1993).

Koperski, Veronica. *What Are They Saying About Paul and the Law?* (Mahwah, New Jersey: Paulist Press, 2001).

Kraus, Hans-Joachim. 'Calvin's Exegetical Principles', *Interpretation*, 31 (1977), 8–18.

Lane, A. N. S. 'Calvin's Use of the Fathers and Medievals', in *John Calvin: Student of the Church Fathers.* (Edinburgh: T & T Clark, 1999), pp. 15–66.

Lane, A. N. S. 'Calvin's Knowledge of the Greek Fathers', in *John Calvin: Student of the Church Fathers.* (Edinburgh: T & T Clark, 1999), pp. 67–86.

Lane, A. N. S. 'Calvin and the Fathers in his *Bondage and Liberation of the Will*', in *John Calvin: Student of the Church Fathers.* (Edinburgh: T & T Clark, 1999), pp. 151–178.

Lang, August. *Der Evangelienkommentar Martin Butzers und die Grundzüge seiner Theologie.* (1900), repr. (Aalen: Scientia, 1972).

Lichtenberger, Hermann. *Das Ich Adams und das Ich der Menschheit: Studien zum Menschenbild in Römer 7.* (Tübingen: Mohr Siebeck, 2004).

Locher, Gottfried W. *Die Zwinglische Reformation im Rahmen der Europäischen Kirchengeschichte.* (Göttingen and Zürich: Vandenhoeck and Ruprecht, 1979).

Lowenich, Walther von. *Martin Luther: The Man and His Work.* Trans. Lawrence W. Denef. (Minneapolis: Augsburg Publishing House, 1982).

McGrath, Alistair. *Luther's Theology of the Cross: Martin Luther's Theological Breakthrough.* (Oxford: Basil Blackwell Press, 1985).

McIndoe, John H. 'John Calvin: Preface to the Homilies of Chrysostom', *Hartford Quarterly*, 5.2 (1965), 19–26.

Markish, Shimon. *Erasmus and the Jews.* (Chicago: University of Chicago Press, 1986).

Markschies, Christoph. 'Innerer Mensch', *Reallexikon für Antike und Christentum*, 18 (1997), 266–312.

Martin, Ralph P. 'Center of Paul's Theology', in *Dictionary of Paul and His Letters.* Eds. Gerald F. Hawthorne and Ralph P. Martin. (Downers Grove: InterVarsity Press, 1993), pp. 92–95.

Matera, Frank J. *Galatians.* Sacra Pagina 9. (Collegeville, Minnesota: Liturgical Press, 1992).

Matheson, Peter. *The Imaginative World of the Reformation.* (Minneapolis: Fortress Press, 2001).

Moltmann, Jurgen. 'Reformation and Revolution', in *Martin Luther and the Modern Mind: Freedom, Conscience, Toleration, Rights,* vol. 22, Toronto Studies in Theology. Ed. Manfred Hoffman. (Lewiston, Maine: Edwin Mellen Press, 1985).

Monheit. M. L. 'Young Calvin, Textual Interpretation and Roman Law', *Bibliotheque d'Humanisme et Renaissance: Travaux et Documents*, 59. 2 (1997), 263–82.

Muller, Richard A. *The Unaccommodated Calvin: Studies in the Foundation of a Theological Tradition.* (Oxford: Oxford University Press, 2000).

Muller, Richard A. '"*Scimus enim quod lex spiritualis est*": Melanchthon and Calvin on the Interpretation of Romans 7.14–23', in *Philip Melanchthon (1497–1560) and the Commentary*. Ed. Timothy J. Wengert and M. Patrick Graham. (Sheffield: Sheffield Academic, 1997), pp. 216–37.

Oberman, Heiko A. *The Two Reformations. The Journey from the Last Days to the New*. Ed. David Daniell. (New Haven: Yale University Press, 2003).

Oberman, Heiko A. 'The Gospel of Social Unrest: 450 Years after the So-Called "German Peasants' War" of 1525', in *The Dawn of the Reformation: Essays in Late Medieval and Early Reformation Thought*. Ed. Heiko Oberman. (Grand Rapids: Eerdmans, 1992).

Oberman, Heiko A. *Luther. Man between God and the Devil*. (New Haven: Yale University Press, 1990).

O'Connell, Robert J. *St. Augustine's "Confessions": The Odyssey of the Soul*. (Cambridge: Harvard University Press, 1969).

Oort, Johannes van. 'John Calvin and the Church Fathers', in *The Reception of the Church Fathers in the West: From the Carolingians to the Maurists*. Ed. Irena Backus. (Leiden: Brill, 1997).

Opitz, Peter. 'Bullingers Lehre vom Munus Propheticum', in *Heinrich Bullinger: Life – Thought – Influence. Zurich, Aug. 25–29, 2004 International Congress Heinrich Bullinger (1504–1575)*, Eds. Emidio Campi and Peter Opitz. (Zurich: Theologicsher Verlag Zurich, 2007), pp. 493–513.

Opitz, Peter. *Heinrich Bullinger als Theologe. Studien zu den "Dekaden"*. (Zurich: Theologischer Verlag Zurich, 2004).

Parker, T. H. L. *Calvin's New Testament Commentaries*. 2nd ed. (Louisville: Westminster John Knox Press, 1993).

Parker, T. H. L. *Commentaries on the Epistle to the Romans 1532–1542*. (Edinburgh: T & T Clark, 1986).

Patte, Daniel. *Ethics of Biblical Interpretation*. (Louisville, Kentucky: Westminster John Knox Press 1995).

Pauck, Wilhelm. 'General Introduction', in Martin Luther, *Lectures on Romans*, Library of Christian Classics 15. (Philadelphia: Westminster Press, 1961).

Payne, John B. 'Erasmus: Interpreter of Romans', in *Sixteenth Century Essays and Studies*, 2 (Jan., 1971), 1–35.

Pesch, Otto. 'Free by Faith: Luther's Contributions to Theological Anthropology', in *Martin Luther and the Modern Mind: Freedom, Conscience, Toleration, Rights*, vol.

22, Toronto Studies in Theology. Ed. Manfred Hoffman. (Lewiston, Maine: Edwin Mellen Press, 1985).

Peter, Rodolphe. *Bibliotheca Calviniana: Les Oevres de Jean Calvin publiées au xvie Siècle.* (Geneva: Librairie Droz, 1991).

Pitkin, Barbara. *What Pure Eyes Could See: Calvin's Doctrine of Faith in Its Exegetical Context.* (Oxford: Oxford University Press, 1999).

Rabil, Albert Jr. *Erasmus and the New Testament: The Mind of a Christian Humanist.* (San Antonio: Trinity University Press, 1972).

Ridderbos, Herman N. *Paul: An Outline of His Theology.* (Grand Rapids: Eerdmans, 1975).

Rummel, Erika. *Erasmus and his Catholic Critics.* (Nieuwkoop: De Graaf Publishers, 1989).

Rummel, Erika. *Erasmus'* Annotations *on the New Testament: From Philologist to Theologian.* (Toronto: University of Toronto Press, 1986).

Roussel, Bernard. *Martin Bucer, lecteur de l'épitre aux Romains* (unpublished doctoral dissertation) (Strasbourg, 1970).

Sanders, E. P. *Paul and Palestinian Judaism.* (Philadelphia: Fortress Press, 1977).

Schäfer, Rolf. 'Melanchthon's Interpretation of Romans 5.15: His Departure from the Augustinian Concept of Grace Compared to Luther's', in *Philip Melanchthon (1497-1560) and the Commentary.* Ed. Timothy J. Wengert and M. Patrick Graham. (Sheffield: Sheffield Academic, 1997), pp. 79–104.

Schultz, Robert. 'Introduction', to 'On the Robbing and Murdering Hordes of Peasants', in *Luther's Works.* v. 46. (Philadelphia: Fortress Press, 1955–1976).

Schüssler Fiorenza, Elisabeth. *Rhetoric and Ethic: The Politics of Biblical Studies.* (Minneapolis: Fortress Press, 1999).

Schüssler Fiorenza, Elisabeth. 'The Ethics of Interpretation : De-Centering Biblical Scholarship', *Journal of Biblical Literature*, 107 (1988), 3–17.

Snodgrass, Klein. 'Spheres of Influence: A Possible Solution to the Problem of Paul and the Law', in *The Pauline Writings.* Ed. Stanley E. Porter and Craig A. Evans. (London: T & T Clark, 2004), pp. 154–158.

Sorabji, Richard. *Self: Ancient and Modern Insights about Individuality, Life, and Death.* (Chicago: University of Chicago Press, 2006).

Stendahl, Krister. *Paul Among Jews and Gentiles.* (Philadelphia: Fortress, 1976).

Stendahl, Krister. 'The Apostle Paul and the Introspective Conscience of the West', *Harvard Theological Review*, 56 (1963), 199–215.

Stephens, W. P. *The Holy Spirit in the Thought of Martin Bucer*. (Cambridge: Cambridge University Press, 1970).

Steinmetz, David. 'John Calvin as an Interpreter of the Bible', in *Calvin and the Bible*. Ed. Donald K. McKim. (New York: Cambridge University Press, 2006), pp. 282–91.

Steinmetz, David. 'Divided by a Common Past: The Reshaping of the Christian Exegetical Tradition in the Sixteenth Century', in *Journal of Medieval and Early Modern Studies*, 27.2 (1997), 245–64.

Steinmetz, David. 'Calvin and the Civil Magistrate', in *Calvin in Context*. (Oxford: Oxford University Press, 1995), pp. 199–211.

Steinmetz, David. 'Calvin and the Divided Self of Romans 7', in *Calvin in Context*. (Oxford: Oxford University Press, 1995), pp. 110–121.

Steinmetz, David. 'Calvin and the Natural Knowledge of God', in *Calvin in Context*. (Oxford: Oxford University Press, 1995), pp. 23–39.

Steinmetz, David. 'Calvin and the Patristic Exegesis of Paul', in *The Bible in the 16th Century*. Ed. David Steinmetz. (Durham: Duke University Press, 1990), 100–118.

Steinmetz, David. 'The Superiority of Pre-critical Exegesis', *Ex Auditu*, 1 (1985), 74–82.

Stowers, Stanley, K. 'Paul as Hero of Subjectivity', in *Paul and the Philosophers*. Ed. Hent De Vries and Ward Blanton. (Durham: Duke University Press, forthcoming).

Stowers, Stanley, K. 'What is Pauline Participation in Christ', in *New Views of Jewish and Christian Self-Definition: Essays in Honor of E. P. Sanders*. Ed. Susannah Heschel and Fabian Udoh. (South Bend: Notre Dame University Press, forthcoming).

Stowers, Stanley, K. 'Apostrophe, *prosopopoiia* and Paul's Rhetorical Education', in *Early Christianity and Classical Culture: Comparative Studies in Honor of Abraham J. Malherbe*. Ed. John T. Fitzgerald, Thomas Olbricht and L. Michael White. (Leiden: Brill, 2003), pp. 351–69.

Stowers, Stanley K. *A Rereading of Romans. Justice, Jews and Gentiles*. (New Haven: Yale University Press, 1994).

Stowers, Stanley K. *The Diatribe and Paul's Letter to the Romans*. (Atlanta: Scholars Press Dissertation Series, 1981).

Tait, Edwin. *A Method for the Christian Life: Martin Bucer and the Sermon on the Mount* (unpublished doctoral dissertation) (Duke University, 2005).

Taylor, Charles. *Sources of the Self: The Making of the Modern Identity*. (Cambridge, Massachusetts: Harvard University Press, 1989).

Wasserman, Emma. *The Death of the Soul in Romans 7: Sin, Death, and the Law in Light of Hellenistic Moral Psychology*, Wissenschaftliche Untersuchungen zum Neuen Testament. (Tübingen: Mohr Siebeck, forthcoming).

Wasserman, Emma. 'The Death of the Soul in Romans 7: Revisiting Paul's Anthropology in Light of Hellenistic Moral Psychology', *Journal of Biblical Literature*, forthcoming.

Wasserman, Emma. 'Paul Among the Philosophers: The Case of Sin in Romans 6–8', *Journal for the Study of the New Testament*, forthcoming.

Watson, Francis. *Paul, Judaism and the Gentiles: A Sociological Approach*. (Cambridge: Cambridge University Press, 1986).

Wendel, François. *Calvin: Origins and Development of His Religious Thought* (1950), Trans. Philip Mairet. (Durham, NC: Labyrinth Press, 1987).

Wengert, Timothy J. 'Philip Melanchthon's 1522 Annotations on Romans and the Lutheran Origins of Rhetorical Criticism', in *Biblical Interpretation in the Era of the Reformation*. Ed. Richard A. Muller and John L. Thompson. (Grand Rapids: Eerdmans, 1996), pp. 118–140.

Westerholm, Stephen. *Perspectives Old and New on Paul: The 'Lutheran' Paul and His Critics*. (Grand Rapids: Eerdmans, 2004).

Westerholm, Stephen. 'Bucer and the Law in Romans 9–11', in James D. G. Dunn (ed.), *Paul and the Mosaic Law*. Ed. James D. G. Dunn. (Tübingen: J. C. B. Mohr, 1996; Grand Rapids: Eerdmans, 2001), pp. 215–37.

Williams, Rowan. *Christian Spirituality: A Theological History from the New Testament to Luther and St. John of the Cross*. (Atlanta: John Knox Press, 1980).

Zachman, Randall. *Image and Word in the Theology of John Calvin*. (South Bend: Notre Dame University Press, 2007).

Zeeden, Ernst Walter. *Die Entstehung der Konfessionen: Grundlagen und Formen der Konfessionsbildung*. (Munich: Ouldenbourg, 1965).

Index

Patristic, Medieval and Early Modern Authors

Index of Modern Authors

Index of Subjects